When should I travel t
Where do I go for answer
What's the best and easiest v

frommers.travelocity.com

Frommer's, the travel guide leader, has teamed up with **Travelocity.com**, the leader in online travel, to bring you an in-depth, easy-to-use resource designed to help you plan and book your trip online.

At **frommers.travelocity.com**, you'll find free online updates about your destination from the experts at Frommer's plus the outstanding travel planning and purchasing features of Travelocity.com. Travelocity.com provides reservations capabilities for 95 percent of all airline seats sold, more than 47,000 hotels, and over 50 car rental companies. In addition, Travelocity.com offers more than 2,000 exciting vacation and cruise packages. Travelocity.com puts you in complete control of your travel planning with these and other great features:

> **Expert travel guidance from Frommer's** - over 150 writers reporting from around the world!
>
> **Best Fare Finder** - an interactive calendar tells you when to travel to get the best airfare
>
> **Fare Watcher** - we'll track airfare changes to your favorite destinations
>
> **Dream Maps** - a mapping feature that suggests travel opportunities based on your budget
>
> **Shop Safe Guarantee** - 24 hours a day / 7 days a week live customer service, and more!

Whether traveling on a tight budget, looking for a quick weekend getaway, or planning the trip of a lifetime, Frommer's guides and Travelocity.com will make your travel dreams a reality. You've bought the book, now book the trip!

Travelocity.com
A Sabre Company

Frommer's
TM

A New Star-Rating System & Other Exciting News from Frommer's!

In our continuing effort to publish the savviest, most up-to-date, and most appealing travel guides available, we've added some great new features.

Frommer's guides now include a new **star-rating system.** Every hotel, restaurant, and attraction is rated from 0 to 3 stars to help you set priorities and organize your time.

We've also added **seven brand-new features** that point you to the great deals, in-the-know advice, and unique experiences that separate travelers from tourists. Throughout the guide, look for:

Finds	Special finds—those places only insiders know about
Fun Fact	Fun facts—details that make travelers more informed and their trips more fun
Kids	Best bets for kids—advice for the whole family
Moments	Special moments—those experiences that memories are made of
Overrated	Places or experiences not worth your time or money
Tips	Insider tips—some great ways to save time and money
Value	Great values—where to get the best deals

We've also added a **"What's New"** section in every guide—a timely crash course in what's hot and what's not in every destination we cover.

Other Great Guides for Your Trip:

Frommer's Hawaii

Frommer's Hawaii from $80 a Day

Frommer's Maui

Frommer's Portable Maui

Frommer's Portable Big Island

Frommer's®

Honolulu, Waikiki & Oahu
7th Edition

by Jeanette Foster & Jocelyn Fujii

Here's what the critics say about Frommer's:

"Amazingly easy to use. Very portable, very complete."

—*Booklist*

"The only mainstream guide to list specific prices. The Walter Cronkite of guidebooks—with all that implies."

—*Travel & Leisure*

"Complete, concise, and filled with useful information."

—*New York Daily News*

"Hotel information is close to encyclopedic."

—*Des Moines Sunday Register*

"Detailed, accurate, and easy-to-read information for all price ranges."

—*Glamour Magazine*

Hungry Minds™

Best-Selling Books • Digital Downloads • e-Books • Answer Networks
e-Newsletters • Branded Web Sites • e-Learning
New York, NY • Cleveland, OH • Indianapolis, IN

About the Authors

A resident of the Big Island, **Jeanette Foster** has skied the slopes of Mauna Kea—during a Fourth of July ski meet, no less—and gone scuba diving with manta rays off the Kona Coast. A prolific writer widely published in travel, sports, and adventure magazines, she's also a contributing editor to *Hawaii* magazine and the editor of *Zagat's Survey to Hawaii's Top Restaurants*.

Kauai-born **Jocelyn Fujii,** a resident of Honolulu, is one of Hawaii's leading journalists. She has authored *Under the Hula Moon: Living in Hawaii* and *The Best of Hawaii*, as well as articles for the *New York Times, National Geographic Traveler, Islands, Condé Nast Traveler, Travel Holiday,* and other national and international publications. She is a contributing editor to *Spirit of Aloha* magazine and a columnist for *Hawaii Westways*.

In addition to this guide, Jeanette and Jocelyn are the coauthors of *Frommer's Hawaii, Frommer's Hawaii from $80 a Day,* and *Frommer's Maui.*

Published by:

Hungry Minds, Inc.

909 Third Ave.
New York, NY 10022

ISBN 0-7645-6411-0
ISSN 1088-5986

Edited by Dog-Eared Pages, Inc.
Production Editor: Suzanna R. Thompson
Photo Editor: Richard Fox
Cartographer: Liz Puhl
Production by Hungry Minds Indianapolis Production Services

Front cover photo: Hanauma Bay

Special Sales

For general information on Hungry Minds' products and services, please contact our Customer Care department; within the U.S. at 800-762-2974, outside the U.S. at 317-572-3993 or fax 317-572-4002. For sales inquiries and reseller information, including discounts, bulk sales, customized editions, and premium sales, please contact our Customer Care department at 800-434-3422.

Manufactured in the United States of America
5   4   3   2   1

Contents

8 Shopping   215

by Jocelyn Fujii

9 Oahu After Dark   236

by Jocelyn Fujii

Appendix: Honolulu & Oahu in Depth   243

by Jeanette Foster

Index   261

List of Maps

An Invitation to the Reader

In researching this book, we discovered many wonderful places—hotels, restaurants, shops, and more. We're sure you'll find others. Please tell us about them, so we can share the information with your fellow travelers in upcoming editions. If you were disappointed with a recommendation, we'd love to know that, too. Please write to:

Frommer's Honolulu, Waikiki & Oahu, 7th Edition
Hungry Minds, Inc. • 909 Third Avenue • New York, NY 10022

An Additional Note

Please be advised that travel information is subject to change at any time—and this is especially true of prices. We therefore suggest that you write or call ahead for confirmation when making your travel plans. The authors, editors, and publisher cannot be held responsible for the experiences of readers while traveling. Your safety is important to us, however, so we encourage you to stay alert and be aware of your surroundings. Keep a close eye on cameras, purses, and wallets, all favorite targets of thieves and pickpockets.

New! Frommer's Star Ratings & Icons

Every hotel, restaurant, and attraction listing in this guide has been ranked for quality, value, service, amenities, and special features using a star-rating scale. In country, state, and regional guides, we also rate towns and regions to help you narrow down your choices and budget your time accordingly. Hotels and restaurants in the Very Expensive and Expensive categories are rated on a scale of one (highly recommended) to three stars (exceptional). Those in the Moderate and Inexpensive categories rate from zero (recommended) to two stars (very highly recommended). Attractions, towns, and regions are rated according to the following scale: zero stars (recommended), one star (highly recommended), two stars (very highly recommended), and three stars (must-see).

In addition to the rating system, we also use seven icons to highlight insider information, useful tips, special bargains, hidden gems, memorable experiences, kid-friendly venues, places to avoid, and other useful information:

| *Finds* | *Fun Fact* | *Kids* | *Moments* | *Overrated* | *Tips* | *Value* |

The following abbreviations are used for credit cards:

AE	American Express	DISC	Discover	V	Visa
DC	Diners Club	MC	MasterCard		

FROMMERS.COM

Now that you have the guidebook to a great trip, visit our website at **www.frommers.com** for travel information on nearly 2,000 destinations. With features updated regularly, we give you instant access to the most current trip-planning information available. At Frommers.com, you'll also find the best prices on air fares, accommodations, and car rentals—and you can even book travel online through our travel booking partners. At Frommers.com, you'll also find the following:

- Daily Newsletter highlighting the best travel deals
- Hot Spot of the Month/Vacation Sweepstakes & Travel Photo Contest
- More than 200 Travel Message Boards
- Outspoken Newsletters and Feature Articles on travel bargains, vacation ideas, tips & resources, and more!

What's New in Honolulu & Oahu

Honolulu, Oahu's largest city and the capital of the only U.S. state that is also an island, is emerging as the cultural center and meeting place of the Pacific Rim. Adding to its importance is the spanking-new $250 million Hawaii Convention Center, at the gateway to Waikiki. Always on the cutting edge, Oahu today offers more than just sunsets and mai tais. You'll find everything from heart-pounding ecoadventures to relaxing, island-inspired body treatments and massages in the world's foremost spas.

GETTING THERE The number of direct flights to Hawaii has increased dramatically to an all time high. Nonstop flights from Newark, Chicago, Atlanta, Dallas–Fort Worth, St. Louis, Vancouver, Toronto, Seattle, Portland, San Francisco, Oakland, Las Vegas, Los Angeles, Orange County (Calif.), San Diego, and Phoenix fly to Honolulu almost every day.

THE SPA EXPLOSION The biggest news this year is the explosion in the number of state-of-the-art resort spas.

In 2001, the **Hilton Hawaiian Village Beach Resort & Spa** (© 800/ HILTONS; www.hawaiianvillage. hilton.com) unveiled its 42,000-square-foot **Mandara Spa** and the **Holistica Hawaii Wellness Center.** The Mandara Spa, a blend of Hawaiian, Asian, Western, European relaxation concepts, features 25 treatment rooms, a dramatic infinity pool, a sauna, steam rooms, an indoor whirlpool, and a cardiovascular fitness center with a host of classes. The

separate Holistica Hawaii features diagnostic and therapeutic medical facilities offering individualized exercise training, nutritional instruction, and other personal medical assessments.

Also making its debut in 2001 was the **Abhasa Waikiki Spa in the Royal Hawaiian Hotel** (© 808/922-8200; www.abhasa.com). This contemporary spa, spread out over 7,000 square feet, features natural, organic products in its spa menu, which includes everything from shiatsu massages under the palm trees to a host of unique skin treatments.

The **Outrigger Reef on the Beach** (© 800/OUTRIGGER; www. outrigger.com) opened the Serenity Spa in 2001, and the **Kahala Mandarin Oriental** (© 800/367-2525; www.mandarinoriental.com) is scheduled to open a new 13,000-square-foot spa and fitness center in 2002.

These new additions to the spa scene join the ranks of the **Ihilani Spa at the J.W. Marriott Ihilani Resort & Spa** © 800/626-4446; www. ihilani.com), which offers tranquillity and pampering on the leeward coast of Oahu, far from the bustle of Waikiki. One of Hawaii's finest spas, this free-standing 35,000-square-foot facility combines Hawaiian products with traditional therapies to produce some of the best water treatments in the state.

A NEW WAIKIKI The city and county of Honolulu just completed the first phase of a makeover of **Kuhio Beach Park,** a $12.75 million improvement project that added walkways, rock waterfalls, more coconut trees, plush grass, and hula mounds; one lane of traffic on Kalakaua Avenue was taken out to expand the beach park. The 73-year-old **Waikiki War Memorial Natatorium** just finished the first phase of a $4.4 million restoration of its building; next up is an $11.5 million renovation of its saltwater swimming pool. Construction is about to begin on **Na Iwi Kupuna Waikiki Memorial,** a large octagonal mound that will hold the remains of several graves unearthed during recent work on a water main in Waikiki. Na Iwi Kupuna (which translates as "ancestors' bones") will be located on the intersection of Kalakaua and Kapahula Avenues in Kapiolani Park and will be open to the public during daylight hours.

Visitors now have an opportunity to experience the restaurants and shops in the neighborhoods adjacent to Waikiki with the launch of the new **Kaimuki-Kapahulu-Waikiki Trolley** (© **800/824-8804;** www.enoa.com). The $1 service runs from Koko Head Avenue down Waialae, Kapahulu, and Kuhio avenues into Waikiki and back. The 30-passenger trolleys make the 3.7-mile round-trip journey every 30 minutes from 6am to 10pm.

The **Honolulu Academy of Arts,** 900 S. Beretania St. (© **808/532-8700;** www.honoluluacademy.org), unveiled its new $28-million Henry R. Luce Pavilion Complex in May 2001, and wowed the state with its new exhibition space, courtyard, expanded outdoor cafe, and gift shop.

DINING Someone has lit a fire under Restaurant Row, at one time a restaurant graveyard and now the Grand Central of dining on Oahu. How so many restaurants can coexist successfully is the $64,000 question, but there they are—everything from Sansei to Jameson's to Baci and the ever-hip Ocean Club.

But the buzz in Honolulu is way back in Manoa Valley, where **Donato's,** Manoa Marketplace, 2756 Woodlawn Dr. (© **808/988-2000**), has resurfaced in this new location with a vengeance. This is not dine-and-dash Italian; Donato Loperfido offers upscale, linger-over-your-linguine dining.

Elsewhere in Honolulu, the 16-theater megaplex of the **Victoria Ward** entertainment center is open at the corner of Auahi and Kamakee streets, near the Ward Centre; its restaurant and retail complex is being completed in the summer of 2001. Three restaurants and six to eight retailers are expected to open, and locals eagerly await an end to the construction that has plagued the area.

While superstars George Mavrothalassitis (Chef Mavro Restaurant), Philippe Padovani (Padovani's Restaurant & Wine Bar), and Alan Wong (Alan Wong's Restaurant) continue to reign in the stratosphere of Hawaii Regional Cuisine, the spotlight has widened to include **Hiroshi Fukui** (**L'Uraku,** 1341 Kapiolani Blvd., Honolulu; © **808/955-0552**) and the remarkable **Onjin Kim** (**Onjin's Café,** 401 Kamakee St.; © **808/589-1666**), the Kakaako phenom.

Throughout Oahu, Vietnamese *pho* houses are the rage. Dim sum houses, too, continue to proliferate, and a new breed of restaurants is offering a more gentrified version of the traditional plate lunch.

Despite the burgeoning popularity of informal eateries and ethnic traditions, however, Hawaii Regional Cuisine remains the pillar of dining in Hawaii, embracing new tastes and techniques but anchored, always, in the agriculture and seafood of the islands.

The Best of Oahu

Everyone ventures to Oahu seeking a different experience. Some talk about wanting to find the "real" Hawaii, some are looking for heart-pounding adventure, some yearn for the relaxing and healing powers of the islands, and others are drawn by Hawaii's aloha spirit, where kindness and friendliness prevail. All kinds of memorable experiences can be yours. Imagine yourself hovering weightless over a rainbowed sea of tropical fish, sitting in a kayak watching the brilliant colors of dawn etch themselves across the sky, sipping a mai tai while you take in sweeping views of the south shore and the Waianae Mountains, battling a magnificent game fish on a high-tech sportfishing boat, or listening to melodic voices chant the stories of a proud people and a proud culture that was overthrown little more than a century ago.

This book is designed to help you have the vacation of your dreams. For those too excited to page through from beginning to end, this chapter highlights the very best of what Honolulu and Oahu have to offer.

1 The Best Oahu Experiences

To have the absolute best experiences on Oahu, be prepared for a different culture, language, cuisine, and way of doing things. Slow yourself down— you're now on an island that operates on its own schedule. To really experience the island, we recommend the following:

- **Get Out on the Water:** View the islands the way Mother Nature does—from the sea. There are many different boats to choose from, ranging from tiny kayaks to 100-foot sightseeing vessels. Even state-of-the-art boats guaranteed to prevent seasickness are available. You'll take home memories of an emerald island rising out of the cobalt sea with white wispy clouds set against an azure sky or the Waikiki shoreline colored by the setting sun. See chapter 6, "Fun in the Surf & Sun," for details on all kinds of cruises and watersports.

- **Plunge Under the Water:** Don mask, fins, and snorkel and dive into the magical world beneath the surface, where clouds of colorful tropical fish flutter by, craggy old turtles lumber along, and tiny marine creatures hover over exotic corals. Can't swim? No excuse— take one of the many submarines or semi-submersibles, but don't miss this opportunity. If you come to Hawaii and don't see the underwater world, you're missing half of what makes up this paradise. See chapter 6.

- **Meet Local Folks:** If you go to Hawaii and see only people like the ones back home, you might as well stay home. Extend yourself, leave the resorts and tourist quarters, go out and learn about Hawaii and its people. Just smile and say "howzit?" which means "how is it?" "It's good," is the usual response—and you'll usually make a new friend. Hawaii is remarkably cosmopolitan; every ethnic group in the world seems to be here. It's fascinating to discover the varieties of food, culture, language, and customs.

- **Drive to the North Shore:** Just an hour's drive from Honolulu, the North Shore is another world: a pastoral, rural setting with magnificent beaches and a slower way of life. During the winter months, stop and watch the professionals surf the monster waves. See chapter 7, "Exploring Oahu."

- **Watch the Hula:** This is Hawaii, so you have to experience the hula. There's no excuse—many performances are free. For just about as long as we can remember, the Eastman Kodak Company has been hosting the **Kodak Hula Show** at Kapiolani Park. The show is really more 1950s nostalgia than ancient culture, but it's a good bit of fun any way you slice it. Some 1,500 people flock to the shows at 10am every Tuesday, Wednesday, and Thursday; they last until 11:15am. See chapter 7.

- **Experience a Turning Point in America's History:** The United States could no longer turn its back on World War II after December 7, 1941, the day that Japanese warplanes bombed Pearl Harbor. Standing on the deck of the USS *Arizona* Memorial, which straddles the eternal tomb for the 1,177 sailors and Marines trapped below deck when the battleship sank in 9 minutes, is a moving experience you'll never forget. Admission is free. See chapter 7.

2 The Best Beaches

See chapter 6 for complete details on all these beaches and their facilities.

- **Waikiki Beach:** This famous stretch of sand is the spot that originally put Hawaii on the tourist map. No beach anywhere is so widely known or so universally sought after as this narrow, 1½-mile-long crescent of soft sand (from Molokai) at the foot of a string of high-rise hotels. Home to the world's longest-running beach party, Waikiki attracts nearly five million visitors a year from every corner of the planet. In high season, it's packed towel-to-towel, but there's no denying the beauty of Waikiki.

- **Lanikai Beach:** Hidden, off the beaten tourist path, this beach on the windward side has a mile of powder-soft sand that's safe for swimming and—with the prevailing trade winds—excellent for sailing and windsurfing. It's the perfect isolated spot for a morning of swimming and relaxation. Sunworshipers should arrive in the morning, as the shadow of the Koolau Mountains (which separate Windward Oahu from Honolulu) blocks the sun's rays in the afternoon.

- **Kailua Beach:** Imagine a 30-acre public park with a broad, grassy area with picnic tables, a public boat ramp, restrooms, a pavilion, a volleyball court, and food stands. Add a wide, sandy beach, great for diving, swimming, sailing, snorkeling, and board- and windsurfing, and you've just described Kailua Beach, which is tops on the windward side of the island. On weekends, local families consider it *the* place to go. Great on weekdays, when you practically have the entire place to yourself.

- **Kahana Bay Beach Park:** If you didn't know you were in Hawaii, you would swear this beach was in

The Hawaiian Islands

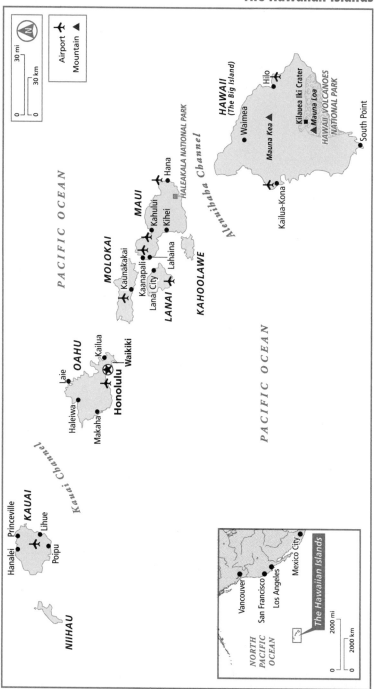

Airport ✈
Mountain ▲

30 mi
30 km

PACIFIC OCEAN

HAWAII
(The Big Island)

Hilo
Kilauea Iki Crater
Waimea
Mauna Kea ▲
■ Mauna Loa
HAWAII VOLCANOES
NATIONAL PARK
Kailua-Kona
South Point

Hana
HALEAKALA NATIONAL PARK

MAUI
Kahului
Kihei

Alenuihaha Channel

MOLOKAI
Kaunakakai
Kaanapali
Lanai City
Lahaina
LANAI

KAHOOLAWE

PACIFIC OCEAN

OAHU
Kailua
Laie
Waikiki
Honolulu
Haleiwa
Makaha

Kauai Channel

KAUAI
Princeville
Lihue
Hanalei
Poipu

NIIHAU

The Hawaiian Islands

Vancouver
San Francisco
Los Angeles
Mexico City

NORTH
PACIFIC
OCEAN

2000 mi
2000 km

Oahu

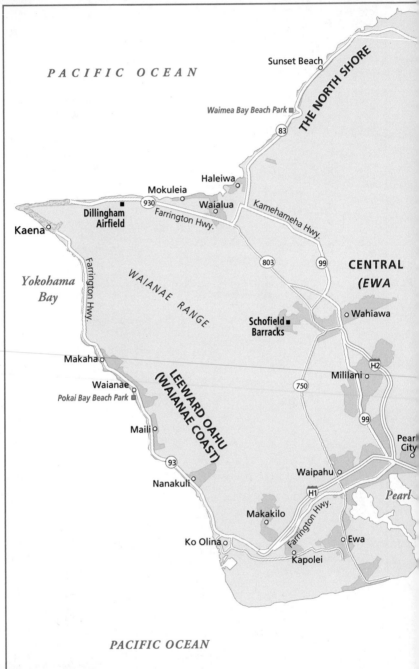

PACIFIC OCEAN

THE NORTH SHORE

Sunset Beach

Waimea Bay Beach Park

83

Haleiwa

Mokuleia

930

Waialua

Dillingham
Airfield

Farrington Hwy.

Kamehameha Hwy.

Kaena

Yokohama
Bay

Farrington Hwy.

WAIANAE RANGE

803

99

CENTRAL
(EWA

Schofield
Barracks

Wahiawa

Makaha

LEEWARD OAHU
(WAIANAE COAST)

750

H2

Mililani

Waianae

Pokai Bay Beach Park

Maili

93

99

Pearl
City

Nanakuli

Waipahu

H1

Farrington Hwy.

Pearl

Makakilo

Ko Olina

Ewa

Kapolei

PACIFIC OCEAN

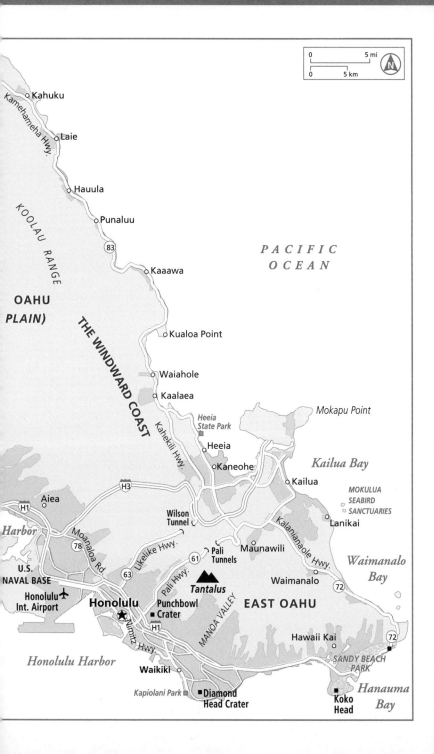

0   5 mi
0   5 km

N

Kahuku

Laie

Kamehameha Hwy.

Hauula

KOOLAU

Punaluu

83

RANGE

Kaaawa

PACIFIC
OCEAN

OAHU
PLAIN)

THE WINDWARD COAST

Kualoa Point

Waiahole

Kaalaea

Mokapu Point

Heeia
State Park

Kahekili Hwy.

Heeia

Kaneohe

Kailua Bay

H3

Kailua

Aiea

MOKULUA
SEABIRD
SANCTUARIES

H1

Harbor

Moanaloa Rd.

78

Wilson
Tunnel

Likelike Hwy.

63

Pali Hwy.

61

Pali
Tunnels

Lanikai

Maunawili

Kalanianaole Hwy.

Waimanalo
Bay

U.S.
NAVAL BASE

Tantalus

Waimanalo

72

Honolulu
Int. Airport

Honolulu

Punchbowl
Crater

MANOA VALLEY

EAST OAHU

H1

Nimitz Hwy.

Hawaii Kai

72

Honolulu Harbor

Waikiki

SANDY BEACH
PARK

Kapiolani Park

Diamond
Head Crater

Koko
Head

Hanauma
Bay

Tahiti or Bora Bora. Picture salt-and-pepper sand, a crescent-shaped beach protected by ironwoods and *kamani* trees, and as a backdrop, a lush junglelike valley disturbed only by jagged cliffs. Kahana offers great swimming (even safe for children), good fishing, and perfect conditions for kayaking. Combine that with picnic areas, camping, and hiking trails, and you have one of the best beaches on the island.

- **Malaekahana Beach:** If you'd like to venture back to the Hawaii before jet planes brought millions of people to Oahu, back to the days when there were few footprints on the sand, then go north to the romantic wooded beach park at Malaekahana. This is a place to sit in quiet solitude or to beachcomb along the shore. There's good swimming most of the time, and good snorkeling when it's calm, but no lifeguard here. Surprisingly, very few visitors come to Malaekahana Beach, one of the best on Oahu—it's a true find.

- **Sunset Beach:** Surfers around the world know this famous site for its spectacular winter surf—the waves can be huge, thundering peaks reaching up to 15 to 20 feet. During the winter surf season, the best activity here is watching the professional surfers attack the giant waves. In the summer months, Sunset calms down and becomes a safe swimming beach. It's a great place to people-watch year-round, as you'll spot everybody from wanna-be *Baywatch* babes to King Kong surfers.

- **Waimea Bay:** Here is one of Oahu's most dramatic beaches. During much of the winter—October to April—huge waves come pounding in, creating strong rip currents. Even expert surfers think twice when confronted with 30-foot waves that crash on the shore with the force of a runaway locomotive. It's hard to believe that during the summer this same bay is glassy and calm—a great place for swimming, snorkeling, and diving. Oh, and by the way, despite what the Beach Boys croon in their hit song "Surfin USA" (Why-a-*mee*-ah), the name of this famous surfing beach is pronounced Why-*may*-ah.

- **Pokai Bay:** If you dream of a powdered-sugar sand beach, a place you can swim, snorkel, and probably be the only one on the beach (on weekdays), try this off-the-beaten-path shoreline. Surrounded by a reef, the waters inside are calm enough for children and offer excellent snorkeling. Come with the aloha spirit and a respect for local customs—the local residents here don't see too many visitors.

3 The Best Snorkeling & Diving Sites

A different Hawaii greets anyone with a mask, snorkel, and fins. Under the sea, you'll find schools of brilliant tropical fish, lumbering green sea turtles, quick-moving game fish, slack-jawed moray eels, and prehistoric-looking coral. It's a kaleidoscope of color and wonder. For more on exploring Oahu's underwater world, see chapter 6.

- **Hanauma Bay:** It can get very crowded, but for clear, warm, calm waters, an abundance of fish that are so friendly they'll swim right up to your face mask, a beautiful setting, and easy access, there's no place like Hanauma Bay. Just wade in waist deep and look down to see more than 50 species of reef and inshore fish common to Hawaiian waters. Snorkelers hug the safe, shallow inner bay—it's really like swimming in an outdoor aquarium. Serious, experienced divers shoot "the slot," a passage through the reef, to gain access to Witch's Brew, a turbulent cove, and other outer reef experiences.

- **Wreck of the *Mahi*:** Oahu is a wonderful place to scuba dive, especially for those interested in wreck diving. One of the more famous wrecks in Hawaii is the *Mahi,* a 185-foot former minesweeper, which is easily accessible just south of Waianae. Abundant marine life makes it a great place to shoot photos—schools of lemon butterflyfish and *taa'pe* are so comfortable with divers and photographers that they practically pose. Eagle rays, green sea turtles, manta rays, and white-tipped sharks occasionally cruise by, and eels peer from the wreck.

- **Kahuna Canyon:** For non-wreck diving, one of the best dive spots in the summer is Kahuna Canyon. In Hawaiian, *kahuna* translates as priest, wise man, or sorcerer. This massive amphitheater near Mokuleia is a perfect example of something a sorcerer might conjure up: Walls rising from the ocean floor create the illusion of an underwater Grand Canyon. Inside the amphitheater, crab,

octopi, slipper, and spiny lobsters abound (be aware that taking them in the summer is illegal), and giant trevally, parrotfish, and unicorn tangs congregate. Outside the amphitheater, you're likely to see the occasional shark in the distance.

- **Shark's Cove:** The braver snorkelers might want to head to Shark's Cove, on the North Shore just off Kamehameha Highway, between Haleiwa and Pupukea. Sounds risky, we know, but we've never seen or heard of any sharks in this cove, and in summer this big, lava-edged pool is one of Oahu's best snorkeling spots. Waves splash over the natural lava grotto and cascade like waterfalls into the pool full of tropical fish. There are deep-sea caves to explore to the right of the cove.

- **Kapiolani Park Beach:** In the center of this beach park, a section known as Queen's Beach or Queen's Surf Beach, between the Natatorium and the Waikiki Aquarium, is great for snorkeling. We prefer the reef in front of the Aquarium because it has easy access to the sandy shoreline and the waters are usually calm. It has the added advantage of being right next door to the Aquarium in case you see any flora or fauna you would like more information about.

4 The Best Golf Courses

Oahu is golf country, with 5 municipal, 9 military, and 20 private courses to choose from. The courses range from 9-hole municipals, perfect for beginners, to championship courses that stump even the pros. See chapter 6 for complete details on these and other courses.

- **Ko Olina Golf Club** (② 808/ 676-5300): Here's a course that's not only in a beautiful setting, but

is also downright challenging. In fact, *Golf Digest* named this 6,867-yard, par-72 course one of "America's Top 75 Resort Courses" when it opened in 1992. The rolling fairways and elevated tees and a few too many water features (always where you don't want them) will definitely improve your game or humble your attitude.

- **Hilton at Turtle Bay Resort** (© **808/293-8574**): Of the two courses to choose from here, we recommend the 18-hole **Arnold Palmer Course** (formerly the Links at Kuilima), designed by Arnold Palmer and Ed Seay; *Golf Digest* rated it the fourth best new resort course in 1994. Palmer and Seay never meant for golfers to get off too easy—this is a challenging course. The front nine holes, with rolling terrain, only a few trees, and lots of wind, play like a course on the British Isles. The back nine holes have narrower, tree-lined fairways and water. In addition to ocean views, the course circles Punahoolapa Marsh, a protected wetland for endangered Hawaiian waterfowl.

- **Makaha Golf Club** (© **800/757-8060** or 808/695-9544): The readers of a local city magazine recently named this challenging course "The Best Golf Course on Oahu," and the readers of *Golfweek* rated it one of Hawaii's top 10. Away from the crowds of Honolulu and about an hour's drive, this William Bell–designed course is in Makaha Valley on the leeward side of the island. Incredibly beautiful, sheer, 1,500-foot volcanic walls tower over the course, and swaying palm trees and neon-bright bougainvillea surround it; an occasional peacock even struts across the fairways. "I was distracted by the beauty" is a great excuse for your score at the end of the day.

- **Olomana Golf Links** (© **808/259-7926**): This is a gorgeous course located in Waimanalo, on the other side of the island from Waikiki. The low-handicap golfer may not find this course difficult, but the striking views of the craggy Koolau mountain ridges are worth the greens fees alone. The par-72, 6,326-yard course is popular with local residents and visitors. The course starts off a bit hilly on the front nine, but flattens out by the back nine. The back nine have their own special surprises, including tricky water hazards.

5 The Best Walks

The weather on Oahu is usually sunny, with trade winds providing cooling breezes—perfect conditions for a walk. Below are some of our favorites, from city strolls to trails through rain forests.

- **Diamond Head Crater:** Most everyone can make this moderate walk to the summit of Hawaii's most famous landmark. Kids love the top of the 760-foot volcanic cone, where they have 360-degree views of Oahu up the leeward coast from Waikiki. The 1.4-mile round-trip takes about an hour. See chapter 6.

- **Makiki–Manoa Cliff Trails:** Just a 15-minute drive from downtown Honolulu, you'll find a walk through a rain forest and along a ridgetop with nonstop views. This somewhat strenuous loop trail is one you'll never forget, but it's more than 6 miles long, gains 1,260 feet in elevation, and takes about 3 hours to finish. The trail is part of the labyrinth of trails in this area. The views of the city and the shoreline are spectacular. See chapter 6.

- **Manoa Falls Trail:** This easy .8-mile (one-way) hike is terrific for families; it takes less than an hour to reach idyllic Manoa Falls. The often-muddy trail follows Waihi Stream and meanders through the forest reserve past guava and mountain apple trees and wild ginger. The forest is moist and humid and inhabited by nothing more dangerous than giant bloodthirsty mosquitoes, so bring repellent. See chapter 6.

- **Chinatown:** Honolulu's Chinatown appeals to the senses: The pungent aroma of Vietnamese *pho* mingles with the ever-present sweet scent of burning incense; a jumble of streets come alive every day with busy residents and meandering visitors; vendors and shoppers speak noisily in the open market; retired men talk story over games of mah-jongg; and the constant buzz of traffic all contribute to the cacophony of sounds. No trip to Honolulu is complete without a visit to this exotic, historic district. See chapter 7.

6 The Best Views

- **Puu Ualakaa State Park:** Watching the sun set into the Pacific from a 1,048-foot hill named after a sweet potato is actually much more romantic that it sounds. Puu Ualakaa State Park translates into "rolling sweet potato hill," which was how the early Hawaiians harvested the crop. Don't miss the sweeping panoramic views, which extend from Diamond Head across Waikiki and downtown Honolulu, over the airport and Pearl City, all the way to the Waianae range. Great photo ops during the day, romantic sunset views in the evening, and starry skies at night. See chapter 7.

- **Nuuanu Pali Lookout:** Oahu's best-looking side, the windward coast, can be seen in its full natural glory from the Nuuanu Pali Lookout, a gusty perch set amid jagged cliffs that pierce the puffy white clouds that go racing by. A thousand sheer feet below, the island is a carpet of green that runs to an azure Pacific dotted by tiny offshore islets. You'll feel like you're standing on the edge of the world. See chapter 7.

- **Diamond Head Crater:** The view from atop this world-famous 720-foot-tall sleeping volcano is not to be missed. The 360-degree view from the top is worth the 560-foot hike. You can see all the way from Koko Crater to Barbers Point and the Waianae mountains. See chapter 6.

- **Lanikai Beach:** This is one of the best places on Oahu to greet the sunrise. Watch the sky slowly move from pitch black to wisps of gray to burnt orange as the sun begins to rise over the two tiny offshore islands of Mokulua. This is a five-senses experience: birds singing the sun up; a gentle breeze on your face; the taste of salt in the air; the smell of the ocean, the sand, and the fragrant flowers nearby; and the kaleidoscope of colors as another day dawns. See chapter 6.

- **Puu O Mahuka Heiau:** Once the largest sacrificial temple on Oahu, today Puu O Mahuka Heiau is a state historic site. Located on a 300-foot bluff, the Heiau encompasses some 5 acres. People still come here to pray—you may see offerings such as ti leaves, flowers, and fruit left at the Heiau. Don't disturb the offerings or walk on the stones (it's very disrespectful). The view from this bluff is awe-inspiring, from Waimea Bay all the way to Kaena Point. See chapter 7.

7 The Best Adventures for Thrill-Seekers

See chapter 7 for details on these and many other adventures.

- **Soar in Silence in a Glider:** Imagine soaring through silence on gossamerlike wings, with a panoramic view of Oahu. A ride on a glider is an unforgettable experience. Glider rides are available at Dillingham Air Field, in Mokuleia, on Oahu's North Shore. The glider is towed behind a plane; at the right altitude, the tow is dropped, and you (and the glider pilot) are left to soar in the thermals.
- **Surf Waikiki in a Hawaiian Outrigger Canoe:** It's summertime and there's a South Pacific swell rolling into Waikiki from Tahiti; here's your chance to try surfing—in a Hawaiian outrigger canoe. Numerous beach concessions on Waikiki Beach offer the chance to paddle an outrigger canoe and surf back into Waikiki. Not only do you get a great view of Waikiki Beach from offshore, but also the thrill of actually catching a wave and gliding back into shore.

- **Float on the Thermals on a Tandem Hang Glider:** See things from a bird's-eye view (literally) as you and an instructor float high above Oahu on a tandem hang glider.
- **Leap into the Ocean:** Even though all the signs say DANGEROUS, STAY OFF THE ROCKS, a favorite pastime on Oahu is climbing the stone precipice next to Waimea Bay and leaping into the ocean. This is for experienced swimmers and is a summer-only experience, as the thundering winter waves drive everyone from the sea, except the professional surfers and the very, very stupid.
- **Venture into the Deep:** It's Hawaii—you have to see what it's like under the waves. Try scuba diving; you can enjoy a "scuba experience" with absolutely no previous diving experience. Here's your opportunity to glide weightlessly through the ocean while you admire the multicolored marine creatures.

8 The Best Places to Discover the Real Oahu

Oahu isn't just any other beach destination. It has a wonderfully rich, ancient history and culture, and people who are worth getting to know. If you want to meet the "local" folks who live on Oahu, check out the following:

- **Watch the Ancient Hawaiian Sport of Canoe Paddling:** From February to September, on weekday evenings and weekend days, hundreds of canoe paddlers gather at Ala Wai Canal and practice the Hawaiian sport of canoe paddling. Find a comfortable spot at Ala Wai Park, next to the canal, and

watch this ancient sport come to life. See the Calendar of Events in chapter 2, "Planning Your Trip to Oahu."
- **Attend a Hawaiian-Language Church Service:** Kawaiahao Church (© 808/522-1333) is the Westminster Abbey of Hawaii; the vestibule is lined with portraits of the Hawaiian monarchy, many of whom were coronated in this very building. The coral church is a perfect setting to experience an all-Hawaiian service, held every Sunday at 10:30am, complete with Hawaiian song. Admission is

free; let your conscience be your guide as to a donation. See chapter 7.

- **Buy a Lei from Vendors in Chinatown:** A host of cultural sights and experiences are to be had in Honolulu's Chinatown. Wander through this several-square-block area with its jumble of exotic shops offering herbs, Chinese groceries, and acupuncture services. Before you leave, be sure to check out the lei sellers on Maunakea Street (near N. Hotel St.), where Hawaii's finest leis go for as little as $2.50. See chapter 7 for a neighborhood walking tour, and see chapter 8, "Shopping," for details on where to buy leis.

- **Observe the Fish Auction:** There is nothing else quite like the Honolulu Fish Auction at the United Fishing Agency, 117 Ahui St. (below John Dominis Restaurant), Honolulu, HI 96814

(© **808/536-2148**). The fishermen bring their fresh catch in at 5:30am (sharp), Monday through Saturday, and the small group of buyers wanders from big fat tunas to weird-looking hapupu, bidding on the price of each fish. Don't be surprised if you don't recognize much of the language the bidders are using; it is an internal dialect developed over decades, which only the buyers and the auctioneer understand. The auction lasts until all the fish are sold. It is well worth getting up early to enjoy this unique cultural experience.

- **Get a Bargain at the Aloha Flea Market:** For 50¢ admission, it's an all-day show at the Aloha Stadium parking lot, where more than 1,000 vendors are selling everything from junk to jewels. Go early for the best deals. Open Wednesday, Saturday, and Sunday from 6am to 3pm.

9 The Best Luxury Hotels & Resorts

See chapter 4, "Accommodations," for complete reviews of all these fabulous hotels.

- **Hilton Hawaiian Village Beach Resort & Spa** (© **800/HILTONS** or 808/949-4321): This is Waikiki's biggest resort—so big it even has its own post office. Some 3,000 rooms are spread over 20 acres with tropical gardens, thundering waterfalls, exotic wildlife, award-winning restaurants, nightly entertainment, two brand-new state-of-the-art spas, 100 different shops, children's programs, fabulous ocean activities, a secluded lagoon, three swimming pools, Hawaiian cultural activities, two mini-golf courses, and Waikiki Beach. This place is so big and so complete, you could spend your entire vacation here and never leave the property.

- **Halekulani** (© **800/367-2343** or 808/923-2311; www.halekulani. com): For the ultimate in a "heavenly" Hawaii vacation, this is the place. In fact, Halekulani translates into "House Befitting Heaven," an apt description. When money is no object, Oahu's only AAA five-diamond resort is the place to stay. This luxury resort is spread over 5 acres of prime Waikiki beachfront property and offers acclaimed restaurants. The atmosphere of elegance envelops you as soon as you step into the lobby. Even if you don't stay here, drop by at sunset to sip on a mai tai at the gracious House without a Key and listen to Sonny Kamehele sing Hawaiian songs as a graceful hula dancer sways to the music.

- **Royal Hawaiian** (℃ **800/ 325-3535** or 808/923-7311; www. sheraton.com): Hidden in the jungle of concrete buildings that make up Waikiki is an oasis of verdant gardens and a shockingly pink building. The Royal Hawaiian Hotel, affectionately called the "pink palace," is known around the world as a symbol of luxury. Since the first day it opened in 1927, the Royal has been the place to stay for celebrities, including Clark Gable, Shirley Temple, President Franklin Roosevelt, the Beatles, Kevin Costner, and others. The location is one of the best spots on Waikiki Beach.

- **Sheraton Moana Surfrider Hotel** (℃ **800/325-3535** or 808/ 922-3111; www.moana-surfrider. com): Step back in time to old Hawaii at the Sheraton Moana Surfrider Hotel, built in 1901. Those days of yesteryear live on today at this grand hotel. Entry is through the original colonial porte-cochère, past the highly polished wooden front porch, with white wooden rocking chairs, and into the perfectly restored lobby with its detailed millwork and intricate plaster detailing on the ceiling. Time seems to slow down here, tropical flowers arranged in huge sprays are everywhere, and people in the lobby all seem to be smiling. At check-in, guests are greeted with a lei and a glass of fruit juice. This is a hotel not only with class, but also with historic charm.

- **W Honolulu** (℃ **877/W-HOTELS** or 808/922-1700; www. whotels. com): It's expensive, but worth every penny, to be totally pampered in a low-key, elegantly casual hotel that caters to the business traveler but takes excellent care of vacationers, too. The W Honolulu can be summed up in a nutshell by the button on your room phone that says "whatever/whenever." That's what we call service! If you're craving peace and quiet—away from the crowds of Waikiki but close enough (about a 15-min. walk) to shops and restaurants—this is a perfect location. Although W is not on the beach, guests still have access to the small, private beach in front of the Colony Surf (great swimming here), about a 30-second walk away; Kapiolani Park is across the street, and the Waikiki Aquarium is just a few steps away.

- **Kahala Mandarin Oriental Hawaii** (℃ **800/367-2525** or 808/739-8888; www.mandarin oriental.com): Since 1964, when Conrad Hilton first opened the hotel as a place for rest and relaxation, far from the crowds of Waikiki, the Kahala has always been rated as one of Hawaii's premier hotels. A venerable who's who of celebrities have stayed at the hotel, including every president since Richard Nixon, a host of rock stars from the Rolling Stones to the Beach Boys, and a range of actors from John Wayne to Bette Midler. The Mandarin is a completely up-to-date resort, with exotic Asian touches, but it retains the grace and elegance of a softer, gentler time in the islands.

- **J.W. Marriott Ihilani Resort & Spa at Ko Olina Resort** (℃ **800/ 626-4446** or 808/679-0070; www.ihilani.com): Located in the quiet of Oahu's west coast, some 17 miles and 25 minutes west of Honolulu International Airport—and worlds away from the tourist scene of Waikiki—the Ihilani (which means "heavenly splendor") is the first hotel in the

640-acre Ko Olina Resort. It features a luxury spa and fitness center, plus championship tennis and golf. The plush rooms are spacious, with huge lanais and lagoon or ocean views from some 85% of the units. Who misses Waikiki with luxury like this?

10 The Best Bargain Accommodations

It is possible to stay on Oahu without having to take out a second mortgage. See chapter 4 for complete reviews of all these accommodations.

- **Aston Coconut Plaza** (© 800/92-ASTON or 808/923-8828; www.aston-hotels.com): Calling itself a "studio apartment boutique hotel," the Coconut Plaza offers free continental breakfast and the kind of personalized service that only a small hotel can provide. Rates start at an astonishingly low $75 for a basic double. The recently renovated property has a tropical-plantation feel, with big, airy, island-style rooms, terra-cotta tile, and lots of greenery; all have private lanais. The units with kitchenettes are especially good deals. Ala Wai Golf Course is just across the canal, and the beach is four blocks away.
- **Royal Kuhio** (© 800/367-5205 or 808/538-7145): Families will appreciate this hotel, one of the best bargains in Waikiki. Each unit in this high-rise condo has a full kitchen, separate bedrooms, and a living area with a lanai. It's 2 blocks from Waikiki Beach and within walking distance of everything else of interest. All for just $95 to $125! Not to mention the free parking—a rarity in Waikiki.
- **Hawaiiana Hotel** (© 800/535-0085 or 808/923-3811; www.hawaiianahotelatwaikiki.com): The lush tropical flowers and carved tiki at the entrance on tiny Beach Walk set the tone for this intimate low-rise hotel. From the moment you arrive, you'll

experience the aloha spirit here: At check-in, guests are given a pineapple; every morning, complimentary Kona coffee and tropical juice are served poolside; at check-out, flower leis are presented to the women as a fragrant reminder of their vacation at the Hawaiiana. The concrete hollow-tile rooms, which start at $85 double, feature kitchenettes and views of the gardens and swimming pool.
- **New Otani Kaimana Beach Hotel** (© 800/35-OTANI or 808/923-1555; www.kaimana.com): This boutique hotel is just outside Waikiki, nestled right on the beach at the foot of Diamond Head. The airy lobby opens to the open-air Hau Tree Lanai restaurant, under the same tree that sheltered Robert Louis Stevenson a century ago; there's also the lovely Sunset Lanai Lounge for cocktails. Double rooms in this quiet section of Waikiki start at $135. Because the hotel overlooks Kapiolani Park, guests have easy access to golf, tennis, kite-flying, jogging, and bicycling.
- **Manoa Valley Inn** (© 800/535-0085 or 808/947-6019; www.aloha.net/~wery/index): It's completely off the tourist trail and far from the beach, but that doesn't stop travelers from heading to this genteel 1915 Carpenter Gothic home on a quiet residential street near the University of Hawaii. This eight-room Manoa landmark—it's on the National Register of Historic Places—offers a glimpse into

the lifestyles of the rich and famous in early Honolulu. Each room has its own unique decor and has been named for a prominent figure in Hawaii's history. Rates are $99 to $120 double with shared bath, $140 to $190 double with a private bath.

- **Santa's by the Sea** (© 800/262-9912 or 808/885-4550; www.bestbnb.com): It's just $125 for two for this apartment right on the ocean. The location, price, and style make this place a must-stay if you plan to spend time on the North Shore. Santa's is not located on just any beach, but the famous Banzai Pipeline. You can go from your bed to the sand in less than 30 seconds to watch the sun rise over the Pacific.
- **Rainbow Inn** (© 808/488-7525): This private tropical garden studio has panoramic views of Pearl Harbor, the entire south coast of Oahu, and the Waianae and Koolau mountains. A large deck and full-size pool are just outside your door. Located close to Pearl Ridge Shopping Center, Rainbow Inn is a short drive from all of Oahu's attractions, yet far enough away to provide you with lots of peace and quiet. At $75 a night, this is one of Oahu's best deals.

- **Lanikai Bed & Breakfast:** (© 800/258-7895 or 808/261-1059; www.lanikaibb.com): This old-time bed-and-breakfast, a *kamaaina* (old-timer) home that reflects the Hawaii of yesteryear, is now into its second generation. The recently renovated 1,000-square-foot upstairs apartment is decorated in an old Hawaii bungalow style and rents for $110 for four. Or you can follow the ginger- and ti-lined path to a 540-square-foot honeymooner's delight, at $90 for two. Access to picture-perfect white-sand Lanikai Beach is right across the street.
- **Aloha B&B** (© 808/395-6694; http://home.hawaii.rr.com/aloha phyllis): Perched on a hillside in the residential community of Hawaii Kai is this very affordable B&B, complete with swimming pool, panoramic ocean views, and continental breakfast on the outdoor lanai. The two bedrooms (one with king bed and one with twins) share a bath and a half. It's just a 10-minute drive to snorkeling in Hanauma Bay and about a 15-minute drive to Waikiki and downtown Honolulu. Hostess Phyllis Young has lots of beach toys she'll loan you for the day. And the price for all this? Just $60 to $70 for two.

11 The Best Resort Spas

- **Na Ho'ola Spa in the Hyatt Regency Waikiki** (Oahu; © 800/233-1234; www.hyattwaikiki.com): Waikiki's first spa, just opened in 2000, is an airy, modern 10,000-square-foot facility with a small fitness center, a sauna, Vichy showers, and a relaxation area. The 19 treatment rooms are twice the usual size, with plenty of room to accommodate couples massage. See chapter 4.
- **Abhasa Waikiki Spa in the Royal Hawaiian Hotel** (© 808/922-8200; www.abhasa.com): This contemporary spa, spread out over 7,000 square feet, concentrates on natural, organic treatments in a soothing atmosphere, where the smell of eucalyptus wafts through the air. You can experience everything from the latest aromatherapy thalassotherpie (soaking in a sweet-smelling hot bath) to shiatsu massages. Their specialty is a

(C) Pampering in Paradise

Hawaii's spas have raised the art of the relaxation and healing to a new level. The traditional Greco-Roman-style spas, with lots of marble and big tubs in closed rooms, have evolved into airy, open facilities that embrace the tropics. Spa goers in Hawaii are looking for a sense of place, seeped in the culture. They want to hear the sound of the ocean, smell the salt air, and feel the caress of the warm breeze. They want to experience Hawaiian products and traditional treatments they can get only in the islands.

The spas of Hawaii, once nearly exclusively patronized by women, are now attracting more male clients. There are special massages for children and pregnant women, and some spas have created programs to nurture and relax brides on their big day.

Today's spas offer a wide diversity of treatments. There is no longer plain, ordinary massage, but Hawaiian lomilomi, Swedish, aromatherapy (with sweet-smelling oils), craniosacral (massaging the head), shiatsu (no oil, just deep thumb pressure on acupuncture points), Thai (another oilless massage involving stretching), and hot stone (with heated, and sometimes cold, rocks). There are even side-by-side massages for couples. The truly decadent might even try a duo massage—not one, but *two* massage therapists working on you at once.

Massages are just the beginning. Body treatments, for the entire body or for just the face, involve a variety of herbal wraps, masks, or scrubs using a range of ingredients from seaweed to salt to mud, with or without accompanying aromatherapy, lights, and music.

After you have been rubbed and scrubbed, most spas offer an array of water treatments—a sort of hydromassage in a tub with jets and an assortment of colored crystals, oils, and scents.

Those are just the traditional treatments. Most spas also offer a range of alternative health care like acupuncture, chiropractic, and other exotic treatments like ayurvedic and siddha from India or reiki from Japan. Many places offer specialized, cutting-edge treatments, like the Grand Wailea Resort's full-spectrum color-light therapy pod (based on NASA's work with astronauts).

Once your body has been pampered, spas also offer a range of fitness facilities (weight-training equipment, raquetball, tennis, golf) and classes (yoga, aerobics, step, spinning, stretch, tai chi, kickboxing, aquacize). Several even offer adventure fitness packages (from bicycling to snorkeling). For the nonadventurous, most spas have salons, dedicated to hair and nail care and makeup.

If all this sounds a bit overwhelming, not to worry, all the spas in Hawaii have individual consultants who will help design you an appropriate treatment program to fit your individual needs.

Of course, all this pampering doesn't come cheap. Massages are generally $95 to $115 for 50 minutes and $145 to $165 for 80 minutes; body treatments are in the $120 to $165 range; and alternative healthcare treatments can be has high as $150 to $220. But you may think it's worth the expense to banish your tension and stress.

cold-laser, anti-aging treatment that promises to give you a refreshed, revitalized face in just 30 minutes.

- **Mandara Spa in the Hilton Hawaiian Village Resort & Spa** (Waikiki; © 808/926-6500; www.mandaraspa.com): Just opened in the summer of 2001, this spa is located in the new Kalia Tower of the sprawling Hilton Hawaiian Village. In the 25 luxury treatment rooms (each with its own exotic private garden), you can choose from a menu of unique treatments like a Javanese Lulur rub, a Balinese facial, or a Hawaiian tropical flower bath. There's also a fitness center with an open-air cardiovascular center, aerobic and fitness classes, a relaxing pool and a meditative area, and a full-service salon.

- **Ihilani Spa at the J.W. Marriott Ihilani Resort & Spa** (© 800/ 626-4446; www.ihilani.com): An oasis by the sea, this freestanding 35,000-square-foot facility is dedicated to the traditional spa definition of "health by water." This modern, multistoried spa, filled with floor-to-ceiling glass looking out on green tropical plants, combines Hawaiian products with traditional therapies to produce some of the best water treatments in the state. You'll also find a fitness center, tennis courts, and a bevy of aerobic and stretching classes.

12 The Best Restaurants

See chapter 5 for complete reviews of these and many other top Oahu restaurants.

- **Akasaka** (© 808/942-4466): The spicy tuna handroll, hamachi sushi, clam miso soup, and sizzling tofu and scallops here are among life's greatest pleasures. This tiny sushi bar with its petite tatami room is hidden among the shadowy nightclubs of Honolulu's Kona Street—off the beaten track, yet always jumping with regulars.

- **Alan Wong's Restaurant** (© 808/949-2526): Master strokes at this shrine of Hawaii Regional Cuisine: warm California rolls made with salmon roe, wasabi, and Kona lobster instead of rice; luau lumpia with butterfish and kalua pig; and gingercrusted fresh onaga. Opihi shooters and day-boat scallops in season are a must, while noriwrapped tempura ahi is a perennial favorite. The menu changes daily, but the flavors never lose their sizzle.

- **C&C Pasta** (© 808/732-5999): This place jumps with Italian food lovers who line up for a chance at Carla Magziar's mushroom risotto and excellent house-made pasta, lasagne, and gourmet salads and pizza. Bruschetta, ravioli, and a spate of specials (including a world-class bread pudding and tiramisu) are perfectly flavored, and the aromas of truffle butter and garlic scent the room.

- **Chef Mavro Restaurant** (© 808/ 944-4714): Honolulu is abuzz over the wine pairings and elegant cuisine of George Mavrothalassitis, the culinary wizard from Provence who turned La Mer (at the Halekulani) and Seasons (at the Four Seasons Resort Wailea) into temples of fine dining. He brought his award-winning signature dishes with him, and continues to prove his ingenuity with dazzling a la carte and prix-fixe menus.

- **Jimbo's Restaurant** (© 808/ 947-2211): From broth to noodles to tempura and vegetable toppings, only the finest ingredients from Japan are used. Noodle lovers delight in the flawless broth with its smoky, toasty undertones, and the homemade udon noodles topped with shrimp tempura and mirin-soaked shiitake mushrooms. The Japanese-style curries are also big sellers, but noodles are king.

- **Olive Tree Cafe** (© 808/ 737-0303): This temple of Greek and Mediterranean delights is the quintessential neighborhood magnet—casual, bustling, and consistently great. Owner Savas Mojarrad has a following of foodies, hipsters, artists, and all manner of loyalists who appreciate his integrity and generosity. Standards are always high, the food reasonable, the dishes fresh and homemade. Order at the counter and grab a table inside or out (the place is small). Bring your own wine, and sit down to fresh fish souvlaki, excellent marinated mussels, and spanakopita made with special sheep's cheese. Mojarrad even makes the yogurt for his famous yogurt-mint-cucumber sauce, the souvlaki's ticket to immortality. And don't miss the chicken saffron, a Tuesday special.

- **Padovani's Restaurant & Wine Bar** (© 808/946-3456): Chef Philippe Padovani's elegant, innovative style is highlighted in everything from the endive salad to

pan-fried moi at his two-tiered approach to fine dining. Downstairs is the swank dining room with its Bernaudaud china and Frette linens; upstairs is the informal Wine Bar, with excellent single-malt Scotches, wines by the glass, and a much more casual, but equally sublime, menu.

- **Roy's Restaurant** (© 808/ 396-7697): Good food still reigns at this busy, noisy flagship Hawaii Kai dining room with the trademark open kitchen. Roy Yamaguchi's deft way with local ingredients, nostalgic ethnic preparations, and fresh fish makes his menu, which changes daily, a novel experience every time. Yamaguchi's special dinners with vintners are a Honolulu staple.

- **Sushi Sasabune** (© 808/ 947-3800): Sushi chef Seiji Kumagawa offers "trust me" sushi for the purists who sit at the sushi bar. The specials of the day are fresh as can be, with no Western mutations such as mayonnaise, avocado, and the resultant California roll. This is Japanese all the way, with halibut, salmon, scallops, oysters, and seafood from around the world, flown in fresh that day and served with warm rice. Sit at a table if you want to order; at this sushi bar, you must be submissive and receive what the chef serves.

13 The Best Shopping

Products of Hawaii now merit their own festivals and trade shows throughout the year. "Made in Hawaii" is a label to be touted. See chapter 8 for a complete shopper's guide.

- **Academy Shop** (in the Honolulu Academy of Arts; © 808/ 523-8703): The recent expansion

of the Honolulu Academy of Arts made a good thing even better. You'll find a stunning selection of art books, stationery, jewelry, basketry, beadwork, ikats, saris, ethnic fabrics, fiber vessels, accessories, and contemporary gift items representing the art and craft traditions of the world.

- **Alii Antiques of Kailua II** (℡ **808/261-1705**): Make a bee-line here, particularly if you have a weakness for vintage Hawaiiana. Koa lamps and rattan furniture from the 1930s and '40s, hula nodders, rare 1940s koa tables, and a breathtaking array of vintage etched-glass vases and trays are some of the items in this unforgettable shop.

- **Avanti Fashion** (℡ **808/ 924-1688,** and 808/922-2828): In authentic prints from the 1930s and '40s reproduced on silk, Avanti aloha shirts and sportswear elevate tropical garb from high kitsch to high chic. Casual, comfortable, easy care, and light as a cloud, the silks look vintage but cost a fraction of collectibles prices. The nostalgic treasures are available in retail stores statewide, but the best selection is at the retail stores in Waikiki.

- **Bibelot** (℡ **808/738-0368**): Bibelot is the perfect local gallery: tiny, tasteful, and luminous with fine works of glass, paintings, ceramics, jewelry, textiles, and other objects of beauty. Kudos to Paul Sakai and Tom Tierney for giving island artists this new and refreshing venue. More than 30 artists, some of them the finest in the islands (Doug Britt, Margaret Ezekiel, Charles Higa, Kenny Kicklighter) make their works available here. Fantastic gifts to go.

- **Contemporary Museum Gift Shop** (in the Contemporary Museum; ℡ **808/523-3447**):

This gets our vote as the most beautiful setting for a gift shop, and its contents are a bonus: extraordinary art-related books, avant-garde jewelry, cards and stationery, home accessories, and gift items made by artists from Hawaii and across the country. Only the best here.

- **Vagabond House** (℡ **808/ 593-0288**): Gracious island living is translated here into home accessories, one-of-a-kind island crafts, fine porcelain and pottery, children's books, luxury soaps, hand-screened table linens, china, furniture, and designer toys and teapots. A browser's (and shopper's!) paradise.

- **Native Books & Beautiful Things** (℡ **808/596-8885,** and 808/599-5511): Hawaii is the content and the context in this shop of books, crafts, and gift items made by island artists and crafters. Musical instruments, calabashes, jewelry, leis, books, fabrics, clothing, home accessories, jams and jellies—they're all high quality and made in Hawaii—a celebration of Hawaiiana.

- **Silver Moon Emporium** (℡ **808/637-7710**): This is an islandwide phenomenon, filled with the terrific finds of owner Lucie Talbot-Holu, who has a gift for discovering fashion treasures. Exquisite clothing and handbags, reasonably priced footwear, hats, jewelry, scarves, and a full gamut of other treasures pepper the attractive boutique.

14 The Best Spots for Sunset Cocktails

- **Sunset Lanai** (in the New Otani Kaimana Beach Hotel; ℡ **808/ 923-1555**): The hau tree shaded Robert Louis Stevenson as he wrote poems to Princess Kaiulani. Today it frames the ocean view

from the Sunset Lanai, next to the Hau Tree Lanai restaurant. Sunset Lanai is the favorite watering hole of Diamond Head–area beach-goers who love Sans Souci Beach, the ocean view, the mai tais and sashimi platters, and the live music during weekend sunset hours.

- **House Without a Key** (in the Halekulani; ℂ 808/923-2311): Oahu's quintessential sunset oasis claims several unbeatable elements: It's outdoors on the ocean, with a view of Diamond Head, and it offers great hula and steel guitar music—and one of the best mai tais on the island. You know it's special when even jaded Honoluluans declare it their favorite spot for send-offs, reunions, and an everyday gorgeous sunset.

- **Mai Tai Bar** (in the Royal Hawaiian Hotel; ℂ 808/923-7311): This bar without walls is perched a few feet from the sand, with sweeping views of the South Shore and the Waianae Mountains. Surfers and paddlers ride the waves while the light turns golden and Diamond Head acquires a

halo. This is one of the most pleasing views of Waikiki Beach; sip a mighty mai tai while Carmen and Keith Haugen serenade you.

- **Duke's Canoe Club** (in the Outrigger Waikiki Hotel; ℂ 808/923-0711): It's crowded at sunset, but who can resist listening to the top Hawaiian musicians in this upbeat atmosphere a few feet from the sands of Waikiki? Come in from the beach or from the street—it's always a party at Duke's. Entertainment here is tops, and it reaches a crescendo at sunset.

- **Jameson's by the Sea** (ℂ 808/637-6272): The mai tais here are dubbed the best in surf city, and the view, although not perfect, isn't hurting either. Across the street from the harbor, this open-air roadside oasis is a happy stop for North Shore wave watchers and sunset-savvy sightseers.

15 The Best Oahu Websites

- **Hawaii Visitors & Convention Bureau** (www.gohawaii.com): An excellent, all-around guide to activities, tours, lodging, and events, plus a huge section on weddings and honeymoons. But keep in mind that only members of the HVCB are listed.

- **Planet Hawaii** (www.planet-hawaii.com): Click on "Island" for an island-by-island guide to activities, lodging, shopping, culture, the surf report, weather, and more. Mostly, you'll find short listings with links to companies' own websites. Click on "Hawaiian Eye" for live images from around the islands.

- **Internet Hawaii Radio** (www.hotspots.hawaii.com): A great way to get into the mood, this

eclectic site features great Hawaiian music, with opportunities to order a CD or cassette. You can also purchase a respectable assortment of Hawaiian historical and cultural books.

- **Visit Oahu** (www.visit-oahu.com): An extensive guide to activities, dining, lodging, parks, shopping, and more from the Oahu chapter of the Hawaii Visitors and Convention Bureau.

- **The Hawaiian Language Website** (http://hawaiianlanguage.com): This fabulous site not only has easy lessons on learning the Hawaiian language, but also a great cultural calendar, links to other Hawaiiana websites, a section on the hula, and lyrics (and translations) to Hawaiian songs.

2

Planning Your Trip to Oahu

by Jeanette Foster

Oahu has so many places to explore, things to do, sights to see—where do you start? That's where we come in. In the pages that follow, we've compiled everything you need to know to plan your ideal trip: information on airlines, seasons, a calendar of events, how to make camping reservations, and much more (even how to tie the knot).

Actually, Oahu is a relatively small island, measuring 26 miles long and some 44 miles across at its widest, totaling 608 square miles of land, with 112 miles of coastline. From outer space, Oahu looks somewhat like a frayed Indian arrowhead with two mountain ridges shoring up each side: the 4,000-foot Waianae Mountains on the leeward (western) coast and the 3,000-foot Koolau Mountains on the windward (eastern) side. At night you can see the lights of suburban Oahu pouring down and out of the mountain valleys and reaching toward the shoreline.

In the minds of many, Oahu and its most famous city, Honolulu, are synonymous. In fact, some people think the name of the island is Honolulu, a misnomer further compounded by the islandwide county calling itself the "City and County of Honolulu." Honolulu's best-known neighborhood, Waikiki, is actually pretty small, but its spectacular beach and array of resort hotels are the attractions that originally put Hawaii on the tourist map.

1 The Island in Brief

HONOLULU

Hawaii's largest city looks like any other big metropolitan center with tall buildings. In fact, some cynics refer to it as "Los Angeles West." But within Honolulu's boundaries, you'll find rain forests, deep canyons, valleys and waterfalls, a nearly mile-high mountain range, coral reefs, and gold-sand beaches. The city proper—where most of Oahu's residents live—is approximately 12 miles wide and 26 miles long, running east to west, roughly between Diamond Head and Pearl Harbor. Within the city are seven hills laced by seven streams that run to Mamala Bay.

Surrounding the central area is a plethora of neighborhoods, ranging from the quiet suburbs of **Hawaii Kai** to *kamaaina* (old-timer) neighborhoods like **Manoa.** These areas are generally quieter and more residential than Waikiki, but they're still within minutes of beaches, shopping, and all the activities Oahu has to offer.

WAIKIKI Some say that Waikiki is past its prime—that everybody goes to Maui now. If it has fallen out of favor, you couldn't prove it by us. Waikiki is the very incarnation of Yogi Berra's comment about Toots Shor's famous New York restaurant: "Nobody goes there anymore. It's too crowded."

When King Kalakaua played in Waikiki, it was "a hamlet of plain cottages . . . its excitements caused by the activity of insect tribes and the

---

Tips Finding Your Way Around, Oahu Style

Mainlanders sometimes find the directions given by locals a bit confusing. Seldom will you hear the terms east, west, north, and south; instead, islanders refer to directions as either **makai** (ma-*kae*), meaning toward the sea, or **mauka** (*mow*-kah), toward the mountains. In Honolulu, people use **Diamond Head** as a direction meaning to the east (in the direction of the world-famous crater called Diamond Head), and **Ewa** as a direction meaning to the west (toward the town called Ewa, on the other side of Pearl Harbor).

So, if you ask a local for directions, this is what you're likely to hear: "Drive 2 blocks makai (toward the sea), then turn Diamond Head (east) at the stoplight. Go 1 block, and turn mauka (toward the mountains). It's on the Ewa (western) side of the street."

---

occasional fall of a coconut." The Merrie Monarch, who gave his name to Waikiki's main street, would love the scene today. Some 5 million tourists visit Oahu every year, and 9 out of 10 of them stay in Waikiki. This urban beach is where all the action is; it's backed by 175 high-rise hotels with more than 33,000 guest rooms and hundreds of bars and restaurants, all in a 1½-square-mile beach zone. Waikiki means honeymooners and sun seekers, bikinis and bare buns, a round-the-clock beach party every day of the year—and it's all because of a thin crescent of sand that was shipped over from Molokai. Staying in Waikiki puts you in the heart of it all, but also be aware that this is an on-the-go place with traffic noise 24 hours a day and its share of crime—and it's almost always crowded.

ALA MOANA A great beach as well as a famous shopping mall, Ala Moana is the retail and transportation heart of Honolulu, a place where you can both shop and suntan in one afternoon. All bus routes lead to the open-air **Ala Moana Shopping Center,** across the street from **Ala Moana Beach Park.** This 50-acre, 200-shop behemoth attracts 56 million customers a year (people fly up from Tahiti just to buy their Christmas gifts here). Every European designer from Armani to Vuitton is represented in Honolulu's answer to Beverly Hills's Rodeo Drive. For our purposes, the neighborhood called "Ala Moana" extends along Ala Moana Boulevard from Waikiki in the direction of Diamond Head to downtown Honolulu in the Ewa direction (west), and includes the **Ward Centre** and **Ward Warehouse** complexes as well as **Restaurant Row.**

DOWNTOWN A tiny cluster of high-rises west of Waikiki, downtown Honolulu is the financial, business, and government center of Hawaii. On the waterfront stands the iconic 1926 Aloha Tower, now the centerpiece of a harbor-front shopping and restaurant complex known as the **Aloha Tower Marketplace.** The whole history of Honolulu can be seen in just a few short blocks: Street vendors sell papayas from trucks on skyscraper-lined concrete canyons; joggers and BMWs rush by a lacy palace where U.S. Marines overthrew Hawaii's last queen and stole her kingdom; burly bus drivers sport fragrant white ginger flowers on their dashboards; Methodist churches look like Asian temples; and businessmen wear aloha shirts to billion-dollar meetings.

Honolulu Neighborhoods in Brief

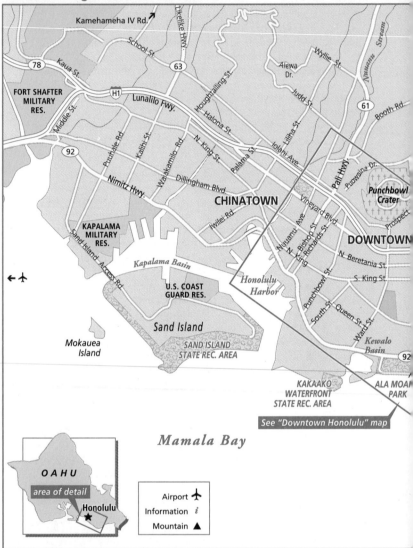

On the edge of downtown is the **Chinatown Historic District,** the oldest Chinatown in America and still one of Honolulu's liveliest neighborhoods, a nonstop pageant of people, sights, sounds, smells, and tastes—not all Chinese, now that Southeast Asians, including many Vietnamese, share the old storefronts. Go on Saturday morning, when everyone shops here for fresh goods such as gingerroot, fern fronds, and hogs' heads.

Among the historic buildings and Pan-Pacific corporate headquarters are a few hotels, mainly geared toward business travelers. Most visitors prefer

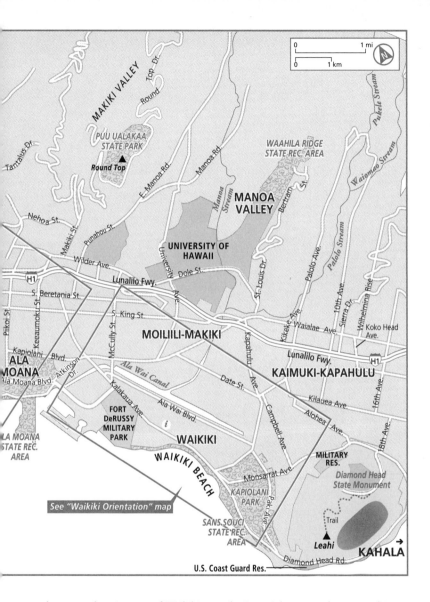

MAKIKI VALLEY

Top Dr.

Round

Tantalus Dr.

PUU UALAKAA
STATE PARK
▲ Round Top

E. Manoa Rd.

Manoa Rd.

Manoa Stream

WAAHILA RIDGE
STATE REC. AREA

Pukele Stream

Waiomao Stream

Nehoa St.

Makiki St.

Punahou St.

Wilder Ave.

University Ave.

Dole St.

Lunalilo Fwy.

MANOA
VALLEY

Bertram St.

UNIVERSITY OF
HAWAII

Palolo Ave.

Palolo Stream

H1

S. Beretania St.

S. King St.

McCully St.

S. King St.

Kapahulu Ave.

St. Louis Dr.

10th Ave.

Sierra Dr.

Wilhelmina Rise

Koko Head
Ave.

Kikele Ave.

Waialae Ave.

MOILIILI-MAKIKI

Lunalilo Fwy.

H1

Piikoi St.

Kapiolani Blvd.

Keeaumoku St.

Atkinson Dr.

Ala Wai Canal

Kalakaua Ave.

Ala Wai Blvd.

Date St.

KAIMUKI-KAPAHULU

Kilauea Ave.

Alohea Ave.

16th Ave.

18th Ave.

ALA
MOANA

Ala Moana Blvd.

ALA MOANA
STATE REC.
AREA

FORT
DeRUSSY
MILITARY
PARK

i

WAIKIKI

WAIKIKI BEACH

Campbell Ave.

Monsarrat Ave.

KAPIOLANI
PARK

Paki Ave.

MILITARY
RES.

Diamond Head
State Monument

Trail

See "Waikiki Orientation" map

SANS SOUCI
STATE REC.
AREA

▲ Leahi

KAHALA →

Diamond Head Rd.

U.S. Coast Guard Res.

0   1 mi
0   1 km

the sun and excitement of Waikiki or choose a quieter neighborhood outside the city.

MANOA VALLEY   First inhabited by white settlers, the Manoa Valley above Waikiki still has vintage *kamaaina* (old-timer) homes, one of Hawaii's premier botanical gardens in the Lyon Arboretum, the ever-gushing Manoa Falls, and the 320-acre campus of the University of Hawaii, where 50,000 students hit the books when they're not on the beach.

TO THE EAST: KAHALA   Except for the estates of world-class millionaires and the luxurious Kahala

Waikiki Orientation

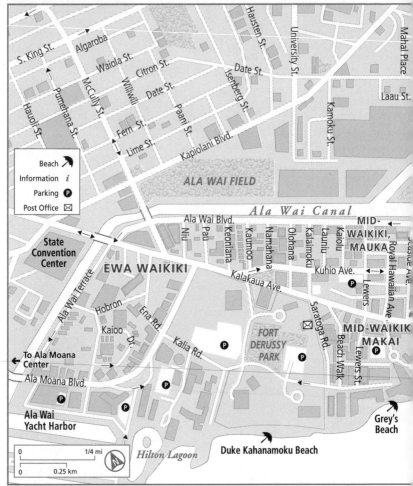

Beach 🏖
Information *i*
Parking 🅿
Post Office ✉

Mandarin Oriental Hotel (home of Hoku's, an outstanding beachfront restaurant), there's not much out this way that's of interest to visitors.

EAST OAHU

Beyond Kahala lies East Honolulu and suburban bedroom communities like Aina Haina, Niu Valley, and Hawaii Kai, among others, all linked by the Kalanianaole Highway and loaded with homes, condos, fast-food joints, and shopping malls. It looks like Southern California on a good

day. There are only a few reasons to come here: to have dinner at **Roy's,** the original and still-outstanding Hawaii Regional Cuisine restaurant, in Hawaii Kai; to snorkel at **Hanauma Bay** or watch daredevil surfers at **Sandy Beach;** or just to enjoy the natural splendor of the lovely coastline, which might include a hike to **Makapuu Lighthouse.**

THE WINDWARD COAST

The windward side is the opposite side of the island from Waikiki. On this

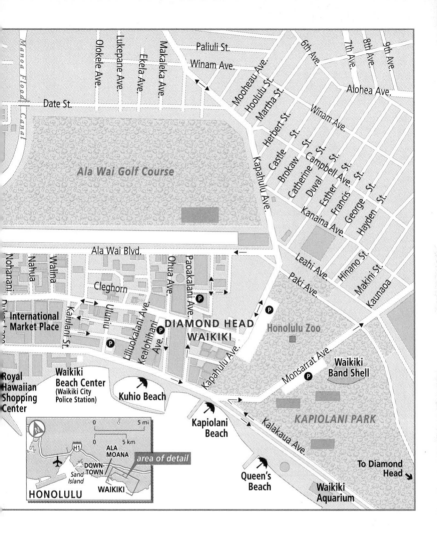

coast, trade winds blow cooling breezes over gorgeous beaches; rain-squalls inspire lush, tropical vegetation; and miles of subdivisions dot the landscape. Bed-and-breakfasts, ranging from oceanfront estates to tiny cottages on quiet residential streets, are everywhere. Vacations here are spent enjoying ocean activities and exploring the surrounding areas. Waikiki is just a quick 15-minute drive away.

KAILUA The biggest little beach town in Hawaii, Kailua sits at the foot of the sheer green Koolau Mountains, on a great bay with two of Hawaii's best beaches. The town itself is a funky low-rise cluster of timeworn shops and homes. Kailua has become the B&B capital of Hawaii; it's an affordable alternative to Waikiki, with rooms and vacation rentals from $60 a day and up. With the prevailing trade winds whipping up a cooling breeze,

Downtown Honolulu

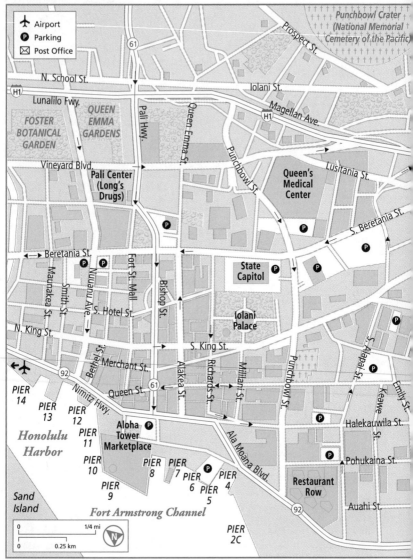

✈ Airport
🅿 Parking
✉ Post Office

Punchbowl Crater
(National Memorial
Cemetery of the Pacific)

Prospect St.

61

N. School St.
Iolani St.

H1
Lunalilo Fwy.
Magellan Ave.

QUEEN
EMMA
GARDENS

H1

FOSTER
BOTANICAL
GARDEN

Pali Hwy.

Queen Emma St.

Punchbowl St.

Lusitania St.

Vineyard Blvd.

Pali Center
(Long's
Drugs)

Queen's
Medical
Center

Beretania St.

S. Beretania St.

Maunakea St.

Smith St.

Nuuanu Ave.

Fort St. Mall

Bishop St.

State
Capitol

S. Hotel St.

N. King St.

Iolani
Palace

S. King St.

S. Alapai St.

Merchant St.

Bethel St.

92

61

Alakea St.

Richards St.

Mililani St.

Punchbowl St.

Keawe St.

Emily St.

✈

PIER
14

Nimitz Hwy.

Queen St.

Halekauwila St.

PIER
13

PIER
12

Aloha
Tower
Marketplace

Honolulu
Harbor

PIER
11

PIER
10

PIER
8

PIER
7

PIER
6

Ala Moana Blvd.

Pohukaina St.

PIER
4

Restaurant
Row

Sand
Island

PIER
9

PIER
5

Auahi St.

Fort Armstrong Channel

92

0   1/4 mi
0   0.25 km

N

PIER
2C

Kailua attracts windsurfers from around the world.

KANEOHE Helter-skelter suburbia sprawls around the edges of Kaneohe, one of the most scenic bays in the Pacific. A handful of B&Bs dots its edge. After you clear the trafficky maze of town, Oahu returns to its more natural state. This great bay beckons you to get out on the water; you can depart from Heeia Boat Harbor on snorkel or fishing charters and visit Ahu a Laka a, the sandbar that appears and disappears in the middle of the bay. From here, you'll have a panoramic view of the Koolau Range.

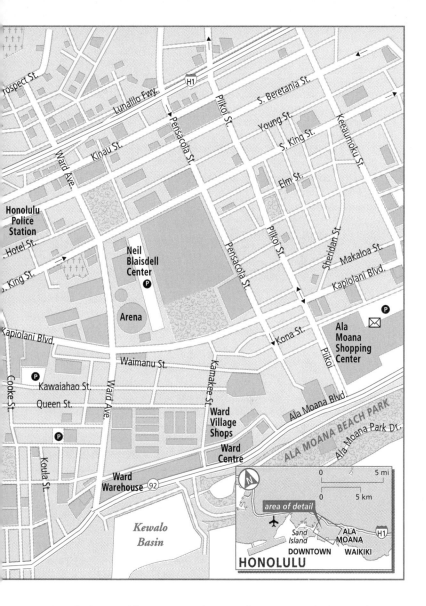

KUALOA/LAIE The upper northeast shore is one of Oahu's most sacred places, an early Hawaiian landing spot where kings dipped their sails, cliffs hold ancient burial sites, and ghosts still march in the night. Sheer cliffs stab the reef-fringed seacoast, while old fishponds are tucked along the two-lane coast road that winds past empty gold-sand beaches around beautiful Kahana Bay. Thousands "explore" the South Pacific at the **Polynesian Cultural Center,** in Laie, a Mormon settlement with its own Tabernacle Choir of sweet Samoan harmony.

THE NORTH SHORE

Here's the Hawaii of Hollywood—giant waves, surfers galore, tropical jungles, waterfalls, and mysterious Hawaiian temples. If you're looking for a quieter vacation, closer to nature, and filled with swimming, snorkeling, diving, surfing, or just plain hanging out on some of the world's most beautiful beaches, the North Shore is your place. The artsy little beach town of **Haleiwa** and the surrounding shoreline seem a world away from Waikiki. The North Shore boasts good restaurants, shopping, and cultural activities—but here they come with the quiet of country living. Bed-and-breakfasts are the most common accommodations, but there's one first-class hotel and some vacation rentals as well. *Be forewarned:* It's a long trip—nearly an hour's drive—to Honolulu and Waikiki, and it's about twice as rainy on the North Shore as in Honolulu.

CENTRAL OAHU: THE EWA PLAIN

Flanked by the Koolau and Waianae mountain ranges, the hot, sun-baked Ewa Plain runs up and down the center of Oahu. Once covered with sandalwood forests (hacked down for the China trade) and later the sugarcane and pineapple backbone of Hawaii,

Ewa today sports a new crop: suburban houses stretching to the sea. But let your eye wander west to the Waianae Range and Mount Kaala, at 4,020 feet the highest summit on Oahu; up there in the misty rain forest, native birds thrive in the hummocky bog. In 1914, the U.S. Army pitched a tent camp on the plain; author James Jones would later call **Schofield Barracks** "the most beautiful army post in the world." Hollywood filmed Jones's *From Here to Eternity* here.

LEEWARD OAHU: THE WAIANAE COAST

The west coast of Oahu is a hot and dry place of dramatic beauty: white-sand beaches bordering the deep blue ocean, steep verdant green cliffs, and miles of Mother Nature's wildness. Except for the luxurious J. W. Marriott Ihilani Resort and Spa in the Ko Olina Resort and the Makaha Golf Course, you'll find virtually no tourist services out here. The funky west coast villages of Nanakuli, Waianae, and Makaha are the last stands of native Hawaiians. This side of Oahu is seldom visited, except by surfers bound for **Yokohama Bay** and those coming to see needle-nose **Kaena Point** (the island's westernmost outpost), which has a coastal wilderness park.

2 Visitor Information

For advance information, contact the **Hawaii Visitors and Convention Bureau (HVCB),** Suite 801, Waikiki Business Plaza, 2270 Kalakaua Ave., Honolulu, HI 96815 (© **800/GO-HAWAII** or 808/923-1811; www.gohawaii.com). Among other things, the bureau publishes the helpful *Accommodations and Car Rental Guide* and supplies free brochures, maps, and the *Islands of Aloha* magazine, the official HVCB magazine.

The **Oahu Visitors Bureau,** 1001 Bishop St., Pauahi Tower, Suite 47,

Honolulu, HI 96813 (© **800/ OAHU-678** or 808/524-0722; www.visit-oahu.com), distributes a free 64-page visitors booklet.

A number of free publications, including *This Week* and *Guide to Oahu,* are packed with money-saving coupons offering discounts on dining, shops, and activities around the island; look for them on the visitors' publication racks at the airport and around town.

If you want information about working and living in Hawaii, contact

**The Chamber of Commerce of
Hawaii,** 1132 Bishop St., Suite 200,
Honolulu, HI 96815 (© **808/
545-4300**).

HAWAII ON THE WEB
Listed below are some of the most useful sites.

• **Hawaii Visitors & Convention
Bureau:** www.gohawaii.com

• **Hawaii State Vacation Planner:**
www.hshawaii.com
• **Planet Hawaii:** www.planet-
hawaii.com/travel
• **Oahu Visitors Bureau:** www.
visit-oahu.com
• **State of Hawaii:** www.hawaii.gov
• **City and County of Honolulu:**
www.co.honolulu.hi.us
• **Hawaii Yellow Pages:** www.
surfhi.com

3 Money

Hawaii pioneered the use of **ATMs**
more than 2 decades ago, and now
they're everywhere. You'll find them at
most banks, in supermarkets, at
Long's Drugs, and in some resorts and
shopping centers like Ala Moana Center and Aloha Tower Market Place.
Cirrus (© **800/424-7787**; www.
mastercard.com/atm) and **PLUS**
(© **800/843-7587**; www.visa.com/
atms) are the two most popular networks; check the back of your ATM
card to see which network your bank
belongs to (most banks belong to both
these days).

With the convenience of ATMs,
traveler's checks seem less necessary.
But you may want to go with traveler's
checks if you want to avoid ATM
withdrawal charges, or if you still prefer the security they offer—provided
you don't mind showing identification
every time you want to cash one. You
can get traveler's checks at almost any

bank, paying a service charge ranging
from 1% to 4%. You can also get
American Express traveler's checks
over the phone by calling © **800/
221-7282** or 800/721-9768; you can
also purchase checks online at **www.
americanexpress.com**. AmEx gold or
platinum cardholders can avoid paying the fee by ordering over the telephone; platinum cardholders can also
purchase checks fee-free in person at
AmEx Travel Service locations (check
the website for the office nearest you).
American Automobile Association
members can obtain checks with no
fee at most AAA offices.

Credit cards are accepted all over
the island. They're a safe way to carry
money and keep track of your
expenses. Still, be sure to keep some
cash on hand for small expenses, or for
that rare occasion when a restaurant or
small shop doesn't take plastic.

4 When to Go

Most visitors don't come to Hawaii
when the weather's best in the islands;
rather, they come when it's at its
worst everywhere else. Thus, the **high
season**—when prices are up and
resorts are booked to capacity—
generally runs from mid-December
through March or mid-April. The last
2 weeks of December in particular are
the prime time for travel to Oahu; if
you're planning a holiday trip, make

your reservations as early as possible,
count on holiday crowds, and expect
to pay top dollar for accommodations,
car rentals, and airfare.

The **off-seasons,** when the best
bargain rates are available, are spring
(mid-Apr to mid-June) and fall (Sept
to mid-Dec)—a paradox, since these
are the best seasons in terms of reliably
great weather. If you're looking to save
money, or if you just want to avoid the

crowds, this is the time to visit. Hotel rates tend to be significantly lower during these off-seasons. Airfares also tend to be lower—again, sometimes substantially—and good packages and special deals are often available.

Note: If you plan to come between the last week in April and mid-May, be sure to book your accommodations, interisland air reservations, and car rental in advance. In Japan, the last week of April is called **Golden Week,** because three Japanese holidays take place one after the other; the islands are especially busy with Japanese tourists during this time.

Due to the large number of families traveling in **summer** (June–Aug), you won't get the fantastic bargains of spring and fall. However, you'll still do much better on packages, airfare, and accommodations than you will in the winter months.

THE WEATHER

Because Hawaii lies at the edge of the tropical zone, it technically has only two seasons, both of them warm. There's a **dry season** that corresponds to summer, and the **rainy season** generally runs during the winter from November to March. It rains every day somewhere in the islands at all times of the year, but the rainy season can cause "gray" weather and spoil your tanning opportunities. Fortunately, it seldom rains for more than 3 consecutive days.

The year-round temperature usually varies no more than 10°F, but this does depend on where you are. Oahu is like a ship in that it has a leeward and a windward side. The leeward side (the west and south, from Waianae to Honolulu and Waikiki) is usually hot and dry, while the windward side (east and north, from Haleiwa to Waimanalo) is generally cooler and moist. When you want arid, sun-baked weather, go leeward. When you want lush, often wet, junglelike weather, go windward.

Hawaii also has many micro-climates, thanks to its interior valleys, coastal plains, and mountain peaks. It can be pouring rain at the University of Hawaii in Manoa, and sunny and dry in Waikiki, a 15-minute drive away.

The **best months** to be in Hawaii are April, May, September, and October, when the nearly perfect weather is even better—not too windy, not too humid, but just right. And this is the off-season: The kids are in school, and the tourists have thinned out. The state's "carrying capacity," as they say here, isn't maxed out. Hotels, restaurants, and attractions aren't as crowded, and everyone is more relaxed.

On rare occasions, the weather can be disastrous. The official hurricane season is June to November. (Remember Hurricane Iniki in Sept 1992? It was the most powerful Pacific storm in history, and it crushed Kauai with 225-mph winds.) Tsunamis, huge tidal waves caused by far-off earthquakes, have swept the shores of the islands. But those are extreme exceptions. Usually one sunny day simply follows another here, each quite like the other.

HOLIDAYS

When Hawaii observes holidays, especially those over a long weekend, travel between the islands increases, interisland airline seats are fully booked, rental cars are at a premium, and hotels and restaurants are busier than usual.

Federal, state, and county government offices are closed on all federal holidays: January 1 (New Year's Day); third Monday in January (Martin Luther King Jr. Day); third Monday in February (Presidents' Day, Washington's Birthday); last Monday in May (Memorial Day); July 4 (Independence Day); first Monday in September (Labor Day); second Monday in October (Columbus Day); November 11

(Veterans' Day); fourth Thursday in November (Thanksgiving Day); and December 25 (Christmas).

State and county offices also are closed on local holidays, including Prince Kuhio Day (Mar 26), honoring the birthday of Hawaii's first delegate to the U.S. Congress; King Kamehameha Day (June 11), a statewide holiday commemorating Kamehameha the Great, who united the islands and ruled from 1795 to 1819; and Admission Day (third Fri in Aug), which honors Hawaii's admission as the 50th state in the United States on August 21, 1959.

Other special days celebrated by many people in Hawaii but that do not involve the closing of federal, state, or county offices are Chinese New Year (in Jan or Feb), Girls' Day (Mar 3), Buddha's Birthday (Apr 8), Father Damien's Day (Apr 15), Boys' Day (May 5), Samoan Flag Day (in Aug), Aloha Festivals (in Sept or Oct), and Pearl Harbor Day (Dec 7).

OAHU CALENDAR OF EVENTS

As with any schedule of upcoming events, the following information is subject to change; always confirm the details before you plan your schedule around an event. For an updated calendar, point your browser to **www.visit-oahu.com**.

January

Morey World Bodyboarding Championship, Banzai Pipeline, North Shore. Competition is determined by the best wave selection and maneuvers on the wave. Call ℰ **808/396-2326.** Early January.

Sony Open, Waialae Country Club. A $1.2-million PGA golf event featuring the top men in golf. Call ℰ **808/734-2151.** Second week in January.

Ala Wai Challenge, Ala Wai Park, Waikiki. This all-day event features ancient Hawaiian games, like *ulu*

maika (bowling a round stone through pegs), *oo ihe* (spear-throwing at an upright target), *huki kaula* (tug of war), and a quarter-mile outrigger canoe race. It's also a great place to hear Hawaiian music. Call ℰ **808/923-1802.** Last weekend in January.

February

NFL Pro Bowl, Aloha Stadium, Honolulu. The National Football League's best pro players square off in this annual gridiron all-star game. Call ℰ **808/486-9300.** First Sunday in February.

Chinese New Year. A big celebration takes place in Chinatown; call ℰ **808/533-3181** for details. February 12, 2002, starts the Year of the Horse, and on February 1, 2003, the Year of the Ram begins.

Narcissus Festival, Honolulu. Taking place around the Chinese New Year, this cultural festival includes a queen pageant, cooking demonstrations, and a cultural fair. Call ℰ **808/533-3181** for details.

Sand Castle Building Contest, Kailua Beach Park. Students from the University of Hawaii School of Architecture compete against professional architects to see who can build the best, most unusual, and most outrageous sand sculpture. Call ℰ **808/956-7225.**

The Great Aloha Run, Honolulu. Thousands run 8.25 miles from Aloha Tower to Aloha Stadium. Always held on Presidents' Day (third Mon in Feb). Call ℰ **808/528-7388.**

Buffalo's Big Board Classic, Makaha Beach. A traditional Hawaiian surfing, longboarding, and canoe-surfing contest. Call ℰ **808/951-7877.** Depending on the surf, it can be held in February or March.

March

Hawaii Challenge International Sportkite Championship, Kapiolani Park. The longest-running sportkite competition in the world attracts top kite pilots from around the globe. Call ℂ **808/735-9059.** First weekend in March.

Annual St. Patrick's Day Parade, Waikiki (Fort DeRussy to Kapiolani Park). Bagpipers, bands, clowns, and marching groups parade through the heart of Waikiki, with lots of Irish celebrating all day. Call ℂ **808/524-0722.** March 17.

Prince Kuhio Celebration. This event commemorates the birth of Jonah Kuhio Kalanianaole, born March 26, 1871. He might have been one of Hawaii's kings if the Hawaiian monarchy had not been overthrown. After Hawaii's annexation to the United States, Prince Kuhio was elected to Congress (1902). Ceremonies are held at the Prince Kuhio Federal Building, at Kuhio Beach in Waikiki, and other locations throughout Oahu. Check the local newspapers for details.

Kamehameha Schools Song Contest, Neal Blaisdell Center, Honolulu. For more than three-quarters of a century, Hawaii's top Hawaiian school has conducted this traditional Hawaiian chorale contest. Call ℂ **808/842-8338.**

Annual Easter Sunrise Service, National Cemetery of the Pacific, Punchbowl Crater, Honolulu. For a century, people have gathered at this famous cemetery for Easter sunrise services. March 31, 2002; April 20, 2003. Call ℂ **808/ 566-1430.**

April

Buddha Day, at various Hongwanji missions throughout the island. Some Buddhist missions have a flower pageant honoring the birth of Buddha. April 6. Call ℂ **808/595-2144.**

Hawaiian Slack Key Concert, Honolulu Academy of Arts, Honolulu. A great opportunity to listen to this traditional form of music. The date of the concert varies from year to year; call ℂ **808/532-8701** for details.

Honolulu International Bed Race Festival, Honolulu. This popular fund-raiser event allows visitors a small taste of Honolulu, with food booths sponsored by local restaurants, live entertainment, a *keiki* (children's) carnival with games and rides, and a race through the streets of Honolulu with runners pushing beds to raise money for local charities. Call ℂ **808/696-2424.** Mid-April.

May

Annual Lei Day Celebration. May Day is Lei Day in Hawaii, celebrated with lei-making contests, pageantry, arts and crafts, and a concert at the Waikiki Shell. May 1. Call ℂ **808/924-8934.**

World Fire-Knife Dance Championships & Samoan Festival, Polynesian Cultural Center, Laie. Junior and adult fire-knife dancers from around the world converge on the center in the most amazing performance you'll ever see. Authentic Samoan food and cultural festivities. Mid-May. Call ℂ **808/293-3333.**

Outrigger Canoe Season, all islands. From May to September, nearly every weekend, canoe paddlers across the state participate in outrigger canoe races. Call ℂ **808/ 261-6615** or www.y2kanu.com for this year's schedule of events.

Outrigger Hotels Hawaiian Oceanfest, various Oahu locations. This weeklong celebration of ocean sports includes the Hawaiian International Ocean Challenge, which features teams of the world's best professional lifeguards; the Outrigger Waikiki Kings Race, an ocean iron-man race; the Diamond Head Wahine Windsurfing Classic, the only all-women professional windsurfing competition; and the Diamond Head Biathlon, a run/swim event. Great athletes, serious competition, a variety of evening events, and more. Call © **808/521-4322.** End of May.

Shinnyo-en Hawaii Temple Floating Lanterns Festival, Keehi Lagoon. A ceremonial floating of some 700 lanterns takes place at sunset, representing an appeal for peace and harmony. Hula and music follows. Generally around Memorial Day weekend. Call © **808/947-2814.**

Memorial Day, National Memorial Cemetery of the Pacific, Punchbowl, Honolulu. The Armed Forces hold a ceremony recognizing those who died for their country, beginning at 9am. Call © **808/532-3720.**

June

King Kamehameha Celebration, a state holiday with a massive floral parade, *hoolaulea* (party), and much more. First weekend in June. On Oahu, call © **808/586-0333.**

King Kamehameha Hula Competition, Neal Blaisdell Center, Honolulu. One of the top hula competitions with dancers from as far away as Japan. Third weekend in June. Call © **808/586-0333.**

Taste of Honolulu, Civic Center Grounds, Honolulu. Hawaii's premier outdoor food festival features tastings from 30 restaurants. Entertainment, beer and wine tasting, cooking demos, gourmet marketplace, and children's activities. End of June. Call © **808/536-1015.**

July

Pacific Island Taro Festival, Windward Community College, Kaneohe. Music, storytelling, dance, an arts-and-crafts fair, and a farmers' market help explain and celebrate the cultures and traditions of the Pacific Islands. Usually first Saturday in July. Call © **808/ 235-7433.**

Fourth of July Fireworks, Desiderio and Sills Field, Schofield Barracks. A free daylong celebration, with entertainment, food, and games, that ends with a spectacular fireworks show. Call © **808/ 656-0110.**

Walter J. McFarlane Regatta and Surf Race, Waikiki. An outrigger canoe regatta featuring 30 events. July 4. Call © **808/259-7112.**

Bankoh Na Wahine O Hawaii, Sheraton Waikiki, Honolulu. The top female hula dancers, singers, musicians, and entertainers in Hawaii perform in this free concert. Call © **808/239-4336** or e-mail kahokuproductions@yahoo.com.

Hawaii International Jazz Festival, Sheraton Waikiki, Honolulu. Evening concerts and daily jam sessions plus scholarship giveaways, the University of Southern California jazz band, and many popular jazz and blues artists. Call © **808/ 941-9974.** Mid-July.

Ukulele Festival, Kapiolani Park Bandstand, Waikiki. This free concert has some 600 kids (ages 4–92) strumming the ukulele. Hawaii's top musicians all pitch in. Call © **808/732-3739** or check out www.ukulele-roysakuma.com. Last Sunday in July.

Hawaiian Open Ice Skating Competition, Ice Palace, Honolulu. Top skaters compete for honors. Date varies. For information, call © **808/487-9921.**

Kenwood Cup. This international yacht race is held during July in even-numbered years only (2002, 2004, etc.). Sailors from the United

States, Japan, Australia, New Zealand, Europe, and Hawaii participate in a series of races around the state. For information, call ℅ **808/949-7141.**

August

Hawaii State Fair, Aloha Stadium, Honolulu. The annual state fair is a great one: It features displays of Hawaii agricultural products (including orchids), educational and cultural exhibits, entertainment, and local-style food. Call ℅ **808/531-3531.** Early August.

Duke Kahanamoku Beach Doubles Volleyball Championship, Waikiki. First held in 1958, this is the oldest-running beach volleyball tournament in the state. Championship-caliber men can enter. Register at least a month in advance; fee is $20 per team. Mid-August. Call ℅ **808/923-1585.**

Admissions Day. Hawaii became the 50th state on August 21, 1959. The state takes a holiday (all state-related facilities are closed) on the third Friday in August.

Bankoh Ki-ho'alu Gabby Style Hawaiian Slack-Key Guitar Festival, Sheraton Waikiki, Honolulu. The best of Hawaii's folk music—slack-key guitar—performed by the best musicians in Hawaii. It's 5 hours long and absolutely free. Call ℅ **808/239-4336** or e-mail kahokuproductions@yahoo.com. Third Sunday in August.

September

Waikiki Rough-Water Swim. This popular 2.4-mile, open-ocean swim from Sans Souci Beach to Duke Kahanamoku Beach in Waikiki takes place on Labor Day. Early registration is encouraged, but they will take last-minute entries on race day. For information, call ℅ **808/587-0300.**

Aloha Festivals, various sites across Oahu. Parades and other events celebrate Hawaiian culture. Call ℅ **800/852-7690** or 808/545-1771 for a schedule of events.

Na Wahine O Ke Kai. This invitational, 41-mile, open-ocean Hawaii outrigger canoe race from Hale O Lono, Molokai, to Duke Kahanamoku Beach, Waikiki, attracts international teams. Usually held the last weekend in September. For information, call ℅ **808/262-7567.**

October

Molokai Hoe, Molokai to Oahu. The course of this men's 40.8-mile outrigger race runs across the channel from Molokai to finish at Fort DeRussy Beach in Waikiki. Call ℅ **808/261-6615.** Mid-October.

Hawaii International Rugby Tournament, Kapiolani Park, Waikiki. Teams from around the world gather to compete in this exciting tournament. The event has a division for all players including Masters, Social, Championship, 7-side, 9-side, and touch. Second week in October. Call ℅ **808/971-2750.**

November

Hawaii International Film Festival, various locations throughout the state. A cinema festival with a cross-cultural spin featuring filmmakers from Asia, the Pacific Islands, and the United States. Call ℅ **808/528-FILM,** or look up www.hiff.org. First 2 weeks in November.

World Invitational Hula Festival, Waikiki Shell. Competitors from all over the world dance for the prizes. Early to mid-November. Call ℅ **808/486-3185;** www.world hula.com.

Triple Crown of Surfing, North Shore. The world's top professional surfers compete in six events for more than $1 million in prize money. Call ✆ **808/638-7266.** Mid-November to mid-December.

December

Honolulu Marathon, Honolulu. One of the largest marathons in the world, with more than 30,000 competitors. Call ✆ **808/734-7200** or check out www.honolulu marathon.org. Early December.

Pacific Handcrafters Guild's Christmas Faire, Thomas Square. One of the largest and finest fairs in the state selling art and fine crafts takes place the first weekend in December, with local entertainment and food booths to liven up the atmosphere. Call ✆ **808/ 223-8482.**

Festival of Trees, Honolulu. A downtown display of one-of-a-kind decorated trees, wreaths, and decorations to benefit Queen's Medical Center. The lighting takes place the first or second week of the month. Call ✆ **808/547-4371.**

Aloha Bowl, Aloha Stadium, Honolulu. A Pac-10 team plays a Big 12 team in this nationally televised collegiate football classic. Call ✆ **808/ 545-7171** or go to www.aloha games.com. Christmas Day.

Rainbow Classic, University of Hawaii, Manoa Valley. Eight of the best NCAA basketball teams compete at the Special Events Arena. Call ✆ **808/956-6501.** The week after Christmas.

5 Health & Insurance

STAYING HEALTHY

If you suffer from a chronic illness, consult your doctor before your departure. For conditions like epilepsy, diabetes, or heart problems, wear a **Medic Alert Identification Tag** (✆ **888/633-4298;** www.medic alert.org), which will immediately alert doctors to your condition and give them access to your records through Medic Alert's 24-hour hot line.

Pack prescription medications in your carry-on luggage. Carry written prescriptions in generic, not brand-name, form and dispense all prescription medications from their original labeled vials. If you wear contact lenses, pack an extra pair in case you lose one.

ON LAND

As in any tropical climate, there are lots of bugs in Hawaii. Most of them won't harm you; however, three insects—mosquitoes, centipedes, and scorpions—do sting, and they can cause anything from mild annoyance to severe swelling and pain.

MOSQUITOES There's not a whole lot you can do about them, except to apply repellent, or burn mosquito punk or citronella candles to keep them out of your area. If they've bitten you, head to the drugstore for sting-stopping ointments (antihistamine creams, such as Benadryl, or homeopathic creams, such as Sting Stop or Florasone); they'll ease the itching and swelling. Most bites disappear in anywhere from a few hours to a few days.

CENTIPEDES These segmented insects with a jillion legs come in two varieties: 6- to 8-inch-long brown ones and the smaller 2- to 3-inch-long blue guys; both can really pack a wallop with their sting. Centipedes are generally found in damp places, like under woodpiles or compost heaps; wearing closed-toe shoes can help prevent stings if you accidentally unearth a centipede. If you're stung, the reaction can range from something similar to a mild bee sting to severe pain; apply ice at once to prevent swelling. See a doctor if you experience extreme pain, swelling, nausea, or any other severe reaction.

SCORPIONS   Rarely seen, scorpions are found in arid, warm regions; their stings can be serious. Campers in dry areas should always check their boots before putting them on, and shake out sleeping bags and bedrolls. Symptoms of a scorpion sting include shortness of breath, hives, swelling, and nausea. In the unlikely event that you're stung, apply diluted household ammonia and cold compresses to the area of the sting and seek medical attention immediately.

Hiking Safety

In addition to taking the appropriate cautions regarding Oahu's bug population (see above), hikers should let someone know where they're heading, when they're going, and when they plan to return.

Always check weather conditions with the **National Weather Service** (© **808/877-5111**) before you go. Hike with a pal, never alone. Wear hiking boots, a sun hat, clothes to protect you from the sun and from getting scratches, and high-SPF sunscreen on all exposed areas of skin. Take water. Stay on the trail. Watch your step. It's easy to slip off precipitous trails and into steep canyons. Many experienced hikers and boaters today pack a cellular phone in case of emergency; just dial © **911.**

Vog

The volcanic haze dubbed "vog" is caused by gases released when molten lava—from the continuous eruption of the volcano on the flank of Kilauea on the Big Island—pours into the ocean. This hazy air, which looks like urban smog, limits viewing from scenic vistas and wreaks havoc with photographers trying to get clear panoramic shots. Some people claim that long-term exposure to vog has even caused bronchial ailments.

There actually is a "vog" season in Hawaii: the fall and winter months, when the trade winds that blow the fumes out to sea die down. The vog is felt not only on the Big Island, but also as far away as Oahu.

OCEAN SAFETY

Because most people coming to Hawaii are unfamiliar with the ocean environment, they're often unaware of the natural hazards it holds. But with just a few precautions, your ocean experience can be a safe and happy one. An excellent book to get is *All Stings Considered: First Aid and Medical Treatment of Hawaii's Marine Injuries* (University of Hawaii Press, 1997) by Craig Thomas (an emergency-medicine doctor) and Susan Scott (a registered nurse). These avid water people have put together the authoritative book on first aid for Hawaii's marine injuries.

SEASICKNESS   The waters off Oahu can range from calm as glass to downright frightening (in storm conditions), and they usually fall somewhere in between; in general, expect rougher conditions in winter than in summer.

If you've never been out on a boat or if you've gotten seasick in the past, you might want to heed the following suggestions: Avoid alcohol; caffeine; citrus and other acidic juices; and greasy, spicy, or hard-to-digest foods the day before you go out. Take or use whatever seasickness prevention works best for you—medication, an acupressure wristband, gingerroot tea or capsules, or any combination—*before* you board; once you set sail, it's generally too late.

Once you're on the water, stay as low and as near the center of the boat as possible. Avoid the fumes (especially if it's a diesel boat); stay out in the fresh air and watch the horizon. Do not read. If you start to feel

Tips Don't Get Burned: Smart Tanning Tips

Tanning just ain't what it used to be. Hawaii's Caucasian population has a higher incidence of deadly skin cancer, malignant melanoma, than anywhere else in the United States. But none of us are safe from the sun's harmful rays: People of all skin types and races can burn when exposed to the sun too long.

To ensure that your vacation won't be ruined by a painful, throbbing sunburn, here are some helpful tips on how to tan safely and painlessly:

- **Wear a strong sunscreen at all times, and use lots of it.** Use a sunscreen with a sun-protection factor (SPF) of 15 or higher; people with a light complexion should use 30. Apply sunscreen as soon as you get out of the shower in the morning, and at least 30 minutes before you're exposed to the sun. No matter what the label says— even if the sunscreen is waterproof—reapply it every 2 hours and immediately after swimming.
- **Read the labels.** To avoid developing allergies to sunscreens, avoid those that contain para-aminobenzoic acid (PABA). Look for a sunscreen with zinc oxide, talc, or titanium dioxide, which reduce the risk of developing skin allergies. For the best protection from UVA rays (which can cause wrinkles and premature aging), check the label for zinc oxide, benzophenone, oxybenzone, sulisobenzone, titanium dioxide, or avobenzone (also known as Parsol 1789).
- **Wear a hat and sunglasses.** And make sure that your sunglasses have UV filters.
- **Avoid being in the sun between 9am and 3pm.** Use extra caution during these peak hours. Remember that a beach umbrella is not protection enough from the sun's harmful UV rays; in fact, with the reflection from the water, the sand, and even the sidewalk, some 85% of the ultraviolet rays are still bombarding you.
- **Protect children from the sun, and keep infants out of the sun altogether.** Infants under 6 months should not be in the sun at all. Older babies need zinc oxide to protect their fragile skin, and children should be slathered with sunscreen every hour. The burns that children get today predict what their future will be with skin cancer tomorrow.

If you start to turn red, **get out of the sun.** Contrary to popular belief, you don't have to turn red to tan; if your skin is red, it's burned—and that's serious. The redness from a burn may not show until 2 to 8 hours after you get out of the sun, and the full force of that burn may not appear for 24 to 36 hours. During that time, you can look forward to pain, itching, and peeling. The best **remedy** for a sunburn is to get out of the sun immediately and stay out of the sun until all the redness is gone. Aloe vera (straight from the plant or from a commercial preparation), cool compresses, cold baths, and anesthetic benzocaine may also help with the pain of sunburn.

queasy, drink clear fluids like water, and eat something bland, such as a soda cracker.

STINGS   The most common stings in Hawaii come from jellyfish, particularly Portuguese man-of-war and box jellyfish. Because the poisons they inject are very different, you need to treat each sting differently.

A bluish-purple floating bubble with a long tail, the **Portuguese man-of-war** causes thousands of stings a year. Stings, although painful and a nuisance, are rarely harmful; fewer than one in a thousand requires medical treatment. The best prevention is to watch for these floating bubbles as you snorkel (look for the hanging tentacles below the surface). Get out of the water if anyone near you spots these jellyfish.

Reactions to stings range from mild burning and redness to severe welts and blisters. *All Stings Considered* recommends the following treatment: First, pick off any visible tentacles with a gloved hand, a stick, or anything handy; rinse the sting with salt or fresh water; and apply ice to prevent swelling and to help control pain.

Hawaiian folklore advises using vinegar, meat tenderizer, baking soda, papain, or alcohol, or even urinating on the wound. Studies have shown that these remedies may actually cause further damage. Most Portuguese man-of-war stings will disappear by themselves within 15 to 20 minutes if you do nothing to treat them. Still, be sure to see a doctor if pain persists or if a rash or other symptoms develop.

Box jellyfish, transparent, square-shaped bell jellyfish, are nearly impossible to see in the water. Fortunately, they seem to follow a monthly cycle: 8 to 10 days after the full moon, they appear in the waters on the leeward side of the island and hang around for about 3 days. Also, they seem to sting more in the morning hours, when they're on or near the surface. The best prevention is to get out of the water.

Stings range from no visible marks to red, hivelike welts, blisters, and pain (a burning sensation) lasting from 10 minutes to 8 hours. *All Stings Considered* recommends the following course of treatment: First, pour regular household vinegar on the sting; this may not relieve the pain, but it will stop additional burning. Do not rub the area. Pick off any vinegar-soaked tentacles with a stick. For pain, apply an ice pack. Seek additional medical treatment if you experience shortness of breath, weakness, palpitations, muscle cramps, or any other severe symptoms. Again, ignore any folk remedies. Most box jellyfish stings disappear by themselves without treatment.

PUNCTURES   Most sea-related punctures come from stepping on or brushing against the needlelike spines of sea urchins (known locally as *wana*). Be careful when you're in the water; don't put your foot down (even if you have booties or fins on) if you cannot clearly see the bottom. Waves can push you into wana in a surge zone in shallow water (the wana's spines can even puncture a wet suit).

A sea urchin sting can result in burning, aching, swelling, and discoloration (black or purple) around the area where the spines have entered your skin. The best thing to do is to pull out any protruding spines. The body will absorb the spines within 24 hours to 3 weeks, or the remainder of the spines will work themselves out. Again, contrary to popular wisdom, do not urinate or pour vinegar on the embedded spines—this will not help.

CUTS   All cuts obtained in the marine environment must be taken seriously, because the high level of bacteria present can quickly cause the cut to become infected. The most common cuts are from **coral.** Contrary to popular belief, coral cannot grow inside your body. However, bacteria can—and very often does—grow inside a cut. The best way to prevent cuts is to wear a wet suit, gloves, and reef shoes. Never, under any circumstances, should you touch a coral head; not only can you get cut, but you can also damage a living organism that took decades to grow.

The symptoms of a coral cut can range from a slight scratch to severe welts and blisters. *All Stings Considered* recommends gently pulling the edges of the skin open and removing any embedded coral or grains of sand with tweezers, or rinsing well with fresh water. Next, scrub the cut well with fresh water. Never use ocean water to clean a cut. If the wound is bleeding, press a clean cloth against it until it stops. If bleeding continues, or the edges of the injury are jagged or gaping, seek medical treatment.

TRAVEL INSURANCE

Most travelers' needs are met by their existing insurance policies (your homeowners' insurance should cover lost or stolen luggage, for example), but if you have any concerns, contact your insurance company before you leave home and ask them to detail what they'll cover. Some credit- and charge-card companies may insure you against travel accidents if you buy plane, train, or bus tickets with their cards. If you do decide you need additional specific travel coverage, most travel agents can sell you any number of insurance packages tailored to fit your specific needs. But check your existing policies first, and don't buy more than you need.

Among the companies offering specialized travel insurance policies are **Access America** (© 800/284-8300; www.accessamerica.com); **Travel Guard** (© 877/216-4885; www.travel-guard.com); and **Travelex Insurance Services** (© 888/457-4602; www.travelex-insurance.com).

Trip-cancellation insurance may be a good idea if you've paid a large portion of your vacation expenses up front, say, by purchasing a package tour. (But don't buy it from your tour operator—talk about putting all of your eggs in one basket! Buy it from an outside vendor instead.) Coverage should cost approximately 6% to 8% of the total value of your vacation, so a $3,000 trip could be insured for around $210.

Your homeowner's or renter's insurance should cover stolen luggage. The airlines are responsible for losses up to $2,500 on domestic flights if they lose your luggage; if you plan to carry anything more valuable than that, keep it in your carry-on bag.

6 Tips for Travelers with Special Needs

FOR TRAVELERS WITH DISABILITIES

Travelers with disabilities are made to feel very welcome in Hawaii. There are more than 2,000 ramped curbs in Oahu alone, hotels are usually equipped with wheelchair-accessible rooms, and tour companies provide many special services. The **Hawaii Center for Independent Living,** 414 Kauwili St., Suite 102, Honolulu, HI 96817 (© 808/522-5400; fax 808/586-8129; www.hawaii.gov/health/cpd; cpdppp@aloha.net), can provide information and send you a copy of the *Aloha Guide to Accessibility* ($15).

Moss Rehab ResourceNet (**www.mossresourcenet.org**) is a great source for information, tips, and resources relating to accessible travel. You'll find links to a number of travel agents who specialize in planning trips for disabled travelers here and through **Access-Able Travel Source** (© 303/232-2979; www.access-able.com), another excellent online source. You'll also find relay and voice numbers for hotels, airlines, and car-rental companies on Access-Able's user-friendly site, as well as links to accessible accommodations, attractions, transportation, tours, local medical resources and equipment repair, and much more.

Membership organizations that offer excellent general information, links to trip-planning resources, and publications dedicated to accessible travel include the **Society for Accessible Travel & Hospitality,** or SATH (© 212/447-7284; www.sath.org); **Mobility International USA** (© 541/343-1284; www.miusa.org); and **Travelin' Talk** (© 303/232-2979; www.travelintalk.net).

For travelers with disabilities who wish to do their own driving, hand-controlled cars can be rented from **Avis** (© 800/331-1212; www.avis.com) and **Hertz** (© 800/654-3131; www.hertz.com). The number of hand-controlled cars in Hawaii is limited, so be sure to book well in advance—at least a week.

For wheelchair-accessible vans, contact **Accessible Vans of Hawaii** (© 800/303-3750 or 808/879-5521; www.accessiblevanshawaii.com).

Vision-impaired travelers who use a Seeing Eye dog can now come to Hawaii without the hassle of quarantine. A recent court decision ruled that visitors with Seeing Eye dogs only need to present documentation that the dog is a trained Seeing Eye dog and has had rabies shots. For more information, contact the **Animal Quarantine Facility** (© 808/483-7171; www.hawaii.gov).

FOR GAY & LESBIAN TRAVELERS

Known for its acceptance of all groups, Hawaii welcomes gays and lesbians just as it does anybody else.

The best guide for gay and lesbian visitors is Matthew Link's ***Rainbow Handbook Hawaii,*** which not only covers travel on every island, but also has information on Hawaii's gay history, gay and lesbian businesses in the state, and interviews with Hawaii residents. The book is available for $14.95 by writing to P.O. Box 100, Honaunau, HI 96726 (© 800/260-5528; www.rainbowhandbook.com).

The **Gay and Lesbian Community Center,** 2424 S. Beretania St., between Isenberg and University, Honolulu (© 808/951-7000; glccnews@juno.com), open Monday through Saturday from 10am to 7pm, is a referral center for nearly every kind of gay-related service you can think of.

Another Oahu-based referral service is the **Gay Community Director** (© 808/532-9000), which can point you to all kinds of gay-friendly organizations, from hotels to doctors to support groups, and can also tell you where to pick up gay-oriented publications.

For the latest happenings on Oahu, pick up a copy of the monthly magazine ***Da Kine*** (ha@gte.net).

For the latest information on the gay marriage issue, contact the **Hawaii Marriage Project** (© 808/532-9000).

Pacific Ocean Holidays (© 800/735-6600 or 808/923-2400; www.gayhawaii.com) offers vacation packages that feature gay-owned and gay-friendly lodgings. It also publishes the *Pocket Guide to Hawaii: A Guide for Gay Visitors & Kamaaina,* a list of gay-owned and gay-friendly businesses throughout the islands. Send $5 for a copy (mail order only; no phone orders, please), or access the online version on the website.

If you want help planning your trip, the **International Gay & Lesbian**

Travel Association (IGLTA; C 800/ 448-8550 or 954/776-2626; www. iglta.org) can link you up with the appropriate gay-friendly service organization or tour specialist. **GayWired Travel Services** (www.gaywired.com) is another great trip-planning resource; click on "Travel Services."

Out and About (C **800/929-2268** or 415/486-2591; www.outandabout. com) offers a monthly newsletter packed with good information on the global gay and lesbian scene. Its website features links to gay and lesbian tour operators and other gay-themed travel links, plus extensive online travel information to subscribers only. Out and About's guidebooks are available at most major bookstores and through www.adlbooks.com.

FOR SENIORS

Discounts for seniors are available at almost all of Hawaii's major attractions, and occasionally at hotels and restaurants. The Outrigger hotel chain, for instance, offers travelers ages 50 and older a 20% discount off regular published rates—and an additional 5% off for members of AARP. Always inquire when making hotel reservations, and especially when you're buying your airline ticket—most major domestic airlines offer senior discounts.

Members of the **American Association of Retired Persons** (AARP; C **800/424-3410** or 202/434-2277; www.aarp.org) are usually eligible for such discounts; AARP also puts together organized tour packages at moderate rates. The **National Council of Senior Citizens** (C **301/ 578-8800;** www.ncscinc.org), a nonprofit organization, offers members hotel, condominium, and car-rental

discounts, as well as a 24-hour emergency alert service for accident, injury, or illness.

Some great, low-cost trips to Hawaii are offered to people 55 and older through **Elderhostel** (C **617/ 426-8056;** www.elderhostel.org), a nonprofit group that arranges travel and study programs around the world. You can obtain a complete catalog of offerings by writing to Elderhostel, P.O. Box 1959, Wakefield, MA 01880-5959.

FOR FAMILIES

Hawaii is paradise for children: beaches to frolic on, water to splash in, unusual sights to see, and a host of new foods to taste. Be sure to check out "Family-Friendly Hotels" in chapter 4, "Family-Friendly Restaurants" in chapter 5, and "Especially for Kids," in chapter 7.

The larger hotels and resorts have supervised programs for children and can refer you to qualified baby sitters. You can also contact **People Attentive to Children** (PATCH; C **808/ 242-9232**), which will refer you to individuals who have taken their training courses on child care.

Baby's Away (C **800/942-9030** or 808/875-9093; www.babysaway.com) rents cribs, strollers, highchairs, playpens, infant seats, and the like, to make your baby's vacation (and yours) much more enjoyable.

Hawaii's sun is probably much stronger than what you're used to at home, so it's important to protect your kids from the sun, and keep infants out of the sun altogether. Older babies need zinc oxide to protect their fragile skin, and children should be slathered with sunscreen every hour.

7 Getting Married on Oahu

Whatever your budget, Oahu is a great place for a wedding. Not only does the entire island exude romance and natural beauty, but after the ceremony, you're also only a few steps away from the perfect honeymoon.

And the members of your wedding party will most likely be delighted, since you've given them the perfect excuse for their own island vacation.

Nearly half of the couples married here are from somewhere else. This booming business has spawned dozens of companies that can help you organize a long-distance event and stage an unforgettable wedding, Hawaiian style or your style.

The easiest way to plan your wedding is to let someone else handle it at the resort or hotel where you'll be staying. All of the major resorts and hotels (and even most of the small ones) have wedding coordinators, whose job is to make sure that your wedding day is everything you've dreamed about. They can plan everything from a simple (relatively) low-cost wedding to an extravaganza. Remember that resorts can be pricey—catering, flowers, musicians, and so on, may cost more at a resort, but sometimes a resort will at least throw in a free stay. Be frank with your wedding coordinator if you want to keep costs down.

You can also plan your own island wedding, even from afar, and not spend a fortune doing it.

THE PAPERWORK

The state of Hawaii has some very minimal procedures for obtaining a marriage license. The first thing you should do is contact the **Marriage License Office,** State Department of Health Building, 54 S. High St., Wailuku, HI 96793 (© **808/ 984-8210;** www.hawaii.gov), open Monday through Friday from 8am to 4pm. The staff will mail you a brochure, *Getting Married,* and direct you to the marriage-licensing agent closest to where you'll be staying on Oahu.

Once on Oahu, the prospective bride and groom must go together to the marriage-licensing agent to get a license. A license costs $50 and is good for 30 days; if you don't have the

ceremony within the time allotted, you'll have to pay another $50 for another license. The only requirements for a marriage license are that both parties are 15 years of age or older (couples 15–17 years old must have proof of age, written consent of both parents, and the written approval of the judge of the family court) and are not more closely related than first cousins. That's it.

Contrary to some reports from the media, gay couples cannot marry in Hawaii. After a protracted legal battle, and much discussion in the state legislature, in late 1999 the Hawaii Supreme Court ruled the state won't issue a marriage license to a couple of the same sex. For the latest information on this issue, contact the **Hawaii Marriage Project** (© **808/532-9000**).

PLANNING THE WEDDING

DOING IT YOURSELF   The marriage licensing agents, which range from the governor's satellite office to private individuals, are usually friendly, helpful people who can steer you to a nondenominational minister or someone who's licensed by the state of Hawaii to perform the ceremony. These marriage performers are great sources of information for budget weddings. They usually know great places to have the ceremony for free or for a nominal fee.

If you don't want to use a wedding planner (see below) but want to make arrangements before you arrive on Oahu, get a copy of some local publications. People willing and qualified to conduct weddings advertise in the classifieds. They're great sources of information, as they know the best places to have the ceremony and can recommend caterers, florists, and everything else you need. Check out the *Honolulu Advertiser,* P.O. Box 3110, Honolulu, HI 96802 (© **808/ 525-8000;** www.honoluluadvertiser. com); the *Honolulu Star Bulletin,* 7 Waterfront Plaza, Suite 500,

Honolulu, HI 96813 (℗ **808/ 529-4700;** www.honolulustarbulletin. com); and *MidWeek,* 45–525 Luluku Rd., Kaneohe, HI 96744 (℗ **808/ 235-5881;** www.midweek.com).

USING A WEDDING PLANNER Wedding planners—many of whom are marriage licensing agents as well— can arrange everything for you, from a small, private, outdoor affair to a full-blown formal ceremony in a tropical setting. They charge anywhere from $450 to a small fortune—it all depends on what you want. The Hawaii Visitors and Convention Bureau (℗ **800/GO-HAWAII** or 808/923-1811; www.gohawaii.com) can supply contact information on wedding coordinators.

If you want to get married at sea, call Capt. Ken Middleton, of **Tradewind Charters,** based in Honolulu (℗ **800/829-4899** or 808/973-0311;

www.tradewindcharters. com) for a private wedding and reception on the ocean waves.

For a wedding and reception in Waimea Valley Adventure Park, contact the wedding coordinator, **Waimea Valley Adventure Park,** 59-88864 Kamehameha Hwy., Haleiwa, at ℗ **808/638-8511.**

If you want a romantic wedding in an exotic setting, such as near a waterfall, on the beach, or in a garden chapel, **AAA Above Heaven's Gate** (℗ **800/800-2WED** or 808/259-5429; www.hawaiiweddings.com), can arrange it.

Other wedding planners include **Affordable Weddings of Hawaii** (℗ **800/942-4554** or 808/923-4876; www.wedhawaii.com), and **Aloha Wedding Planners** (℗ **800/ 288-8309** or 808/943-2711; www. alohaweddingplanners.com).

8 Money-Saving Package Deals

Booking an all-inclusive travel package that includes some combination of airfare, accommodations, rental car, meals, airport and baggage transfers, and sightseeing can be the most cost-effective way to travel to Hawaii.

Package tours are not the same as escorted tours. They are simply a way to buy airfare and accommodations (and sometimes extras, such as sightseeing tours and rental cars) at the same time. You can sometimes save so much money by buying all the pieces of your trip through a packager that your transpacific airfare ends up, in effect, being free. That's because packages are sold in bulk to tour operators, who then resell them to the public at a cost that drastically undercuts standard rates.

Packages, however, vary widely. Some offer a better class of hotels than others. Some offer the same hotels for lower prices. With some packagers, your choice of accommodations and

travel days may be limited. Which package is right for you depends entirely on what you want.

Start out by **reading this guide.** Do a little homework; read up on Hawaii so that you can be a smart consumer. Compare the rack rates that we've published to the discounted rates being offered by the packagers to see what kinds of deals they're offering— if you're actually being offered a substantial savings, or if they've just gussied up the rack rates to make their offer *sound* like a deal. If you're being offered a stay in a hotel we haven't recommended, do more research to learn about it, especially if it isn't a reliable franchise. It's not a deal if you end up at a dump.

Be sure to **read the fine print.** Make sure you know *exactly* what's included in the price you're being quoted, and what's not. Are hotel taxes and airport transfers included, or will you have to pay extra? Before you

> **Tips   Package-Buying Tip**
>
> For one-stop shopping on the Web, go to **www.vacationpackager.com**, a search engine that can link you up to many different package-tour operators, who can then help you plan a custom-tailored trip to Hawaii. Be sure to look under "Honolulu," "Oahu," "Hawaii," and the "Hawaiian Islands."

commit to a package, make sure you know how much flexibility you have, say, if your kid gets sick or your boss suddenly asks you to adjust your vacation schedule. Some packagers require ironclad commitments, while others will go with the flow, charging only minimal fees for changes or cancellations.

The best place to start looking for a package deal is in the travel section of your local Sunday newspaper. Also check the ads in the back of such national travel magazines as *Arthur Frommer's Budget Travel* and *Travel Holiday.*

Liberty Travel (✆ **888/271-1584;** www.libertytravel.com), one of the biggest packagers in the Northeast, usually boasts a full-page ad in Sunday papers. At press time, Liberty was offering a 7-day/6-night package to Hawaii for $979 (from New York; $745 from Los Angeles) per person, double occupancy. The package included round-trip airfare, all airport transfers, accommodations on Waikiki Beach, and some sightseeing—not a bad deal, considering that you can spend $700 to $800 on airfare alone.

American Express Travel (✆ **800/ AXP-6898;** www.americanexpress. com/travel) can also book you a well-priced Hawaiian vacation; it also advertises in many Sunday travel sections.

Excellent deals can also be found through **More Hawaii For Less** (✆ **800/967-6687;** www.hawaii4less. com), a California-based company that specializes in air-condominium packages at unbelievable prices.

Pleasant Hawaiian Holidays (✆ **800/2-HAWAII** or 800/242-9244; www.pleasantholidays.com) is by far the biggest and most comprehensive packager to Hawaii; it offers an extensive, high-quality collection of 50 condos and hotels in every price range.

Other reliable packagers include the airlines themselves, which often package their flights together with accommodations. Among the airlines offering good-value package deals to Hawaii are **American Airlines Fly-Away Vacations** (✆ 800/321-2121; www.aa.com), **Continental Airlines Vacations** (✆ 800/634-5555 or 800/ 301-3800; www.coolvacations.com), **Delta Dream Vacations** (✆ 800/ 872-7786; www.deltavacations.com), and **United Vacations** (✆ 800/ 328-6877; www.unitedvacations. com). If you're traveling to the islands from Canada, ask your travel agent about package deals through **Air Canada Vacations** (✆ 800/776-3000; www.aircanada.ca).

Hawaii's major hotel chains also have a host of packages that will save you money. For years, the name **Outrigger** has been synonymous with excellent affordable accommodations, all with consistently clean and well-appointed rooms. The Outrigger chain divides its properties into two categories: the 15 moderately priced "Ohana" (Hawaiian for family) Hotels in Waikiki (and one in Maui), offering quality accommodations (with air-conditioning, in-room safe, TV, refrigerator, and coffeemaker) from $109 to

$139; and the 14 more upscale "Outrigger" resorts and condominiums on Oahu, Maui, Kauai, and the Big Island. The **Ohana Hotels** (✆ 800/462-6262; www.ohanahotels.com) offer a range of affordable package deals, while the **Outrigger** properties (✆ 800/OUTRIGGER; www.outrigger.com) also offer discounts for multinight stays, family plans, cut rates for seniors, and even packages for golfers and lovers.

The **Aston** chain (✆ 800/92-ASTON; www.aston-hotels.com) has some 37 hotels, condominiums, and resort properties scattered throughout the islands. They range dramatically in price and style. Aston offers package deals galore, including family packages; discounted senior rates; car, golf, and shopping packages; and multinight deals. The wonderful Island Hopper deal allows you to travel from island to island and get 25% off on 7 nights or more at Aston properties.

9 Getting There

All major American and many international carriers fly to **Honolulu International Airport.**

United Airlines (✆ 800/225-5825; www.ual.com) offers the most frequent service from the U.S. mainland to Honolulu. **Aloha Airlines** (✆ 800/367-5250 or 808/484-1111; www.alohaair.com) has direct flights from Oakland and Orange County (Calif.) with connecting flights from Las Vegas. **American Airlines** (✆ 800/433-7300; www.americanair.com) offers flights from Dallas, Chicago, San Francisco, San Jose, and Los Angeles to Honolulu. **Continental Airlines** (✆ 800/231-0856; www.continental.com) offers the only daily nonstop from the New York area (Newark) to Honolulu, in addition to flights from other cities. **Delta Air Lines** (✆ 800/221-1212; www.delta.com) flies nonstop from the West Coast. **Hawaiian Airlines** (✆ 800/367-5320; www.hawaiianair.com) offers nonstop flights to Honolulu from several West Coast cities (including new daily service from San Diego). **Northwest Airlines** (✆ 800/225-2525; www.nwa.com) has a daily nonstop from Detroit to Honolulu, as well as service from other cities. **TWA** (✆ 800/221-2000; www2.twa.com) flies nonstop from its St. Louis hub and from the West Coast.

For information on airlines serving Hawaii from places other than the U.S. mainland, see chapter 3, "For International Visitors."

FLY FOR LESS: TIPS FOR GETTING THE BEST AIRFARES

Keep your eye out for periodic **sales.** You'll almost never see a sale during the peak winter vacation months, and especially not around the holidays, but before fuel prices went through the stratosphere last year, deals in the off-season were as low as $300 round-trip from Los Angeles to Honolulu. Just before we went to press that rate had climbed to $360. Note, however, that the lowest-priced fares are often nonrefundable, require advance purchase of 1 to 3 weeks and a certain length of stay, and carry penalties for changing dates of travel. So when you're quoted a fare, make sure you know exactly what the restrictions are before you commit.

If your schedule is flexible, you can almost always get a cheaper fare by **staying over a Saturday night** or by **flying during midweek.** Many airlines won't volunteer this information, so be sure to ask.

Consolidators, also known as bucket shops, are a good place to find low fares, often below even the airlines' discounted rates. There's

Tips Your Departure: Agricultural Screening at the Airports

All baggage and passengers bound for the mainland must be screened by agricultural officials before boarding. This takes a little time, but isn't a problem unless you happen to be carrying a football-sized local avocado home to Aunt Emma. Officials will confiscate fresh avocados, bananas, mangoes, and many other kinds of local produce in the name of fruit-fly control. Pineapples, coconuts, and papayas inspected and certified for export, boxed flowers, leis without seeds, and processed foods (macadamia nuts, coffee, jams, dried fruit, and the like) will pass. Call federal agricultural officials (© **808/877-8757**) before leaving for the airport if you're not sure about your trophy.

nothing shady about the reliable ones—basically, they're just big travel agents that get discounts for buying in bulk and pass some of the savings on to you. But be aware that consolidator tickets are usually nonrefundable or come with stiff cancellation penalties.

We've gotten great deals on many occasions from **Cheap Tickets** (© 800/377-1000; www.cheap tickets.com). **Council Travel** (© 800/226-8624; www.counciltravel.com) and **STA Travel** (© 800/781-4040; www.sta.travel.com) cater especially to young travelers, but their bargain-basement prices are available to people of all ages. Other reliable consolidators include **Lowestfare.com** (© 888/278-8830; www.lowestfare.com); **1-800-AIRFARE** (www.1800airfare.com); **Cheap Seats** (© 800/451-7200; www.cheapseatstravel.com); and **1-800-FLY-CHEAP** (www.flycheap.com).

Search the Internet for cheap fares, though it's still best to compare your findings with the research of a dedicated travel agent, especially if you're booking more than just a flight. Among the major online travel agents are **Expedia** (www.expedia.com), **Travelocity** (www.travelocity.com), and **Yahoo! Travel** (http://travel.yahoo.com).

ARRIVAL AT HONOLULU INTERNATIONAL AIRPORT

Honolulu International Airport sits on the south shore of Oahu, west of downtown Honolulu and Waikiki, near Pearl Harbor.

While the airport is large and constantly expanding, the layout is quite simple and easy to navigate. You can walk or take the **Wiki-Wiki Bus,** a free airport shuttle, from your arrival gate to the main terminal and baggage claim, which is on the ground level. After collecting your bags, exit to the palm-lined street, where uniformed attendants flag down taxis, Waikiki shuttles, and rental car vans; they can also direct you to **TheBus** (see below).

GETTING TO & FROM THE AIRPORT

BY RENTAL CAR   All major rental companies have cars available at Honolulu International Airport (see "Getting Around," later in this chapter). Rental agency vans pick you up at the middle curbside outside baggage claim and take you to their off-site lot.

BY TAXI   Taxis are abundant at the airport; an attendant will be happy to flag one down for you. Taxi fare from Honolulu International to downtown Honolulu is about $16; to Waikiki, about $23 to $25. If you need to call a taxi, see "Getting Around," later in this chapter, for a list of cab companies.

For a flat fee of $18, **Star Taxi** (© **800/671-2999** or 808/942-STAR) will take up to five passengers from the airport to Waikiki (with no extra charges for baggage); however, you must book in advance. After you have arrived and before you pick up your luggage, re-call Star to make sure that they will be outside waiting for you when your luggage arrives.

BY AIRPORT SHUTTLE Shuttle vans operate 24 hours a day every day of the year between the airport and all 350 hotels and condos in Waikiki. At a rate of $8 one-way to Waikiki and $13 round-trip, it's a much better bargain than taking a taxi—if there's only one or two of you. If you're in a group of three or more, it's probably more cost-efficient to grab a cab.

Trans-Hawaiian Services (© **800/533-8765** or 808/566-7000; www.transhawaiian.com) serves the airport with passenger vans every 20 to 30 minutes, depending on traffic. Children small enough to sit on your lap ride for free. No reservation is necessary, but do book ahead for hotel pickup for a departing flight. Look for attendants in red shirts that say shuttle vehicle; pickup is at the middle curb outside baggage claim. You can board with two pieces of luggage and a carry-on at no extra charge; surfboards and bicycles are prohibited for safety reasons. Backpacks are okay. Tips are welcome.

BY TheBus TheBus is by far the cheapest way to get to Waikiki—but you've got to be traveling light to use it. Bus nos. 19 and 20 (Waikiki Beach and Hotels) run from the airport to downtown Honolulu and Waikiki. The first bus from Waikiki to the airport is at 4:50am on weekdays and 5:25am on weekends; the last bus departs the airport for Waikiki at 11:45pm on weekdays, 11:25pm on

weekends. There are two bus stops on the main terminal's upper level; a third is on the second level of the Inter-Island terminal.

You can board TheBus with a carry-on or small suitcase as long as it fits under the seat and doesn't disrupt other passengers; otherwise, you'll have to take a shuttle or taxi. The approximate travel time to Waikiki is an hour. The one-way fare is $1.50 (exact change only). For information on routes and schedules, call © **808/848-5555,** or point your browser to **www.thebus.org**.

INTERISLAND FLIGHTS

If you want to see another island in addition to Oahu, you'll have to fly there. Don't expect to jump a ferry between any of the Hawaiian islands. Today, everyone island-hops by plane. In fact, almost every 20 minutes of every day from just before sunrise to well after sunset (usually around 8pm), a plane takes off or lands at Honolulu International Airport on the interisland shuttle service. If you miss a flight, don't worry; they're like buses—another one will be along soon.

Aloha Airlines (© **800/367-5250** or 808/484-1111; www.alohaair.com) is the state's largest provider of interisland air transport service. It offers 175 regularly scheduled daily jet flights throughout Hawaii and has one of the lowest complaint records in the airline industry. Aloha's sister company, **Island Air** (© **800/323-3345** or 808/484-2222), operates eight deHavilland Twin Otter turboprop aircraft and serves Hawaii's small interisland airports in West Maui, Hana (Maui), Lanai, and Molokai.

Hawaiian Airlines (© **800/367-5320** or 808/835-3700; www.hawaiianair.com), Hawaii's oldest interisland airline, has carried more than 100 million passengers around the state on its jets and prop planes.

C The Welcoming Lei

Nothing makes you feel more welcome than a lei. The tropical beauty of the delicate garland, the deliciously sweet fragrance of the blossoms, the sensual way the flowers curl softly around your neck—there's no doubt about it: Getting lei'd in Hawaii is a sensuous experience.

Leis are much more than just a decorative necklace of flowers; they're also one of the nicest ways to say hello, good-bye, congratulations, I salute you, my sympathies are with you, or I love you. The custom of giving leis can be traced back to Hawaii's very roots: According to chants, the first lei was given by Hiiaka, the sister of the volcano goddess, Pele, who presented Pele with a lei of lehua blossoms on a beach in Puna.

During ancient times, leis given to *alii* (royalty) were accompanied by a bow, since it was *kapu* (forbidden) for a commoner to raise his arms higher than the king's head. The presentation of a kiss with a lei didn't come about until World War II; it's generally attributed to an entertainer who kissed an officer on a dare, then quickly presented him with her lei, saying it was an old Hawaiian custom. It wasn't then, but it sure caught on fast.

Lei-making is a tropical art form. All leis are fashioned by hand in a variety of traditional patterns; some are sewn of hundreds of tiny blooms or shells, or bits of ferns and leaves. Some are twisted, some braided, some strung. Every island has its own special flower lei. On Oahu, the choice is *ilima*, a small orange flower. Big Islanders prefer the *lehua*, a large, delicate red puff. Maui likes the *lokelani*, a small rose. On Kauai, it's the *mokihana*, a fragrant green vine and berry. Molokai prefers the *kukui*, the white blossom of a candlenut tree. And Lanai's lei is made of *kaunaoa*, a bright yellow moss, while Niihau uses its abundant seashells to make leis that were once prized by royalty and are now worth a small fortune.

Leis are available at lei stands at Honolulu International Airport. Other places to get creative, inexpensive leis are the half-dozen lei shops on **Maunakea Street** in Honolulu's Chinatown, and **Flowers by Jou & T Jr.,** 2653 S. King St. (near University Ave.), Honolulu (© **808/941-2022**). They're also available from florists, and even at supermarkets.

Leis are the perfect symbol for Hawaii: They're given in the moment, their fragrance and beauty are enjoyed in the moment, and when they fade, their spirit of aloha lives on. Welcome to the islands!

MULTI-ISLAND PASSES At press time, the standard interisland fare was around $100 one way between islands. However, both airlines offer multiple-flight deals that you might want to consider.

Aloha Airlines offers the **Seven-Day Island Pass,** which allows visitors unlimited travel on Aloha and Island Air flights for 7 consecutive days. The price is $321. For $376, you can buy a **Coupon Book,** which contains six blank one-way tickets that you can use—for yourself or any other traveler—any time within a year of purchase. If you and a companion are island-hopping two or three times during your stay, this is an excellent deal.

The six-coupon book for Hawaiian Airlines is $391.50. Hawaiian also offers the Hawaiian Island Pass, which gives you unlimited interisland flights for $324 per person for 5 consecutive days, $345 for 7 days, $409 for 10 days. Because Hawaiian Airlines also flies to and from the mainland United States, you may be able to apply your transpacific flight toward discounts on your interisland travel; be sure to inquire when booking.

10 Getting Around

BY CAR

Oahu residents own 600,000 registered vehicles, but they have only 1,500 miles of mostly two-lane roads. That's 400 cars for every mile, a fact that becomes abundantly clear during morning and evening rush hours. You can avoid the gridlock by driving between 9am and 3pm or after 6pm.

State law mandates that all passengers in a car must wear a seat belt. The law is enforced with vigilance and the fine is quite stiff—so buckle up.

RENTALS

Hawaii has some of the lowest car-rental rates in the country. The average nondiscounted, unlimited-mileage rate for a one-day rental for an intermediate-sized car in Honolulu was $41 in 2001; that's the lowest rate in the country, compared with the national average of $53.50 a day. To rent a car in Hawaii, you must be at least 25 years of age and have a valid driver's license and credit card.

At Honolulu International Airport, you'll find most major rental-car agencies, including **Alamo** (© 800/327-9633; www.goalamo.com), **Avis** (© 800/321-3712; www.avis.com), **Budget** (© 800/935-6878; www.budgetrentacar.com), **Dollar** (© 800/800-4000; www.dollarcar.com), **Enterprise** (© 800/325-8007; www.enterprise.com), **Hertz** (© 800/654-3011; www.hertz.com), **National** (© 800/227-7368; www.nationalcar.com), and **Thrifty** (© 800/367-2277; www.thrifty.com). It's almost always cheaper to rent a car at the airport than in Waikiki or through your hotel (unless there's one already included in your package deal).

Most of the local, "Rent-A-Wreck"–type car rental companies have gone by the wayside on Oahu. However, one reliable, affordable, and accessible company remains: **Tradewinds,** 2875-A Koapaka St., Honolulu (© **888/388-7368** or 808/834-1465; Rent-a-Car@gte.net), a small, family-run company with a fleet of some 300 cars. Depending on the time of year, daily rentals are at least $5 less than what the national chains charge; weekly and monthly rentals at Tradewinds offer super savings; and collision coverage is also cheaper—$9 per day versus $14 to $20. It's best to book in advance. When you arrive at Honolulu airport, get your luggage, go to the courtesy phones for car rentals, and push the button for Tradewinds—they'll send a van to pick you up.

Hawaii is a no-fault state, which means that if you don't have collision-damage insurance, you are required to pay for all damages before you leave the state, whether or not the accident was your fault. Your personal car insurance back home may provide rental-car coverage; read your policy or call your insurer before you leave

Easy Riding on Oahu

If your dream is to go screaming down the highway on the back of a big Harley Hog, here's your chance. **Cruzin Hawaii Motorcycles,** 1980 Kalakaua Ave (at Kuhio Ave., next to Tony Roma's), Waikiki (© **808/ 945-9595**), has a range of bikes starting at $99 (insurance is included in the price). Also try **Thrifty's,** 1778 Ala Moana Blvd., Discovery Bay Plaza, Honolulu (© **808/971-2660**), which has brand-new Harley Fat Boys, Wide Glides, and Heritages starting at $139 a day (includes helmet), or **Coconut Cruisers,** 2301 Kalakaua Ave., across the street from the International Market Place, Honolulu (© **808/924-1644**), which has a range of bikes from $160 to $240 a day. You must have a valid motorcycle license to rent a bike.

home. Bring your insurance identification card if you decline the optional insurance, which usually costs from $12 to $20 a day. Obtain the name of your company's local claim representative before you go. Some credit-card companies also provide collision-damage insurance for their customers; check with yours before you rent.

MAIN STREETS & HIGHWAYS

Navigating around Oahu is actually easy—there are only a few roads that circle the perimeter of the island and a handful that cut across the island.

TO & FROM THE AIRPORT

The main thoroughfare that runs from the airport to Honolulu and Waikiki is the **H-1 Freeway.** The H-1 also runs in the opposite direction to Pearl Harbor and Ewa. The artery that runs from the airport to Honolulu and Waikiki is **Nimitz Highway** (which has stoplights). In downtown Honolulu, Nimitz Highway becomes **Ala Moana Boulevard.**

HONOLULU The myriad of one-way streets in Honolulu can be confusing and frustrating. If you want to travel in the Diamond Head direction, **King Street** is one-way going toward Diamond Head. **Beretania Street** is one-way in the opposite, or Ewa, direction. In the mauka and makai direction: **Punchbowl** and **Bishop streets** run toward the ocean (makai),

and **Alakea** and **Bethel streets** run toward the mountains (mauka).

There are three parallel main streets in **Waikiki: Kalakaua Avenue** (which is one-way going toward Diamond Head and eventually fronts Waikiki Beach), **Kuhio Avenue** (one block mauka of Kalakaua Avenue, which has two-way traffic), and **Ala Wai Boulevard** (which fronts the Ala Wai Canal and runs one-way in the Ewa direction).

AROUND OAHU From Waikiki, **Highway 72 (the Kalanianaole Hwy.)** takes you around Makapuu Point into Kailua and Kaneohe. From Kailua and Kaneohe, **Highway 83 (the Kamehameha Hwy.)** takes you around the North Shore to Haleiwa, where it is still called the Kamehameha Highway, but the number of the highway changes to 99, and then cuts through mid-Oahu past Schofield Barracks and Wahiawa, and swings out to Pearl City.

On the leeward coast, H-1 Freeway becomes two-lane **Highway 93 (the Farrington Hwy.);** after Makaha, the number changes to Highway 930, but it is still called Farrington Highway all the way out to Kaena Point. Although you cannot drive around Kaena Point, Farrington Highway (still called Hwy. 930) picks up on the north side of the point and goes through Mokuleia and Waialua.

ACROSS OAHU Highways that cut across the island are **Highway 99** (see above), the **Likelike Highway** (also called Hwy. 63, which goes from Honolulu to Kaneohe), and the **Pali Highway** (also called Hwy. 61, which goes from Honolulu to Kailua). The H-3 Freeway, which starts at Pearl Harbor, is the fastest way to get to Kaneohe and Kailua.

STREET MAPS

One of the best general maps of the island is the *Map of Oahu,* cartography by James A. Bier, published by the University of Hawaii Press, available at bookstores or online at www.uhpress.hawaii.edu.

For a more specific street map, the best one we have found is *TMK Maps: Oahu Streets and Condos,* published by Hawaii TMK Service, Inc. (© **808/536-0867**).

BY BUS

One of the best deals anywhere, **The-Bus** (© **808/848-5555**, or © 808/296-1818 for recorded information; www.thebus.org) will take you around the whole island for $1.50. In fact, on a daily basis, more than 260,000 people use the system's 68 lines and 4,000 bus stops.

TheBus goes almost everywhere almost all the time. The most popular route is no. 8 (Waikiki/Ala Moana), which shuttles people between Waikiki and Ala Moana Center every 10 minutes or so (the ride is 15–20 min.). The no. 19 (Airport/Hickam), no. 20 (Airport/Halawa Gate), no. 47 (Waipahu), and no. 58 (Waikiki/Ala Moana) also cover the same stretch. Waikiki service begins daily at 5am and runs until midnight; buses run about every 15 minutes during the day and every 30 minutes in the evening.

The Circle Island–North Shore route is no. 52 (Wahiawa/Circle Island); it leaves from Ala Moana Shopping Center every 30 minutes and takes about 4½ hours to circle the island. The Circle Island–South Shore route is no. 55 (Kaneohe/Circle Island) and also leaves Ala Moana every half hour and takes about 3 to 4½ hours to circle the island.

You can buy a **Visitors Pass** for $15 at any ABC store in Waikiki (ABC stores are literally everywhere in Waikiki). It's good for unlimited rides anywhere on Oahu for 4 days.

BY TROLLEY

It's fun to ride the 34-seat, open-air, motorized **Waikiki Trolley** (© **800/824-8804** or 808/593-2822; www.enoa.com), which looks like a San Francisco cable car. It loops around Waikiki and downtown Honolulu, stopping every 40 minutes at 12 key places: Hilton Hawaiian Village, Iolani Palace, Wo Fat's in Chinatown, the State Capitol, King Kamehameha's Statue, the Mission House Museum, Aloha Tower, Honolulu Academy of Arts, Hawaii Maritime Museum, Ward Centre, Fisherman's Wharf, and Restaurant Row. A one-day pass at $18 for adults, $8 for children ages 11 and under, allows you to jump on and off all day long. Four-day passes cost $30 for adults, $10 for children under 12.

BY TAXI

Oahu's major cab companies offer islandwide, 24-hour radio-dispatched service, with multilingual drivers, air-conditioned cars, limos, vans, and

Warning

Recently, visitors waiting for a bus along the North Shore have been attacked and robbed in broad daylight. You might want to consider splurging on a rental car to visit the North Shore.

TheBus

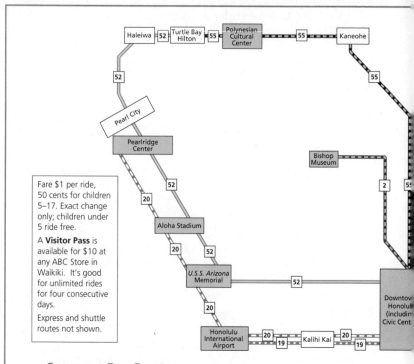

Fare $1 per ride, 50 cents for children 5–17. Exact change only; children under 5 ride free.

A **Visitor Pass** is available for $10 at any ABC Store in Waikiki. It's good for unlimited rides for four consecutive days.

Express and shuttle routes not shown.

Common Bus Routes:

Ala Moana Shopping Center: Take bus #19 & #20 AIRPORT. Return via #19 WAIKIKI, or cross Ala Moana Blvd. for #20.

Bishop Museum: Take #2 SCHOOL STREET. Get off at Kapalama St., cross School St., walk down Bernice St. Return to School St. and take #2 WAIKIKI.

Byodo-In Temple: Take bus #2 to Hotel-Alakea St. (TRF) to #55 KANEOHE-KAHALUU. Get off at Valley of the Temple cemetery. Also #19 and #20 AIRPORT to King-Alakea St., (TRF) on Alakea St. to #55 KANEOHE-KAHALUU.

Circle Island: Take a bus to ALA MOANA CENTER (TRF) to #52 WAHIAWA CIRCLE ISLAND or #55 KANEOHE CIRCLE ISLAND. This is a 4-hour bus ride.

Chinatown or Downtown: Take any #2 bus going out of Waikiki, to Hotel St. Return, take #2 WAIKIKI on Hotel St., or #19 or #20 on King St.

The Contemporary Museum & Punchbowl (National Cemetery of the Pacific): Take #2 bus (TRF) at Alapai St. to #15 MAKIKI-PACIFIC HGTS. Return, take #15 and get off at King St., area (TRF) #2 WAIKIKI.

Diamond Head Crater: Take #22 HAWAII KAI-SEA LIFE PARK to the crater. Take a flashlight. Return to the same area and take #22 WAIKIKI.

Dole Plantation: Take bus to ALA MOANA CENTER (TRF) to #52 WAHIAWA CIRCLE ISLAND.

Foster Botanic Gardens: Take #2 bus to Hotel-Riviera St. Walk to Vineyard Blvd. Return to Hotel St. Take #2 WAIKIKI, or take #4 NUUANU and get off at Nuuanu-Vineyard. Cross Nuuanu Ave. and walk one block to the gardens.

Aloha Tower Marketplace & Hawaii Maritime Center: Take #19-#20 AIRPORT and get off at Alakea–Ala Moana. Cross the street to the Aloha Tower.

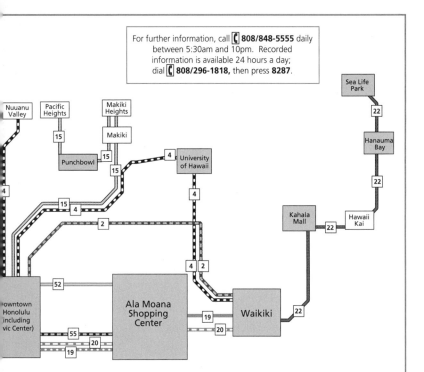

For further information, call 808/848-5555 daily between 5:30am and 10pm. Recorded information is available 24 hours a day; dial 808/296-1818, then press 8287.

Honolulu Zoo: Take any bus on Kuhio Ave. going DIAMOND HEAD direction to Kapahulu Ave.

Iolani Palace (also **State Capitol, Honolulu Hale, Kawaihao Church, Mission Houses, Queen's Hospital, King Kamehameha Statue, State Judiciary Bldg.**) Take any #2 bus and get off at Punchbowl and Beretania St. Walk to King St. Return #2 WAIKIKI on King St.

Kahala Mall: Take #22 HAWAII KAI–SEA LIFE PARK to Kilauea Ave. Return, #22 WAIKIKI.

Pearl Harbor (*Arizona* Memorial): Take #20 AIRPORT. Get off across from Memorial, or take a bus to ALA MOANA CENTER (TRF) to #52.

Polynesian Cultural Center: Take a bus to ALA MOANA CENTER (TRF) to #55 KANEOHE CIRCLE ISLAND. Bus ride takes 2 hours one-way.

Queen Emma's Summer Home: Take #4 NUUANU, or board a bus to ALA MOANA CENTER (TRF) to #55 KANEOHE.

Sea Life Park: Take #22 HAWAII KAI-SEA LIFE PARK. #22 will stop at Hanauma Bay en route to the park.

University of Hawaii: Take #4 NUUANU. The bus will go to the University en route to Nuuanu.

Waimea Valley & Adventure Park: Take a bus to ALA MOANA CENTER (TRF) to #52 WAHIAWA CIRCLE ISLAND or #55 KANEOHE CIRCLE ISLAND.

vehicles equipped with wheelchair lifts. Fares are standard for all taxi firms; from the airport, expect to pay about $23 (plus tip) to Waikiki, about $16.50 to downtown, about $35 to Kailua, about $35 to Hawaii Kai, and about $75 to the North Shore.

Try **Aloha State Cab** (© 808/ 847-3566), **Charley's Taxi & Tours** (© 808/531-1333), **City Taxi** (© 808/524-2121), **Royal Taxi & Tour** (© 808/944-5513), **Sida Taxi & Tours** (© 808/836-0011), **Star Taxi** (© 808/942-7827), or **TheCab** (© 808/422-2222). **Coast Taxi** (© 808/261-3755) serves Windward Oahu; **Hawaii Kai Hui/Koko Head Taxi** (© 808/396-6633) serves East Honolulu/Southeast Oahu.

There is a discount taxi service, offering a fixed-price fare of $15 (up to five passengers) to Waikiki, with no additional charge for baggage, from **Star Taxi** (© **800/671-2999** or 808/ 942-STAR). You must book it in advance.

⊘ FAST FACTS: Oahu

American Express The Honolulu office is at 1440 Kapiolani Blvd., Suite 104 (© **808/946-7741**), and is open Monday through Friday from 8am to 5pm. There's also an office at **Hilton Hawaiian Village**, 2005 Kalia Rd. (© **808/947-2607** or 808/951-0644), and one at the **Hyatt Regency Waikiki**, 2424 Kalakaua Ave. (© **808/926-5441**); both offer financial services daily from 8am to 8pm.

Area Code All of the Hawaiian Islands, including Oahu, are in the **808** area code.

Business Hours Most offices open at 8am and close by 5pm. The morning commute usually runs from 6am to 8am, and the evening rush is from 4pm to 6pm. Many people work at two or three jobs and drive their children to and from private schools, which creates extra traffic. Bank hours are Monday to Thursday from 8:30am to 3pm, Fridays from 8:30am to 6pm. Some banks open on Saturdays. Shopping centers are open Monday through Friday from 10am to 9pm, Saturdays from 10am to 5:30pm, and Sundays from noon to 5pm or 6pm.

Dentists If you need dental attention on Oahu, contact the **Hawaii Dental Association** (© **808/593-2135**).

Doctors **Straub Doctors on Call**, 2222 Kalakaua Ave., at Lewers Street, Honolulu (© **808/971-6000**), can dispatch a van if you need help getting to the main clinic or to any of their additional clinics at the Royal Hawaiian Hotel, Hyatt Regency Waikiki, Hawaiian Regent Hotel, Hilton Hawaiian Village, Kahala Mandarin Oriental, and Ihilani Resort and Spa.

Emergencies Call © **911** for police, fire, and ambulance. The **Poison Control Center** is at 1319 Punahou St. (© **808/941-4411**).

Hospitals Hospitals offering 24-hour emergency care include **Queens Medical Center**, 1301 Punchbowl St. (© 808/538-9011); **Kuakini Medical Center**, 347 Kuakini St. (© 808/536-2236); **Straub Clinic and Hospital**, 888 S. King St. (© 808/522-4000); **Moanalua Medical Center**, 3288 Moanalua Rd. (© 808/834-5333); **Kapiolani Medical Center for Women and Children**, 1319 Punahou St. (© 808/973-8511); and **Kapiolani Medical Center** at Pali Momi, 98–1079 Moanalua Rd. (© 808/486-6000). Central Oahu has **Wahiawa General Hospital,** 128 Lehua St. (© 808/621-8411). On the windward side is **Castle Medical Center,** 640 Ulukahiki St., Kailua (© 808/263-5500).

Internet Access If your hotel doesn't have Web access, head to **Web Site Story Café,** 2555 Cartwright Rd. (in the Hotel Waikiki), Waikiki (© 808/922-1677). It's open daily from 7am to 1am, and serves drinks.

Legal Aid Call the **Legal Aid Society of Hawaii,** 1108 Nuuanu Ave., Honolulu HI 96817 (© **808/536-4302**).

Liquor Laws The legal drinking age in Hawaii is 21. Bars are allowed to stay open daily until 2am; places with cabaret licenses are able to keep the booze flowing until 4am. Grocery and convenience stores are allowed to sell beer, wine, and liquor 7 days a week.

Newspapers The *Honolulu Advertiser* and *Honolulu Star-Bulletin* are Oahu's daily papers. *Midweek, Pacific Business News,* and *Honolulu Weekly* are weekly papers. *Honolulu Weekly,* available free at restaurants, clubs, shops, bookstores, and newspaper racks around Oahu, is the best source for what's going on around town. It features discriminating restaurant reviews and an informed critique of the nightclub scene, plus a weekly Calendar of Events.

Poison Control Center Call © 808/941-4411.

Post Office To find the location nearest you, call © **800/275-8777.** The downtown location is in the old U.S. Post Office, Customs, and Court House Building (referred to as the "old Federal Building") at 335 Merchant St., across from Iolani Palace and next to the Kamehameha Statue (bus: 2). Other branch offices include the Waikiki Post Office, 330 Saratoga Ave. (Diamond Head side of Fort DeRussy; bus: 19 or 20), and in the Ala Moana Shopping Center (bus: 8, 19, or 20).

Radio & TV Honolulu has a score of radio stations that broadcast in English, Hawaiian, Japanese, and Filipino throughout the islands. The most popular are KCCN (1420 AM), which features Hawaiian music; KHPR (88.1 or 90.7 FM), the National Public Radio station; KGU (760 AM), for news and talk radio; KUMU (94.7 FM), for easy listening; and KSSK (590 AM), the pop-music station and the top morning-drive DJs.

All major Hawaiian islands are equipped with cable TV and get major mainland network broadcast programs, which local stations delay by several hours so they appear as "prime time" in Hawaii's time zone. This includes sports events, so fans who want to follow their teams "live" should seek out establishments with satellite dishes. CNN is the prime source of 24-hour news.

Safety Although Hawaii is generally safe, visitors have been crime victims, so stay alert. The most common crime against tourists is rental car break-ins. Never leave any valuables in your car, not even in your trunk. Thieves can be in and out of your trunk faster than you can open it with your own keys. Be leery of high-risk areas, such as beaches and resort areas. Also, never carry large amounts of cash in Waikiki and other tourist zones. Stay in well-lighted areas after dark. Don't hike on deserted trails alone.

Recently, there has been a series of purse-snatching incidents in Oahu. Thieves in slow-moving cars or on foot have snatched handbags from female pedestrians (in some instances, dragging women who refuse to let go of their pocketbooks down the street). The Honolulu police department advises women to carry their purses on the shoulder away from the street or, better yet, to wear the strap across the chest instead of on one shoulder. Women with clutch bags should hold them close to their chest.

Smoking It's against the law to smoke in public buildings, including the airports, grocery stores, retail shops, movie theaters, banks, and all government buildings and facilities. Hotels have nonsmoking rooms available, restaurants have nonsmoking sections, and car-rental agencies have nonsmoking cars. Most bed-and-breakfasts prohibit smoking inside their buildings.

Taxes Hawaii's sales tax is 4%. Hotel occupancy tax is 7%, and hoteliers are allowed by the state to tack on an additional .42% excise tax. Thus, expect taxes of about 11.42% to be added to every hotel bill.

Telephone Hawaii's telephone system operates like any other state's. Local calls costs 35¢ at a pay phone (if you can find one). Interisland calls are billed at the same rate as long distance. Hotels add a surcharge on local, interisland, mainland, and international calls.

Time For the time, call ℂ 808/983-3211. Hawaii standard time is in effect year-round. Hawaii is 2 hours behind Pacific standard time and 5 hours behind eastern standard time. In other words, when it's noon in Hawaii, it's 2pm in California and 5pm in New York during standard time on the mainland. There's no daylight saving time here, so when daylight saving time is in effect on the mainland (Apr–Oct), Hawaii is 3 hours behind the West Coast and 6 hours behind the East Coast—so in summer, when it's noon in Hawaii, it's 3pm in California and 6pm in New York.

Hawaii is east of the international dateline, putting it in the same day as the U.S. mainland and Canada, and a day behind Australia, New Zealand, and Asia.

Transit Info For information on TheBus, call ℂ 808/848-5555; www.thebus.org.

Weather For National Weather Service recorded forecasts for Honolulu, call ℂ 808/973-4380; for elsewhere on the island, call ℂ 808/973-4381. For marine reports, call ℂ 808/973-4382. For surf reports, call ℂ 808/973-4383.

For International Visitors

by Jeanette Foster

The pervasiveness of American culture around the world may make the United States feel like familiar territory to foreign visitors, but leaving your own country for the States—especially the unique island state of Hawaii—still requires some additional planning.

1 Preparing for Your Trip

ENTRY REQUIREMENTS

Check at any U.S. embassy or consulate for current information and requirements. You can also obtain a visa application and other information online at **U.S. State Department**'s website, at **travel.state.gov.** Click on "Visas for Foreign Citizens" for the latest entry requirements, while "Foreign Consular Offices" and "Links to Foreign Embassies" will provide you with contact information for U.S. embassies and consulates worldwide.

VISAS The U.S. State Department has a **Visa Waiver Program** that allows citizens of certain countries to enter the United States without a visa for stays of up to 90 days. At press time, this visa waiver program applied to citizens of Andorra, Argentina, Australia, Austria, Belgium, Brunei, Denmark, Finland, France, Germany, Iceland, Ireland, Italy, Japan, Liechtenstein, Luxembourg, Monaco, the Netherlands, New Zealand, Norway, Portugal, San Marino, Singapore, Slovenia, Spain, Sweden, Switzerland, the United Kingdom, and Uruguay. Citizens of these countries need only a valid passport and a round-trip air or cruise ticket in their possession upon arrival. Further information is available from any U.S. embassy or consulate.

Canadian citizens may enter the United States without visas; they need only proof of residence.

Citizens of all other countries must have: (1) a valid passport that expires at least 6 months later than the scheduled end of their visit to the United States, and (2) a tourist visa, which may be obtained from any U.S. consulate.

To obtain a visa, you must submit a completed application form (either in person or by mail) with two 1½-inch-square photos and a US$45 fee, and must demonstrate binding ties to a residence abroad. Usually you can obtain a visa at once or within 24 hours, but it may take longer during the summer rush from June through August. If you cannot go in person, contact the nearest U.S. embassy or consulate for directions on applying by mail. Your travel agent or airline office may also be able to provide you with visa applications and instructions. The U.S. consulate or embassy that issues your visa will determine if you will be issued a multiple- or single-entry visa and any restrictions regarding the length of your stay.

Inquiries about visa cases and the application process can be made by calling © **202/663-1225.** U.K. citizens can obtain up-to-date passport and visa information by calling the **U.S. Embassy Visa Information Line** (☎ 0891/200-290) or the **London Passport Office** (☎ 0990/210-410** for recorded information).

Foreign driver's licenses are recognized in Hawaii, although you may want to get an international driver's license if your home license is not written in English.

MEDICAL   REQUIREMENTS

Inoculations are not needed to enter the United States unless you are coming from or have stopped over in areas known to be suffering from epidemics, particularly cholera or yellow fever. If you have a disease requiring treatment with medications containing narcotics or requiring a syringe, carry a valid signed prescription from your physician to allay suspicions that you are smuggling drugs.

Upon entering the United States, foreign nationals are required to declare any dangerous contagious diseases they carry, which includes infection with HIV, the AIDS virus. Anyone who has such a disease is excluded from entry as a tourist. However, you may be able to apply for a waiver if you are attending a conference or have another compelling non-tourism reason for your visit (call the **INS** at ☎ 800/375-5283 to inquire). Doubtless many HIV-positive visitors come in without declaring their condition, their way of dealing with an archaic law that was originally intended to halt the spread of tuberculosis and the like.

CUSTOMS
WHAT YOU CAN BRING IN

Every visitor over 21 years of age may bring in, free of duty, the following: (1) 1 liter of wine or hard liquor; (2) 200 cigarettes, 150 cigars (but not from Cuba), or 3 pounds of smoking tobacco; and (3) $100 worth of gifts. These exemptions are offered to travelers who spend at least 72 hours in the United States and who have not claimed them within the preceding 6 months. In addition, you cannot bring fresh fruits and vegetables into Hawaii, even if you're coming from the U.S. mainland and have no need to clear customs. Every passenger is asked shortly before landing to sign a certificate declaring that he or she does not have fresh fruits and vegetables in his or her possession.

Foreign tourists may bring in or take out up to $10,000 in U.S. or foreign currency with no formalities; larger sums must be declared to U.S. Customs upon entering or leaving, which includes filing form CM 4790.

Declare any medicines you are carrying and be prepared to present a letter or prescription from your doctor demonstrating you need the drugs; you may bring in no more than you would normally use in the duration of your visit.

For many more details on what you can and cannot bring, check the informative U.S. Customs website at **www.customs.ustreas.gov/** and click "Traveler Information," or call ☎ **202/927-1770.**

WHAT YOU CAN BRING HOME

Rules governing what you can bring back duty-free vary from country to country and are subject to change, but they're generally posted on the Web. **Canadians** should check the booklet *I Declare,* which you can download or order from Revenue Canada (☎ 613/993-0534; www.ccra-adrc.gc.ca). **British** citizens should contact HM Customs & Excise (☎ 020/7202 4227; www.hmce.gov.uk). **Australians** can contact the Australian Customs Service (☎ 1-300/363-263 within Australia, 612/6275-6666 from outside Australia; www. customs. ov.au/). **New Zealand** citizens should contact New Zealand Customs (☎ 09/359-6655; www.customs. govt.nz/).

INSURANCE

Although it's not required of travelers, health insurance is highly recommended. Unlike many European countries, the United States does not usually offer free or low-cost medical care to its citizens or visitors. Doctors and hospitals are expensive, and in most cases will require advance payment or proof of coverage before they render their services. Travel insurance policies can cover everything from the loss or theft of your baggage and trip cancellation to the guarantee of bail in case you're arrested. Good policies will also cover the costs of an accident, repatriation, or death. Packages such as **Europ Assistance** in Europe are sold by automobile clubs and travel agencies at attractive rates. **Worldwide Assistance Services, Inc.** (✆ **800/ 821-2828,** or 703/204-1897; www. worldwideassistance.com) is the agent for Europe Assistance in the United States.

Though lack of health insurance may prevent you from being admitted to a hospital in nonemergencies, don't worry about being left on a street corner to die: The American way is to fix you now and bill the living daylights out of you later.

MONEY

CURRENCY The most common **bills** (all ugly, all green) are the $1 (colloquially, a "buck"), $5, $10, and $20 denominations. There are also $2 bills (seldom encountered), $50 bills, and $100 bills (the last two are usually not welcome as payment for small purchases). Note that redesigned bills were introduced in the last few years, but the old-style bills are still legal tender.

There are six denominations of **coins:** 1¢ (1 cent, or a penny); 5¢ (5 cents, or a nickel); 10¢ (10 cents, or a dime); 25¢ (25 cents, or a quarter); 50¢ (50 cents, or a half dollar); and the rare $1 piece (the older, large silver

dollar and the newer, small Susan B. Anthony coin). In 2000, a new gold-toned $1 coin was introduced.

EXCHANGING CURRENCY Exchanging foreign currency for U.S. dollars is usually painless in Oahu. Generally, the best rates of exchange are available through major banks, most of which exchange foreign currency. In Waikiki, go to **A-1 Foreign Exchange,** which has offices in the Royal Hawaiian Shopping Center, 2301 Kalakaua Ave., and in the Hyatt Regency Waikiki Tower, 2424 Kalakaua Ave. (✆ **808/922-3327**), or **Pacific Money Exchange,** 339 Royal Hawaiian Ave. (✆ **808/924-9318**). There also are currency services at **Honolulu International Airport.** Most of the major hotels offer currency-exchange services, but generally the rate of exchange is not as good as what you'll get at a bank.

On the other islands, it's not so easy. None of the other airports have currency-exchange facilities. You'll need to either go to a bank (call first to see if currency exchange is available) or use your hotel.

TRAVELER'S CHECKS Though traveler's checks are widely accepted at most hotels, restaurants, and large stores, *make sure that they're denominated in U.S. dollars,* as foreign-currency checks are often difficult to exchange. The three traveler's checks that are most widely recognized—and least likely to be denied—are **Visa, American Express,** and **Thomas Cook/MasterCard.** Be sure to record the numbers of the checks, and keep that information separately in case they get lost or stolen. Most businesses are pretty good about taking traveler's checks, but you're better off cashing them at a bank (in small amounts, of course) and paying in cash. Remember that you'll need identification, such as a driver's license or passport, to change a traveler's check. It's generally easier to use ATMs than to bother with traveler's checks.

CREDIT CARDS   Credit cards are widely used in Hawaii. You can save yourself trouble by using plastic rather than cash or traveler's checks in most hotels, restaurants, retail stores, and a growing number of food and liquor stores. You must have a credit card to rent a car in Hawaii.

SAFETY

GENERAL   SAFETY   Although tourist areas are generally safe, visitors should always stay alert, even in laid-back Hawaii (and especially in Waikiki). It's wise to ask the island tourist office if you're in doubt about which neighborhoods are safe. Avoid deserted areas, especially at night. Don't go into any city park at night unless there's an event that attracts crowds—for example, the Waikiki Shell concerts in Kapiolani Park. Generally speaking, you can feel safe in areas where there are many people and open establishments.

Avoid carrying valuables with you on the street, and don't display expensive cameras or electronic equipment. Hold onto your pocketbook, and place your billfold in an inside pocket. In theaters, restaurants, and other public places, keep your possessions in sight.

Recently, there has been a series of purse-snatching incidents in Oahu. Thieves in slow-moving cars or on foot have snatched handbags from female pedestrians (in some instances, dragging women who refuse to let go of their pocketbooks down the street). The Honolulu police department advises women to carry their purses on the shoulder away from the street or, better yet, to wear the strap across the chest instead of on one shoulder. Women with clutch bags should hold them close to their chest.

Remember also that hotels are open to the public and that, in a large hotel, security may not be able to screen everyone entering. Always lock your room door—don't assume that once inside your hotel, you're automatically safe.

DRIVING SAFETY   Safety while driving is particularly important. Ask your rental agency about personal safety, or request a brochure of traveler safety tips when you pick up your car. Get written directions or a map with the route marked in red showing you how to get to your destination.

Recently, crime has involved more burglary of tourist rental cars in hotel parking structures and at beach parking lots. Park in well-lighted and well-traveled areas if possible. Never leave any packages or valuables visible in the car. If someone attempts to rob you or steal your car, do not try to resist the thief or carjacker—report the incident to the police department immediately.

For more information on driving rules and getting around by car in Hawaii, see "Getting There" and "Getting Around," in chapter 2.

2 Getting to & Around the United States

Airlines serving Hawaii from places other than the U.S. mainland include **Air Canada** (✆ 800/776-3000; www.aircanada.ca); **Canadian Airlines** (✆ 800/426-7000; www.cdnair.ca); **Canada 3000** (✆ 888/CAN-3000; www.canada3000.com); **Air New Zealand** (✆ 0800/737-000 in Auckland, 64-3/379-5200 in Christchurch, 800/926-7255 in the U.S.; www.airnewzealand.co.nz), which runs 40 flights per week between Auckland and Hawaii; **Qantas** (✆ 008/177-767 in Australia, 800/227-4500 in the U.S.; www.qantas.com.au), which flies between Sydney and Honolulu daily (plus additional flights 4 days a week); **Japan Air Lines** (✆ 03/5489-1111 in

Tokyo, 800/525-3663 in the U.S.; www.jal.co.jp); **All Nippon Airways (ANA)** (© 03/5489-1212 in Tokyo, 800/235-9262 in the U.S.; www.ana. co.jp); **China Airlines** (© 02/715-1212 in Taipei, 800/227-5118 in the U.S.; www.china-airlines.com); **Air Pacific,** serving Fiji, Australia, New Zealand, and the South Pacific (© 800/227-4446; www.airpacific. com); **Korean Airlines** (© 02/656-2000 in Seoul, 800/223-1155 on the East Coast, 800/421-8200 on the West Coast, 800/438-5000 from Hawaii; www.koreanair.com); and **Philippine Airlines** (© 631/816-6691 in Manila, 800/435-9725 in the U.S.; www.philippineair.com).

Operated by the European Travel Network, **www.discount-tickets.com** is a great online source for regular and discounted airfares to destinations around the world. You can also use this site to compare rates and book accommodations, car rentals, and tours. Click on "Special Offers" for the latest package deals. Students should also try **Campus Travel** (© 0870/240-1010 in England, 0131/668-3303 in Scotland; www. usitcampus.co.uk).

If you're traveling in the United States beyond Hawaii, some large American airlines—such as **American, Delta, Northwest, TWA,** and **United**—offer travelers on transatlantic or transpacific flights special discount tickets under the name **Visit USA,** allowing travel between any U.S. destinations at reduced rates. These tickets must be purchased before you leave your foreign point of departure. This system is the best, easiest, and fastest way to see the United States at low cost. You should obtain information well in advance from your travel agent or the office of the airline concerned, since the conditions attached to these discount tickets can change without advance notice.

Visitors arriving by air should cultivate patience and resignation before setting foot on U.S. soil. Getting through immigration control may take as long as 2 hours on some days, especially summer weekends. Add the time it takes to clear customs, and you'll see that you should allow plenty of time for making connections between international and domestic flights—an average of 2 to 3 hours at least.

For further information about travel to Hawaii, see "Getting There" and "Getting Around," in chapter 2.

✐ FAST FACTS: **For the International Traveler**

Automobile Organizations Auto clubs supply maps, suggested routes, guidebooks, accident and bail-bond insurance, and emergency road service. The major auto club in the United States, with 955 offices nationwide, is the **American Automobile Association** (AAA; often called "Triple A"). Members of some foreign auto clubs have reciprocal arrangements with the AAA and enjoy its services at no charge. If you belong to an auto club, inquire about AAA reciprocity before you leave. The AAA can also provide you with an **International Driving Permit** validating your foreign license. You may be able to join the AAA even if you are not a member of a reciprocal club. To inquire, call © **800/736-2886** or visit www.aaa.com.

Oahu's local AAA office is at 1270 Ala Moana Blvd., Honolulu (© **808/593-2221**). Some car-rental agencies now provide automobile club–type services, so inquire about their availability when you rent your car.

Automobile Rentals To rent a car in the United States, you need a valid driver's license, a passport, and a major credit card. The minimum age is usually 25, but some companies will rent to younger people and add a surcharge. It's a good idea to buy maximum insurance coverage unless you're positive your own auto or credit-card insurance is sufficient. Rates vary, so it pays to call around.

Business Hours See "Fast Facts: Oahu," in chapter 2.

Climate See "When to Go," in chapter 2.

Electricity Hawaii, like the U.S. mainland and Canada, uses 110–120 volts (60 cycles), compared to the 220–240 volts (50 cycles) used in most of Europe and in other areas of the world, including Australia and New Zealand. Small appliances of non-American manufacture, such as hair dryers or shavers, will require a plug adapter with two flat, parallel pins; larger ones will require a 100-volt transformer.

Embassies & Consulates All embassies are in Washington, D.C. Some countries have consulates general in major U.S. cities, and most have a mission to the United Nations in New York City. If your country isn't listed below, call for directory information in Washington, D.C. (© 202/555-1212), or point your Web browser to **www.embassy.org/embassies** for the location and phone number of your national embassy.

The embassy of **Australia** is at 1601 Massachusetts Ave. NW, Washington, D.C. 20036 (© **202/797-3000**; www.austemb.org). There is also an Australian consulate in Hawaii at 1000 Bishop St., Penthouse Suite, Honolulu, HI 96813 (© 808/524-5050).

The embassy of **Canada** is at 501 Pennsylvania Ave. NW, Washington, D.C. 20001 (© **202/682-1740**; www.canadianembassy.org). Canadian consulates are also at 1251 Avenue of the Americas, New York, NY 10020 (© 212/596-1628), and at 550 South Hope St., 9th floor, Los Angeles, CA 90071 (© 213/346-2700).

The embassy of **Japan** is at 2520 Massachusetts Ave. NW, Washington, D.C. 20008 (© **202/238-6700**; www.embjapan.org). The consulate general of Japan is located at 1742 Nuuanu Ave., Honolulu, HI 96817 (© 808/543-3111; www.embjapan.org/honolulu).

The embassy of **New Zealand** is at 37 Observatory Circle NW, Washington, D.C. 20008 (© **202/328-4800**; www.nzemb.org). The only New Zealand consulate in the United States is at 780 Third Ave., New York, NY 10017 (© 202/328-4800).

The embassy of the **Republic of Ireland** is at 2234 Massachusetts Ave. NW, Washington, D.C. 20008 (© **202/462-3939**; www.irelandemb.org). There's a consulate office in San Francisco at 44 Montgomery St., Suite 3830, San Francisco, CA 94104 (© 415/392-4214).

The embassy of the **United Kingdom** is at 3100 Massachusetts Ave. NW, Washington, D.C. 20008 (© **202/588-6640**; www.fco.gov.uk/directory). British consulates are at 845 Third Ave., New York, NY 10022 (© 212/745-0200), and 11766 Wilshire Blvd., Suite 400, Los Angeles, CA 90025 (© 310/477-3322).

Emergencies Call © **911** to report a fire, call the police, or get an ambulance.

Gasoline (Petrol) One U.S. gallon equals 3.8 liters, while 1.2 U.S. gallons equal 1 Imperial gallon. You'll notice that there are several grades (and price levels) of gasoline available at most gas stations. You'll also notice that their names change from company to company. The ones with the highest octane are the most expensive, but most rental cars take the least expensive "regular" gas, with an octane rating of 87.

Holidays See "When to Go," in chapter 2.

Legal Aid The ordinary tourist will probably never become involved with the American legal system. If you're pulled over for a minor infraction (for example, driving faster than the speed limit), never attempt to pay the fine directly to a police officer; you may wind up arrested on the much more serious charge of attempted bribery. Pay fines by mail or directly into the hands of the clerk of the court. If accused of a more serious offense, it's wise to say and do nothing before consulting a lawyer (under the U.S. Constitution, you have the rights both to remain silent and to consult an attorney). Under U.S. law, an arrested person is allowed one telephone call to a party of his or her choice; call your embassy or consulate.

Mail Mailboxes, which are generally found at intersections, are blue with a blue-and-white eagle logo and carry the inscription "U.S. Postal Service." If your mail is addressed to a U.S. destination, don't forget to add the five-figure postal code, or ZIP code, after the two-letter abbreviation of the state to which the mail is addressed. The abbreviation for Hawaii is HI.

At press time, domestic postage rates were 22¢ for a postcard and 34¢ for a letter. For international mail, a first-class letter of up to 1 ounce costs 80¢ (60¢ to Canada and Mexico); a first-class postcard costs 70¢ (50¢ to Canada and Mexico); and a preprinted postal aerogramme costs 70¢. Point your Web browser to www.usps.com for complete U.S. postal information, or call ✆ 800/275-8777 for information on the nearest post office. Most branches are open Monday through Friday from 8am to 5 or 6pm, Saturday from 9am to noon or 3pm.

Taxes The United States has no VAT (value-added tax) or other indirect taxes at a national level. Every state, and every city in it, has the right to levy its own local tax on all purchases, including hotel and restaurant checks, airline tickets, and so on. In Hawaii, sales tax is 4%; there's also a 7.25% hotel-room tax and a small excise tax, so the total tax on your hotel bill will be 11.42%.

Telephone & Fax The telephone system in the United States is run by private corporations, so rates, particularly for long-distance service and operator-assisted calls, can vary widely—especially on calls made from public telephones. Local calls—that is, calls to other locations on the island you're on—made from public phones in Hawaii cost 35¢.

Generally, hotel surcharges on long-distance and local calls are astronomical. You are usually better off using a **public pay telephone,** which you will find clearly marked in most public buildings and private establishments as well as on the street. Many convenience stores and newsstands sell **prepaid calling cards** in denominations up to $50.

Most **long-distance** and **international calls** can be dialed directly from any phone. **For calls within the United States and to Canada,** dial 1 followed by the area code and the seven-digit number. **For other international calls,** dial 011 followed by the country code, city code, and the telephone number of the person you are calling. Some country and city codes are as follows: **Australia** 61, Melbourne 3, Sydney 2; **Ireland** 353, Dublin 1; **New Zealand** 64, Auckland 9, Wellington 4; **United Kingdom** 44, Belfast 232, Birmingham 21, Glasgow 41, London 71 or 81.

If you're calling the **United States from another country,** the country code is 01.

In Hawaii, interisland phone calls are considered long-distance and are often as costly as calling the U.S. mainland. The international country code for Hawaii is 1, just as it is for the rest of the United States and Canada.

For **reversed-charge** or **collect calls,** and for **person-to-person calls,** dial 0 (zero, not the letter "O"), followed by the area code and number you want; an operator will then come on the line, and you should specify that you are calling collect, person-to-person, or both. If your operator-assisted call is international, ask for the overseas operator.

Note that all phone numbers with the area code 800, 888, and 877 are toll-free. However, calls to numbers in area codes 700 and 900 (chat lines, "dating" services, and so on) can be very expensive—usually a charge of 95¢ to $3 or more per minute.

For **local directory assistance** ("information"), dial 411. For **long-distance information,** dial 1, then the appropriate area code and 555-1212; for **directory assistance for another island,** dial 1, then 808, then 555-1212.

Fax facilities are widely available and can be found in most hotels and many other establishments. Try **Mail Boxes, Etc.** or **Kinko's** (check the local Yellow Pages) or any photocopying shop.

Telephone Directories There are two kinds of telephone directories in the United States. The general directory, the so-called White Pages, lists private and business subscribers in alphabetical order. The inside front cover lists the emergency numbers for police, fire, and ambulance, along with other vital numbers. The first few pages are devoted to community-service numbers, including a guide to long-distance and international calling, complete with country codes and area codes.

The second directory, printed on yellow paper (hence its name, Yellow Pages), lists all local services, businesses, and industries by type of activity, with an index at the front. The listings cover not only such obvious items as automobile repairs and drugstores (pharmacies), but also restaurants by type of cuisine and geographical location, bookstores by special subject and/or language, places of worship by religious denomination, and other information that the visitor might not otherwise readily find. The Yellow Pages also include detailed maps, postal ZIP codes, and a calendar of events.

Time Zone See "Fast Facts: Oahu," in chapter 2.

Tipping It's part of the American way of life to tip. Many service employees receive little direct salary and must depend on tips for their income. The following are some general rules:

In **hotels,** tip bellhops at least $1 per piece of luggage ($2–$3 if you have a lot of luggage), and tip the housekeeping staff $1 per person, per day. Tip the doorman or concierge only if he or she has provided you with some specific service (for example, calling a cab for you or obtaining difficult-to-get theater tickets). Tip the valet-parking attendant $1 every time you get your car.

In **restaurants, bars,** and **nightclubs,** tip service staff 15% to 20% of the check, tip bartenders 10% to 15%, and tip valet-parking attendants $1 per vehicle. Tip the doorman only if he or she has provided you with some specific service (such as calling a cab for you). Tipping is not expected in cafeterias and fast-food restaurants.

Tip **cab drivers** 15% of the fare.

As for **other service personnel,** tip skycaps at airports at least $1 per piece ($2–$3 if you have a lot of luggage), and tip hairdressers and barbers 15% to 20%. Tipping ushers at theaters is not expected.

Toilets Foreign visitors often complain that public toilets are hard to find in most U.S. cities. True, there are none on the streets, but visitors can usually find one in a bar, fast-food outlet, restaurant, hotel, museum, or department store—and it will probably be clean. (The cleanliness of toilets at service stations, parks, and beaches is more open to question.) Note, however, a growing practice in some restaurants and bars of displaying a notice that toilets are for the use of patrons only. You can ignore this sign or, better yet, avoid arguments by paying for a cup of coffee or soft drink, which will qualify you as a patron.

Accommodations

by Jeanette Foster

The island of Oahu, while not the biggest in the Hawaiian chain, offers the widest variety of accommodations. You can stay in near-palatial surroundings where kings, heads of state, billionaires, and rock stars have spent the night, or in a quaint bed-and-breakfast on the North Shore where the rolling surf lulls you to sleep at night. You can opt for the bright lights and action of Waikiki, the quiet comforts of Kahala, or the rural calm of the windward side. Oahu has the perfect place for everyone.

Before you reach for the phone to reserve a place, consider when you will be traveling to Hawaii. Hawaii has two seasons—high and low. The **highest season** is mid-December to March. This is the time of year when rooms are always booked and rates are at the top end. The second "high" season is June to September, when rates are high, but bookings are somewhat easier. The **low season,** with fewer tourists, cheaper rates—and sometimes, even "deals" on rooms—is April to June and September to mid-December.

Be sure to factor in Hawaii's 11.42% hotel tax to all the listed rates to get a true picture of your bill. Don't forget to include parking, which, at Waikiki hotels, can quickly add up.

TYPES OF ACCOMMODATIONS

HOTELS In Hawaii, *hotel* can mean a wide range of options, from few or no on-site amenities to enough extras to call it a mini-resort. Generally, a hotel offers daily maid service and has a restaurant, on-site laundry facilities, a swimming pool, and a sundries/convenience-type shop (rather than the shopping arcades most resorts have these days). Top hotels also have activities desks, concierge and valet service, room service (although it may be limited), business centers, an airport shuttle, a bar and/or lounge, and maybe a few more shops. The advantage of staying in a hotel is privacy and convenience. The disadvantage is generally noise: either thin walls between rooms or loud music from a lobby lounge late into the night.

Hotels are often a short walk from the beach instead of being beachfront (but some, like the Sheraton Moana Surfrider and the New Otani in Waikiki, are right on the sand). Because they come with fewer amenities than full-fledged resorts, hotels tend to be cheaper, but not always.

RESORTS In Hawaii, a resort offers everything a hotel offers and more. What you get varies from property to property, of course, but expect facilities, services, and amenities such as direct beach access, with beach cabanas and chairs; pools (often more than one) and a Jacuzzi; a spa and fitness center; restaurants, bars, and lounges; a 24-hour front desk; concierge, valet, and bell services; room service (often around the clock); an activities desk; tennis and golf (some of the world's best courses are at Hawaii resorts); ocean activities; a business center; kid's programs; and more.

⌒ *Tips* Nickel-and-Dime Charges at High-Priced Hotels

Several upscale resorts in Hawaii have begun a practice that we find dis-tasteful, dishonest, and downright discouraging: charging a so-called "resort fee." This daily fee is added on to your bill (and can range from $8–$12 a day), for such "complimentary" items as a daily newspaper, local phone calls, use of the fitness facilities, and so on. Amenities that the resort has been happily providing its guests for years are now tacked on to your bill under the guise of a "fee." In most cases you do not have an option to decline the resort fee—in other words, this is a sneaky way to further increase the prices without telling you. We are very opposed to this practice and urge you to voice your complaints to the resort man-agement. Otherwise, what'll be next—a charge for using the tiny bars of soap or miniature shampoo bottles?

The advantages of a resort are that you have everything you could possibly want in the way of services and things to do; the disadvantage is that the price generally reflects this. Don't be misled by a name—just because a place is called "ABC Resort" doesn't mean it actually *is* a resort. Make sure you're getting what you pay for.

CONDOS   The roominess and convenience of a condo—which is usually a fully equipped, multiple-bedroom apartment—makes it a great choice for fam-ilies. Condominium properties in Hawaii are generally several apartments set in a single high-rise or a cluster of low-rise units. Condos generally have amenities such as limited maid service (ranging from daily to weekly; it may or may not be included in your rate, so be sure to ask), a swimming pool, laundry facilities (either in your unit or in a central location), and an on-site front desk or a live-in property manager. The advantages of a condo are privacy, space, and conveniences—which usually include full kitchen facilities, a washer and dryer, a private phone, and more. The downsides are the standard lack of an on-site restaurant and the density of the units (versus the privacy of a single-unit vaca-tion rental).

Condos vary in price according to size, location, and amenities. Many of them are located on or near the beach, and they tend to be clustered in resort areas. While there are some very high-end condos, most tend to be quite afford-able, especially if you're traveling in a group that's large enough to require more than one bedroom.

BED-AND-BREAKFASTS   Hawaii has a wide range of places that call them-selves B&Bs, everything from a traditional B&B—several bedrooms (which may or may not share a bathroom) in a home, with breakfast served in the morning—to what is essentially a vacation rental on an owner's property that comes with fixings to make your own breakfast. Make sure that the B&B you're thinking about booking matches your own mental picture. Would you prefer conversation around a big dining-room table as you eat a hearty breakfast, or just a muffin and juice to enjoy in your own private place? Laundry facilities and a private phone are not always available at B&Bs. If you have to share a bath-room, we've spelled it out in the listing; otherwise, you can assume that you will have a private bathroom.

Tips B&B Etiquette

In Hawaii, it is traditional and customary to remove your shoes before entering anyone's home. The same is true for most bed-and-breakfast facilities. Most hosts post signs or will politely ask you to remove your shoes before entering the B&B. Not only does this keep the B&B clean, but also you'll be amazed how relaxed you feel walking around barefoot. If this custom is unpleasant to you, a B&B may not be for you. Consider a condo or hotel, where no one will be particular about your shoes.

Hotels, resorts, condos, and vacation rentals generally allow smoking in the guest rooms (most also have no-smoking rooms available), but the majority of bed-and-breakfast units forbid smoking in the rooms. If this matters to you, be sure to check the policy of your accommodation before you book.

The advantage of a traditional B&B is its individual style and congenial atmosphere. B&Bs are great places to meet other visitors to Hawaii, and the host is generally happy to act as your own private concierge, giving you tips on where to go and what to do. In addition, they're usually an affordable way to go (although fancier ones can run $150 or more a night). The disadvantages are lack of privacy, usually a set time for breakfast, few amenities, generally no maid service, and the fact that you'll have to share the quarters beyond your bedroom with others. In addition, B&B owners usually require a minimum stay of 2 or 3 nights, and it's often a drive to the beach.

VACATION RENTALS   This is another great choice for families and for long-term stays. "Vacation rental" usually means that there's no one on the property where you're staying. The actual accommodation can range from an apartment in a condominium building to a two-room cottage on the beach to an entire fully equipped house. Generally, vacation rentals are the kind of places you can settle into and make yourself at home for a while. They have kitchen facilities (either a complete kitchen or just a kitchenette with microwave, refrigerator, burners, and coffeemaker), on-site laundry facilities, and a phone; some also come outfitted with such extras as a TV, VCR, and stereo. The advantages of a vacation rental are complete privacy, your own kitchen (which can save you money on meals), and lots of conveniences. The disadvantages are a lack of an on-site property manager and generally no maid service; often, a minimum stay is required (sometimes as much as a week). If you book a vacation rental, be sure you have a 24-hour contact so that when the toilet won't flush or you can't figure out how to turn on the air-conditioning, you have someone to call.

HOW TO GET THE BEST RATES

Like the price of a car, accommodation rates can sometimes be bargained down, but it depends on the place. In general, each type of accommodation allows a different amount of latitude in bargaining on their rack (or published) rates.

The best bargaining can be had at **hotels** and **resorts.** Hotels and resorts regularly pay travel agents as much as 30% of the rate they're getting for sending clients their way; if business is slow, some hotels may give you the benefit of at least part of this commission if you book directly instead of going through an airline or travel agent. Most also have *kamaaina* or "local" rates for islanders, which they may extend to visitors during slow periods. It never hurts to ask politely for a discounted or local rate; there is also a host of special rates available for the military, seniors, members of the travel industry, families, corporate travelers, and long-term stays. Ask about package deals, where for the same price as a room, you can get a car rental or free breakfast. Hotels and resorts have packages for everyone: golfers, tennis players, families, honeymooners, and more (for more on these, see "Money-Saving Package Deals," on p. 45). We've found that it's worth the extra few cents to make a local call to the hotel; sometimes the local reservations person knows about package deals that the 800 operators are unaware of. If all else fails, try to get the hotel or resort to upgrade you to a better room for the same price as a budget room, or waive the extra fees for children or the parking fee. Persistence and asking politely can pay off.

The rates for a **bed-and-breakfast** are the hardest to bargain on. Sometimes you can be successful in bargaining down the minimum stay, or you might be able to negotiate a discount if you're staying a week or longer. Generally, however, a B&B owner has only a few rooms and has already priced the property at a competitive rate; expect to pay what's asked.

You have somewhat more leeway to negotiate on **vacation rentals** and **condos.** In addition to asking for a discount on a multi-night stay, ask if they can throw in a rental car to sweeten the deal; believe it or not, they often will.

USING A BOOKING AGENCY VS. DOING IT YOURSELF

Sometimes you can save money by making the arrangements yourself—not only can you bargain on the phone, but some accommodations might be willing to pass on a percentage of the commission they normally pay a travel agent or a booking agency.

However, if you don't have the time or money to call several places to make sure they offer the amenities you'd like and to bargain for a price you're comfortable with, then you might consider a booking agency. The time they spend on your behalf could well be worth any fees you have to pay.

The top reservations service in the state is **Hawaii's Best Bed & Breakfasts** ★, P.O. Box 563, Kamuela, HI 96743 (✆ **800/262-9912** or 808/885-4550; fax 808/885-0559; www.bestbnb.com). The service charges you $15 to book the first two locations and $5 for each additional location. Barbara and Susan Campbell personally select the traditional homestays, cottages, and inns throughout the islands they represent, based on each one's hospitality, distinctive charm, and attention to detail. They also book vacation rentals, hotels, and resorts.

Another great statewide booking agent is **Bed & Breakfast Hawaii,** P.O. Box 449, Kapaa, HI 96746 (✆ **800/733-1632** or 808/822-7771; fax 808/822-2723; www.bandb-hawaii.com), offering a range of accommodations from vacation homes to B&Bs, starting at $65 a night.

For vacation rentals, contact **Hawaii Beachfront Vacation Homes** (✆ **808/ 247-3637** or 808/235-2644; www.hotspots.hawaii.com/beachrent1.html). **Hawaii Condo Exchange** (✆ **800/442-0404;** http://hawaiicondoexchange.com) acts as a consolidator for condo and vacation-rental properties.

A Note on Smoking

Hotels, resorts, condos, and vacation rentals generally allow smoking in the rooms (most have no-smoking rooms, too), but the majority of the bed-and-breakfast units forbid smoking in the rooms. Be sure to check the policy of your accommodation before you book.

1 Waikiki

Some 5 million tourists visit Oahu every year, and 9 out of 10 of them choose accommodations in Waikiki, a 500-acre beachfront neighborhood of Honolulu. This is where the action is: fast food to fine dining, nightlife including everything from the sweet sounds of Hawaiian melodies to spicy dance music, shopping from bargains to brand names, and every ocean activity you can imagine. Staying here puts you in the heart of it all, but be aware that Waikiki is an on-the-go city with crowds, traffic noise, and its fair share of crime.

WAIKIKI, EWA END

All the hotels listed below are located from the ocean to Ala Wai Blvd., and between Ala Wai Terrace in the Ewa direction (or western side of Waikiki) and Olohana Street and Fort DeRussy Park in the Diamond Head direction (or eastern side of Waikiki).

VERY EXPENSIVE

Hawaii Prince Hotel Waikiki 🎔🎔   The first hotel at the entrance to Waikiki is this striking $150 million modern structure (actually, twin 33-story high-tech towers with a view). The high-ceilinged lobby is a mass of pink Italian marble with English slate accents; a grand piano sits in the midst of the raised seating area, where high tea is served every afternoon. A glass-encased elevator with views of all of Honolulu whisks you up to your room. All bedrooms face the Ala Wai Yacht Harbor, with floor-to-ceiling sliding-glass windows that let you enjoy the view (sorry, no lanais). All of the comfortably appointed rooms are basically the same, but the higher the floor, the higher the price.

Following Japanese standards, the level of service is impeccable; no detail is ignored, no request is too small. The location is perfect for shopping—Ala Moana Center is a 10-minute walk away—and Waikiki's beaches are just a 5-minute walk away (both are also accessible via the hotel's own shuttle).

100 Holomoana St. (just across Ala Wai Canal Bridge, on the ocean side of Ala Moana Blvd.), Honolulu, HI 96815. ✆ 800/321-OAHU or 808/965-1111. Fax 808/946-0811. www.princeresortshawaii.com. 521 units. $300–$440 double; from $550 suite. Extra person $40; children 17 and under stay free using existing bedding. AE, DC, MC, V. Valet parking $14, self-parking $10. TheBus: 19 or 20. **Amenities:** 2 excellent restaurants (1 Japanese, 1 serving Hawaii Regional cuisine and a terrific buffet at a great price; see the review of the Prince Court on p. 111); outdoor bar; outdoor pool; 27-hole golf club a half-hour drive away in Ewa Beach (reached by hotel shuttle); small but newly renovated fitness room; Jacuzzi; concierge; car-rental desk; business center; room service (6am–midnight); baby-sitting; coin-op washer/dryers; laundry/dry cleaning; executive-level rooms. *In room:* A/C, TV, dataport, fridge, coffeemaker, hair dryer, iron, safe.

Hilton Hawaiian Village Beach Resort & Spa 🎔🎔 *Kids*   Sprawling over 20 acres, this is Waikiki's biggest resort—a minicity unto itself, so big it even has its own post office. You'll find tropical gardens dotted with exotic wildlife (flamingos, peacocks, even tropical penguins!), award-winning restaurants (see p. 108), 100 different shops, a secluded lagoon, two minigolf courses, and a gorgeous stretch of Waikiki Beach. This is a great place to stay with the kids.

There's a wide choice of accommodations. Rooms, which range from simply lovely to ultradeluxe, are housed in five towers: Rainbow, Tapa, Diamond Head, Alii, and the brand-new-in-2001 Kalia. Despite the hotel's mega-Vegas size, this division into towers, each with its own restaurants and shopping, cuts down on the chaotic, impersonal feeling that might have resulted. Still, this is the place for a lively, activity-packed vacation; those seeking a more intimate, relaxing experience might want to look elsewhere.

All rooms are large and beautifully furnished; if you can afford it, we highly recommend the ones in the Alii Tower, located right on the ocean. Guests in these 348 amenity-laden rooms and suites get the royal treatment, including in-room registration, an exclusive health club and pool, and the full attention of a multilingual staff. Each room has no fewer than three phones (one of which is PC-compatible) and even a mini-TV on the bathroom vanity. But if you choose a room in one of the more affordable towers, you'll still be happy.

In 2001, the new Kalia Tower opened, along with two new spas: Holistica Hawaii (a wellness center with high-tech equipment) and Mandara Spa (a state-of-the-art fitness center and traditional body-treatment spa). Also new at the Hilton is Waikiki's first full-service, 24-hour hotel business center, located on the ground floor of the Diamond Head tower.

2005 Kalia Rd. (at Ala Moana Blvd.), Honolulu, HI 96815. ⓒ **800-HILTONS** or 808/949-4321. Fax 808/ 947-7898. www.hawaiianvillage.hilton.com. 2,998 units. $355–$445 double; $385–$460 Alii Tower double; from $430 suite. Ask about Bounce Back rates, starting at $219, including breakfast. Extra person $35; children 18 and under stay free in parents' room. AE, DISC, MC, V. Valet parking $14, self-parking $9. TheBus: 19 or 20. **Amenities:** 18 restaurants (including an award-winning Cantonese/Szechuan eatery in exquisite Asian-style surroundings; a romantic oceanview dining room serving Pacific Rim cuisine; a sushi bar; a branch of Benihana); 6 bars; 3 outdoor pools; fitness center with free classes and high-tech equipment; brand-new superplush Mandara Spa; watersports equipment rentals; 2 minigolf courses; year-round children's program (one of Waikiki's best); game room; concierge; activity desk; car-rental desk; Waikiki's only 24-hr. business center; huge shopping arcade; salon; room service (6am–midnight); in-room massage; baby-sitting; coin-op washer/dryers; same-day laundry service; dry cleaning; concierge-level rooms. *In room:* A/C, TV, dataport, fridge, coffeemaker, hair dryer, iron, safe.

EXPENSIVE
Doubletree Alana Waikiki ⚐ This boutique hotel is a welcome oasis of beauty, comfort, and prompt service. It's an intimate choice, offering the amenities of a much larger, more luxurious hotel at more affordable prices. The guest rooms are comfortable and homey; they're small, but make good use of the space and offer all the amenities you'd expect from a more expensive hotel. Many guests are business travelers who expect top-drawer service—and the Alana Waikiki delivers. The staff is attentive to detail and willing to go to any lengths to make you happy. Waikiki Beach is a 10-minute walk away.

1956 Ala Moana Blvd. (on the Ewa side, near Kalakaua Ave.), Honolulu, HI 96815. ⓒ **800/222-TREE** or 808/ 941-7275. Fax 808/949-0996. www.alana-doubletree.com. 313 units. $195–$215 double; from $240 suite. Extra person $30; children under 18 stay free in parents' room. AE, DC, DISC, MC, V. Valet parking $10. TheBus: 19 or 20. **Amenities:** 2 excellent restaurants (Padovani's, review on p. 111, serves Mediterranean cuisine prepared with an innovative island flair; there's also a wine bar offering appetizers); 1 bar; outdoor heated pool; small fitness center with sauna and massage services; concierge; well-equipped business center; room service (6am–10pm); in-room massage; baby-sitting; coin-op washer/dryers; laundry/dry cleaning. *In room:* A/C, TV, dataport, fridge, coffeemaker, hair dryer, iron, safe.

MODERATE
Renaissance Ilikai Waikiki Hotel   In 2001, this oceanfront hotel, which faces the Ala Wai Yacht Harbor, underwent a multi-million dollar renovation. Even before the renovation, the hotel had several pluses: excellent location, ocean views, huge rooms with spacious lanais, and all the activities, restaurants, and shops you can imagine. The only thing missing was the much-needed remodeling to bring it into the 21st century. Rooms are extraordinarily spacious, with large lanais overlooking the ocean and the mountains. Some of the top rooms have whirlpool spas, fax machines, and a mini-library of bestsellers for purchase. There are great deals for seniors, and good family packages that include rooms with a full kitchen, a midsize car, and free parking.

Waikiki Accommodations

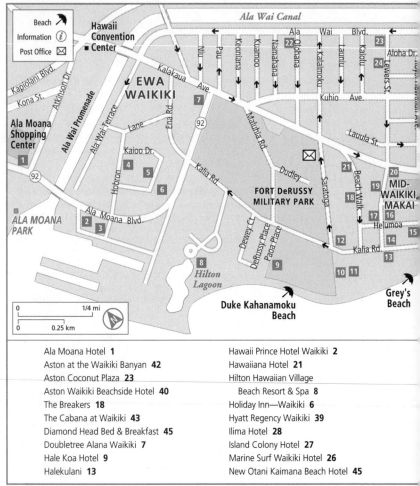

Ala Moana Hotel **1**

Aston at the Waikiki Banyan **42**

Aston Coconut Plaza **23**

Aston Waikiki Beachside Hotel **40**

The Breakers **18**

The Cabana at Waikiki **43**

Diamond Head Bed & Breakfast **45**

Doubletree Alana Waikiki **7**

Hale Koa Hotel **9**

Halekulani **13**

Hawaii Prince Hotel Waikiki **2**

Hawaiiana Hotel **21**

Hilton Hawaiian Village

  Beach Resort & Spa **8**

Holiday Inn—Waikiki **6**

Hyatt Regency Waikiki **39**

Ilima Hotel **28**

Island Colony Hotel **27**

Marine Surf Waikiki Hotel **26**

New Otani Kaimana Beach Hotel **45**

1777 Ala Moana Blvd. (ocean side of Ala Moana Blvd., at Hobron Lane), Honolulu, HI 96815. ℭ **800/367-8434** or 808/949-3811. Fax 808/947-0892. www.ilikaihotel.com. 783 units. $149–$169 double; $425–$525 suite. Extra person $30. AE, DC, DISC, MC, V. Parking $12. TheBus: 19 or 20. **Amenities:** 4 restaurants ranging from American cuisine to Japanese; 6 bars; 2 outdoor pools; 6 Plexipave tennis courts; fitness room; Jacuzzi; concierge; activity desk; car-rental desk; business center; shopping arcade; salon; room service; massage; baby-sitting; coin-op washer/dryers; laundry/dry cleaning; concierge-level rooms. *In room:* A/C, TV/VCR, dataport, kitchen (in some rooms), fridge, coffeemaker, hair dryer, iron, safe.

Royal Garden at Waikiki ℛ *(Finds)*   This elegant boutique hotel, tucked away on a quiet, tree-lined side street, offers a lobby filled with European marble and chandeliers. The plush guest rooms feature pantry kitchenettes, marble bathrooms, lanais, lots of closet space, and views. The beach is a few blocks away, but at these prices, it's worth the hike.

440 Olohana St. (between Kuhio Ave. and Ala Wai Blvd.), Honolulu, HI 96815. ℭ **800/367-5666** or 808/943-0202. Fax 808/946-8777. www.royalgardens.com. 220 units. $150–$250 double; $325–$425 1-bedroom double; $600 2-bedroom (sleeps up to 4). Packages galore. Extra person $25; children under 12 stay free in parents' room. AE, DC, DISC, MC, V. Parking $8. TheBus: 19 or 20. **Amenities:** 2 restaurants

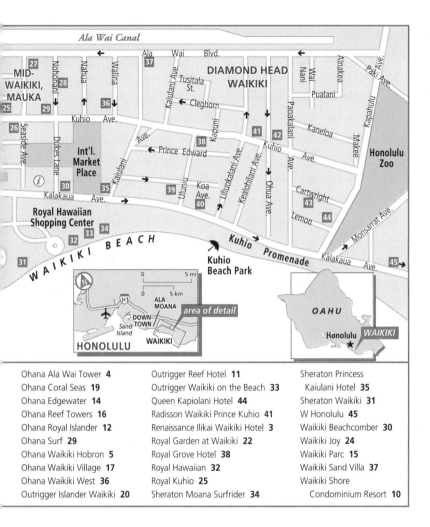

(country French, Japanese); 2 freshwater outdoor pools (1 with cascading waterfall); small fitness room; 2 Jacuzzis; 2 saunas; concierge; small business center; complimentary shuttle service to Honolulu shopping centers; baby-sitting; coin-op washer/dryers; laundry/dry cleaning. *In room:* A/C, TV, dataport, kitchenette, fridge, coffeemaker, hair dryer, iron, safe.

INEXPENSIVE

Holiday Inn–Waikiki   Just 2 blocks from the beach, 2 blocks from Ala Moana Shopping Center, and a 7-minute walk from the Convention Center, this Holiday Inn has a great location and offers this chain's usual amenities for prices that are quite reasonable (for Waikiki, anyway). All rooms, which have a modern Japanese look, come with either a king or two double beds. The property sits back from the street, so noise is at a minimum. The staff is unbelievably friendly.

1830 Ala Moana Blvd. (between Hobron Lane and Kalia Rd.), Honolulu, HI 96815. *©* **888/9WAIKIKI** or 808/955-1111. Fax 808/947-1799. www.holiday-inn-waikiki.com. 199 units. $120–$130 double. Extra person $15; children 19 and under stay free in parents' room using existing bedding. AE, DC, DISC, MC, V. Parking $6. TheBus: 19 or 20. **Amenities:** 1 restaurant (Chinese/seafood); outdoor lap pool; small fitness room;

concierge; limited room service; coin-op washer/dryers; laundry/dry cleaning. *In room:* A/C, TV, dataport, fridge, coffeemaker, hair dryer, iron, safe.

Ohana Ala Wai Tower ☆ *Value*   This skyscraper complex, which sits back from busy Ala Moana Boulevard, is just 4 blocks from the beach and close to Ala Moana Shopping Center and the Hawaii Convention Center. The rooms were renovated in 1995; views are stunning from the upper floors. The doubles are in the Tower, whose glass elevators offer breathtaking views every time you ride up and down (but with 40 floors and only 2 elevators, the wait for an elevator can challenge your patience); each has a well-equipped kitchenette. The one-bedroom suites are in the 16-story Annex; these have a separate bedroom, living room, lanai, and kitchen. (Mobility-impaired travelers should book in the Tower, as you have to climb a flight of stairs to reach the elevator in the Annex.)

There are no restaurants on site, but several are within walking distance. *Hot tip for views:* In the Tower, the best views are from floors 21 and above; ask for a room facing Ewa (west) for spectacular sunset views.

1700 Ala Moana Blvd. (between Hobron Lane and Ala Wai Canal), Honolulu, HI 96815. © 800/462-6262 or 808/942-7722. Fax 808/943-7272 or 800/622-4852. www.ohanahotels.com. 167 units. $129–$139 double with kitchenette; $189 one-bedroom suite for 5. Extra person $20. Ask about Simple Saver rates, which were $79 at press time. Extra person $20. AE, DC, DISC, MC. V. Parking $8. TheBus: 19 or 20. **Amenities:** Outdoor pool; 1 tennis court (lit for night play); Jacuzzi; children's program; activity desk; car-rental desk; business center; coin-op washer/dryers; laundry/dry cleaning. *In room:* A/C, TV, kitchenette, fridge, coffeemaker, iron, safe.

Ohana Waikiki Hobron ☆ *Value*   Attention, visitors attending an event at the Hawaii Convention Center: This is the best bargain accommodation within walking distance. This 44-story outpost of the reliable Outrigger chain is located on a quiet side street, just a 10-minute walk from Waikiki Beach, the Ala Moana Shopping Center, and the Convention Center. There are 16 rooms on each floor: Four rooms have ocean views, four look toward the mountains, four face Diamond Head, and the last four show you Honolulu's city lights. The rooms are small (only 200–240 sq. ft.), with not much dancing room between the bed and the walls, but they're blissfully outfitted with blackout drapes for those mornings you want to sleep in. The studios are a bit larger, and have well-equipped kitchenettes. You might want to invest in earplugs—the walls seem paper thin. But at $109 a day for a couple or $69 to $89 for "Simple Saver" rates (call the hotel for details), you're getting a lot of bang for your buck.

343 Hobron Lane (just off Ala Moana Blvd.), Honolulu, HI 96815. © 800/462-6262 or 808/942-7777. Fax 808/943-7373 or 800/622-4852. www.ohanahotels.com. 612 units. $109 double; $119 double with kitchenette; $169 1-bedroom suite with kitchenette. Extra person $15. Ask about promotions and packages, including Simple Saver rates. AE, DC, DISC, MC. V. Parking $8. TheBus: 19 or 20. **Amenities:** 1 restaurant (coffee shop); 1 lounge with Hawaiian music Fri–Sat nights; small outdoor pool; Jacuzzi; sauna; activity desk; sundries store; coin-op washer/dryers; laundry/dry cleaning. *In room:* A/C, TV, dataport, kitchenette (some rooms), fridge, coffeemaker available on request, hair dryer, iron available on request, safe.

MID-WAIKIKI, MAKAI

All the hotels listed below are between the ocean and Kalakaua Avenue, and between Fort DeRussy in the Ewa (west) direction and Kaiulani Street in the Diamond Head (east) direction.

VERY EXPENSIVE

Halekulani ☆☆☆ *Kids*   Here's the ultimate heavenly Hawaii vacation. Halekulani translates as "House Befitting Heaven"—an apt description of this luxury resort, selected the number-one hotel in the world by *Gourmet* magazine in 2000. It's spread over 5 acres of prime Waikiki beachfront in five buildings

What to Do If Your Dream Hotel Turns Out to Be a Nightmare

Don't panic! Even if you've booked into a small B&B and you absolutely hate your room, usually the host wants to make you happy and may even get on the phone and book you at another place that suits you better. Hotels, resorts, and condominiums are generally easier to deal with, since they have numerous units to offer and can probably satisfy your requests by moving you to another room.

Here are some tips on how to avoid getting a room you dislike or how to complain if you've checked in and can't stand your room:

- Find out beforehand exactly what the accommodation is offering you: the cost, the minimum stay, the included amenities. Ask if there's any penalty for leaving early. Read the small print in the contract—especially the information on cancellation fees.

- Discuss ahead of time with the B&B, vacation rental, condominium agent, or booking agency what their cancellation policy is if the accommodation doesn't meet your expectations. Get this policy in writing (so there are no misunderstandings later).

- When you arrive, if your room doesn't meet your expectations, notify the front desk, rental agent, or booking agency immediately.

- Approach the management in a calm, reasonable manner. Voice your complaint clearly and suggest a solution. Be reasonable and be willing to compromise. Do not make threats or leave. If you leave, it may be harder to get your deposit returned.

- If all else fails, when you get home, write your credit-card company or any association the accommodation may be a member of (such as the Hawaii Visitors and Convention Bureau, a resort association, or an island association). In the letter, state the name of the accommodation, the name you registered under, the date of the complaint, the exact nature of the complaint, and why the issue was not resolved to your satisfaction. And be sure to let us know if you have a problem with a place we've recommended in this book!

that are connected by open courtyards and lush, tropical gardens. Upon arrival, you're immediately greeted and escorted to your room, where registration is handled in comfort and privacy.

There are so many things that set this luxury hotel apart from the others, the most important being the rooms: About 90% face the ocean, and they're big (averaging 620 sq. ft.), each with a separate sitting area and a large, furnished lanai. Each bathroom features a deep soaking tub, a separate glassed-in shower, and a marble basin.

Other perks include complimentary tickets to any or all of the following: Ihilani Palace, Bishop Museum, Contemporary Art Museum, Honolulu Academy of Art, and the Honolulu Symphony (about $100 per person worth of art and culture). The hotel's restaurants are outstanding (see the reviews of La Mer on p. 107 and Orchids on p. 110), and the **House Without a Key** ★★ is surely one of the world's most romantic spots for sunset cocktails, light meals, and entertainment. You can't find a better location on Waikiki Beach or a more luxurious hotel.

2199 Kalia Rd. (at the ocean end of Lewers St.), Honolulu, HI 96815. ℂ 800/367-2343 or 808/923-2311. Fax 808/926-8004. www.halekulani.com. 456 units. $325–$520 double; from $720 suite. Extra person $125; 1 child under 17 stays free in parents' room using existing bedding; maximum 3 people per room. AE, DC, MC, V. Parking $10. TheBus: 19 or 20. **Amenities:** 4 superb restaurants (including one serving award-winning neoclassic French cuisine, and an excellent seafood eatery with one of Waikiki's best views); 2 bars; gorgeous outdoor pool; small fitness room; watersports equipment rentals; bike rental; children's program during the summer and at Christmas; concierge; activity desk; complete business center; top-drawer shops; salon; 24-hr. room service; in-room massage; baby-sitting; same-day laundry and dry cleaning. *In room:* A/C, TV, dataport, minibar, hair dryer, iron, safe.

Royal Hawaiian ✪✪   This shocking-pink oasis, hidden away among blooming gardens within the concrete jungle of Waikiki, is a symbol of luxury. Built by Matson steamship lines and inspired by popular silent-screen star Rudolph Valentino (*The Sheik*), the Spanish-Moorish "Pink Palace" opened in 1927 on the same spot where Queen Kaahumanu had her summer palace—on one of the best stretches of Waikiki Beach.

Entry into the hotel is past the lush gardens, with their spectacular banyan tree, into the black terrazzo-marble lobby, which features handwoven pink carpets and giant floral arrangements. My heart was won over by the rooms in the Historic Wing, which contain carved wooden doors, four-poster canopy beds, flowered wallpaper, and period furniture. Historic touches abound, including Hawaiian craft displays (Hawaiian quilts, leis, weaving, and more) by local artists every Monday, Wednesday, and Friday. Another plus: 24-hour medical services on property.

The Surf Room is known for its elaborate seafood buffets; the casual Beach Club features an oceanfront patio that's a great place to start your day. The Royal Hawaiian luau is done in grand style on Monday nights. The hotel's **Mai Tai Bar** ✪✪ is one of the most popular places in Waikiki for its namesake drink, which supposedly originated here.

2259 Kalakaua Ave. (at Royal Hawaiian Ave., on the ocean side of the Royal Hawaiian Shopping Center), Honolulu, HI 96815. ℂ 800/325-3535 or 808/923-7311. Fax 808/924-7098. www.sheraton.com. 527 units. $335–$625 double; from $800 suite. Extra person $50. Ask about Sheraton's Sure Saver rates, which could save you as much as 32%. AE, MC, V. Valet parking $13; self-parking at Sheraton Waikiki $9. TheBus: 19 or 20. **Amenities:** 2 restaurants; 1 landmark bar; good-sized outdoor pool; preferential tee times at Makaha Resort and Golf Club (about 1 hr. away); nearby fitness room (next door at the Sheraton Waikiki); watersports equipment rentals; bike rental; excellent year-round children's program ($30 a day, $20 for half-day); game room; multilingual concierge desk; activity desk; car-rental desk; business center; elegant shopping arcade; 24-hr. room service; in-room massage; baby-sitting; 24-hr. laundry service/dry cleaning (except Sun). *In room:* A/C, TV, dataport, fridge, hair dryer, iron, safe.

Sheraton Moana Surfrider ✪✪ *(Kids)*   Step back in time at Waikiki's first hotel, which dates from 1901 and is listed on the National Register of Historic Places. Considered an innovation in the travel industry, the Moana featured a private bathroom and a telephone in each guest room—an unheard-of luxury at the turn of the 20th century. Yesteryear lives on at this grand hotel: Entry is through the original colonial porte cochere, past the highly polished front porch dotted with rocking chairs, and into the perfectly restored lobby with detailed millwork and intricate plasterwork. The female employees even wear traditional Victorian-era muumuus. The aloha spirit that pervades this classy and charming place is infectious.

The hotel consists of three wings: the original (and totally restored) Banyan Wing, the Diamond Wing, and the Tower Wing. It's hard to get a bad room here; most have ocean views, and all come with pampering amenities like bed-side controls and plush robes. But we're especially taken with the Banyan Wing rooms: What they lack in size (they're on the smallish side and don't have lanais), they make up for in style; even the fixtures in the smallish bathrooms are modern-day replicas of 19th-century hardware. You get the feel for Old Hawaii here, with daily activities like Hawaiian arts and crafts, such as coconut-palm weaving and Hawaiian quilting; be sure to visit the Historical Room, where a variety of memorabilia is on display.

One of the best reasons to stay here is the hotel's prime stretch of beach, with lifeguard, beach chairs, towels, and any other service you desire. The Beach Bar and a poolside snack bar are located in the oceanfront courtyard that's centered around a 100-year-old banyan tree, where there's live music in the evenings.

2365 Kalakaua Ave. (ocean side of the street, across from Kaiulani St.), Honolulu, HI 96815. ℂ **800/ 325-3535** or 808/922-3111. Fax 808/923-0308. www.moana-surfrider.com. 793 units. $265–$530 double; from $950 suite. Extra person and rollaway bed $45; children under 18 stay free in parents' room using exist-ing bedding. Ask about Sure Saver rates, which could save you as much as 32%. AE, DC, MC, V. Valet park-ing $15; self-parking at sister property $9. TheBus: 19 or 20. **Amenities:** 5 restaurants (ranging from casual to fine dining, plus Sun brunch and high tea each afternoon); 2 bars; outdoor pool; nearby fitness room (about a 2-min. walk down the beach at the Sheraton Waikiki); watersports equipment rentals; children's program (featuring both on-site activities and excursions to the Honolulu Zoo and the Waikiki Aquarium); nearby game room (a stroll down the beach at the Sheraton Waikiki); concierge; activity desk; car-rental desk; nearby busi-ness center (a few minutes away at the Royal Hawaiian); very upscale shopping arcade; salon; room service; massage; baby-sitting; coin-op washer/dryers; same-day laundry service/dry cleaning. *In room:* A/C, TV, data-port, fridge, coffeemaker, hair dryer, iron, safe.

EXPENSIVE

Outrigger Reef Hotel ⨶ ⟨*Kids*⟩ Location, location, location! This Outrigger is right on Waikiki Beach, across from Ft. DeRussy, with beautifully appointed rooms, excellent service and a myriad of activities, shops, and restaurants. This is a big hotel with three towers and a megalobby connecting them. Off the lobby is an enormous swimming pool, with some 300 chaise longues surrounding it, three whirlpool spas, and food and cocktail service within hailing distance. Throughout the lobby are enough shops to qualify as a mini-shopping mall. And, of course, beautiful Waikiki is in the back yard. The rooms have the usual well-designed, well-appointed Outrigger furnishings and decorations with great views and plenty of extra room to have a couple of kids bedding down. Black-out drapes are a nice touch for jet-lagged travelers, as is a hospitality room for early check-ins or late checkouts.

2169 Kalia Rd. (ocean side of Kalia Rd., Ewa side of the Halekulani Hotel, and across the street from Beach Walk), Honolulu, HI 96815. ℂ **800/OUTRIGGER** or 808/923-3111. Fax 800/622-4852. www.outrigger.com. 883 units. $220–$440 double; $365–$485 Voyagers Club; $440–$1,300 suite. Extra person $30. Children under 17 free in parents' room. Seniors 50 and older 20% off, AARP members 25% off. Ask about room-and-breakfast packages. AE, DC, DISC, MC, V. Parking $10. TheBus: 19 or 20. **Amenities:** 3 restaurants (including the Shorebird Beach Broiler, an immensely popular oceanside spot offering buffet breakfasts and broil-your-own dinners); 3 bars with Hawaiian entertainment plus poolside sports bar; giant outdoor pool; 24-hr. fitness room; 3 Jacuzzis; children's program; concierge; activity desk; business center (Mon–Fri 8am–4pm); large shopping arcade; salon; room service 7am–10pm; massage; baby-sitting; coin-op washer/dryers; concierge-level rooms. *In room:* A/C, TV, dataport, kitchenette in some units, fridge, coffeemaker, hair dryer, iron, safe.

Outrigger Waikiki on the Beach ⨶ ⟨*Kids*⟩ The same value and quality that we've come to expect in every Outrigger hotel are definitely in evidence here, only multiplied by a factor of 10. Even the standard rooms in this 16-story oceanfront hotel are large and comfortable. And the prime beachfront location and loads of facilities help make this one of the chain's most attractive properties. The guest

⌒Kids Family-Friendly Hotels

If you're traveling with the kids, you'll be welcomed with open arms by many of Oahu's resorts, condos, and B&Bs. Our favorite family-friendly accommodations on the island are listed below. If you're looking for a hotel that has supervised activities for your youngster, you might want to consider the **Sheraton Moana Surfrider** (see p. 78), which has a great children's program. If you're looking for a more moderately priced option, look at the **Waikiki Sand Villa** (see p. 94) in Waikiki, **Schrader's Windward Marine Resort** (see p. 99) in Kaneohe and **Ke Iki Beach Bungalows** (see p. 101) on the North Shore, all of which love to accommodate kids and their well-behaved parents.

Waikiki

Halekulani *(see p. 76)* Between early June and mid-August and during Christmastime (Dec 18–30), the Halekulani, possibly our favorite hotel in the islands, has a wonderful complimentary supervised program for children ages 6 to 11. The only charges are for lunch and admission to activities. Daily programs include crafts, games, sightseeing, and excursions. Another plus is the Family Program, which allows a family to book a second room at special rates; depending on the category, this can bring savings of $115 to $210 per day.

Hilton Hawaiian Village *(see p. 72)* The Rainbow Express is Hilton's year-round daily program of activities for children ages 5 to 12. The program costs $32 for a full day, including lunch, or $17 for a half day. It offers a wide range of educational and fun activities: Hawaiian arts and crafts, nature walks, wildlife feedings, shell hunting, fishing, and much more. Everything about this hotel is kid-friendly, from the wildlife parading about the grounds to the submarine dives offered just out front. In three of the resort's restaurants, kids ages 11 and under eat for free.

Ilima Hotel *(see p. 87)* This hotel was designed with families in mind. The units are large, and all have full-sized kitchens. Although there's no formal children's program, you'll find free HBO, the Disney Channel, and Super Nintendo video games in each room, and the coin-operated laundry is a big help to mom and dad. The beach and the International Market Place are both only a short walk away, and TheBus stops just outside. Very popular with neighbor-island families.

Outrigger/Ohana Hotels Kids staying at any of the many Outrigger or Ohana Hotels in Waikiki can enjoy a special activities program with a surfing theme. Located at the Outrigger Reef, the Cowabunga Kids Club offers daily programs for children ages 5 to 13. The half-day ($28) and full-day ($38 including lunch, snack, and Cowabunga T-shirt) programs include games, arts and crafts, beach walks, shoreline fishing, and excursions around Waikiki. Professional counselors are in charge. A special benefit: Parents have the option of taking a free pager while their children are enrolled in the program. Transportation to the Outrigger Reef is provided from other hotels in the chain. Reservations are necessary; call ℰ **808/923-3111.**

Royal Kuhio *(see p. 90)* If you have active kids, this is the place for you. The seventh-floor recreation area has volleyball courts, billiards, basketball courts, shuffleboard, an exercise room, and even a putting green. Located just across the street from the International Market Place and 2 blocks from the beach, the Royal Kuhio features one-bedroom apartments with sofa sleepers and full kitchens. You're allowed up to four people per unit at the regular rate, and can even have five at an extra charge of $15 for a rollaway or crib.

Sheraton Waikiki Hotel *(see p. 82)* The Keiki Aloha Sunshine Club offers year-round activities for children ages 5 to 12 ($30 for a full day, $20 for a half day). On arrival, your kids are greeted with a complimentary candy lei; afterwards, they can boogie board, fly a kite, compete in a photo contest, watch nightly movies, and more.

Honolulu Beyond Waikiki

Kahala Mandarin Oriental Hawaii *(see p. 97)* The Keiki Club is the year-round activities program for kids ages 5 to 12. Your youngsters will have a blast dancing the hula, making leis, designing sand sculptures, putting on puppet shows, learning to strum a ukulele, making shell art and fish prints, listening to Hawaiian folk tales and legends, playing Hawaiian games, and more. The cost is $50 for a full day (including lunch), $30 for a half day.

The North Shore

Best Inn Hukilau Resort *(see p. 101)* There's no charge for kids under 18 to stay with you at this two-story, plantation-style North Shore hotel. Within walking distance of the Polynesian Cultural Center, the Rodeway is set up for families, with features like free continental breakfast, a pool, and laundry. A terrific white-sand beach is just across the street.

Hilton at Turtle Bay Resort *(see p. 100)* This North Shore resort offers a year-round program for children ages 5 to 12. The Turtle Keiki Program offers Hawaiian-style arts and crafts, coconut painting, sand sculpturing, swimming, movies, storytelling, and a host of other fun activities to keep the kids busy while you relax. The cost is $30 a day, which includes lunch.

Leeward Oahu: The Waianae Coast

J. W. Marriott Ihilani Resort & Spa *(see p. 102)* The Keiki Beachcomber Club, for children ages 4 to 12, is available every day of the year. Outdoor activities include kite-flying, tide-pool exploration, snorkeling, golf, tennis, swimming, aerobics, and international games like les boules (similar to bocce ball), Indian kickball, and tinikling (a bamboo dance from the Philippines); Hawaiian cultural activities include lei-making and hula dancing. There's also a state-of-the-art Computer Learning Center (complete with SEGA Genesis and Super Nintendo) and so many other activities that you're unlikely to even see the kids until you're ready to get on the plane to go home. The cost is $55 per child, which includes all activities, lunch, and a T-shirt.

rooms are big and comfortable, all with huge closets, roomy bathrooms, and plenty of amenities, plus a spacious lanai; the price is entirely dependent on the view. Rooms on the top four floors are part of the Voyager Club, where guests have the use of the private lounge serving continental breakfast and evening pupu. Among the hotel's restaurants is **Duke's Canoe Club** ⚐⚐ (see the review on p. 113), a wonderful spot right on the beach where great island-style seafood and steaks are complemented by Hawaiian entertainment.

2335 Kalakaua Ave. (on the ocean, between the Royal Hawaiian Shopping Center and the Sheraton Moana Surfrider), Honolulu, HI 96815. ⓒ 800/OUTRIGGER or 808/923-0711. Fax 800/622-4852. www.outrigger. com. 530 units. $230–$450 double; $370–$645 Voyager Club rooms and suites; from $600 suite. 20% discount for seniors 50 and over, 25% discount for AARP members; free rental car when booking at rack rates; ask about other package deals. Extra person $30; children 17 and under stay free in parents' room using existing bedding. AE, DC, DISC, MC, V. Parking $10. TheBus: 19 or 20. **Amenities:** 5 restaurants; 3 bars; showroom with nightly entertainment; giant outdoor pool; fitness center; Jacuzzi; watersports equipment rentals; year-round children's program; concierge; activity desk; car-rental desk; business center; large shopping arcade; salon; limited room service (7am–2pm and 5–9:45pm); baby-sitting; coin-op washer/dryers; laundry service; dry cleaning; concierge-level rooms. *In room:* A/C, TV, dataport, some kitchenettes, fridge, coffeemaker, hair dryer, iron, safe.

Sheraton Waikiki ⚐ *Kids*   Occupying two 30-story towers, this is by far the biggest of the four Sheratons on the beach. The lobby is immense and filled with shops, travel desks, and people. Not surprisingly, this hotel hosts numerous conventions; if you're not comfortable with crowds and conventioneers, book elsewhere. However, size has its advantages: The Sheraton has everything from a fabulous kids' program to historical walks and cooking demonstrations for Mom and Dad. Plus, you can "play and charge" at Waikiki's other Sheraton hotels.

It's hard to get a bad room here. A whopping 1,200 units have some sort of ocean view, and 650 rooms overlook Diamond Head. Accommodations are spacious, with big lanais to take in those magnificent views. For the budget-conscious, the Sheraton Manor Annex occupies a separate adjacent wing and offers all the services and beachfront of the main hotel. The views aren't the best, and the rooms are small (two people, max) and modestly appointed (no lanai), but the price is hard to beat.

2255 Kalakaua Ave. (at Royal Hawaiian Ave., on the ocean side of the Royal Hawaiian Shopping Center and west of the Royal Hawaiian), Honolulu, HI 96815. ⓒ 800/325-3535 or 808/922-4422. Fax 808/923-8785. www.sheraton.com. 1,852 units. $100 Sheraton Manor Annex double; $270–$510 Waikiki double; from $705 suite. Extra person $45; children under 18 stay free in parents' room. Ask about Sure Saver rates, which could save you as much as 32%. AE, DC, DISC, MC, V. Valet parking $13, self-parking $9. TheBus: 19 or 20. **Amenities:** 4 restaurants (including an open-air spot for casual buffet meals and the glamorous Hanohano Room, which offers gourmet dining in a spectacular setting); 3 bars; nightclub; 2 large outdoor pools, including one of the biggest and sunniest along the Waikiki beachfront; access to Makaha Golf Club's golf and tennis facilities (about 1 hr. away); fitness center; watersports equipment rentals; bike rental; children's program with activities ranging from catamaran sailing to nightly movies; organized activities and outings; game room; concierge; activity desk; car-rental desk; business center; shopping arcade; room service (6am–midnight); in-room massage; baby-sitting; coin-op washer/dryers; same-day laundry service/dry cleaning (except holidays). *In room:* A/C, TV, dataport, kitchenette, minibar, fridge, coffeemaker, hair dryer, iron, safe.

Waikiki Parc ⚐   Terrifically located just 100 yards from the beach, this hotel is for people who want a taste of the Halekulani's elegance, grace, and style but at a more reasonable price. It's tucked just behind the Halekulani and is owned and operated by the same company. The compact, beautifully appointed rooms all have lanais with ocean, mountain, or city views; ceramic-tile floors with plush carpeting; and conversation areas with a writing desk and rattan couch and chair. A nice extra: the adjustable floor-to-ceiling shutters for those who want to sleep in.

The Parc features the same level of service that has made the Halekulani famous, and offers two excellent restaurants. On a recent visit, we asked room service for a few items that were not on the menu—not only did they happily comply, but the manager also checked back later to make sure we got what we wanted.

2233 Helumoa Rd. (at Lewers St.), Honolulu, HI 96815. ℭ **800/422-0450** or 808/921-7272. Fax 808/ 923-1336. www.waikikiparchotel.com. 298 units. $190–$270 double. Extra person $40; children 14 and under stay free in parents' room. Ask about room/car, bed-and-breakfast, and family packages. AE, DC, MC, V. Self- or valet parking $10. TheBus: 19 or 20. **Amenities:** 2 restaurants (1 with fine buffets—see the review of the Parc Cafe on p. 113; 1 Kyoto-style Japanese restaurant); concierge; activity desk; business center; limited room service; baby-sitting; coin-op washer/dryers; same-day laundry/dry cleaning. *In room:* A/C, TV, dataport (in some rooms), fridge, hair dryer, safe.

Waikiki Shore Condominium Resort ★★
As soon as you arrive, you'll see why everyone wants to stay here: the location (right on Waikiki beach) and the view (a spectacular panoramic vista of the entire shoreline from Diamond Head to Honolulu). The apartments—which are privately owned and decorated and then rented out through Outrigger—range in size from studio to two-bedroom. Each has a fully equipped kitchen, a big lanai, a spacious sitting area, washer/dryer, and those fabulous views. There are full-time residents who live in this complex, so it tends to be quiet, and entry to the units is through a locked gate and keyed elevators, so security is tight. The building sits on an excellent beach, close to restaurants and shopping. As you might expect, reservations are hard to get; book *way* in advance. Because this establishment is part of the Outrigger chain, guests have full access to the Outrigger Reef (located right next door), including its pool, exercise room, and business center. Daily maid service, a few on-site shops, and plenty of assistance from the front desk give this condominium stay all the benefits of hotel service with the roominess of your own apartment.

2161 Kalia Rd. (on the ocean at Saratoga Rd., across the street from Ft. DeRussy), Honolulu, HI 96815. ℭ **800/OUTRIGGER.** Fax 800/622-4852. www.outrigger.com. 168 units. $205–$230 studio double; $285–$310 one-bedroom apt (sleeps up to 4); $400–$600 two-bedroom apt (up to 6). Ask about Outrigger package deals including free car rental, bed-and-breakfast, and other deals. AE, DC, DISC, MC, V. Parking $10. TheBus: 19 or 20. **Amenities:** Outdoor pool; access to all the facilities at the Outrigger Reef hotel next door (including 3 restaurants, 3 bars, 24-hr. fitness room, Jacuzzi, children's program, concierge, activity desk, business center, shopping arcade, salon, massage, baby-sitting, dry cleaning). *In room:* A/C, TV/VCR, dataport, kitchen, fridge, coffeemaker, hair dryer, iron, safe, washer/dryer.

MODERATE
Hawaiiana Hotel ★ *Finds*
"The spirit of old Hawaii"—the hotel's slogan says it all. The lush tropical flowers and carved tiki at the entrance on tiny Beach Walk set the tone for this intimate low-rise hotel. From the moment you arrive, you'll be embraced by the aloha spirit: At check-in, you're given a pineapple, and every morning, complimentary Kona coffee and tropical juice are served poolside. All the concrete hollow-tiled guest rooms feature kitchenettes, two beds (a double and a single or a queen and a sofa bed), and a view of the gardens and two swimming pools. Hawaiian entertainment is featured every week. The hotel is and a single or a queen plus a sofa bed), and a view of the gardens and two about a block from the beach and within walking distance of Waikiki shopping and nightlife.

260 Beach Walk (near Kalakaua Ave.), Honolulu, HI 96815. ℭ **800/367-5122** or 808/923-3811. Fax 808/ 926-5728. www.hawaiianahotelatwaikiki.com. 95 units (some with shower only). $85–$95 double; $165–$190 studio with kitchenette; $135 1-bedroom with kitchenette (sleeps up to 4). Extra person $10.

AE, DC, DISC, MC, V. Parking $8. TheBus: 19 or 20. **Amenities:** 2 good-sized outdoor pools; coin-op washer/dryers. *In room:* A/C, TV, kitchenette, fridge, coffeemaker, iron, safe.

Outrigger Islander Waikiki *🅕* If you're looking for a moderately priced hotel in the midst of Waikiki, here's your place. In 1997, the Outrigger chain completely gutted the old Pleasant Holiday Isle Hotel, and then dropped more than $7 million for renovations to bring the property up to Outrigger standards. The location on Lewers and Kalakaua is fabulous: just across the street from the Royal Hawaiian Shopping Center, and 1 block to the beach. An escalator takes you up to the glass-encased lobby, with the pool at one end and shops and a Starbuck's Cafe at the other. The rooms, which are all interconnected, range in size from 240 to 342 square feet and have been refurbished in Berber carpets, with Italian tile entryways, blond island-style furniture, and matching wallpaper and artwork by Hawaiian artists. All rooms have small semicircular balconies, either a king or two double beds, coffeemakers, safes, hair dryers, and irons and ironing boards. Also available are rooms with bathtubs, no-smoking rooms, and wheelchair-accessible rooms.

270 Lewers St. (entry on ocean, Ewa side of Lewers St. at Kalakaua Ave.), Honolulu, HI 96815. *🅒* **800/OUT-RIGGER** or 808/923-7711. Fax 800/622-4852. www.outrigger.com. 287 units. $175–$195 double; $205 studio. Extra person $20; children 17 and under stay free when using existing bedding. Seniors 50 and older 20% discount, AARP members 25% discount. Ask about room-and-breakfast packages. Parking $8. TheBus: 19 or 20. **Amenities:** Food court–style restaurant in lobby; outdoor pool; children's program; concierge; activity desk; car-rental desk; business center; shopping arcade; room service (7am–9pm); baby-sitting; coin-op washer/dryers; laundry/dry cleaning. *In room:* A/C, TV, dataport, fridge, coffeemaker, hair dryer, iron, safe.

INEXPENSIVE

The Breakers *🅕* *Value* The Breakers is full of old-fashioned Hawaiian aloha—and it's only steps from the sands of Waikiki. This two-story hotel has a friendly staff and a loyal following. Its six buildings are set around a pool and a tropical garden blooming with brilliant red and yellow hibiscus; wooden jalousies and shoji doors further the tropical ambience. Each of the tastefully decorated, slightly oversized rooms comes with a lanai and a kitchenette. Every Wednesday and Friday, you're invited to a formal Japanese tea ceremony from 10am to noon. One of the best things about the Breakers is the location, just a 2-minute walk to numerous restaurants, shopping, and Waikiki beach.

250 Beach Walk (between Kalakaua Ave. and Kalia Rd.), Honolulu, HI 96815. *🅒* **800/426-0494** or 808/923-3181. Fax 808/923-7174. www.breakers-hawaii.com. 64 units (shower only). $94–$100 double. Extra person $8. AE, DC, MC, V. Limited free parking; $6–$8 across the street. TheBus: 19 or 20. **Amenities:** 1 restaurant (poolside bar and grill for lunch); outdoor pool; coin-op washer/dryers. *In room:* A/C, TV, kitchenette, fridge, coffeemaker, iron, safe.

Ohana Coral Seas *Value* In the heart of Waikiki, on a busy little street lined with a number of Ohanas, you'll find this small, older budget hotel. It's one of the area's great bargains at $69 to $79 a night. That's the Simple Saver rate, which was available at press time, giving you "run of the house," meaning whatever room they have at the time—if you want a kitchenette or one-bedroom, book the regular rack rates. The rooms are small but comfortable, with two double beds and a desk. They don't have ocean views and aren't grand, but the hotel's location can't be beat—just a short stroll to Waikiki Beach. If you get a room overlooking Lewers Street, you can sit on your semi-private lanai and watch the incredible parade of humanity go by; Lewers may be noisy, but it's the best free show in town. There's no pool, but you're welcome to use the one at neighboring Ohana Waikiki Tower.

250 Lewers St. (between Kalakaua Ave. and Helumoa St.), Honolulu, HI 96815. (*C*) **800/462-6262** or 808/923-3881. Fax 800/622-4852 or 808/922-2330. www.ohanahotels.com. 109 units (with shower only). Simple Saver rate $69. Rack rates: $109 double; $119 double with kitchenette; $169 one-bedroom with kitchenette for up to 4. Extra person $15. AE, DC, DISC, MC, V. Parking $8. TheBus: 19 or 20. **Amenities:** 3 restaurants and bars (buffet, rib house, and Chinese); children's program; activity desk; gift shop; room service (7am–9pm); laundry service. *In room:* A/C, TV, dataport, some kitchenettes, coffeemaker on request, hair dryer, iron, safe.

Ohana Edgewater   Although this one is closer to the beach, we don't think it's as nice as the numerous Ohana Hotels on Lewers Street, nor does it have the amenities they offer (for one, limited number of coffeemakers). The Edgewater is an older building with small, cramped rooms and tiny lanais. Still, as in all Ohana Hotels, the rooms are tastefully decorated. But the shortage of elevators—only two for 184 rooms—can cause long, long waits. The hotel shares a swimming pool with the adjacent Outrigger Waikiki Tower. The location really can't be beat—just cross the street and walk behind the Outrigger Reef to get to the beach. It's also convenient to restaurants (including four on site), nightlife, and shopping. Ask yourself: how much time will I spend in the hotel room and is $69 a night worth it?

2168 Kalia Rd. (at Beach Walk), Honolulu, HI 96815. (*C*) **800/800/462-6262** or 808/922-6424. Fax 808/924-6354 or 800/622-4852. www.ohanahotels.com. 184 units. $109 double; $119 double with kitchenette; $169 one-bedroom with kitchenette for up to 4. Extra person $15. Ask about packages and promotions, such as the Simple Saver rates, which were as low as $69–$79 at press time. AE, DC, DISC, MC, V. Parking $8. TheBus: 19 or 20. **Amenities:** 4 restaurants and bars (family-style, steak/seafood, Italian, deli); outdoor pool; children's program; game room; activity desk; shopping arcade; salon; room service (7am–9pm); coin-op washer/dryers; laundry service. *In room:* A/C, TV, dataport, some kitchenettes, fridge, coffeemaker on request, hair dryer, iron, safe.

Ohana Reef Towers *(Kids)*   This is a great deal for families: Four of you can easily stay here for $139, with your own kitchenette to help keep dining costs down. The Reef is one of Outrigger's larger hotels, consisting of two 13-story towers. The recently renovated rooms are larger than those at some nearby Outriggers, and come with a few more amenities than those in the chain's lower-priced hotels. The lanais, however, are very small. The huge lobby is filled with shops. The Polynesian Showroom features some of Hawaii's top entertainers. You can order room service from the Waikiki Broiler.

227 Lewers St. (near Helumoa Rd.), Honolulu, HI 96815. (*C*) **800/462-6262** or 808/924-8844. Fax 808/924-6042 or 800/622-4852. www.ohana.com. 479 units. $129 double; $139 double with kitchenette; $159 studio with kitchenette for up to 4 guests; $189 1-bedroom with kitchenette for up to 4. Ask about packages and promotions, such as the Simple Saver rates, which were as low as $89 at press time. Extra person $15. Children under 17 stay free with parents. AE, DC, DISC, MC, V. Parking $8. TheBus: 19 or 20. **Amenities:** 4 restaurants (deli, casual family restaurant, pasta/seafood, poolside snacks); 3 bars; outdoor pool; children's program; activity desk; shopping arcade; salon; room service (7am–9pm); baby-sitting; laundry service. *In room:* A/C, TV, dataport, some kitchenettes, fridge, coffeemaker, hair dryer, iron, safe.

Ohana Royal Islander   This is about as close as you can get to the beach and still pay budget prices: The sand is just across the street and through the beach access walkway. The elegant lobby of this boutique hotel gives it the look of a luxury hotel. The rooms are small—don't try to squeeze in a third person—but decorated in the same tasteful fashion that characterizes all Ohana Hotels. Ask for room 901, it's high enough up for a view of the ocean and the park and as a corner unit you get more room. You can request coffeemakers from housekeeping, or just bop down to the lobby in the morning, where complimentary coffee awaits. Since the Royal Islander is such a small hotel, it shares some services with the beachfront Outrigger Reef across the street, such as a swimming pool and spill-over parking. Dozens of restaurants are within a five-minute walk.

2164 Kalia Rd. (at Saratoga Rd.), Honolulu, HI 96815. **©** **800/462-6262** or 808/922-1961. Fax 808/923-4632 or 800/622-4852. www.ohanahotels.com. 101 units (with showers only). $129 double; $149 ocean-view suite double; $169 1-bedroom suite for up to 4 with kitchenette. Ask about packages and promotions, such as the Simple Saver rates, which were as low as $89 at press time. Extra person $20. AE, DC, DISC, MC, V. Parking $9. TheBus: 19 or 20. **Amenities:** McDonald's; children's program; activity desk; car-rental desk; room service (7am–9pm); laundry service. *In room:* A/C, TV, some kitchenettes, fridge, coffeemaker available on request, hair dryer, iron, safe.

Ohana Waikiki Village   Deep in the heart of Ohana country (they seem to own Lewers St.) is another recommendable link in the chain. The Ohana Waikiki Village is less than 2 blocks from the beach and in the midst of Waikiki's restaurant, shopping, and nightlife scene. The Village is considered a moderate Ohana hotel: The rooms are small but cozy and recently received new bed-spreads, curtains, carpet, and a fresh paint job. There are no in-room coffee-makers, but you can get your morning cup at the breakfast-only coffee shop. The pool sits in the middle of the open-air lobby, which makes for interesting people-watching as you work on your tan. There's an Internet connection in the lobby that will hook you up for $1 for 7 minutes. Families of three might con-sider the studio kitchenettes, as the hotel rooms sleep only two. *Helpful hint:* If you prefer a king bed, request one when reserving your room, as the hotel has a limited number of them.

240 Lewers St. (near Helumoa Rd.), Honolulu, HI 96815. **©** **800/462-6262** or 808/923-3881. Fax 800/622-4852 or 808/922-2330. www.ohanahotels.com. 441 units (with showers only). $139 double; $149 dou-ble with kitchenette; $179 studio with kitchenette. Ask about packages and promotions, such as the Simple Saver rates, which were as low as $89 at press time. Extra person $15. AE, DC, DISC, MC, V. Parking $8. The-Bus: 19 or 20. **Amenities:** 1 family-style restaurant; 2 bars (1 poolside); outdoor pool; children's program; activity desk; shopping arcade; room service (7am–9pm); coin-op washer/dryers; laundry service. *In room:* A/C, TV, dataport, some kitchenettes, fridge, coffeemaker, hair dryer, iron, safe.

A Hotel for Military Personnel

Hale Koa Hotel ★★ ⓥ*alue*   We wish we could stay here—but we're not allowed. This is a very exclusive hotel, for active-duty and retired military and their families only. This is a first-class hotel, right on Waikiki Beach, with the grassy lawns of Fort DeRussy on the other side. The price structure, which depends on military rank (lower ranks get cheaper rates), is 50% to 75% less than what comparable Waikiki hotels charge. The facilities here include three swimming pools, 66 landscaped acres with picnic tables and barbecues, health club, Jacuzzi, sauna, jogging trails, four lighted tennis courts, racquetball courts, volleyball courts, four restaurants (plus dinner shows), and lounges. The only drawback is that the hotel is always booked; some guests reserve up to a year in advance.

2055 Kalia Rd. (across from Ft. DeRussy, between Dewey Way and Saratoga Rd.), Honolulu, HI 96815. **©** **800/367-6027** or 808/955-0555. Fax 800/HALE-FAX. www.halekoa.com. 814 units. $66–$169 double, depending on views and military rank. Rates include continental breakfast and orientation the morning after check-in. Extra person $10; singles deduct $2 from double rate. AE, DC, DISC, MC, V. Parking $3. TheBus: 19 or 20. **Amenities:** 4 restaurants and bars; 3 outdoor pools; 4 lit tennis courts; fitness room; Jacuzzi; concierge; activity desk; car-rental desk; business center; shopping arcade; salon; room service; baby-sitting; coin-op washer/dryers; laundry/dry cleaning. *In room:* A/C, TV/VCR, dataport, fridge, coffeemaker, hair dryer, iron, safe.

MID-WAIKIKI, MAUKA

These mid-Waikiki hotels, on the mountain side of Kalakaua Avenue, are a lit-tle farther away from the beach than those listed above. They're all between

Kalakaua Avenue and Ala Wai Boulevard, and between Kalaimoku Street in the Ewa direction and Kaiulani Street in the Diamond Head direction.

EXPENSIVE

Sheraton Princess Kaiulani Hotel ⚮ Portraits of the hotel's namesake, Princess Kaiulani, heir to the throne who died in 1899 at the age of 24, fill the large open-air lobby. Her regal, youthful face looks out on the site that was once her royal estate. A huge swimming pool sits behind a row of restaurants and shops facing Kalakaua Ave. The open-air lobby connects the three buildings of the Princess Kuiulani; the 11-story original hotel that opened in 1955, and the 11-story Kaiulani wing and the 29-story Ainahau tower, both of which opened in 1960. The rooms, which are perfectly fine if unremarkable, have been recently renovated, and double-insulated doors with soundproofing have been added. (We wish every hotel in noisy Waikiki had this feature. The soundproofing really works: You can't hear the blaring sirens or the sound of garbage cans being emptied at 3am.) The hotel's dinner and cocktail show "Creation—A Polynesian Odyssey" is a fun, but touristy, musical-theatrical excursion through the South Pacific. We wouldn't pay the rack rates, but it's often possible to get a good package deal here.

120 Kaiulani Ave. (at Kalakaua Ave., across the street from the Sheraton Moana Surfrider), Honolulu, HI 96815. ℂ **800/325-3535** or 808/922-5811. Fax 808/923-9912. www.sheraton.com. 1,150 units. $160–$330 double; from $650 suite. Extra person $45; children under 18 free in parents' room with existing bedding. Inquire about Sheraton's Sure Saver rates, available at different times of the year, which could mean as much as 32% in savings. AE, DC, MC, V. Parking $9. TheBus: 19 or 20. **Amenities:** 4 restaurants (Mandarin, Japanese, poolside garden, international food court); 4 bars; outdoor pool; Jacuzzi; good children's program; concierge; activity desk; room service; massage; baby-sitting; coin-op washer/dryers; laundry/dry cleaning. *In room:* A/C, TV, dataport, fridge, coffeemaker, hair dryer, iron, safe.

Waikiki Beachcomber A room/car package makes this stylish Waikiki hotel a real deal. One of its main pluses is the great location—a block from Waikiki Beach, across the street from the upscale Royal Hawaiian Shopping Center, and next door to bargain shopping at the International Market Place. The rooms feature Berber carpets, TV armoires, contemporary furniture, handheld showers, convenient hot pots for making coffee or tea, and voice mail. Yet another reason to stay at this conveniently located hotel is that it hosts *The Magic of Polynesia*, a show with illusionist John Hirokana and the king of Hawaiian entertainment, Don Ho, a Hawaii legend for more than 40 years.

2300 Kalakaua Ave. (at Duke's Lane), Honolulu, HI 96815. ℂ **800/622-4646** or 808/922-4646. Fax 808/926-9973. www.waikikibeachcomber.com. 495 units (shower only). $200–$240 double; from $350 suite. Extra person $25. Room/car packages from $140. AE, DC, MC, V. Parking $8. TheBus: 19 or 20. **Amenities:** 1 restaurant (poolside coffeeshop); Hawaiian entertainment show; outdoor pool; children's program July–Aug; activity desk; car-rental desk; small shopping arcade; limited room service (6am–11am); coin-op washer/dryers; laundry service; dry cleaning. *In room:* A/C, TV, fridge, coffeemaker, hair dryer, iron on request, safe.

MODERATE

Ilima Hotel ⚮ 𝘒𝘪𝘥𝘴 The Teruya brothers, owners of Hawaii's Times Supermarket, wanted to offer comfortable accommodations that Hawaii residents could afford, and they've succeeded. One of Hawaii's small, well-located condo-style hotels, the 17-story, pale pink Ilima (named for the native orange flower used in royal leis) offers value for your money. Rooms are huge, the location (near the International Market Place and the Royal Hawaiian Shopping Center, 2 blocks to Waikiki Beach) is great, and prices are low. A tasteful koa-wood lobby lined with works by Hawaiian artists greets you upon arrival. Perks include free local phone calls (a nice plus), and a full kitchen in every unit; in addition, all the couches fold out into beds, making this a particularly good deal for families. Some of the beds are waveless waterbeds. Truly nice people staff the front desk, ready to help you enjoy your vacation. The only caveat: no ocean views.

445 Nohonani St. (near Ala Wai Blvd.), Honolulu, HI 96815. © 800/367-5172 or 808/923-1877. Fax 808/924-2617. www.ilima.com. 99 units. $110–$155 double; $150–$195 1-bedroom (rate for 4); $190–$225 2-bedroom (rate for 4, sleeps up to 6); $330 3-bedroom (rate for 6, sleeps up to 8). Extra person $10. Discounts available for seniors and business travelers. AE, DC, DISC, MC, V. Limited free parking, $8 across the street. TheBus: 19 or 20. **Amenities:** 1 restaurant (Italian); outdoor pool with sauna; exercise room; activity desk; coin-op washer/dryers. *In room:* A/C, TV, kitchen, fridge, coffeemaker, hair dryer, iron, safe.

Island Colony Hotel ⋌★

This elegant property combines the spaciousness of a condominium with the amenities of a hotel. Plus the rates include complimentary continental breakfast. All of the units have private lanais and daily maid service, and can sleep up to four. The studio units have kitchenettes, and the one-bedrooms—which can sleep up to five—have full kitchens. And the views are spectacular: either the jagged mountains and lush valleys, Diamond Head, or the sparkling Pacific Ocean. The only caveat is the minuscule bathrooms: Ours was so small that the door didn't clear the toilet (it doesn't sound like a big deal, but it was annoying). The tub/shower combo was also cramped. I found it best to shower with my elbows close to my side to avoid hitting the walls. The hotel features a pool, sun deck, restaurant, jet spa, and sauna. Access via car (always tricky on Waikiki's one-way streets) is very convenient from Ala Wai Boulevard.

445 Seaside Ave. (at Ala Wai Blvd.), Honolulu, HI 96815. © 800/535-0085 or 808/923-2345. Fax 808/921-7105 or 800/633-5085. www.marcresorts.com. 347 units. $129–$149 double; $149–$169 studio with kitchenette; $169–$209 1-bedroom. Rates include continental breakfast. Check for Internet-only deals, which started at $103 double, $127 double with kitchenette, and $151 for a 1-bedroom at press time. Extra person $18. AE, DC, DISC, MC, V. Parking $8. TheBus: 19 or 20. **Amenities:** 1 restaurant (Chinese); outdoor pool; Jacuzzi; activity desk; car-rental desk; gift shop; coin-op washer/dryers. *In room:* A/C, TV, dataport, some kitchens and kitchenettes, fridge, coffeemaker, hair dryer.

Waikiki Joy ⋌★

Tucked away, down a narrow path on a side street, this hidden jewel offers not only outstanding personal service but also a Bose entertainment system and a Jacuzzi in every room! Complimentary continental breakfast is included in the price. The Italian marble–accented open-air lobby and the tropical veranda set the scene for the beautifully decorated guest rooms, each with a marble entry, tropical island decor, and a lanai wide enough for you to sit and enjoy the views. Another plus: All the rooms are soundproof. The suites are even more luxurious: Club suites have either a king bed or two doubles, a fridge, a microwave, a coffeemaker, and a wet bar, while executive suites come with two double beds and a kitchen with microwave and full fridge; the executive king suites add a separate living room and bedroom. Every unit comes with voice mail, as well as fax and modem hookups. There are, however, a couple of downsides: The beach is 4 or 5 blocks away (a 10–15-min. walk), and although there's a sandwich/coffee shop on-site, the food's nothing to brag about, and the fact that smoking is allowed in this tiny restaurant makes for a very unappetizing atmosphere.

320 Lewers St. (between Kuhio and Kalakaua aves.), Honolulu, HI 96815. © 800/92-ASTON or 808/923-2300 Aston Hotels and Resorts. Fax 808/924-4010. www.aston-hotels.com. 94 units. $125–$177 double; $175–$195 club suite; $215–$235 junior suite with kitchen (sleeps up to 4); $265–$285 1-bedroom executive suite with kitchen (up to 3). Rates include continental breakfast. Extra person $20. Ask about the Island Hopper rates (25% off if you stay 7 or more consecutive nights with Aston). AE, DC, DISC, MC, V. Valet

parking $10. TheBus: 19 or 20. **Amenities:** 1 restaurant (smoke-filled coffee-shop); 1 bar (karaoke); miniscule outdoor pool with dry sauna; concierge; activity desk; coin-op washer/dryers; laundry/dry-cleaning services. *In room:* A/C, TV, dataport, kitchenette (full kitchen in suites), fridge, coffeemaker, hair dryer, iron, safe.

INEXPENSIVE

Aston Coconut Plaza ★ *Value*   This small hotel is an island of integrity in a sea of tourist schlock. Calling itself a "studio apartment boutique hotel," the Coconut Plaza offers perks that are rare in Waikiki, such as free continental breakfast and the kind of personalized service that only a small hotel can provide. The recently renovated property has a tropical-plantation feel, with big, airy, island-style rooms, terra-cotta tile, and lots of greenery. The bedrooms have been redone in rattan and earth tones; all have private lanais, ceramic-tile bathrooms, and daily maid service. The units with kitchenettes are especially good deals. Most rooms have views of the Ala Wai Canal and the mountains (if you prefer quiet, ask for a city-view room). Ala Wai Golf Course is just across the canal, and the beach is 4 blocks away.

450 Lewers St. (at Ala Wai Blvd.), Honolulu, HI 96815. ℂ **800/92-ASTON** or 808/923-8828. Fax 808/922-8785. www.aston-hotels.com. 80 units. $75–$125 double; $160–$175 suite with kitchenette. Rates include continental breakfast. Ask about Island Hopper rates, which at press time were 25% off if you stay 7 or more consecutive nights with Aston. Extra person $12. AE, DC, MC, V. Parking $9. TheBus: 19 or 20. **Amenities:** Tiny outdoor pool with sun deck; activity desk; coin-op washer/dryers. *In room:* A/C, TV, some kitchenettes, fridge, coffeemaker, hair dryer, iron, safe.

Marine Surf Waikiki Hotel *Value*   Located in the heart of Waikiki, this high-rise is part privately owned condo units and part spacious studio apartments—only the studios are available for rent. Each one has a complete kitchen, two extra-long double beds, and a small lanai. The price difference depends on the view. *Hot tip:* The best views are from floors 17 to 22. Located just a half-block from Kuhio Mall and the International Market Place, the hotel is less than two blocks from the beach.

364 Seaside Ave. (at Kuhio Ave.), Honolulu, HI 96815. ℂ **888/456-SURF** or 808/923-0277. Fax 808/926-5915. 110 units. www.marine-surf.com $102–$112 double; $185 1-bedroom penthouse suite. Extra person $10. DC, DISC, MC, V. Parking $5. TheBus: 19 or 20. **Amenities:** 1 restaurant (Italian) and bar; outdoor pool; activity desk; coin-op washer/dryers. *In room:* A/C, TV, full kitchen, fridge, coffeemaker, hair dryer, iron, safe.

Ohana Surf *Kids*   The Ohana chain makes sure that it has a hotel to suit every budget and every need; this one has recently renovated kitchenettes in every room. The guest rooms, pool deck, and lobby went through extensive renovations in 1997; the rooms were outfitted with new bedspreads, chairs, lampshades, refurbished furniture, new TVs, and new fridges. The Surf is centrally located, across the street from the Kuhio Mall and 2 blocks from the beach; restaurants and nightlife are also within walking distance.

2280 Kuhio Ave. (at Nohonani St.), Honolulu, HI 96815. ℂ **800/462-6262** or 808/922-5777. Fax 800/622-4852 or 808/921-3677. www.ohanahotels.com. 251 units (with showers only). $129 double with kitchenette; $159 studio with kitchenette. Ask about packages and promotions, such as the Simple Saver rates, which were as low as $79 at press time. Extra person $15. AE, DC, DISC, MC, V. Parking $8. TheBus: 19 or 20. **Amenities:** 1 restaurant and bar (steak/lobster); outdoor pool; children's program; activity desk; laundry service. *In room:* A/C, TV, kitchenette, fridge, coffeemaker, hair dryer, iron, safe.

Ohana Waikiki West   On the upside, this chain hotel has lots of guest services and facilities, including a lounge, room service, and lots of shops (including a pharmacy). The downside is that it's located on a very noisy part of Kuhio Avenue. The rooms were redone in 1995; all have refrigerators, and some have kitchenettes. Waikiki Beach is 2 blocks away, and restaurants, shopping, and nightlife are all no more than a 10-minute walk. International Market Place is across the street.

2330 Kuhio Ave. (between Nahua and Walina sts.), Honolulu, HI 96815. ✆ **800/462-6262** or 808/922-5022. Fax 800/622-4852 or 808/924-6414. www.ohana.com. 663 units (with shower only). $129 double; $139 double with kitchenette. Ask about packages and promotions, such as the Simple Saver rates, which were as low as $89 at press time. Extra person $15. AE, DC, DISC, MC, V. Parking $8. TheBus: 19 or 20. **Amenities:** 2 restaurants (a branch of Chili's and a bakery/deli); 2 bars (1 poolside, 1 country and western); outdoor pool; children's program; activity desk; shopping arcade; coin-op washer/dryers. *In room:* A/C, TV, some kitchenettes, fridge, coffeemaker, hair dryer, iron, safe.

Royal Kuhio *★ Kids Value*   Families, take note: This is one of the best deals in Waikiki. All the units in this high-rise condo are privately owned, and some are owner-occupied. Several companies handle apartments here, but Paradise Management offers some of the best deals. Each of its units has a full kitchen, separate bedrooms, and a living area with a lanai. Because the units are individually owned, they're all decorated and furnished uniquely. It's 2 blocks from Waikiki Beach and within walking distance of everything else of interest. And this is one of the few places in Waikiki where parking is free. *Hot tips:* Ask for a corner unit (they're the nicest); if you plan to go in February, be sure to book a year in advance (it's the condo's busiest month).

2240 Kuhio Ave. (between Royal Hawaiian and Seaside aves.), c/o Paradise Mgmt., 50 S. Beretania St., Suite C207, Honolulu, HI 96813. ✆ **800/367-5205** or 808/538-7145. Fax 808/533-4621. pmchi@gte.net. 389 units. $95–$125 apt for 4. Extra person $15. AE, MC, V. Free parking. TheBus: 19 or 20. **Amenities:** Small fitness room; sauna; volleyball; billiards; basketball court; shuffleboard; putting green; game room; coin-op washer/dryers. *In room:* A/C, TV, dataport, kitchen, fridge, coffeemaker, hair dryer, iron, safe.

A Gay-Friendly Hotel

The Cabana at Waikiki   Located on a quiet street in Waikiki, this boutique hotel caters to a clientele of gay men, and features exquisitely decorated rooms. Each has a queen bed and pullout sofa bed, entertainment center with VCR and CD player, lanai, and well-equipped kitchenette. A free continental breakfast is served every morning. Free Internet access is available in the lobby. A giant, eight-person spa also is on the property. The Cabana is within walking distance of gay nightclubs and the gay scene at Queen's Surf Beach.

2551 Cartwright Rd. (between Paoakalani and Kapahulu aves.), Honolulu, HI 96815. ✆ **877/902-2121** or 808/926-5555. Fax 808/926-5566. www.cabana-waikiki.com. 15 units. $99–$175 double. Rates include continental breakfast. Extra person $15. AE, DC, DISC, MC, V. Parking $7. TheBus: 19 or 20. **Amenities:** Complimentary access to a nearby (about a 15-min. walk) fitness complex; Jacuzzi; concierge; coin-op washer/dryers. *In room:* A/C, TV, dataport, kitchenette, fridge, coffeemaker, hair dryer, iron, safe.

WAIKIKI, DIAMOND HEAD END

You'll find all these hotels between Ala Wai Boulevard and the ocean, and between Kaiulani Street (1 block east of the International Marketplace) and Diamond Head itself.

VERY EXPENSIVE

Hyatt Regency Waikiki *★*   This is one of Waikiki's biggest hotels, a $100 million project sporting two 40-story towers and covering nearly an entire city block, just across the street from the Diamond Head end of Waikiki Beach. Some may love the location, but others will find this behemoth too big and impersonal—you can get lost just trying to find the registration desk. The second-floor lobby is huge, decorated in koa and wrapped around an atrium that rises *40 floors* from the ground level. It's filled with the squawks of parrots, tumbling waterfalls, and traffic noise from busy Kalakaua Avenue outside.

The guest rooms are spacious and luxuriously furnished. But please, when room rates start at $265 a night, do they have to charge you an extra $3.25 per package of coffee for the "free coffeemaker" in your room? (Not only that, but if you want to empty your minibar to use it as a fridge, the cost is $7!) The deluxe oceanview rooms overlooking Waikiki Beach are fabulous but can be noisy (traffic on Kalakaua is constant). For a few dollars more (well, actually more than a few dollars), you can upgrade to the Regency Club floors, where the rooms are nicer (and the coffee is free); you'll also be entitled to an expedited check-in and entry to a private rooftop sun deck and Jacuzzi and the Regency Club, which has concierge service all day and serves complimentary continental breakfast and afternoon pupu.

Just opened in April 2001 is a 10,000-square-foot, two-story luxury spa, with all the massage services, body treatments, and facials you can imagine.

2424 Kalakaua Ave. (at Kaiulani St., across the street from the beach), Honolulu, HI 96815. ℂ 800/ **233-1234** or 808/923-1234. Fax 808/923-7839. www.hyattwaikiki.com. 1,230 units. $265–$400 double; $400–$470 Regency Club double; from $800 suite. Extra person $35 ($50 Regency Club); children under 19 stay free in parents' room using existing bedding. AE, DC, DISC, MC, V. Valet parking $12; self-parking $10. TheBus: 19 or 20. **Amenities:** 7 restaurants (including an indoor/outdoor grill overlooking the ocean; Japanese; steak/seafood; and Ciao Mein, for creative family-style Chinese and Italian cuisine—see the review on p. 112); 4 bars (including a very elegant poolside bar); outdoor pool with a view of Waikiki; fitness room; brand-new elegant spa; Jacuzzi; children's program (Fri–Sat year-round and daily in summer); game room; concierge; activity desk; car-rental desk; business center; large shopping arcade; salon; room service (6am–11pm); in-room massage; baby-sitting; coin-op washer/dryers; same-day laundry service/dry cleaning; concierge-level rooms. *In room:* A/C, TV, dataport, kitchenette (in some units), minibar, coffeemaker (with expensive coffee!), hair dryer, iron, safe.

W Honolulu ★★★ It's expensive but worth every penny to be totally pampered in a low-key, elegantly casual hotel that caters to the business traveler but takes excellent care of vacationers, too. The W Honolulu can be summed up in a nutshell by the button on your room phone that says "whatever/whenever." That's what we call service! If you're craving peace and quiet, away from the crowds of Waikiki but want to be close enough (about a 15-min. walk) to shops and restaurants, this is a perfect location. Formerly part of the Colony Surf (the adjacent, beachside condominium), this newly renovated hotel became part of the upscale W chain in 1999. You'll feel like you've entered a luxurious private world here: The hotel lobby looks like an elegant living room, and check-in occurs in the privacy of the guest rooms, which are decorated with handmade teak furniture from Bali. In addition to the large balconies with great views of Diamond Head, there are numerous excellent touches: from Hawaiian music CDs to dual-line cordless phones, plush robes, top-drawer bathroom amenities, twice-daily maid service (great to have clean towels when you return from the beach), and various business equipment available on request.

Although W is not on the beach, guests still have access to the small, private beach in front of the Colony Surf (great swimming here), about a 30-second walk away; Kapiolani Park is across the street, and the Waikiki Aquarium is just a few steps away.

2885 Kalakaua Ave. (on the ocean side between the Waikiki Aquarium and Outrigger Canoe Club), Honolulu, HI 96815. ℂ **877/W-HOTELS** or 808/922-1700. Fax 808/923-2249. www.whotels.com. 48 units. $350–$600 double. Children under 18 stay free in parents' room. AE, DC, DISC, MC, V. Valet parking $15. TheBus: 19 or 20. **Amenities:** 1 outstanding restaurant serving Hawaii Regional Cuisine (see the review of the Diamond Head Grill on p. 108); 1 elegant bar (jazz every night); outstanding concierge service; 24-hr. room service; in-room massage; baby-sitting; coin-op washer/dryers; laundry service; dry cleaning. *In room:* A/C, TV, dataport, minibar, coffeemaker, hair dryer, iron, safe.

EXPENSIVE

Aston Waikiki Beachside Hotel ⭐ This luxury boutique hotel is right across the street from Waikiki Beach. There's a feeling of elegance and charm throughout this intimate place: You step off busy Kalakaua Avenue into a marble-filled lobby with classical music wafting in the background, sprays of flowers everywhere, and a soothing Italian fountain. The staff is attentive to every detail (including twice-daily maid service). The only caveat: The bedrooms are very, very tiny, but tastefully decorated with artwork and antiques (including hand-painted Oriental screens and 18th-century furnishings). There's no on-site restaurant, but there is a complimentary continental breakfast daily in the lobby. On Saturday and Sunday afternoons, a three-course tea service (with different teas, sandwiches, desserts, and more), served on antique china, is presented in the lobby and courtyard.

2452 Kalakaua Ave. (between Uluniu and Liliuokalani aves.), Honolulu, HI 96815. ℂ **800/922-7866** or 808/931-2100. Fax 808/931-2129. www.aston-hotels.com. 79 units. $190–$340 double; $265–$395 junior suite. Rate includes continental breakfast. No more than 2 adults per room. Some discounts for seniors over 50. Ask about Island Hopper rates, which at press time were 25% off if you stay 7 or more consecutive nights with Aston. AE, DC, DISC, MC, V. Parking $9.50 at nearby hotel. TheBus: 19 or 20. **Amenities:** Concierge; same-day laundry/dry cleaning. *In room:* A/C, TV, dataport, fridge, hair dryer, iron, safe.

MODERATE

Aston at the Waikiki Banyan The one-bedrooms here combine the homey comforts of a condo apartment with the amenities of a hotel. You'll get daily maid service, bellhop service, the assistance of the front desk, and much more, including an enormous sixth-floor recreation deck with a panoramic mountain view, complete with sauna, barbecue areas, snack bar, and children's play area—a great boon for families. Your introduction to this complex is through the open-air lobby with impressive lacquer artwork, hand carved and painted in Hong Kong. All units have a fully equipped full-size kitchen, a breakfast bar that opens to a comfortably furnished living room (with sofa bed), and a separate bedroom with two double beds or a king. The one we stayed in had an old-fashioned air conditioner in the wall, but it did the job. Each apartment opens onto a fairly good-sized lanai with chairs and a small table; there's a partial ocean view, with some buildings blocking the way.

201 Ohua Ave. (on mountain side, at Kuhio Ave.), Honolulu, HI 96815. ℂ **800/922-7866** or 808/922-0555. Fax 808/922-8785. www.aston-hotels.com. 307 1-bedroom apts. $165–$240 double. Some discounts for seniors over 50. Ask about Island Hopper rates, which at press time were 25% off if you stay 7 or more consecutive nights with Aston. Extra person $20. AE, DC, DISC, MC, V. Parking $5. TheBus: 19 or 20. **Amenities:** Huge outdoor pool; tennis courts; sundries store; coin-op washer/dryers. *In room:* A/C, TV, dataport, kitchen, fridge, coffeemaker, hair dryer, iron, safe.

New Otani Kaimana Beach Hotel ⭐ *Finds* This is one of Waikiki's best-kept secrets: a boutique hotel nestled right on a lovely stretch of beach at the foot of Diamond Head, with Kapiolani Park just across the street. Robert Louis Stevenson's description of Sans Souci, the beach fronting the hotel, still holds true: "If anyone desires lovely scenery, pure air, clear sea water, good food, and heavenly sunsets, I recommend him cordially to the Sans Souci." The Waikiki-side guest rooms are tiny but tastefully decorated in pale pastels; they open onto large lanais with ocean and park views. A good budget buy is the park-view studio with kitchen, for just $160 to $180. You can stock up with provisions from the on-site Mini-Mart, open until 11pm.

Since the hotel overlooks Kapiolani Park, guests have easy access to activities such as golf, tennis, jogging, and bicycling; kayaking, and snorkeling are available at the beach. The hotel also arranges for visitors to climb to the top of Diamond Head. The airy lobby opens onto the alfresco **Hau Tree Lanai** restaurant (see the review on p. 110), a delightfully romantic beachfront restaurant, set under the same banyan tree that sheltered Robert Louis Stevenson a century ago. The Miyako Restaurant offers gourmet Japanese dining with an ocean view. The beachfront **Sunset Lanai Lounge** ★ is great for cocktails and has live Hawaii music at lunch on Friday.

2863 Kalakaua Ave. (ocean side of the street just Diamond Head of the Waikiki Aquarium, across from Kapiolani Park), Honolulu, HI 96815. ℭ 800/356-8264 or 808/923-1555. Fax 808/922-9404. www.kaimana.com. 124 units. $135–$320 double; $200–$695 suite. Extra person $25; children 12 and under stay free in parents' room using existing bedding. AE, DC, DISC, MC, V. Valet parking $10. TheBus: 2 or 14. **Amenities:** 2 restaurants; 1 beachfront bar; concierge; activity desk; car-rental desk; small shopping arcade; limited room service (7am–9:30pm); coin-op washer/dryers; laundry/dry cleaning. *In room:* A/C, TV, dataport, some kitchenettes, minibar (on request), fridge, coffeemaker, hair dryer, iron, safe.

Queen Kapiolani Hotel

Named for Queen Kapiolani (1834–99), the wife of Hawaii's last king, David Kalakaua (1836–91), this hotel harks back to the days of the Hawaiian monarchs. The 19th-century flavor of the place reflects those grand days, with 10-foot chandeliers in the main dining room and a full-size portrait of the queen in the lobby. The plush decor, however, doesn't extend to the budget rooms, which are quite small. For just a few bucks more, get the superior room. Not only is it double in size, but also its shoreline views are vastly superior. The property's location is great: just across the street from Kapiolani Park, a half-block to the beach, and within walking distance of the Honolulu Zoo, the Waikiki Aquarium, and the activities of Waikiki, including municipal tennis courts.

150 Kapahulu Ave. (at Lemon Rd., across from Kapiolani Park), Honolulu, HI 96815. ℭ **800/367-5004** or 808/922-1941 Castle Resorts and Hotels. Fax 808/596-0518 or 808/922-2694. www.castle-group.com. 315 units. $120–$175 double; $170–$190 studio double with kitchenette; $265–$405 1-bedroom suite with kitchenette (sleeps up to 4). Extra person $17; children 18 and under stay free in parents' room using existing bedding. AE, DC, DISC, MC, V. Parking $8. TheBus: 19 or 20. **Amenities:** 2 restaurants (1 with a tasty, budget-priced buffet); 1 bar; 1 large outdoor pool; concierge; activity desk; sundries store; salon; baby-sitting; coin-op washer/dryers; laundry/dry cleaning. *In room:* A/C, TV, some kitchenettes, fridge, coffeemaker, hair dryer (on request), iron (on request), safe.

Radisson Waikiki Prince Kuhio

Formerly the Outrigger's Prince Kuhio, this 37-floor hotel, located just 3 blocks from the beach and a couple of blocks from the zoo, offers pleasantly appointed, mid-sized rooms furnished in tropical decor, with a lanai, and the all-important black-out drapes so you can sleep in. All of the rooms are the same; the floor and the view determine the price (from the 18th floor and up, the mountain views overlooking the Ala Wai Canal are spectacular, and not as pricey as the oceanview rooms).

2500 Kuhio Ave. (Liliuokalani Ave.), Honolulu, HI 96815. ℭ **888/557-4422** or 808/922-0811. Fax 808/923-0330. 620 units. $150–$325 double; $245–$265 Kuhio Club floor double; from $450 suite. AE, DC, DISC, MC, V. Parking $8. TheBus: 19 or 20. **Amenities:** 2 restaurants (1 Chinese, 1 Pacific Rim with bargain buffets); 1 bar which features Hawaiian entertainment; outdoor pool; small fitness room; Jacuzzi; concierge; activity desk; car-rental desk; small business center; shopping arcade; limited room service; baby-sitting; coin-op washer/dryers; laundry/dry cleaning; concierge-level rooms. *In room:* A/C, TV, dataport, kitchenette, minibar, fridge, coffeemaker, hair dryer, iron, safe.

INEXPENSIVE

Diamond Head Bed & Breakfast ★ *Finds*

Hostess Joanne and her longtime housekeeper, Sumiko, offer a quiet, relaxing place to stay on the far side of Kapiolani Park, away from the hustle and bustle of Waikiki. Staying here is like venturing back 50 years to a time when *kamaaina* (native-born) families built huge houses with airy rooms opening onto big lanais and tropical gardens. The house is filled with family heirlooms and Joanne's artwork. One of the two rooms features the beyond-king-size carved koa bed that once belonged to Princess Ruth, a member of Hawaii's royal family. You'll feel like royalty sleeping in it.

Noela Dr. (at Paki Ave., off Diamond Head Rd.), Honolulu. c/o Hawaii's Best Bed & Breakfasts, P.O. Box 563, Kamuela, HI 96743. (℃ **800/262-9912** or 808/885-4550. Fax 808/885-0559. www.bestbnb.com. 2 units. $125 double. Rates include large breakfast. Extra person $25. 2-night minimum. No credit cards. Free parking. TheBus: 2. *In room:* TV, fridge, coffeemaker, hair dryer, iron.

Royal Grove Hotel ⋆/*Value* This is a great bargain for frugal travelers. You can't miss the Royal Grove—it's bright pink. Among Waikiki's canyons of corporate-owned high-rises, it's also a rarity in another way: The Royal Grove is a small, family-owned hotel. What you get here is old-fashioned aloha in cozy accommodations along the lines of Motel 6—basic and clean. For years, Frommer's readers have written about the aloha spirit of the Fong family; they love the potluck dinners and get-togethers the Fongs have organized so their guests can get to know one another. And you can't do better for the price—this has to be *the* bargain of Waikiki. For $42.50 (about the same price a couple would pay to stay in a private room at the hostel in Waikiki), you get a clean room in the older Mauka Wing, with a double bed or two twins, plus a kitchenette with refrigerator and stove. We suggest that you spend a few dollars more and go for an air-conditioned room ($57) to help drown out the street noise. Even the most expensive unit, a one-bedroom suite with three beds, a kitchenette, and a lanai, at $85, is half the price of similar accommodations elsewhere. At these rates, you won't mind that maid service is only twice a week.

The hotel is built around a courtyard pool, and the beach is just a 3-minute walk away. All of Waikiki's attractions are within walking distance. *Hot tip:* Book 7 nights or more from April to November, and get a discount on the already low rates.

151 Uluniu Ave. (between Prince Edward and Kuhio aves.), Honolulu, HI 96815. (℃ **808/923-7691.** Fax 808/922-7508. www.royalgrovehotel.com. 85 units. $42.50 double (no A/C); $57 standard double; $75 standard 1-bedroom; $75 deluxe double; $85 deluxe condo double. Extra person $10. AE, DC, MC, V. Parking nearby $6. TheBus: 19 or 20. **Amenities:** Pool; activity desk; coin-op washer/dryers. *In room:* A/C, TV, kitchenette, fridge.

Waikiki Sand Villa /*Kids* Budget travelers, take note: This very affordable hotel is located on the quieter side of Waikiki, across the street from the Ala Wai Canal. The 10-story tower has medium-sized rooms, most with a double bed plus a single bed (convenient for families) and a lanai with great views of the green mountains. The adjacent 3-story building features studio apartments with kitchenettes (refrigerator, stove, and microwave). Another plus for families is the Nintendo system in every room (available for $7.95/hr.). For guests arriving early or catching a late flight there's a hospitality room (complete with shower) for late checkout, and a luggage-storage area.

2375 Ala Wai Blvd. (entrance on Kanekapolei Ave.), Honolulu, HI 96815. (℃ **800/247-1903** or 808/922-4744. Fax 808/923-2541. www.waikiki-hotel.com. 232 units. $82–$136 double; $141–$166 studio with kitchenette. Rates include continental breakfast, served poolside every morning. Extra person $15; children under 12 stay free in parents' room using existing bedding. AE, DC, DISC, MC, V. Parking $7.30. TheBus: 19 or 20. **Amenities:** 70-ft. outdoor pool, which has its own island in the middle and an adjoining whirlpool spa; activity desk; coin-op washer/dryers; laundry/dry cleaning. *In room:* A/C, TV w/ Nintendo, dataport (with free Internet access), some kitchenettes, some fridges, some coffeemakers, safe.

2 Honolulu Beyond Waikiki

The city of Honolulu extends far beyond the tourist zones of Waikiki. It encompasses a fairly large area, and most of Oahu's population calls it home. Downtown Honolulu is relatively small, occupying only a handful of blocks. The financial, government, and corporate headquarters of businesses are found here. Other neighborhoods range from the quiet suburbs of Hawaii Kai to the *kamaaina* (old-timer) neighborhoods like Manoa. With the exception of the heart of downtown, these neighborhoods are generally quieter than Waikiki, more residential, yet within minutes of beaches, shopping, and all the activities Oahu has to offer.

ALA MOANA

Ala Moana Hotel   This hotel's 1,169 rooms on 36 floors make it feel like a metropolis. Its proximity to Waikiki, the downtown financial and business district, the new convention center, and Hawaii's largest mall, Ala Moana Shopping Center, makes it a popular spot for out-of-state visitors and locals alike. Lots of Asian tourists choose the Ala Moana Hotel, probably because the management does an excellent job of providing a multilingual staff and translators. Guests mainly are people attending a convention at the Convention Center, a short 2-minute walk away, or shoppers, mostly from neighboring islands (especially in Dec). The rooms vary in size according to price: The cheaper rooms are small, but all come with two double beds and all the amenities to make your stay comfortable. The views of Waikiki and Honolulu from the upper floors are spectacular.

410 Atkinson Dr. (at Kona St., next to Ala Moana Center), Honolulu, HI 96814. (800/367-6025 or 808/955-4811. Fax 808/944-6839. www.alamoanahotel.com. 1,169 units. $125–$225 double; from $250 suite. Extra person $25; children under 18 stay free in parents' room. AE, DC, DISC, MC, V. Valet parking $12; self-parking $9. TheBus: 19 or 20. **Amenities:** 5 restaurants (from coffee shop to exquisite Japanese food); 2 bars (plus a Polynesian show); large outdoor pool; small fitness room; game room; concierge; activity desk; car-rental desk; business center; shopping arcade; salon; limited room service (6:30am–10:30pm); baby-sitting; coin-op washer/dryers; laundry service; dry cleaning; concierge-level floors. *In room:* A/C, TV, dataport, fridge, coffeemaker, hair dryer, iron, safe.

Pagoda Hotel   This is where local residents from neighbor islands stay when they come to Honolulu. Close to shopping and downtown, the Pagoda has been serving Hawaii's island community for decades. This modest hotel has very plain (motel-ish) rooms: clean and utilitarian with no extra frills. For a quieter room, ask for the mountain view, where you'll be away from the street noise. There's easy access to Waikiki via TheBus—the nearest stop is just a half block away. Ask about the car packages: For the price of most rooms, you can get a free car. Studios and one- and two-bedroom units have kitchenettes.

1525 Rycroft St. (between Keeaumoku and Kaheka sts.), Honolulu, HI 96814. (800/367-6060 or 808/923-4511. Fax 808/922-8061. www.pagodahotel.com. 361 units. $110–$120 double; $115 1-bedroom double (sleeps up to 4); $145 1-bedroom deluxe double (sleeps up to 6); $165 2-bedroom double (sleeps up to 5). Extra person $25; free cribs available. Ask about free breakfast packages and excellent car/room deals. AE, DC, DISC, MC, V. Parking $3. TheBus: 5 or 6. **Amenities:** 1 restaurant (well known among locals for its miniature lake filled with Japanese ornamental carp, not necessarily for its food); 1 bar; 2 outdoor pools; activity desk; sundries store; salon; baby-sitting; coin-op washer/dryers; laundry/dry cleaning. *In room:* A/C, TV, dataport, some kitchenettes, fridge, coffeemaker, hair dryer, iron, safe.

DOWNTOWN

Aston at the Executive Centre Hotel   Located in the heart of downtown, this is the perfect hotel for the business traveler. Not only is it close to the business and financial center of Honolulu, but the staff also goes out of its way to meet every need. The hotel occupies the top 10 floors of a 40-story multiuse, glass-walled tower. Every room is a spacious suite, with three phones (with voice mail), a whirlpool bath, and unobstructed views of the city, the mountains, and Honolulu Harbor. Executive suites add a full kitchen, washer/dryer, and VCR. All guests awaken to the local newspaper outside their door. Free local phone calls and a daily newspaper make this place popular with business travelers.

1088 Bishop St. (at S. Hotel St.), Honolulu, HI 96813. ✆ 800/92-ASTON or 808/539-3000. Fax 808/922-8785. www.aston-hotels.com. 114 suites. $160–$190 suite; $220–$250 executive suite. Some discounts for seniors over 50. Ask about Island Hopper rates, which at press time were 25% off if you stay 7 or more consecutive nights with Aston. Extra person $18. Children under 17 stay free in parents' room. AE, DC, DISC, MC, V. Parking $10. TheBus: 1, 2, 3, 9, or 12. **Amenities:** 1 restaurant (American); outdoor pool; 24-hr. fitness center; concierge; 24-hr. staffed business center; shopping arcade; coin-op washer/dryers; laundry/dry cleaning; concierge-level rooms. *In room:* A/C, TV, dataport, kitchenette, fridge, coffeemaker, hair dryer, iron, safe, some washer/dryers.

NEAR HONOLULU INTERNATIONAL AIRPORT

If you have a long layover between flights, or if your flight gets delayed, consider the services of the **Airport Mini-Hotel** (✆ **808/836-3044**). It's the perfect answer to a traveler's dilemma: The clean, comfortable single rooms come with nothing more than a bed, a nightstand, and a private shower. But bring your earplugs—it tends to be noisy, even at night. On the plus side, the staff will provide a wake-up call if you need it, and if you have something that needs refrigeration (medication or flowers to bring home), the management is happy to help out. Rates are $35 for 8 hours (additional hours $6 each); you can rent just a shower for $8.50. There are only 17 rooms, so book in advance. The hotel does not provide transportation to the terminal, but it's just a short walk away.

If you'd like a regular hotel room near the airport, consider the **Honolulu Airport Hotel,** 3401 N. Nimitz Hwy., at Rodgers Street (✆ **800/800-3477** or 808/833-0661; www.honoluluairporthotel.com), where doubles go for $85 to $146. There's also the **Best Western The Plaza Hotel,** 3253 N. Nimitz Hwy., at Paiea Street (✆ **800/800-4683** or 808/836-3636; www.bestwestern.com), where doubles run $116 to $136. Each of these hotels has hundreds of rooms with all the in-room amenities you'd expect from a chain hotel (including fridges, coffeemakers, and hair dryers), plus a pool, a restaurant and lounge, room service, laundry/dry cleaning, and a free shuttle to and from the airport.

PEARL CITY

Rainbow Inn ✦*Finds*   This private tropical garden studio, downstairs from the home of retired military officer Gene Smith and his wife, Betty, has panoramic views of Pearl Harbor, the entire south coast of Oahu, and the Waianae and Koolau mountains. A large deck and full-sized pool is just outside the apartment's door; inside, the apartment features a double bed, washer/dryer, and kitchen. The Smiths are happy to lend their guests any beach and picnic equipment they might need—ice chest, beach mats and chairs, even wine glasses. Located near Pearl Ridge Shopping Center, Rainbow Inn is close to all of Oahu's attractions, yet far enough away to provide lots of peace and quiet. And at $75 a night, this is one of Oahu's best bed-and-breakfast deals. *Hot tip:* Reserve early—bargains like this book up fast, especially when there's only one room.

98-1049 Mahola Pl. (off Kaonohi St., 2 miles from Kamehameha Hwy.), Pearl Ridge, Aiea, HI 96701. ✆ 808/488-7525. Fax 808/487-1879. gsmith3777@aol.com. 1 apt. $75 double. Rates include refrigerator stocked with breakfast items. Extra person $10. 3-night minimum. No credit cards. Free parking. TheBus: 20, 50, 51, or 52. **Amenities:** Outdoor pool; laundry service. *In room:* A/C, TV/VCR, kitchen, fridge, coffeemaker.

MANOA
MODERATE

Manoa Valley Inn ★ *Finds*   It's completely off the tourist trail and far from the beach, but that doesn't stop travelers from heading to this historic 1915 Carpenter Gothic home, on a quiet residential street near the University of Hawaii. This eight-room Manoa landmark—it's on the National Register of Historic Places—offers a glimpse into the lifestyles of the rich and famous of early Honolulu.

Those who find resorts impersonal will find the eclectically furnished inn refreshing. Each room has its own unique decor, and each has been named for a prominent figure in Hawaii's history. The John Guild Suite, for instance, has a turn-of-the-20th-century parlor with antiques and old-fashioned rose wallpaper; the adjoining bedroom contains a king-size koa bed, while the bathroom features an old-style tub as well as a separate modern shower. The three top-floor rooms share a full bathroom; the others have private bathrooms. A genteel ambience pervades the entire place. Guests regularly gather in the parlor to listen to the Victrola or play the nickelodeon. There's also a billiards room with an antique billiards table, a piano in the living room, and croquet set up in the backyard.

2001 Vancouver Dr. (at University Ave.), Honolulu, HI 96822. © **808/947-6019.** Fax 808/946-6168. www. aloha.net/~wery/index. 8 units (3 with shared bathroom). $99–$120 double with shared bathroom; $140–$190 double with private bathroom (shower only). Rates include continental breakfast. Inquire about packages. AE, DC, MC, V. Free parking. TheBus: 4 or 6. Children 8 and older preferred. *In-room:* A/C, TV, dataport, safe.

TO THE EAST: KAHALA
VERY EXPENSIVE

Kahala Mandarin Oriental Hawaii ★★★ *Kids*   Since 1964, when Conrad Hilton first opened it as a place to relax far from the crowds of Waikiki, the Kahala has always been rated one of Hawaii's premier hotels. A veritable who's who of celebrities has stayed here, including every president since Richard Nixon. This grande dame of hotels has now reached a new level. It retains the traditional feeling of an earlier time in Hawaii, but accents it with exotic Asian touches. The result is a resort hotel for the 21st century coupled with the grace and elegance of a softer, gentler time. And the location offers a similarly wonderful compromise. Situated in one of Oahu's most prestigious residential areas, the Kahala offers the peace and serenity of a neighbor-island vacation, but with the conveniences of Waikiki just a 10-minute drive away. The lush, tropical grounds include an 800-foot crescent-shaped beach, and a 26,000-square-foot lagoon (home to two bottle-nosed dolphins, sea turtles, and tropical fish).

All guest rooms feature 19th-century mahogany reproductions, teak parquet floors with hand-loomed Tibetan rugs, overstuffed chairs, canopy beds covered with soft throw pillows, and works by local artists adorning the grass-cloth-covered walls. Views from the floor-to-ceiling sliding-glass doors are of the ocean, Diamond Head, and Koko Head. In-room amenities include two-line phones, 27-inch TVs, large bathrooms with vintage fixtures, freestanding glass showers, large soaking tubs, "his" and "her" dressing areas, plush bathrobes and slippers, and illuminated makeup mirrors.

Other extras that make this property outstanding: a Hawaiian cultural program, shuttle service to Waikiki and major shopping centers, free scuba lessons in the pool, and daily dolphin-education talks by a trainer from Sea Life Park.

5000 Kahala Ave. (next to the Waialae Country Club), Honolulu, HI 96816. © **800/367-2525** or 808/ 739-8888. Fax 808/739-8800. www.mandarinoriental.com. 371 units. $310–$690 double; from $590 suite. Extra person $100. Children 17 and under stay free in parents' room. AE, DC, DISC, MC, V. Parking $12. **Amenities:** 2 restaurants (including award-winning Hoku's, with international cuisine and casual, open-air setting and a special Sun brunch; see the review on p. 133); 3 bars (the lobby lounge has nightly entertainment); large outdoor pool; great fitness center with steam rooms, dry sauna, and Jacuzzis; watersports equipment rentals; bike rental; children's program; game room; concierge; activity desk; car-rental desk; multilingual business center; shopping arcade; salon; 24-hr. room service; in-room massage; baby-sitting; laundry/dry cleaning. *In room:* A/C, TV, dataport, minibar, hair dryer, iron, safe.

HAWAII KAI
INEXPENSIVE

Aloha B&B ⟡ Perched on a hillside in the residential community of Hawaii Kai is this very affordable B&B, complete with swimming pool, panoramic ocean views and continental breakfast on the outdoor lanai. The two bedrooms (one with king bed, one with twins) share a bath and a half (no waiting for the toilet!). Just a 10-minute drive to snorkeling in Hanauma Bay and about a 15-minute drive to Waikiki and downtown Honolulu. Hostess Phyllis Young has lots of beach toys (including coolers and beach chairs) she will loan you for the day. She'll even do a load of laundry for you for $4. No smoking anywhere on the property.

909 Kahauloa Pl., Honolulu, HI 96825. © **808/395-6694**. Fax 808/396-2020. http://home.hawaii.rr.com/ alohaphyllis. 2 units with shared bathroom. $60-$70 double. Rates include continental breakfast. 2-night minimum. No credit cards. Free parking. TheBus: 22. **Amenities:** Pool. *In room:* TV.

J&B's Haven Brits Joan and Barbara Webb have had a successful bed-and-breakfast on Oahu since 1982. Barbara, who has lived in Hawaii since 1970, and her mother Joan, who moved to Hawaii in 1981, are both knowledgeable about Oahu's attractions and love introducing guests to the Hawaii they love. They recently moved to this beautiful house in Hawaii Kai, just 15 minutes east of Waikiki. It's close to Hanauma Bay, Sandy Beach, and Sea Life Park, and is within easy reach of three shopping centers with excellent restaurants. There are two rooms in the house: the large master bedroom, with private bathroom, king bed, mini-refrigerator, and microwave; and a smaller room with a small refrigerator. *Note:* This is a smoke-free house. They have two very friendly dogs that live inside, so if you're allergic to canine roommates, you might look elsewhere.

Kahena St. (at Ainapo St., off Hawaii Kai Dr.), Hawaii Kai. Reservations: P. O. Box 25907, Honolulu, HI 96825. © **808/396-9462**. www.hits.net/~babe. 2 units. $65–$75 double. Rates include continental breakfast. Extra person $10. 2-night minimum. No credit cards. Free parking. TheBus: 1. *In room:* TV, fridge.

3 The Windward Coast

On the eastern side of the island, the windward side is where the trade winds blow, rainsqualls support lush, tropical vegetation, and subdivisions dot the landscape. The communities of Kailua and Kaneohe dominate here. Numerous bed-and-breakfasts (ranging from oceanfront estates to tiny cottages on quiet residential streets) abound. This is the place for "island" experiences, yet you're still within a 15-minute drive from Waikiki.

KAILUA & KANEOHE

Pat O'Malley of **Pat's Kailua Beach Properties,** 204 S. Kalaheo Ave., Kailua, HI 96734 (© **808/261-1653** or 808/262-4128; fax 808/261-0893; www. 10kvacationrentals.com/pats), books a wide range of houses and cottages on or near Kailua Beach. Rates start at $70 a day for a studio cottage near the beach and go up to $425 per day for a multimillion-dollar home right on the sand with room to sleep eight. All units are fully furnished, with everything from cooking utensils to telephone and TV, even washer/dryers.

MODERATE

Ingrid's *★* Ingrid has impeccable taste. Decorated in modern Japanese style, her cute one-bedroom apartment is straight out of a magazine. The pristine white walls and cabinets are accented with such dramatic touches as black tile counters, black-and-white shoji doors, and a black Oriental screen behind a king-size bed dressed in white quilts and red, red, red throw pillows. The tiled bathroom is done in complementary gray and has a luxurious soaking tub. The kitchenette even has a dishwasher. A huge tiled deck extends out from the apartment, while a small alcove off the bedroom can house a third person or serve as a reading nook. Fresh flowers are everywhere. The apartment is located upstairs, past the Japanese garden and through a private entrance.

Pauku St. (across from Enchanted Lakes School), Kailua. c/o Hawaii's Best Bed & Breakfasts, P.O. Box 563, Kamuela, HI 96743. (✆) **800/262-9912** or 808/885-4550. Fax 808/885-0559. www.bestbnb.com. 1 apt. $135 double. Rates include continental breakfast. Extra person $25. 3-night minimum. No credit cards. Free parking. TheBus: 52, 55, or 56. *In-room:* TV, kitchenette, fridge, coffeemaker, hair dryer, iron.

Lanikai Bed & Breakfast *★* *Finds* This old-time bed-and-breakfast, a *kamaaina* (native) home that reflects the Hawaii of yesteryear, is now into its second generation. For years, Mahina and Homer Maxey ran this large, comfortable, island-style residence; today, their son, Rick, and his wife, Nini, are the hosts. The recently renovated 1,000-square-foot upstairs apartment, which easily accommodates four, is decorated in old Hawaii bungalow style. There's a king-size bed in the bedroom, a separate den, a large living/dining room, a big bathroom, a kitchenette, and all the modern conveniences—VCR, cordless phone with answering machine—plus oversized windows to let you enjoy wonderful views. Or, you can follow the ginger- and ti-lined path to a 540-square-foot honeymooner's delight, with queen-size bed and sitting area with VCR, cordless phone, answering machine, and recently remodeled kitchenette. The units are stocked with breakfast fixings (muffins, juice, fruit, coffee, tea) and all the beach equipment you'll need (towels, mats, chairs, coolers, water jugs). Picture-perfect white-sand Lanikai Beach access is across the street, bus routes are close by, and a 2½-mile biking-walking loop is just outside.

1277 Mokulua Dr. (between Onekea and Aala drs. in Lanikai), Kailua, HI 96734. (✆) **800/258-7895** or 808/ 261-1059. Fax 808/262-2181. www.lanikaibb.com. 2 units. $90 studio double; $125 apt double. Rates include breakfast items in refrigerator. Extra person $10–$20. 3-night minimum. MC, V. Free parking. TheBus: 52, 55, or 56. *In-room:* TV, dataport, kitchenette, fridge, coffeemaker, hair dryer.

Schrader's Windward Marine Resort *Kids* Despite the name, the ambience here is more motel than resort, but Schrader's offers a good alternative for families. The property is nestled in a tranquil, tropical setting on Kaneohe Bay, only a 30-minute drive from Waikiki. The complex is made up of cottage-style motels and a collection of older homes. Cottages contain either a kitchenette with refrigerator and microwave or a full kitchen. There's also a picnic area with barbecue grills. Prices are based on the views; depending on how much you're willing to pay, you can look out over a Kahuluu fishpond, the Koolau Mountains, or Kaneohe Bay. Lots of watersports are available at an additional cost; don't miss the complimentary boat cruise on Wednesday and Saturday. *Hot tip:* When booking, ask for a unit with a lanai; that way, you'll end up with at least a partial view of the bay.

47–039 Lihikai Dr. (off Kamehameha Hwy.), Kaneohe, HI 96744. ℂ 800/735-5711 or 808/239-5711. Fax 808/239-6658. www.hawaiiscene.com/schrader. 20 units. $60–$125 1-bedroom double; $110–$190 2-bedroom for 4; $200–$320 3-bedroom for 6; $400–$450 4-bedroom for 8. Rates include continental breakfast. Extra person $7.50. 2-night minimum. AE, DC, DISC, MC, V. Free parking. TheBus: 52, 55, or 56. **Amenities:** Outdoor pool; watersports equipment rentals. *In room:* TV, kitchenette, fridge, coffeemaker.

4 The North Shore

Here's the Hawaii of Hollywood: giant waves, surfers galore, tropical jungles, waterfalls, and mysterious Hawaiian temples. If you're looking for a quieter vacation, closer to nature, filled with swimming, snorkeling, diving, surfing, or just plain hanging out on some of the world's most beautiful beaches, the North Shore is your place. The North Shore boasts good restaurants, shopping, and cultural activities, but here they come with the quiet of country living. Bed-and-breakfasts are the most common accommodations, but there are some deluxe options to consider. *Be forewarned:* It's nearly an hour's drive from the North Shore to Honolulu and Waikiki, and the ocean is rough in winter.

The North Shore doesn't have many accommodations or an abundance of tourist facilities—some say that is its charm. **Team Real Estate,** 66–250 Kamehameha Hwy., Suite D–103, Haleiwa, HI 96712 (ℂ **800/982-8602** or 808/ 637-3507; fax 808/637-8881; www.teamrealestate.com), manages vacation rentals on the North Shore. Its units range from affordable cottages to condos to oceanfront homes, at rates ranging from $90 to $300 per night. A minimum stay of 1 week is required for some properties, but shorter stays are available as well.

EXPENSIVE

Hilton at Turtle Bay Resort 🎯 *Kids*   This luxurious oceanfront resort is an hour's drive from Waikiki, but eons away in its country feeling. Sitting on 808 acres, this place is loaded with activities (including outstanding golf courses) and 5 miles of shoreline with secluded white-sand coves. It's located on Kalaeokaunu Point ("point of the altar"), where ancient Hawaiians built a small altar to the fish gods. The altar's remains are now at the Bishop Museum, but it's easy to see why the Hawaiians considered this holy ground. The feeling of old Hawaii is carried through to the guest rooms, which are now undergoing a massive renovation and expected to be completed by 2002. (Unfortunately, that renovation is making things uneven at the moment and is the reason behind the hotel's current one-star rating.) The resort is still spectacular, offering breathtaking views and one of the safest swimming beaches on the North Shore, thanks to the large reef offshore.

P.O. Box 187 (Kuilima Dr., off Kamehameha Hwy. [Hwy. 83]), Kahuku, HI 96731. ℂ 800/HILTONS or 808/ 293-8811. Fax 808/293-9147. www.turtlebayresort.hilton.com. 485 units. $249–$289 double; $300 cabana; from $475 suite. Ask about Bounceback rates, starting at $189. Extra person $35; children stay free in parents' room. AE, DC, DISC, MC, V. Self-parking $5.20; valet parking $9.30. TheBus: 52 or 55. **Amenities:** 5 restaurants (from a terrific Sun brunch to casual local cuisine); 2 bars (live entertainment nightly at the Bay View Lounge, plus a poolside bar for sunset cocktails); 2 outdoor pools; 27 holes of golf; 10 Plexipave tennis courts; small fitness room; Jacuzzi; watersports equipment rentals; children's program; game room; concierge; activity desk; business center; shopping arcade; salon; limited room service; baby-sitting; coin-op washer/dryers; laundry service; dry cleaning. *In room:* A/C, TV, fridge, coffeemaker, hair dryer, iron.

MODERATE

Santa's by the Sea 🎯 *Finds*   This certainly must be where Santa Claus comes to vacation: St. Nick knows a bargain when he sees it. The location, price, and style make this a must-stay if you plan to see the North Shore. It's one of the few North Shore B&Bs right on the beach—and not just any beach, but the famous

Banzai Pipeline. You can go from your bed to the sand in less than 30 seconds to watch the sun rise over the Pacific. Hosts Gary and Cyndie renovated this vacation hideaway into an impeccable one-bedroom unit with finely crafted woodwork, bay windows, and a collection of unique Santa figurines and one-of-a-kind Christmas items. It may sound schlocky, but somehow it gives the apartment a country charm. Honeymooners, take note: There's lots of privacy here. The unit has its own entrance; a living room with VCR and stereo; and a full kitchen with everything a cook could need. Fruit, cereal, bread, coffee, tea, and juice are provided on the first morning to get you started.

Ke Waena Rd. (off Kamehameha Hwy.), Haleiwa. c/o Hawaii's Best Bed & Breakfasts, P.O. Box 563, Kamuela, HI 96743. © 800/262-9912 or 808/885-4550. Fax 808/885-0559. www.bestbnb.com. 1 apt (shower only). $125 double. Rate includes breakfast items in refrigerator. Extra person $15. 3-night minimum. No credit cards. Free parking. TheBus: 52 or 55. **Amenities:** Washer/dryers. *In room:* TV, kitchen, fridge, coffeemaker, hair dryer.

INEXPENSIVE

Best Inn Hukilau Resort *Kids*   This two-story, plantation-style hotel is a small, intimate property within walking distance of the Polynesian Cultural Center, Brigham Young University Hawaii, and the Mormon Temple. The rooms are standard, with two double beds, microwave on request, and full bathroom. A continental breakfast with bagels, muffins, fresh fruit, juice, and coffee is included in the price (plus free coffee and juice in the lobby all day). Access to a secluded white-sand beach is just across the street. Other amenities include a sun deck, barbecues with free charcoal, and free local calls.

55–109 Laniloa St. (off Kamehameha Hwy., near the Polynesian Cultural Center), Laie, HI 96762. © 800/526-4562 or 808/293-9282. Fax 808/293-8115. www.hawaiibestinn.com. 49 units $84–$94 for up to 4. Rates include continental breakfast. Children under 18 stay free in parents' room. AE, DISC, MC, V. Free parking. TheBus: 52 or 55. **Amenities:** 1 restaurant; outdoor pool; activity desk; coin-op washer/dryers. *In room:* A/C, TV, fridge.

Ke Iki Beach Bungalows *Kids*   This collection of rustic studio, one- and two-bedroom duplex cottages has a divine location. It's snuggled on 1½ acres, with its own 200-foot stretch of white-sand beach between two legendary surf spots: Waimea Bay and Banzai Pipeline. The winter waves are rough stuff; we regular folks can only venture in to swim in the flat summer seas. But there's a large lava reef nearby with tide pools to explore and, on the other side, Shark's Cove, a relatively protected snorkeling area. Nearby are tennis courts and a jogging path. Ke Iki is not for everyone, though. The furnishings are modest, though clean and comfortable; kitchens, barbecues, and hammocks provide some of the comforts of home. The one-bedrooms have one or two single beds in the living room, a double in the separate bedroom, and a full kitchen. *Note:* The units are now under new ownership and have been remodeled with new paint, new furniture from Bali, and the oceanfront units now have TVs and phones. *Hot tip:* Stay on the beach side, where the views are well worth the extra bucks.

59–579 Ke Iki Rd. (off Kamehameha Hwy.), Haleiwa, HI 96712. © 866/638-8229 or 808/638-8829. Fax 808/637-6100. www.keikibeachbungalows.com. 10 units. $70 double; $80–$170 1-bedroom double; $135–$210 2-bedroom double. Plus a one-time cleaning fee ranging from $30 for studio to $75 for 2-bedroom units. Extra person $15. AE, MC, V. Free parking. TheBus: 52. **Amenities:** Coin-op washer/dryers. *In room:* TV, kitchen, fridge, coffeemaker.

North Shore Bed & Breakfast *Value*   One of the great values of the North Shore, this quaint studio is located above a garage, on a 1-acre lot in the country. The unit has a king-size bed (which can be made into two twins), a dining area, a kitchenette (with large refrigerator, two-burner hot plate, microwave, and toaster), wicker furniture (including a sleeper sofa), its own private entrance, and a big deck with views of the majestic Koolau Range. Just across the street is the world-famous Banzai Pipeline. There's also an outdoor shower to wash off the sand when you return from the beach.

59–420 Kamehameha Hwy. (6 miles from Haleiwa, near Ehukai Beach), Haleiwa, HI 96712. (C) 808/638-7947. flipper@hawaiirr.com. 1 studio (shower only). $95 double. Extra person $5. 3-night minimum. No credit cards. Free parking. TheBus: 52 or 55. **Amenities:** Washer/dryer available for guests' use. *In room:* TV, kitchenette, fridge, coffeemaker.

5 Leeward Oahu: The Waianae Coast

This area is a new frontier for Oahu visitors. Currently, there is only one exquisite resort in this beach-lined rural section of Oahu, but more are planned. Here's a chance to escape and be far, far away from the hustle and bustle of Waikiki. This is the sunny side of the island, with little rain and lots of sandy beaches. People who love to play golf, enjoy the ocean, and explore cultural activities will have plenty to do. However, outside the Ko Olina Resort area, there is little in the way of fine dining or interesting shopping.

J. W. Marriott Ihilani Resort & Spa at Ko Olina Resort ★★★ *Kids*   When the 640-acre Ko Olina Resort community opened, some 17 miles and 25 minutes west of Honolulu Airport (and worlds away from the tourist scene of Waikiki), critics wondered who would want to stay so far from the city. Lots of people, it turns out. Ihilani ("heavenly splendor") is nestled in a quiet location between the Pacific Ocean and the first of four man-made beach lagoons. Featuring a luxury spa and fitness center, plus tennis and one of Hawaii's premier golf courses, it's a haven of relaxation and well-being. The spa alone is reason enough to come here. Treatments include thalassic treatments, Swiss showers, Vichy showers, Roman pools, and various kinds of massages. You can even have a fitness and relaxation program custom designed.

Marriott took over management of the resort in late 1999. It's hard to get a bad room in the 15-story building—some 85% of the units enjoy lagoon or ocean views. Accommodations are luxuriously appointed and spacious (680 sq. ft.) and come with huge lanais outfitted with very comfortable, cushioned teak furniture. There's even a state-of-the-art comfort-control-system panel to operate the ceiling fans, air-conditioning, lights, and so on. Luxurious marble bathrooms have deep soaking tubs, separate glass-enclosed showers, yukata robes, and many more amenities. Other extras include daily newspaper, transportation to Waikiki and Ala Moana Shopping Center, a 3-mile coastal fitness trail, and a stretch of four white-sand beaches for ocean activities.

The Ihilani's children's program puts all others to shame, offering year-round outdoor adventures and indoor learning activities for toddlers and teens alike. There's a Computer Learning Center, a 125-gallon fish tank, an evening lounge for teen-themed parties, and more.

92–1001 Olani St., Kapolei, HI 96707. (C) 800/626-4446 or 808/679-0079. Fax 808/679-0080. www.ihilani. com. 387 units. $339–$600 double; from $800 suite. Extra person $50; children under 18 stay free in parents' room using existing bedding. Ask about Paradise package rates, which include a free car or daily breakfast for 2 starting at $289. AE, DC, MC, V. Free self-parking; valet $10. No bus service. Take H-1 west toward Pearl City/Ewa Beach; stay on H-1 until it becomes Hwy. 93 (Farrington Hwy.); look for the exit sign for Ihilani Resort; exit road is Alinui Dr., which goes into the Ko Olina Resort; turn right on Olani Place. **Amenities:** 3 restaurants (ranging from Mediterranean-inspired cuisine on an intimate terrace overlooking the ocean to light, tropical fare at an informal poolside restaurant); 2 bars (with nightly entertainment); 2 huge outdoor pools; championship 18-hole Ko Olina Golf Course, designed by Ted Robinson; tennis club with pro shop; world-class spa with every imaginable treatment; watersports equipment rentals; excellent children's program; game room; concierge; activity desk; business center; shopping arcade; salon; 24-hr. room service; in-room massage; baby-sitting; same-day laundry/dry cleaning. *In room:* A/C, TV, dataport, minibar, hair dryer, iron, safe.

6 Oahu's Campgrounds & Wilderness Cabins

Oahu's balmy weather allows camping year-round. You can expect rain any time of the year, but in general, winter is the rainy season and summer is the dry season. You should be also prepared for insects (have a good repellent for mosquitoes), water purification (boiling, filtration, or iodine crystals), and sun protection (sunscreen, a hat, and a long-sleeve shirt).

If you don't plan to bring your own camping equipment, you can rent or buy gear at **Omar The Tent Man,** 94-158 Leole St, (from H-2 take the 2nd Waipahu exit, then at the first light, make a right on to Leole St.), Waipahu (© **808/677-8785**).

Oahu is the only Hawaiian island with a public transportation system that serves the entire island (see p. 53). However, one problem with getting to a camping site on TheBus is that carry-ons must fit under your seat or on your lap. Metal-frame packs are not permitted on TheBus. Drivers do use discretion, but be forewarned.

The best places to camp on Oahu are listed below. You can find them on the "Beaches & Outdoor Pursuits on Oahu" map on p. 140.

HONOLULU
SAND ISLAND STATE RECREATION AREA ⟨⋆

Believe it or not, there is a campground in Honolulu. It's located just south of Honolulu Harbor at a waterfront Park. Don't be put off by the heavy industrial area you have to drive through to reach this 102-acre park with grassy lawns, ironwood trees, and sandy beaches. Campers have great views of the entire Honolulu coastline all the way to Waikiki, better than some of the guests in the $400-a-night rooms in Waikiki. In addition to the scenery, the most popular activity here is shoreline fishing, especially along the western shore of Sand Island. Swimming is an option, but watch out for the rocks along the shoreline bottom; the water quality is occasionally questionable too. The park is also a place to base yourself for Honolulu attractions; it's just 15 minutes from Waikiki or Pearl Harbor.

Only tent camping is allowed in this park, and only on Friday, Saturday, and Sunday nights. There are picnic tables (some under small covered shelters), rest rooms with cold showers only, and potable water. You'll need a permit; the fee is $5 per campsite per night. Applications are accepted no earlier than 30 days in advance. Write to the **Department of Land and Natural Resources,** State Parks Division, P.O. Box 621, Honolulu, HI 96809 (© **808/587-0300;** www.state.hi.us/dlnr). Permits are only given for a maximum of 5 days in every 30-day period (and since you can only stay on weekends, 5 consecutive days aren't possible). The gates close at 6:45pm in the fall and winter (from the weekend after Labor Day until Mar 31) and 7:45pm in the spring and summer (Apr 1 to Fri after Labor Day). The gates do not open until 7am the next morning; cars cannot enter or leave during that period. TheBus 19 stops at Nimitz Highway and Puuhale Road, just over a mile walk to the park entrance.

To get here from the Honolulu International Airport, take Nimitz Highway toward Honolulu and Waikiki. Turn right at the Sand Island Access Road (Hwy. 64) and follow it to the end of the road and the park entrance.

CENTRAL OAHU

KEAIWA HEIAU STATE RECREATION AREA ✦

At the southern end of central Oahu, above Halawa Heights, this 385-acre wooded park offers a cool mountain retreat with hiking trails and picnic facilities. This area, in the foothills of the Koolaus, is filled with eucalyptus, ironwood, and Norfolk pines. The remains of the *heiau ho'ola* (temple of treating the sick) are on the grounds, and specimens of Hawaiian medicinal plants are on display. An excellent 5-mile hiking trail, the Aiea loop, offers magnificent views of Pearl Harbor and the mountains. There's tent camping only; campers have the choice of flat, open grassy areas or slightly sloping areas with shade trees. Facilities include picnic tables, restrooms with cold showers, outdoor grills, a dishwashing area, a covered pavilion, drinking water, and a public phone. Supplies are available in Aiea, 2 miles away.

You'll need a permit, the fee is $5 per campsite per night; applications are accepted no earlier than 30 days in advance. Write to the **Department of Land and Natural Resources** (see "Sand Island State Recreation Area," above for address and telephone number). Permits are limited to a 5-day stay in every 30-day period. Camping is permitted Friday through Tuesday nights; no camping on Wednesday and Thursday nights. The gates close at 6:45pm in the fall and winter (from the weekend after Labor Day until Mar 31) and 7:45pm in the spring and summer (Apr 1 to Fri after Labor Day). The gates do not open until 7am the next morning; cars cannot enter or leave during that period.

From Waikiki, take the H-1 Freeway to Highway 78 and exit at Aiea (Exit 13A). Follow Moanalua Road to Aiea Heights Drive and turn right; the park entrance is at the end of the road. There is no bus service to this area.

THE WINDWARD COAST

HOOMALUHIA BOTANICAL GARDENS ✦

This relatively unknown windward-side camping area, outside Kaneohe, is a real find. *Hoomaluhia* means "peace and tranquility," an apt description for this 400-acre botanical garden. In this lush garden setting with rare plants and craggy cliffs in the background, it's hard to believe you're just a half-hour from downtown Honolulu. The gardens are laid out in areas devoted to the plants specific to tropical America, native Hawaii, Polynesia, India–Sri Lanka, and Africa. A 32-acre lake sits in the middle of the scenic park (no swimming or boating is allowed, though), and there are numerous hiking trails. The Visitors Center can suggest a host of activities, ranging from guided walks to demonstrations of ancient Hawaiian plant use. The facilities for this tent-camp area include restrooms, cold showers, dishwashing stations, picnic tables, grills, and water. A public phone is available at the Visitors Center, and shopping and gas are available in Kaneohe, 1 mile away.

Permits are free, but you have to get here on a Friday no later than 3pm, as the office is not open on weekends. Stays are limited to Friday, Saturday, and Sunday nights only. For information, contact **Hoomaluhia Botanical Gardens,** 45–680 Luluku Rd. (at Kamehameha Hwy.), Kaneohe, HI 96744 (© **808/ 233-7323**). The gate is locked at 4pm; it is open again from 5:30 to 6:30pm, and then closed for the night after that until 9am the next morning. TheBus no. 55 (Circle Island) stops 4 miles from the park entrance.

From Waikiki, take H-1 to the Pali Highway (Hwy. 61) and turn left on Kamehameha Highway (Hwy. 83); at the fourth light, turn left on Luluku Road.

KUALOA REGIONAL PARK ✹✹

Located on a peninsula on Kaneohe Bay, this park has a spectacular setting. The gold-sand beach is excellent for snorkeling, and fishing can be rewarding (see "Beaches," p. 146). There are two campgrounds: Campground A—in a wooded area with a sandy beach and palm, ironwood, kamani, and monkeypod trees—is mainly used for groups, but has a few sites for families, except during the summer, when the Department of Parks and Recreation conducts a children's camping program here. Campground B is on the main beach; it has fewer shade trees, but a great view of Mokolii Island. Facilities at both sites include restrooms, showers, picnic tables, drinking fountains, and a public phone. Campground A also has sinks for dishwashing, a volleyball court, and a kitchen building. Gas and groceries are available in Kaaawa, 2½ miles away. The gate hours are 7am to 8pm; if you're not back to the park by 8pm, you're locked out for the night.

Permits are free, but limited to 5 days (no camping on Wed and Thurs). Contact the **Honolulu Department of Parks and Recreation,** 650 S. King St., Honolulu, HI 96713 (© **808/523-4525;** www.co.honolulu.hi.us), for information and permits. Kualoa Regional Park is located in the 49–600 area of Kamehameha Highway, across from Mokolii Island. Take the Likelike Highway (Hwy. 63); after the Wilson Tunnel, get in the right lane and turn off on Kahakili Highway (Hwy. 83). Or, take TheBus no. 55.

KAHANA BAY BEACH PARK ✹✹

Under Tahiti-like cliffs, with a beautiful, gold-sand crescent beach framed by pine-needle casuarina trees, Kahana Bay Beach Park is a place of serene beauty. You can swim, bodysurf, fish, hike, and picnic, or just sit and listen to the trade winds whistle through the beach pines.

Both tent and vehicle camping are allowed at this oceanside oasis. Facilities include restrooms, picnic tables, drinking water, public phones, and a boat-launching ramp. Note that the restrooms are at the north end of the beach, far away from the camping area, and there are no showers. You'll need a permit; the fee is $5 per campsite per night. There's a 5-night limit, and no camping at all on Wednesday or Thursday nights. You can get a permit at the **Department of Land and Natural Resources,** State Parks Division, P.O. Box 621, Honolulu, HI 96809 (© **808/587-0300;** www.state.hi.us/dlnr). Note that although information is available on the website, you cannot apply for permits online.

Kahana Bay Beach Park is in the 52–222 block of Kamehameha Highway (Hwy. 83) in Kahana. From Waikiki, take the H-1 west to the Likelike Highway (Hwy. 63). Continue north on the Likelike, through the Wilson Tunnel, turning left on Highway 83; Kahana Bay is 13 miles down the road on the right. You can also get there via TheBus no. 55.

WAIMANALO BAY STATE RECREATION AREA ✹

Just outside the town of Waimanalo is one of the most beautiful beachfront camping grounds on Oahu: Steep verdant cliffs in the background, a view of Rabbit Island off shore, and miles of white-sand beach complete the picture of Waimanalo Bay State Recreation Area. This campground is close to Sea Life Park and relatively close to Hanauma Bay, Makapuu, and Sandy Beach.

Ocean activities abound: great swimming offshore, good surfing for beginners, and plentiful fishing grounds. There is tent camping only at the 12 sites, which ensures plenty of privacy. The campsites (in numbered slots) are all in the open grassy lawn between the ironwood trees and the shoreline. Each campsite has its own picnic table, barbecue grill, and garbage can. Other facilities in the area include a central restroom with showers, water fountains, and a dishwashing sink. A public telephone is located by the caretaker's house.

Permits are free, but limited to 5 nights (no camping on Wed or Thurs nights). Contact the **Honolulu Department of Parks and Recreation,** 650 S. King St., Honolulu, HI 96713 (© 808/523-4525; www.co.honolulu.hi.us), for information and permits. Permits are not issued until 2 weeks before your camping dates.

TheBus no. 57 stops on Kalanianaole Highway (Hwy. 72), about a mile walking distance to the park entrance. From Honolulu, take the H-1 Freeway east until it ends. Continue on Highway 72 into Waimanalo. Turn right on Whiteman Road and then right again on Walker Road, which leads to the park entrance.

THE NORTH SHORE

MALAEKAHANA BAY STATE RECREATION AREA ★★★

This beautiful beach camping site has a mile-long gold-sand beach. There are two areas for tent camping. Facilities include picnic tables, restrooms, showers, sinks, drinking water, and a phone. Stays are limited to 5 nights (no camping on Wed or Thurs nights). Camping fees are $5 per campsite per night; permits can be obtained at any state parks office, including the **Department of Land and Natural Resources,** State Parks Division, P.O. Box 621, Honolulu, HI 96809 (© 808/587-0300; www.state.hi.us/dlnr). The park gate is closed between 6:45pm and 7am; vehicles cannot enter or exit during those hours. Groceries and gas are available in Laie and Kahuku, less than a mile away.

The recreation area is located on Kamehameha Highway (Hwy. 83) between Laie and Kahuku. To get there, take the H-2 Freeway to Highway 99 to Highway 83 (both roads are called Kamehameha Hwy.); continue on Highway 83 just past Kahuku. Or take TheBus no. 55.

CAMP MOKULEIA ★★

A quiet, isolated beach on Oahu's North Shore, 4 miles from Kaena Point, is the centerpiece of this 9-acre campground. Camping is available on the beach or in a grassy, wooded area. Activities include swimming, surfing, shore fishing, and beachcombing.

Facilities include tent camping, cabins, and lodge accommodations. The tent-camping site has portable chemical toilets, a water spigot, and outdoor showers; there are no picnic tables or barbecue grills, so come prepared. The cabins have bunk beds and can sleep up to 14 people in the small cabins and 22 in the large cabins. The lodge facilities include rooms with and without a private bathroom. The cabins are $160 per night for the 14-bed cabin and $200 per night for the 18-bed cabin. The rooms at the lodge are $55 for a shared bathroom and $65 for a private bathroom (an additional $10 will buy you breakfast). Many groups use the camp, but it's still a very peaceful place. The tent area is separated from the buildings—but you can use all the facilities if you opt for it—and there's a real sense of privacy. Tent camping is $8 per person per night (kids ages 4–17 are $4, and children under 4 stay free). Reservations for permits are needed; contact **Camp Mokuleia,** 68–729 Farrington Hwy., Waialua, HI 96791 (© **808/ 637-6241;** fax 808/637-5505, www.campmokuleia.org).

Camp Mokuleia is located on Farrington Highway, west of Haleiwa. To get here from Waikiki, take the H-1 to the H-2 exit; stay on H-2 until the end. Where the road forks, bear left to Waialua on Highway 803, which turns into Highway 930, to Kaena Point. Look for the green fence on the right, where a small sign at the driveway reads CAMP MOKULEIA, EPISCOPAL CHURCH OF HAWAII.

5

Dining

by Jocelyn Fujii

On Oahu, the full range of choices includes chef-owned glamour restaurants, neighborhood eateries, fast-food joints, ethnic spots, and restaurants and food courts in shopping malls.

The recommendations below are organized by location, beginning with Waikiki, then neighborhoods west of Waikiki, neighborhoods east of Waikiki, and finally the Windward Coast and the North Shore.

1 Waikiki

VERY EXPENSIVE

La Mer ★★★ NEOCLASSICAL FRENCH   This is the splurge restaurant of Hawaii, the oceanfront bastion of haute cuisine where two of the state's finest chefs (George Mavrothalassitis and Philippe Padovani, each with his own eponymous restaurant now) quietly redefined fine dining in Hawaii. La Mer is romantic, elegant, and expensive; dress up not to be seen, but to match the ambience and food. It's the only AAA Five-Diamond restaurant in the state, a second-floor, open-sided room with views of Diamond Head and the sound of trade winds rustling the nearby coconut fronds. Michelin-award–winning chef Yves Garnier melds classical French influences with fresh island ingredients: elegant soups with saffron, chanterelles, and savory fresh fish filets; *moano* (a delicate goatfish) in strudel with basil and niçoise olives; ruby snapper, skin crisped, in exotic sauces hinting of truffle and herbs. The wine list, desserts, and service—formal without being stiff—complete the dining experience.

In the Halekulani, 2199 Kalia Rd. ℂ 808/923-2311. Reservations recommended. Long-sleeve collared dress shirts for men; jackets provided if necessary. Main courses $36–$45; prix fixe $85, $105. AE, DC, MC, V. Daily 6–10pm.

Michel's ★★ FRENCH/HAWAII REGIONAL   The room on the sand at Sans Souci Beach has windows that open to the ocean air. Manager Phil Shaw, a charming host with a following all his own, presides over a room with one side open to the sunset, torches on the breakwater, a hula moon above the palm fronds, and the entire Waikiki skyline visible to the leeward side. All tables have an ocean view, and dining here is less stiff and more welcoming than in bygone years. Jackets are no longer required for men, and the live music (slack-key and classical guitar with a vocalist Thurs–Sat, and strolling musicians on Sun) attracts sunset and music lovers too. Chef Hardy Kintscher has added his touch to the classics (onion soup, steak tartare, chateaubriand, bouillabaisse) and prepares fresh seafood, vegetarian creations, and rack of lamb with restraint and creativity.

In the Colony Surf Hotel, 2895 Kalakaua Ave. ℂ 808/923-6552. Reservations recommended. No shorts or beach wear. Main courses $26–$39. AE, DC, DISC, MC, V. Daily 5:30–9:30pm.

Waikiki Dining

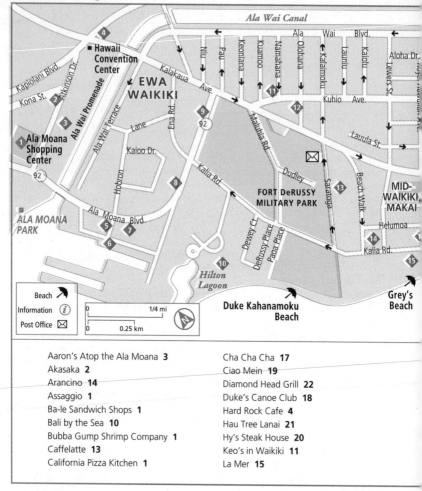

Aaron's Atop the Ala Moana **3**
Akasaka **2**
Arancino **14**
Assaggio **1**
Ba-le Sandwich Shops **1**
Bali by the Sea **10**
Bubba Gump Shrimp Company **1**
Caffelatte **13**
California Pizza Kitchen **1**

Cha Cha Cha **17**
Ciao Mein **19**
Diamond Head Grill **22**
Duke's Canoe Club **18**
Hard Rock Cafe **4**
Hau Tree Lanai **21**
Hy's Steak House **20**
Keo's in Waikiki **11**
La Mer **15**

EXPENSIVE

Bali by the Sea ★ CONTINENTAL/PACIFIC RIM   Another memorable oceanfront dining room—pale and full of light, with a white grand piano at the entrance and sweeping views of the ocean. The menu merges island cooking styles and ingredients with the chef's Alsatian roots: an excellent herb-infused rack of lamb coated with macadamia nuts, escargots in phyllo, and fresh seafood in sauces hinting of plum wine, kaffir lime, black bean, ginger, and lemongrass.

In the Hilton Hawaiian Village, 2005 Kalia Rd. ✆ **808/941-2254**. Reservations recommended. Main courses $22.50–$34. AE, DC, DISC, MC, V. Mon–Sat 6–9pm.

Diamond Head Grill ★★ HAWAII REGIONAL   Talk about buzz. From judges and fashionistas to politicos and the boy next door, they're all here, either dining in the sleek and stylish dining room or being seen at the "bar with the bed," the serpentine DHG Bar that is the social nexus of Friday-night Honolulu. But it's not all flash at this dining room of W Honolulu.

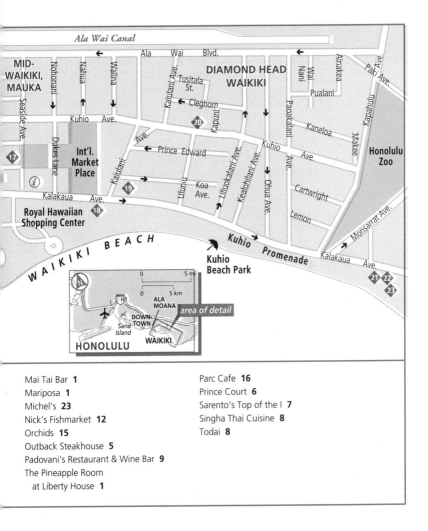

Executive chef Todd Constantino offers noteworthy fare that highlights the flavors and ingredients of Hawaii teamed with a "chop house" menu of prime dry-aged beef, corn-fed and flown in from the Midwest. The filet mignon and New York strip steak are rubbed with sea salt, organic fresh herbs, and roasted garlic, and prepared with homemade Worcestershire; or you can choose oak-aged soy sauce or a demi-glace of roasted shallots. The fresh fish comes grilled, sautéed, steamed, or wok-fried. Among DHG's staples are opakapaka with Kahuku corn and truffled clam broth and guava-mustard rack of lamb. The room features burnished copper columns, large windows overlooking Kapiolani Park and Diamond Head, a private dining room for the "Chef's Table" of up to 10 people, and the notorious DHG Bar, where there really is a bed and the drinks are as stylish as the crowd. There's live jazz entertainment nightly (see p. 239).

In the W Honolulu, 2885 Kalakaua Ave. ✆ **808/922-3734**. Reservations recommended. Main courses $7–$14 breakfast; $18–$34 dinner. AE, DC, DISC, MC, V. Daily 7–10:30am, 6–10pm; Bistro menu nightly 10–11:30pm; live entertainment daily 8:30pm–midnight.

Hau Tree Lanai ⭐ PACIFIC RIM   Informal and delightful, this Honolulu institution scores higher on ambience than on food. The outdoor setting and earnest menu make it a popular informal dining spot; an ancient hau tree provides shade and charm for diners. A diverse parade of beachgoers at Sans Souci Beach (called "Dig Me Beach" for its eye-candy sunbathers) is part of the scenery. Breakfast here is a must: salmon Florentine, served with a fresh-baked scone; poi pancakes and Belgian waffles; eggs Benedict; and the Hawaiian platter of miniature poi pancakes, eggs, and a medley of island sausages. Lunchtime offerings include house-cured Atlantic salmon and an assortment of burgers, sandwiches, salads, and fresh-fish and pasta specialties. Dinner selections are more ambitious and less reliable: fresh moonfish, red snapper, opakapaka, ahi, and chef's specials, in preparations ranging from plain grilled to stuffed and over-the-top rich.

In the New Otani Kaimana Beach Hotel, 2863 Kalakaua Ave. ℂ **808/921-7066.** Reservations recommended. Main courses $19–$32.95. AE, DC, DISC, MC, V. Mon–Sat 7–11am, 11:30am–2pm, and 5:30–9pm; Sun 7–11:30am, noon–2pm, and 5:30–9pm. Late lunch in the open-air bar, daily 2–4pm.

Hy's Steak House ⭐⭐ AMERICAN   This is as good as it gets in steakhouses. Think dark, clubby, lots of leather, good Scotch, and filet mignon. This is a great choice for steak lovers with hefty pocketbooks or for those who have tired of Hawaii Regional Cuisine. Hy's has demonstrated admirable staying power in the cult of the low fat, still scoring high among carnivores while offering ample alternatives, such as a grilled vegetable platter and excellent salads prepared tableside (spinach and Caesar are textbook perfect). "The Only" is its classic best, a kiawe-grilled New York strip steak served with a mysterious signature sauce. Garlic lovers swear by the Garlic Steak Diane, a richly endowed rib eye with sliced mushrooms.

2440 Kuhio Ave. ℂ **808/922-5555.** Reservations recommended. Main courses $17.95–$49 or market price. AE, DC, DISC, MC, V. Sun–Thurs 6–10pm; Fri–Sat 6–11pm.

Nick's Fishmarket ⭐ SEAFOOD   With its extensive fish and lobster specialties, Nick's is the restaurant for seafood lovers with upscale tastes. It's a bit of a time warp (extravagant 1980s) and the atmosphere is unremarkable, but you will find first-rate seafood and professional service from crisp, formally clad servers. Come here for the classics: bouillabaisse, Alaskan crab legs, lobster tail (prepared six different ways), fresh fish in a medley of preparations. Meat lovers can order veal, rack of lamb, chicken, New York steak, or filet mignon; appetizers range from Beluga caviar and escargots to ahi and salmon tartare, oysters Rockefeller, and blackened sashimi. The kids' menu appeals to families, the pasta and risotto to less-formal tastes. The Kalakaua Room has a window for people-watching, but we prefer the intimacy of the banquettes on the opposite side of the room. Live entertainment and dancing in the lounge attract the after-dinner crowd (see p. 239).

In the Waikiki Gateway Hotel, 2070 Kalakaua Ave. ℂ **808/955-6333.** Reservations recommended. Main courses $24.50 to market price; complete dinners $20–$55. AE, DC, DISC, MC, V. Sun–Thurs 5:30–10pm, cafe menu 5:30–10pm; Fri–Sat 5:30–11pm, cafe menu 5:30–11pm. Late-night entertainment Thurs–Sat 9:30pm–1:30am.

Orchids ⭐ INTERNATIONAL SEAFOOD   Orchids highlights fresh local produce and seafood in elegant presentations, in a fantasy setting with consummate service. It's an extraordinary setting and the food is good to excellent. Blinding white linens and a view of Diamond Head from the open oceanfront dining room will start you off with a smile. (The parade of oiled bodies traversing the seawall is part of the entertainment.) At lunch, the seafood and vegetable curries, though pricey, are winners, and the steamed ehu (short-tail red snapper) is an Orchids signature. For dinner, onaga (ruby snapper) is steamed with ginger, Chinese parsley, shiitake mushrooms, and soy sauce, then drizzled with hot sesame oil for a delightful taste explosion. Delicately textured pink snapper (opakapaka) is sautéed and presented with wasabi mashed potatoes and wasabi cream, another pleaser with Asian undertones. There are lamb, chicken, and beef entrees as well, and the desserts, especially the chocolate brioche pudding and haupia lemongrass brûlée, are extraordinary. From 6 to 8pm, the seafood buffet is a $10.50 appetizer if you order an entree.

In the Halekulani, 2199 Kalia Rd. ⓒ 808/923-2311. Reservations recommended. Dinner main courses $25–$34.50. AE, DC, MC, V. Daily 7:30–11am and 6–10pm; Mon–Sat 11:30am–2pm; Sun brunch 9:30am–2:30pm.

Padovani's Restaurant & Wine Bar ✩✩✩ FRENCH/MEDITERRANEAN Expect excellent fare, Frette linens, Riedel stemware, romantic lighting, and highly polished service and presentation. It won't be inexpensive, and don't wear jeans. This is the land of extravagant wines by the glass or bottle to complement the culinary inspirations of chef Philippe Padovani. He has worked at Halekulani's La Mer, the erstwhile Ritz-Carlton Mauna Lani, and the Manele Bay Hotel, so of course his own swank dining room (and fantasy kitchen) would be top-drawer, with food and service that overcome a windowless room with not-so-soaring ceilings. Upstairs from the main dining room, the wine bar offers an extraordinary selection of single-malt scotches and an oenophile's wine list. A bamboo floor (a la Hoku's in the Kahala Mandarin), custom-made 1930s-style lamps, Bernardaud china, and a 16-bottle Cruvinet (which keeps wines fresh for by-the-glass orders) are other impressive features of this Waikiki winner.

The menu is pure Padovani: *ogo* (seaweed) bread, the best clam chowder in town, a panfried veal chop with sun-dried tomatoes and chervil sauce, grilled John Dory with fresh asparagus and tomatoes, and a wildly popular risotto of Dungeness crab and asparagus. Although the menu changes regularly, you can count on the sautéed portabello mushrooms with polenta or the herbed endive salad with toasted almonds and Roquefort—superb.

At the Wine Bar upstairs, you can order from the Bistro menu or choose less expensive offerings that include sandwiches, salads, pastas, and excellent appetizers (ahi tartar with ogo, wild mushrooms in puff pastry). The extensive wine list offers more than 50 wines by the glass.

In the Doubletree Alana Waikiki Hotel, 1956 Ala Moana Blvd. ⓒ 808/946-3456. Reservations recommended. Dinner main courses $16–$42; prix fixe $45, $85. AE, DC, DISC, MC, V. Bistro open Mon–Sat 6–9:30pm; Wine Bar daily 6–10am, 11:30am–2pm, 4pm–midnight.

Prince Court ✩ CONTEMPORARY ISLAND CUISINE Floor-to-ceiling windows, sunny views of the harbor, and buffets a cut above are Prince Court's attractions, especially at lunch, when locals and visitors line up at the international buffet. Chef Goran Streng, formerly of Mauna Kea Beach Hotel's Batik room, keeps the menu fresh and the dining room busy. The harbor view is particularly pleasing at sunset, or on Friday nights when fireworks light up the sky. Monday through Thursday, diners can sample the shellfish appetizer bar with a half entree ($34) from the varied a la carte menu, which features fresh island seafood, Hawaii Regional specialties (melt-in-your-mouth ahi carpaccio), and excellent grilled and roasted meats. Desserts, too, are legendary, especially the custard-drenched bread pudding and the macadamia nut flan.

In the Hawaii Prince Hotel Waikiki, 100 Holomoana St. ✆ **808/944-4494.** Reservations recommended. Main courses $18–$28; breakfast buffet $17.50; weekend brunch $24.50; luncheon buffet $18.95; shellfish appetizer bar $34; dinner buffet $38. AE, DC, MC, V. Daily 6–10:30am; Mon–Fri 11:30am–2pm; Sat–Sun brunch 11:15am–1pm; Mon–Thurs 6–9:30pm; Fri–Sun 5:30–9:30pm.

Sarento's Top of the I✦ITALIAN   The ride up in the glass elevator at this special-occasion Italian restaurant is an event in itself, but Sarento's is not all show. Diners rave about the romantic view of the city, the stellar Greek salad (a trademark of this restaurant chain, whose president is Aaron Placourakis), the Opakapaka Portofino (with asparagus, in a lemon-dill-butter sauce), and the Seafood Fra Diavolo in marinara sauce. Things can be buttery here, so leave your inhibitions at the door. The pasta selections include lobster ravioli and the simple (and divine) capellini pomodoro. Veal lovers come for the osso buco with saffron risotto and the veal saltimbocca, served with a special touch: shiitake mushrooms.

In the Renaissance Ilikai Waikiki hotel, 1777 Ala Moana Blvd. ✆ **808/955-5559.** Reservations recommended. Main courses $16–$32. AE, DC, MC, V. Sun–Thurs 5:30–9:30pm; Fri–Sat 5:30–10pm.

MODERATE

ArancinoITALIAN   When jaded Honolulu residents venture into Waikiki for dinner, it had better be good. Arancino is worth the hunt. Here's what you'll find: a cheerful cafe of Monet-yellow walls and tile floors, respectable pastas, wonderful pizzas, fabulous red-pepper salsa and rock-salt focaccia, we-try-harder service, and reasonable prices. The risotto changes daily. Don't miss the Gorgonzola-asparagus pizza if it's on the menu. The line to get in is worth the wait.

255 Beach Walk. ✆ **808/923-5557.** Main courses $7.50–$14. AE, DC, DISC, MC, V. Daily 11:30am–2:30pm and 5–10pm.

Caffelatte ✦NORTHERN ITALIAN   Chef/owner Laura Proserpio makes everything from scratch and to order; you won't catch her near a microwave oven. As a result, you won't find a better bruschetta, pasta carbonara, marinara, or risotto in Waikiki. The menu is built on uncompromising basics such as generations-old recipes and long hours of simmering soups and sauces. The prix-fixe dinner consists of appetizer or salad, soup (usually fish, lentil, or vegetable, and always good), and entree, which could be a porcini risotto, homemade ravioli, or any of several veal selections.

339 Saratoga Rd. ✆ **808/924-1414.** Reservations recommended. Prix fixe $35. MC, V. Wed–Mon 6:30–10pm.

Ciao MeinITALIAN/CHINESE   Risotto with chopsticks, fried rice with a fork—such is the cross-cultural way of Ciao Mein, 10 years old and still going strong. The large, pleasant dining room, efficient service, surprisingly good Chinese food (especially for a hotel restaurant), and award-winning menu items have made this a haven for noodle lovers. The honey-walnut shrimp, with snap peas and honey-glazed walnuts, is a hit. The angel hair pasta with spicy ginger-garlic shrimp is a big seller, and few who have tasted Ciao Mein's tiramisu will forget its creamy, ambrosial kick. The antipasto is Italian, the seafood fun (as in chow fun) is a form of lasagna, and the Chinese roast duck is cannelloni "collision cuisine." Choose from six different pastas and six sauces.

In the Hyatt Regency Waikiki, 2424 Kalakaua Ave. ✆ **808/923-2426.** Reservations recommended. Main courses $14–$35; prix fixe $27–$39. AE, DC, DISC, MC, V. Daily 6–10pm.

Duke's Canoe Club ⌒★ STEAK/SEAFOOD   Hip, busy, and oceanfront, this is what dining in Waikiki should be. There's hardly a time when the open-air dining room isn't filled with good Hawaiian music. It's crowded at sunset, though. Just because Duke's is popular among singles, don't dismiss it as a pickup bar—its ambience is stellar. Named after fabled surfer Duke Kahanamoku, this casual, upbeat hot spot buzzes with diners and Hawaiian-music lovers throughout the day. Lunch and the Barefoot Bar menu include pizza, sandwiches, burgers, salads, and appetizers such as mac-nut and crab wontons and the ever-popular grilled chicken quesadillas. Dinner fare is steak and seafood, with decent marks for the fresh catch, prepared in your choice of the five styles. There's live entertainment nightly from 4pm to midnight, with no cover.

In the Outrigger Waikiki on the Beach, 2335 Kalakaua Ave. ℂ **808/922-2268**. Reservations recommended for dinner. Main courses $10–$20; breakfast buffet $10.95. AE, DC, MC, V. Daily 7am–midnight.

Keo's in Waikiki ⌒★ THAI   With freshly spiced and spirited dishes and familiar menu of Thai delights, Keo's arrived in Waikiki with a splashy tropical ambience and a menu that islanders and visitors love. Owner Keo Sananikone grows his own herbs, fruits, and vegetables without pesticides on his North Shore farm. Satay shrimp, basil-infused eggplant with tofu, evil jungle prince (shrimp, chicken, or vegetables in a basil-coconut-chile sauce), Thai garlic shrimp with mushrooms, pad Thai noodles, and the ever-delectable panang, green, and yellow curries are among his abiding delights. The menu includes a heat rating for spiciness, a plus for the delicate palate.

2028 Kuhio Ave. ℂ **808/951-9355**. Reservations recommended. Main courses $8.95–$13.95; prix fixe $29.95. AE, DC, DISC, MC, V. Daily 7:30am–2pm; Sun–Thurs 5–10:30pm; Fri–Sat 5–11pm.

Parc Cafe ⌒★ GOURMET BUFFETS   As the saying goes, Wow! Laulau! The Halekulani's sister hotel has redefined the buffet and made it—surprise!—a culinary attraction. Breakfast, sushi lunch, noodles, Hawaiian, and seafood/prime rib are among the buffet themes featured throughout the week. My favorite is the Hawaiian buffet, which maintains the integrity of real, down-home Hawaiian food with an elegance that is nonthreatening. It's multicultural too, so you have roast duck and Portuguese bean soup among the Hawaiian staples of laulau, beef stew, chicken long rice, kalua pig, squid luau, and the pièce de résistance, Kauai (or sometimes, Molokai) taro au gratin, a brilliant treatment of the Hawaiian corn that is too often misunderstood. Regulars flock to the dining room for the $16.95 Wednesday and Friday Hawaiian lunch buffet, which is also featured (for $2 more) on Wednesday evenings. Chafing dishes notwithstanding, this is gourmet fare, using fresh, fine ingredients. A carving station serves up rotisserie duck and prime rib, and the seafood soup is reliably good.

In the Waikiki Parc Hotel, 2233 Helumoa Rd. ℂ **808/931-6643**. Reservations recommended. Breakfast, lunch, and dinner buffets $12.95–$25.95. AE, DC, DISC, MC, V. Daily 5:30–10am; Sun sushi brunch 11am–2pm; Mon–Tues, Thurs, Sat noodle buffet 11am–2:30pm; Wed and Fri Hawaiian buffet 11:30am–2pm; dinner buffet 5:30–9:30pm (Prime rib on Mon–Tues, Thurs; Hawaiian on Wed; seafood/prime rib Fri–Sun).

Singha Thai Cuisine THAI   The Royal Thai dancers arch their graceful fingers nightly in classical Thai dance on the small center stage, but you may be too busy tucking into your Thai chile fresh fish or blackened ahi summer rolls to notice. Imaginative combination dinners and the use of local organic ingredients are among the special touches of this Thai-Hawaiian fusion restaurant. Complete dinners for two to five cover many tastes and are an ideal way for the uninitiated to sample this cuisine, as well as the elements of Hawaii Regional Cuisine that have had considerable influence on the chef. Some highlights of a diverse menu: local fresh catch with Thai chile and light black-bean sauce; red, green, yellow, and vegetarian curries; ginseng chicken soup; and many seafood dishes. Such extensive use of fresh fish (mahimahi, ono, ahi, opakapaka, onaga, and uku) in traditional Thai preparations is unusual for a Thai restaurant. The entertainment and indoor-outdoor dining add to this first-class experience.

1910 Ala Moana Blvd. (at the Ala Moana end of Waikiki). ✆ 808/941-2898. Reservations recommended. Main courses $11–$27. AE, DC, DISC, MC, V. Daily 4–11pm.

INEXPENSIVE

Cha Cha Cha MEXICAN/CARIBBEAN   Its heroic margaritas, cheap happy-hour beer, pupu, excellent homemade chips, and all-around lovable menu make this a Waikiki treasure. From the beans to the salsa to the gilled Jamaican chicken, there's nothing wimpy about the flavors here. The lime, coconut, and Caribbean spices make Cha Cha Cha more than plain ol' Mex, adding zing to the blackened mahimahi and fresh fish burritos, the jerk chicken breast, and the grilled veggies in a spinach tortilla. Tacos, tamales, quesadillas, soups, enchiladas, chimichangas, and a host of spicy pork, chicken, and fish ensembles are real pleasers. Ask about the specials, because they're likely to be wonderful. Blackened swordfish, curried fresh grilled vegetables, and homemade desserts (including a creamy toasted coconut custard you won't want to miss) are some of the highlights. Its location, across from two of Waikiki's three movie theaters, makes it a choice spot for pre- and after-theater dining.

342 Seaside Ave. ✆ 808/923-7797. Complete dinners $7–$12.95. MC, V. Daily 11:30am–1am; happy hour 4–6pm and 9–11pm.

2 Honolulu Beyond Waikiki

ALA MOANA & KAKAAKO
EXPENSIVE

Aaron's Atop the Ala Moana ✦ AMERICAN/CONTINENTAL/SEAFOOD   Take the express elevator to the 36th floor, where the circular dining room reveals the city in its mountain-to-sea splendor. This may be the best view from a Honolulu restaurant that isn't on the beach. Tables line the sweeping windows while intimate banquettes curve around the interior. A private dining room next to the wine cellar serves parties of up to 10. Aaron's offers beluga caviar, its famous black-and-blue ahi (sliced asymmetrically and seared in Cajun spices), and seafood entrees such as the famous Opakapaka Gabriella, in lemon butter and capers. This is rich Continental fare with some lively local touches and some heavy sauces. Among the excellent salads, the Greek Maui Wowie—chopped tomatoes, bay shrimp, avocado, Maui onions, feta cheese, lettuce—is tops.

Ala Moana Hotel, 410 Atkinson Dr. ✆ 808/955-4466. Reservations recommended. Main courses $20.95–$42.95. AE, DC, DISC, MC, V. Daily 5:30–11:30pm; live music Sun–Thurs until 2am, Fri–Sat until 3am.

Mariposa ✦ PACIFIC RIM/SOUTHWESTERN   Once you get past the gourmet food department of the new Neiman Marcus, you'll be in Mariposa, a popular lunch spot in town (along with Onjin's Café, another fave). High ceilings for indoor diners, plus tables on the deck with views of Ala Moana Park and its Art Deco bridges, add up to a pleasing ambience, with or without the shopping. Instead of Neiman Marcus attitude, you'll find cordial service, nearly four dozen reasonably priced wines by the glass, and a menu of Pacific and American (called "heritage cuisine") specialties that include everything from opakapaka with a three-pepper vinaigrette to an excellent seared salmon salad. Chef Doug Lum's mashed potatoes and steamed Manila clams are legendary, and the Hamakua Meyer lemon tart is a force of nature. But the lunchtime favorite is invariably the starter of chicken broth—like the towering, eggy popover with poha (cape gooseberry) butter, it's the perfect welcome. The food can be spotty, though, so don't expect perfection. You'll take your chances with the sandwiches, especially the Reuben.

In Neiman Marcus, Ala Moana Center, 1450 Ala Moana Blvd. (📞 **808/951-3420.** Reservations recommended. Lunch main courses $9.50–$20; dinner main courses $18.50–$34.50. AE, DC, MC, V. Daily 11am–3pm; dessert and appetizer menu 3–5pm; Mon–Sat 5–10pm; Sun 5–9pm.

The Pineapple Room 🏝 HAWAII REGIONAL   Yes it's in a department store, but it's Alan Wong, a culinary icon. The food is usually great, the ambience so-so, and recent reports in the media had servers complaining about diners who order light and stay long. Oy! Attitude. Still, the food is terrific, particularly anything with kalua pig (for example, the kalua pig BLT), which Wong conjures up in a miraculous greaseless form. The room features an open kitchen with a lava-rock wall and abundant natural light, but these are details in a room where food is king. The menu changes regularly, but keep an eye out for the ginger scallion shrimp scampi, nori-wrapped tempura salmon, and superb gazpacho made of yellow and red Waimea tomatoes.

In Macy's West (formerly Liberty House), 1450 Ala Moana Blvd. (📞 **808/945-8881.** Reservations recommended for lunch and dinner. Main courses $11–$15 lunch; $19–$32 dinner. AE, DC, DISC, MC, V. Mon–Fri 11am–9pm; Sat 8am–9pm; Sun 9am–3pm.

Sushi Sasabune 🏝🏝 *Finds* SUSHI   If dinner here is too steep (and it *is* steep), come for lunch. Sushi Sasabune is one of the marvels of the edible world. There are four lunch specials, each with salad, miso soup, and ice cream: the sushi combo, the tekka don/tuna bowl (sushi rice with nine pieces of sliced tuna), and a roll each of Louisiana blue crab, salmon belly, and tuna. Priced at $7.50 to $12.50, the specials are a fabulous value. My passionate favorite is the chirashi/fish bowl, a neat rectangular box with warm rice, several types of tuna and white fish, marinated octopus, and other slices of sashimi. If you wish to order from the regular menu, by all means grab a table. But if you sit at the sushi bar, you must submit to the Japanese version of the Seinfeld Soup Nazi, otherwise known as omakase. You obey the chef, eat what's served, and God help you if you drop a grain of rice or dip something in wasabi without permission. The payoff is that whatever you eat is freshly shipped in that day, and often exotic. Whether it's salmon from Nova Scotia, sea urchin from Japan, halibut from Boston, Louisiana blue crab, or farmed oyster from Washington, chef Seiji Kumagawa's sushi comes with a strict protocol: Dip only with permission, and then with restraint. This is an extraordinary experience for sushi aficionados—a journey into new tastes, textures, and sensations, expensive but well worth it.

1419 S. King St. (📞 **808/947-3800.** Reservations recommended. Sushi $4–$7; lunch combinations $7.50–$12.50. AE, DC, DISC, MC, V. Mon–Fri noon–2pm; Mon–Sat 5:30–10pm.

MODERATE
Akasaka 🏝🏝 JAPANESE/SUSHI BAR   Cozy, busy, casual, and occasionally smoky, with a tiny tatami room for small groups, Akasaka wins high marks for sushi, sizzling tofu and scallops, miso-clam soup, and the overall quality of its cuisine. Highlights include the zesty spicy tuna hand-roll (temaki), scallop roll

Honolulu Dining Beyond Waikiki

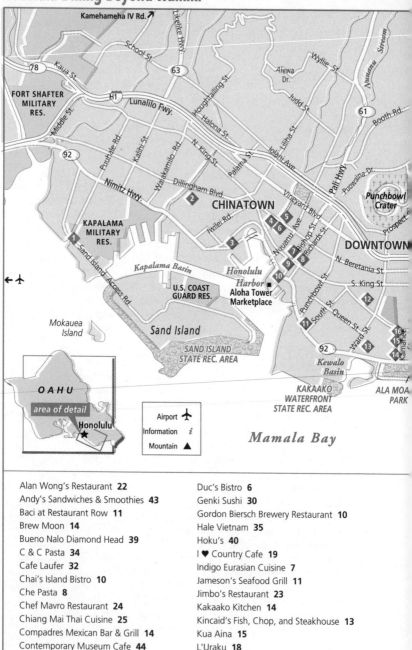

Alan Wong's Restaurant **22**
Andy's Sandwiches & Smoothies **43**
Baci at Restaurant Row **11**
Brew Moon **14**
Bueno Nalo Diamond Head **39**
C & C Pasta **34**
Cafe Laufer **32**
Chai's Island Bistro **10**
Che Pasta **8**
Chef Mavro Restaurant **24**
Chiang Mai Thai Cuisine **25**
Compadres Mexican Bar & Grill **14**
Contemporary Museum Cafe **44**
Don Ho's Island Grill **10**
Donato's **42**

Duc's Bistro **6**
Genki Sushi **30**
Gordon Biersch Brewery Restaurant **10**
Hale Vietnam **35**
Hoku's **40**
I ♥ Country Cafe **19**
Indigo Eurasian Cuisine **7**
Jameson's Seafood Grill **11**
Jimbo's Restaurant **23**
Kakaako Kitchen **14**
Kincaid's Fish, Chop, and Steakhouse **13**
Kua Aina **15**
L'Uraku **18**
La Mariana **1**
Legend Seafood Restaurant **5**

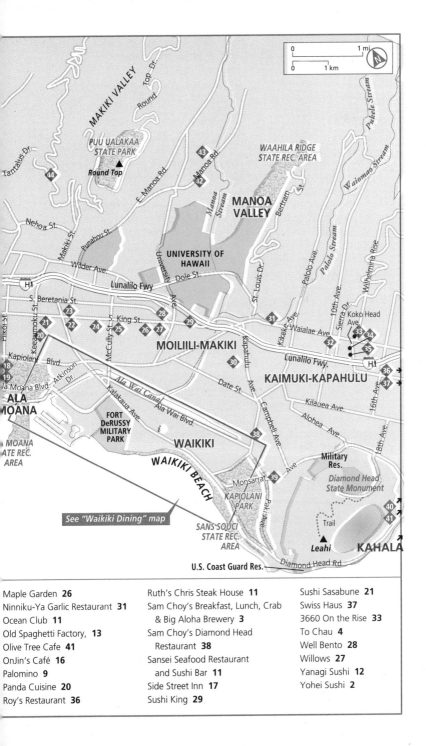

Maple Garden **26**
Ninniku-Ya Garlic Restaurant **31**
Ocean Club **11**
Old Spaghetti Factory, **13**
Olive Tree Cafe **41**
OnJin's Café **16**
Palomino **9**
Panda Cuisine **20**
Roy's Restaurant **36**

Ruth's Chris Steak House **11**
Sam Choy's Breakfast, Lunch, Crab
  & Big Aloha Brewery **3**
Sam Choy's Diamond Head
  Restaurant **38**
Sansei Seafood Restaurant
  and Sushi Bar **11**
Side Street Inn **17**
Sushi King **29**

Sushi Sasabune **21**
Swiss Haus **37**
3660 On the Rise **33**
To Chau **4**
Well Bento **28**
Willows **27**
Yanagi Sushi **12**
Yohei Sushi **2**

with flyingfish roe, hamachi, and soft-shell crab in season. Lunch and dinner specials help ease the bite of the bill, and ordering noodles or other less expensive a la carte items can also reduce the cost considerably.

1646B Kona St. (✆ 808/942-4466. Reservations recommended. Main courses $10–$25. AE, DC, DISC, MC, V. Mon–Sat 11am–2:30pm and 5pm–2am.

Assaggio ★ ITALIAN   The wildly popular chain, until recently the toast of suburban Oahu (see p. 135 for the Kailua location), moved into Ala Moana Center to a roar of approval and immediate success. Townies can now enjoy Assaggio's extensive, high-quality Italian offerings—at good prices. The lighter lunch menu features pasta dishes and house specialties (shrimp scampi, rigatoni alla ricotta) at prices around $10 and less. At dinner, a panoply of pastas and specialties streams out of the kitchen: at least nine chicken entrees, pasta dishes ranging from mushroom and clam to linguine primavera, and eight veal choices. One of Assaggio's best features is its prodigious seafood selection: shrimp, scallops, mussels, calamari, and fresh fish in so many preparations, ranging from plain garlic and olive oil to spicy tomato and wine sauces. Assaggio's excellent service and the fact that entrees are priced under $20 deserve our applause.

In the Ala Moana Center, 1450 Ala Moana Blvd. (✆ 808/942-3446. Reservations recommended. Main courses $8.90–$14.90 lunch; $10.90–$20.90 dinner. AE, DC, DISC, MC, V. Daily 11am–3pm; Sun–Thurs 4:30–9:30pm; Fri–Sat 4:30–10pm.

Brew Moon PACIFIC RIM/AMERICAN   Award-winning beers and an eclectic menu of sandwiches, pizza, seafood, and ethnic specialties (the ahi sampler of poke, blackened ahi and sashimi is popular) are featured at this industrial-tropical microbrewery in the Ward Centre. Diners, many of them under 30, can sit indoors or on the terrace to sample the wide-ranging menu. Poke, chicken curry, barbecued ribs and items from East and West draw the lunchtime and late-night crowd. Brew Moon's physical space was an attempt at an architectural statement, featuring curved banquettes, high ceilings, surprising niches, and views of mountain and sea.

Live entertainment begins at 9pm on Friday nights, when R&B, jazz, funk or contemporary Hawaiian music takes center stage. Sunday brunch is offered from 11am to 2pm and lunch from 2 to 4pm, when dinner service begins. Zero Gravity Hours, when drink prices are slashed ($2 for beer, $3 for house wines) are daily from 3 to 6pm and again Monday through Thursday 11pm to closing.

In the Ward Centre, 1200 Ala Moana Blvd. (✆ 808/593-0088. Reservations recommended. Main courses $8–$27.50. AE, DC, MC, V. Daily 11am–10pm; bar until 2am.

Compadres Mexican Bar & Grill *Value* MEXICAN   Memorable margaritas, tequila festivals, Cinco de Mayo, fundraisers, live Hawaiian music on Fridays, and every excuse for a party make this place an all-around good deal. The atmosphere here is festive, with one wall of glass windows looking out toward Ala Moana Park. The food—from chimichangas to enchilada platters to the simple pleasures of guacamole and salsa—includes some nifty choices for children, who get their own special keiki menu. Those with heftier appetites can choose huevos rancheros; eight different types of enchiladas; steak, chicken, and fish combination plates; fajitas; and nachos. For the reckless: the back-bar margarita, made with Gold tequila, Grand Marnier, fresh lime, sweet-and-sour, and orange juice.

In the Ward Centre, 1200 Ala Moana Blvd. (✆ 808/591-8307. Reservations recommended. Main courses $8–$19. AE, DC, DISC, MC, V. Mon–Thurs 11am–11pm; Fri–Sat 11am–midnight; Sun 11am–10pm; bar daily 11am–2am, depending on business.

gglers, dancers and an assortment of acrobats fill the street.

e shoots you a wide-eyed look as a seven-foot cartoon character approaches.

hat brought you here was wanting the kids

see something magical while they still believed in magic.

merica Online Keyword: Travel

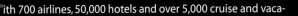

ith 700 airlines, 50,000 hotels and over 5,000 cruise and vaca-

on getaways, you can now go places you've always dreamed of.

Travelocity.com
A Sabre Company
Go Virtually Anywhere.

ORLD'S LEADING TRAVEL WEB SITE, 5 YEARS IN A ROW" WORLD TRAVEL AWARDS

Kincaid's Fish, Chop, and Steakhouse ⭐ SEAFOOD/STEAKS   Kincaid's is always winning surveys for one thing or another—best place for a business lunch, best seafood restaurant—because it pleases wide-ranging tastes and pocketbooks. Brisk service, a harbor view, and an extensive seafood menu keep the large dining room full. Fresh-fish sandwiches, seafood chowders and French onion soups, kiawe-grilled and herb-buttered salmon, fresh mahimahi with key-lime butter, and garlic prawns are among the extensive choices. We love the devil-may-care Dungeness crab and artichoke sandwich—open-faced, rich, and fabulous. You might want to save room for the true-blue key lime pie. Kincaid's is also a popular happy-hour rendezvous, with inexpensive beer and appetizers and live entertainment from 8:30 to 11:30 Friday and Saturday nights.

In the Ward Warehouse, 1050 Ala Moana Blvd. ✆ **808/591-2005.** Reservations recommended. Lunch $8.95–$15.95; dinner main courses $14.95–$49.95. AE, DC, DISC, MC, V. Daily 11am–10pm (open later for pupu).

L'Uraku ⭐⭐ *(Value)* EURO-JAPANESE   L'Uraku's pleasant, light-filled dining room and expanded fusion menu make it a great spot for lunch or dinner. It's not overly fussy, but still has the right touch of elegance for dining in style without breaking the bank. Chef Hiroshi Fukui, born in Japan and raised in Hawaii, was trained in the formal Japanese culinary tradition called *kaiseki;* he combines this training with fresh island ingredients and European cooking styles. Dishes such as seared scallops, garlic steak, and superb misoyaki butterfish are among the many stellar offerings. The $15 "Weekender lunch" is an unbelievable value: crab cake or shrimp, salad, and a choice of entree such as fresh salmon, almond-crusted fresh snapper, or the succulent misoyaki butterfish. Vegetarians should find comfort and pleasure in the Vegetarian's Dream, a medley of grilled tomatoes, eggplant, portabello mushrooms, and seasonal vegetables with a lively tofu sauce. L'Uraku is a find that has only gotten better with the years.

1341 Kapiolani Blvd. ✆ **808/955-0552.** Reservations recommended. Main courses $8.95–$17.50 lunch; $15.75–$27.75 dinner; $34 prix fixe. AE, DC, MC, V. Daily 11am–2pm and 5:30–10pm

OnJin's Café ⭐ *(Value)* FRENCH/ASIAN   OnJin's could appear in both "moderate" and "inexpensive" categories because it's fabulously inexpensive for lunch (gourmet fare at plate-lunch prices) and, although more expensive for dinner, is still a noteworthy value. OnJin Kim is a brilliant chef (formerly of the erstwhile Bagwell's in the Hyatt Regency and her own former Hanatei) who serves excellent fare at excellent prices. Expect long lines at lunch, a more relaxed mood at dinner, pleasant service, and an indoor-outdoor ambience in a rapidly developing part of Kakaako. (A movie multiplex is coming up nearby.) At lunch, you order and pay at the counter, but your superbly prepared snapper with lemon caper beurre blanc or salmon misoyaki arrives on a real plate—for under $7. Specials (beef bourguignonne, seafood jambalaya) change daily. For dinner, there's charred ahi with seven Japanese spices and a selection of entrees remarkable not only for their friendly prices, but also for the sophisticated execution that is OnJin's signature. Whether it's soft-shell crab lightly fried in almond flour or the top-of-the-line bouillabaisse (an OnJin signature), you'll know you've arrived in OnJin heaven.

401 Kamakee St. ✆ **808/589-1666.** Reservations not accepted for lunch; recommended for dinner. Lunch main courses and specials $4.95–$6.95; dinner main courses $14–$21. AE, DISC, MC, V. Mon–Fri 11am–2pm; Tues–Sat 5–9pm.

INEXPENSIVE

I ♥ Country Cafe *(Kids)* INTERNATIONAL   Give yourself time to peruse the lengthy list of specials posted on the menu board, as well as the prodigious printed menu. Stand in line at the counter, place your order and pay, and find a Formica-topped table; or wait about 10 minutes for your takeout order to appear on a Styrofoam plate heaped with salad and other accompaniments. The mind-boggling selection includes nine types of cheese steaks (including vegetarian tofu), Cajun meat loaf, Thai curries, various stir-fries, shoyu chicken, vegetarian or eggplant lasagna, chicken Dijon, Cajun-style ahi, and other choices spanning many cultures and tastes. Take a good look at the diners and notice that the menu appeals equally to bodybuilders and hedonists.

In Ala Moana Plaza, 451 Piikoi St. ℂ **808/596-8108.** Main courses $5–$8.75. AE, DC, DISC, MC, V. Mon–Thurs 10am–9pm; Fri 10am–9:30pm; Sat 8am–9:30pm; Sun 8am–9pm.

Kakaako Kitchen GOURMET PLATE LUNCHES   This popular industrial-style plate-lunch haven is busier than ever since it moved to the trendy Ward Centre in March 2000, with an expanded concept that includes dinner service. The trademark Styrofoam plates, warehouse ambience, and home-style cooking remain, only now there's more dining space and, occasionally, adequate Ward Centre parking. The menu, which changes every 3 to 4 months, includes a seared ahi sandwich with tobiko (flyingfish roe) aioli; the signature charbroiled ahi steak; sandwiches; beef stew; five-spice shoyu chicken; the very popular meat loaf; and other multiethnic entrees. The three-bean chili is a winner, but a recent order of sautéed mahimahi disappointed.

In the Ward Centre, 1200 Ala Moana Blvd. ℂ **808/596-7488.** Lunch and dinner main courses $5.95–$11.95. MC, V for bills over $100. Mon–Fri 7–10am, 10:30am–9pm; Sat–Sun 7–11am; Sat 11:30am–9pm; Sun 11:30am–5pm.

Kua Aina ℛ AMERICAN   The ultimate sandwich shop, for years a North Shore fixture, expanded to the Ward Centre area (near Borders and Starbucks), and the result is dizzying. Phone in your order if you can. During lunch and dinner hours, people wait patiently in long lines for the famous burgers and sandwiches: the beef burgers with heroic toppings; mahimahi with ortega and cheese (a legend); grilled eggplant and peppers; roast turkey; tuna-avocado; roast beef and avocado; and about a dozen other selections on Kaiser roll, multigrain wheat, or rye breads. The sandwiches are excellent, the fries legendary, and the outdoor section with tables, thank God, has grown—but there still may be a wait during lunch hour. The takeout business is brisk.

In Ward Village, 1116 Auahi St. ℂ **808/591-9133.** Sandwiches $3.50–$5.70. No credit cards. Daily 10:30am–9pm.

Panda Cuisine ℛ DIM SUM/SEAFOOD/HONG-KONG STYLE CHINESE   This is dim sum heaven, not only for the selection, but also for the late-night dim sum service, a rare thing for what is a morning and lunchtime tradition in Hong Kong. Panda's dim sum selection—spinach-scallop, chive, taro, shrimp dumplings, pork hash, and some 50-plus others—is a real pleaser. (*Tip:* the spinach-scallop and taro puff varieties are a cut above.) The reckless can spring for the live Maine lobster and Dungeness crab in season, or the king clam and steamed fresh fish, but the steaming bamboo carts yielding toothsome surprises are hard to resist. Noodles and sizzling platters are good accompaniments to the dim sum.

641 Keeaumoku St. ℂ **808/947-1688.** Main courses $7.95–$28.95. AE, MC, V. Mon–Sat 10:30am–2:30pm, 5pm–2am; Sun 5–10pm.

Side Street Inn ℛ *Finds* LOCAL   After their own fancy kitchens have closed, some of Honolulu's top chefs head to this smoky room with TV sets over the bar and a back room with a dart board and Miller Lite and Budweiser neon lights. Very camp. The terrific food is a surprise, as this small side street near Ala Moana Center is noted more for its seedy bars than for pesto-crusted ahi and gourmet Nalo greens. But hey—the grinds (that's local slang for eats) are fabulous, with no pretensions and a spirited local feeling. The barbecued baby back ribs in lilikoi sauce are tender, flavorful, and a steal at $10.75, and you can find 10- to 16-ounce steaks, charbroiled or on sizzling platters, for $13.50 to $15. Our faves are the blackened ahi, pesto-crusted ahi, fresh steamed manila clams (tender, in a wine-garlic broth), shrimp scampi, and escargots. High on calories, but worth it. By the end of the meal, your clothes may smell like smoke—but chances are, you'll return.

1225 Hopaka St. ☎ **808/591-0253.** Reservations accepted. Main courses $7.25–$16. AE, DC, DISC, MC, V. Daily 10:30am–1:30pm and 4pm–12:30am.

ALOHA TOWER MARKETPLACE

Chai's Island Bistro ✦ PACIFIC RIM/ASIAN   We give Chai's high marks for food but have less enthusiasm for service and ambience, especially at dinner, when the overamped music can detract from the dining experience. Also, the dinner entree prices have risen significantly. But the food is generally of high quality and creativity. The 200-seat restaurant has high ceilings, a good location (though not on the waterfront), indoor-outdoor seating, and a discreetly placed (not in-your-face) open kitchen. The appetizer sampler for two appears on a boat-size platter—a feast of ahi katsu with yellow curry sauce and wasabi; crisp duck lumpia, tasty and greaseless; macadamia nut–crusted tiger prawns; and Alaskan king crab cakes. This is an appetizer that could be an entree, or a starter for two, and is my favorite item on the menu. The fusion dishes include steamed, fresh, Chinese-style onaga, and an ample selection of vegetarian dishes. *A caveat:* The nightly entertainment tends to be excruciatingly loud, especially when Hapa plays on Thursday and Friday (see p. 237).

In the Aloha Tower Marketplace, 1 Aloha Tower Dr. ☎ **808/585-0011.** Reservations recommended. Lunch main courses $10.95–$19.95; dinner main courses $28.95–$39.95. AE, DC, MC, V. Sun buffet 10am; Mon–Fri 11am–4pm; daily 4–10pm.

Don Ho's Island Grill HAWAIIAN/CONTEMPORARY ISLAND   Don Ho's shrine to Don Ho is a mix of nostalgic interior elements: koa paneling, thatched roof, split-bamboo ceilings, old pictures of Ho with celebrities, faux palm trees, and open sides looking out onto the harbor. It's kitschy and charming, down to the vinyl pareu-printed tablecloths and the flower behind the server's ear. Don Ho's has become one of the significant late-night musical venues of Honolulu, packing in sold-out crowds for special concerts by local musical icons like Amy Gilliom and Willie K.

In the Aloha Tower Marketplace, 1 Aloha Tower Dr. ☎ **808/528-0807.** Reservations recommended. Main courses $6.95–$15.95. AE, DC, DISC, MC, V. Daily 10am–10pm; nightclub (days vary) open until 2am.

Gordon Biersch Brewery Restaurant NEW AMERICAN/PACIFIC RIM German-style lagers brewed on the premises would be enough of a draw, but the food is also a lure at Gordon Biersch, one of Honolulu's liveliest after-work hangouts. Pacific and Island fresh seafood highlight the eclectic menu. The lanai bar and the brewery bar—open until 1am—are the brightest spots in the marketplace, teeming with downtown types who nosh on pot stickers, grilled steaks, baby back ribs, chicken pizza, garlic fries, and any number of American classics with deft cross-cultural touches. Extensive renovations in 1999 created a stage area for live music, a popular weekend feature.

Kids Family-Friendly Restaurants

Honolulu is constantly battling its image as an expensive destination. It's true that accommodations on Oahu are pricey, but the abundance of ethnic restaurants (born of burgeoning new ethnic populations) and the high percentage of working mothers in Hawaii creates an entirely different scenario for dining. Even with a sluggish economy, residents eat out—because they're busy, because they want to, and because many popular ethnic traditions aren't so easy to duplicate at home. What makes a good family restaurant in Hawaii? More than the presence of high chairs, we think it's friendliness, affordability, and menu choices that take into consideration the tastes and preferences of multiple generations. Not including the usual fast-food burger joints that are perenially popular with the kids, here are some suggestions for family-friendly eateries in Honolulu.

Genki Sushi, 900 Kapahulu Ave. (✆ **808/735-8889**), is part entertainment, part assertiveness training, and part culinary pleasure. Kids love to lunge for their favorites among the freshly made, individually wrapped sushis that parade by on conveyor belts, and the slower ones who miss out the first time around get a chance on the next revolution. Sit with your family around the curvy counters and empty your plates without emptying your pocketbook. See p. 132.

Blockbuster Video outlets are often adjacent to places that kids and teenagers love. And because this may mean less cooking, these places are popular among parents, too. Adjacent to Ala Moana Center, Honolulu's busiest Blockbuster is smack dab next to I ♥ **Country Cafe,** 451 Piikoi St., Ala Moana Plaza (✆ **808/596-8108**). I ♥ Country Cafe offers everything from meat loaf to shoyu chicken, burgers, vegetarian

In the Aloha Tower Marketplace, 1 Aloha Tower Dr. ✆ 808/599-4877. Reservations recommended. Main courses $8–$20. AE, DC, DISC, MC, V. Sun–Wed 10:30am–10:30pm; Thurs–Sat 10:30am–midnight.

DOWNTOWN

Downtowners love the informal walk-in cafes lining one side of attractive **Bishop Square,** at 1001 Bishop St. (at King St.), in the middle of the business district, where free entertainment is offered every Friday during lunch hour. The popular **Che Pasta** is a stalwart here, chic enough for business meetings and not too formal (or expensive) for a spontaneous rendezvous over pasta and minestrone. Some places in Bishop Square open for breakfast and lunch, others just for lunch, but most close when business offices empty.

Note: Keep in mind that **Restaurant Row,** which features several hot new establishments, offers free validated parking in the evening.

Baci at Restaurant Row 🎉 ITALIAN   This is the place for good Italian food in a hip, stylish ambience—dressier than the neighborhood trattoria, with latenight entertainment and a highly visible Restaurant-Row presence. Baci is for women and men in serious black seeking noteworthy ravioli, scampi, and the full range of Italian specialties. The intimately lit, two-story dining room has a small stage upstairs where live entertainment is offered on Fridays and rave dishes, and stir-frys, for takeout or dining in—and there's a new branch in Kahala Mall. See p. 119.

In Ward Warehouse, the classic pre-teen pleaser is the **Old Spaghetti Factory,** 1050 Ala Moana Blvd. (© **808/591-2513**), where kids have been sucking in spaghetti and meatballs for years. Ornate Italianate decor, beveled glass everywhere, and an affordable "Just for Kids" menu for those 12 years old and under (offering a $3.75 spaghetti with choice of sauce, meatballs, or macaroni and cheese), make this a bonanza for the fun-loving younger set.

On the outskirts of Honolulu, the **Swiss Inn,** 5730 Kalanianaole Hwy., Niu Valley Shopping Center (© **808/377-5447**), is another family favorite—not just for its children's-portion spaghetti, but also because it serves European-style frankfurters, with Swiss potato salad or french fries. The new owners haven't changed the affordable, pleasing elements that made Swiss Inn such a hit for decades. Children can feel much more elegant dining here than at a sandwich shop, and they don't have to dress up. Swiss Inn offers a combination of good value, pleasing service, and good food, including a cheese fondue for those too young to consider cholesterol.

Finally, we come to **Zippy's,** the mecca of chili and saimin. There are nearly two dozen locations on Oahu alone (call © **808/955-6622** for the one nearest you). All branches feature cheap, tasty chili, burgers, sandwiches, salads, and all-day American fare that's popular among parents and kids. Tasty vegetarian chili and meatless, smoky Boca Burgers are among the healthy choices for vegetarians.

parties 3 nights a week. Although Baci is still tweaking its entertainment offerings and searching for its late-night identity, it's a viable choice for the Italian classics. The three-course set menu (soup or salad, entree, dessert) for $12.95, and the dinner prix fixe for $22.95 are noteworthy values.

On Restaurant Row, 500 Ala Moana Blvd. © **808/550-8005**. Reservations recommended. Lunch main courses $7.95–$14.95, lunch set menu $12.95; dinner main courses $10–$24.50, dinner set menu $22.95. AE, DC, DISC, MC, V. Mon–Fri 11am–2pm, nightly 5:30–10pm; Wed–Thurs and Sat rave parties from 10pm–2am; Fri late-night appetizer menu 10pm–1:30am.

Duc's Bistro FRENCH/VIETNAMESE   Surrounded by lei stands, marked by a cheery neon sign, this cozy 80-seater stands out at the mauka end of Maunakea in Chinatown. Narrow and quietly elegant, the restaurant has three components: the front room with its windows looking out to Maunakea Street, the windowless back room, and the tiny bar. It has an edgy chic more like Manhattan than Honolulu, and the food is—sometimes—beautifully prepared and presented. Sauces for the meats hint of Grand Marnier (duck supreme), Bordeaux (lamb Raymond Oliver), VSOP cognac (steak au poivre), Pernod (prawns and oysters), and fresh herbs and vegetables. From the seafood spring rolls with shrimp, taro, and mushrooms, to the Meal in a Bowl (rice noodles heaped with fresh herbs and julienned vegetables, topped with lime dressing—excellent!), creative touches abound. There's live jazz nightly except Thursday, when Hawaiian music takes over and surprise vocalists and hula dancers are known to join in the fun.

1188 Maunakea St., Chinatown. © 808/531-6325. Reservations recommended. Lunch main dishes $9.95–$15.95; dinner main dishes $12.95–$27.95. AE, MC, V. Mon–Fri 11:30am–1:30pm; daily 5–10pm; bar open later.

Indigo Eurasian Cuisine ✪ EURASIAN   Hardwood floors, red brick, wicker, high ceilings, and an overall feeling of Indochine luxury give Indigo a stylish edge. You can dine indoors or in a garden setting, on menu offerings such as pot stickers, Buddhist bao buns, savory brochettes, tandoori chicken breast, vegetable tarts, Asian-style noodles and dumplings, lilikoi-glazed baby back ribs, and cleverly named offerings from East and West. Chef Glenn Chu is popular, but too many claim that Indigo is more style than flavor. The adjoining Green Room is packed and smoky.

1121 Nuuanu Ave. © 808/521-2900. Reservations recommended. Lunch $6–$16.25; dinner main dishes $12.50–$22.50. DC, DISC, MC, V. Tues–Fri 11:30am–2pm; Tues–Sat 6—9:30pm; martini time in the Green Room Tues–Fri 5–6:30pm.

Jameson's Seafood Grill SEAFOOD   Ed Greene of the Haleiwa Jameson's has expanded his domain from the barefoot-in-the-sand North Shore to the business core of Honolulu. His new, 80-seat Restaurant Row digs have an open-air section, a private room for up to 30, and a time-tested menu of seafood favorites. This is not dazzling cuisine, but it's popular, especially if you're not counting calories. The grilled crab and shrimp sandwich is guilt-laden and scrumptious, and the salmon paté, a Jameson's signature, could make your day. For lunchtime vegetarians, there are sautéed mushrooms, garden burgers, and Caesar and other salads. For others, there are fresh fish entrees, burgers, black-bean shrimp, and appetizers of calamari and oysters. Although prices escalate for dinner, the lunch menu is offered throughout the day, a nice touch for those seeking lighter and more reasonable fare in a convivial atmosphere. At the adjacent Row Bar, you can order appetizers from Jameson's.

In Restaurant Row, 500 Ala Moana Blvd. © 808/521-6488. Reservations recommended. Lunch main courses $11.95–$13.95, dinner main courses $13.95–$29.95; dinner includes lunch menu. AE, DC, DISC, MC, V. Mon–Fri 11am–9pm; Sat 6–9pm.

Legend Seafood Restaurant ✪ DIM SUM/SEAFOOD   It's like dining in Hong Kong here, with a Chinese-speaking clientele poring over Chinese newspapers and the clatter of chopsticks punctuating conversations. Excellent dim sum comes in bamboo steamers that beckon seductively from carts. Although dining here is a form of assertiveness training (you must wave madly to catch the server's eye and then point to what you want), the system doesn't deter fans from returning. Among our favorites: deep-fried taro puffs and prawn dumplings, shrimp dim sum, vegetable dumplings, and the open-faced seafood with shiitake, scallops, and a tofu product called *aburage.* Dim sum is served only at lunch, but dinnertime seafood dishes comfort sufficiently. Not a very elegant restaurant, but the food is serious and great.

In the Chinese Cultural Plaza, 100 N. Beretania St. © 808/532-1868. Reservations recommended. Most items under $15. AE, DC, MC, V. Mon–Fri 10:30am–2pm and 5:30–10pm; Sat–Sun 8am–2pm and 5:30–10pm.

Ocean Club ✪ SEAFOOD   Ocean Club could be listed as a restaurant or a nightclub. This sleek, chic magnet has redefined happy hour with its extended hours of slashed prices, excellent appetizer-only seafood menu, and ultracool ambience for the 30 and under set. Galvanized steel counters, mahogany bars lined with shoyu bottles, linoleum tile floors, and oddly attractive pillars resembling *pahu* (Hawaiian drums) make for a wonderfully eclectic mix. Add DJs in hip garb spinning hip-hop, and you get the picture. The menu of appetizers lives up to its "ultimate cocktail hour" claim, especially from 4:30 to 8pm nightly, when great seafood is slashed to half-price and the upbeat mood starts spiraling. A happy-hour sampling: toothsome dips of spinach, artichoke or crab, served with tortilla chips, salsa, and sour cream; ahi tacos and sashimi for a pittance; and standards such as buffalo wings and fried calamari.

On Restaurant Row, 500 Ala Moana Blvd. (C) 808/526-9888. No T-shirts or beachwear allowed. Minimum age 23. All items $5–$9 ($2–$5 at happy hour). AE, DISC, MC, V. Tues–Thurs 4:30pm–2am; Fri 4:30pm–3am; Sat 6pm–3am.

Palomino ✦ AMERICAN REGIONAL   Palomino offers splendid harbor views, interesting architecture, conscientious service, and respectable food. Combined, they make up for the dubious (and ubiquitous) artworks. It is more Chicago than Hawaii, lacking in a sense of place but proffering dishes that will likely bring you back. I return for the wild mushroom salad and cedar-plank roasted salmon, and because it's walking distance from Hawaii Theatre. The pizzas (one with caramelized onion and spinach), roasted garlic, shrimp in grape leaves, and kiawe-grilled fish get high marks, as does the devastating dessert called Caffè Affogato (white-chocolate ice cream, espresso, and whipped cream).

In the Harbor Court Building, 66 Queen St., mezzanine. (C) 808/528-2400. Reservations recommended. Main dishes $6.95–$26.95. AE, DC, DISC, MC, V. Mon–Thurs 11am–11:30pm; Fri 11am–1am; Sat 4pm–1am; Sun 4–11:30pm.

Sansei Seafood Restaurant and Sushi Bar ✦ SUSHI/ASIAN-PACIFIC RIM   Perpetual award winner D. K. Kodama, who built Kapalua's Sansei into one of Maui's most popular eateries, has become something of a local legend with his exuberant brand of sushi and fusion cooking. Although some of the flavors (sweet Thai chile sauce with cilantro, for example) may be too fussy for sushi purists, there are ample choices for a full range of palates. On the extensive menu appear Sansei's trademark, award-winning Asian rock shrimp cake, and Sansei special sushi (crab, cilantro, cucumber, and avocado with a sweet chile sauce), as well as Spam musubi (help!), and miso scallops. I favor the quieter traditional selections, such as the elegant yellowtail sushi and the Japanese miso eggplant. Kodama has added karaoke and late-night programs beginning at 10pm.

On Restaurant Row, 500 Ala Moana Blvd. (C) 808/536-6286. Reservations recommended. Main courses $10.95 (appetizer size) to $37.95. AE, DISC, MC, V. Mon–Fri 11am–2pm; daily 5–10pm; local DJ Thurs 10pm–2am.

To Chau ✦✦ (Value) VIETNAMESE PHO   The three stars are strictly for the pho, which many think is the best in a city studded with pho houses. Ambience is nil, you'll have to stand in a line that normally numbers 13 to 15 hopefuls, and service can be brusque. But that is all part of the charm of this no-nonsense Formica-style pho house, located in a stone building along a river and marked, without fail, by a queue of Asian diners who bespeak authority regarding what is and is not the real Vietnamese beef and noodle soup. This is. The anticipation is heightened by the view of diners relishing their steaming, long-awaited orders, visible through the windows as you wait your turn on the sidewalk. There are shrimp and spring rolls and chicken and pork chop plates, but I've never seen anyone order anything but pho. And what a soup this is! The broth is clear, hearty, and marvelously flavored with hints of cinnamon and spice. You can order it with several choices of steak, and it comes with a heaping platter of fresh bean sprouts, basil, hot green peppers, and an Asian green called boke (*bo-kay*). It's worth the wait, and so inexpensive.

1007 River St., Chinatown. © **808/533-4549.** Pho $3.85–$5.20. No credit cards. Daily 8am–2:30pm.

Yanagi Sushi ⭐ JAPANESE   We love the late-night hours, the sushi bar, and the extensive choices of combination lunches and dinners. But we also love the a la carte Japanese menu, which covers everything from *chazuke* (a comfort food of rice with tea, salmon, seaweed, and other condiments) to shabu-shabu and other steaming earthenware-pot dishes. Complete dinners come with choices of sashimi, shrimp tempura, broiled salmon, New York steak, and many other possibilities. You can dine here affordably or extravagantly, on $6 noodles or a $30 lobster *nabe* (cooked in a single pot of seasoned broth). Consistently crisp tempura and fine spicy ahi hand-rolled sushi also make Yanagi worth remembering.

762 Kapiolani Blvd. © **808/597-1525.** Reservations recommended. Main courses $8–$33; complete dinners $11.50–$17.95. AE, DC, DISC, MC, V. Daily 11am–2pm; Mon–Sat 5:30pm–2am; Sun 5:30–10pm.

KALIHI/SAND ISLAND

La Mariana AMERICAN   Just try to find a spot more evocative or nostalgic than this South Seas oasis at lagoon's edge in the bowels of industrial Honolulu, with carved tikis, glass balls suspended in fishing nets, shell chandeliers, and old tables made from koa trees. In the back section, the entire ceiling is made of tree limbs. This unique 46-year-old restaurant is popular for lunch, sunset appetizers, and impromptu Friday- and Saturday-night sing-alongs at the piano bar, where a colorful crowd (including some Don Ho look-alikes) gathers to sing Hawaiian classics like a 1950s high school Glee Club. It is delightful. The seared Cajun-style ahi is your best bet as appetizer or entree; La Mariana is more about spirit and ambience than food.

50 Sand Island Rd. © **808/848-2800.** Reservations recommended, especially on weekends. Lunch items $6–$7.75; dinner main courses $12.75–$20.95. AE, MC, V. Daily 11am–3pm; pupu 3–5pm; Mon 5–8pm; Tues, Thurs, and Sun 5–9pm; Fri–Sat 5–10pm. Turn makai (toward the ocean) on Sand Island Rd. from Nimitz Hwy.; immediately after the first stoplight on Sand Island, take a right and drive toward the ocean; it's not far from the airport.

Sam Choy's Breakfast, Lunch, Crab & Big Aloha Brewery ISLAND CUISINE/SEAFOOD   This is a happy, carefree eatery—elegance and cholesterol be damned. Chef/restaurateur Sam Choy's crab house features great fun and gigantic meals (a Choy trademark). Imagine dining in an all-wood sampan (the centerpiece of the 11,000-sq.-ft. restaurant) and washing your hands in an oversized wok in the center of the room. A 2,000-gallon live-crab tank lines the open kitchen with an assortment of crabs in season: Kona, Maryland, Samoan, Dungeness, and Florida stone crabs. Clam chowder, seafood gumbos, oysters from the oyster bar, and assorted poke are also offered at dinner, which, in Choy fashion, comes complete with soup, salad, and entree. Children's menus are an additional family feature. Several varieties of "Big Aloha Beer," brewed on-site, go well with the crab and poke.

580 Nimitz Hwy., Iwilei. © **808/545-7979.** Reservations recommended for lunch and dinner. Main courses $5–$10 breakfast; $6–$27 lunch; $19–$35 dinner. AE, DC, DISC, MC, V. Daily 6:30am–4pm (breakfast until 10:30 Mon–Fri, 11:30 Sat–Sun) and 5–10pm. Located in the Iwilei industrial area near Honolulu Harbor, across the street from Gentry Pacific Center

Local Chains & Familiar Names

Todai, 1910 Ala Moana Blvd. (© **808/947-1000**), a string of Japanese seafood buffet restaurants with locations ranging from Dallas to Portland to Beverly Center, is packing 'em in at the gateway to Waikiki with bountiful tables of sushi (40 kinds), hot seafood entrees (tempura, calamari, fresh fish, gyoza, king crab legs, teppanyaki), and delectable desserts. Not much ambience, but no one cares; the food is terrific, the selection impressive, and the operation as smooth as the green tea cheesecake.

Ala Moana Center's third floor is a mecca for dining and schmoozing. The open-air **Mai Tai Bar** is a popular watering hole. Next door are the boisterous **Bubba Gump Shrimp Company** (© **808/949-4867**) and the **California Pizza Kitchen** (© **808/941-7715**), which also maintains branches in Kahala Mall, 4211 Waialae Ave. (© **808/737-9446**), and Pearlridge, 98–1005 Moanalua Road (© **808/487-7741**).

L&L Drive-Inn remains a plate-lunch bonanza islandwide, with 45 locations in Hawaii (36 on Oahu alone). **Zippy's Restaurants** —at last count 21 of them on Oahu—is the maestro of quick meals, with a surprisingly good selection of fresh seafood, saimin, chili, and local fare, plus the wholesome new low-fat, vegetarian "Shintani Cuisine," sold in selected branches and deli counters. Every restaurant offers a daily Shintani special, and at several locations (Kahala, Vineyard, Pearlridge, Kapolei, Waipio) you can order cold Shintani items in 2-pound portions to take home and heat up.

It's hard to spend more than $7 for the French and Vietnamese specials at the **Ba-le Sandwich Shops:** *pho,* croissants as good as the espresso, and wonderful taro/tapioca desserts. Among Ba-le's 20 locations are those at Ala Moana Center (© **808/944-4752**) and 333 Ward Ave. (© **808/591-0935**). A Ba-le location at Manoa Marketplace, 2855 E. Manoa Rd. (© **808/988-1407**), serves a terrific selection of Thai dishes in an enlarged dining area, making it as much a restaurant as a place for takeout food. For smoothies, head to **Jamba Juice,** with seven locations at last count, from Kahala Mall to Ward Village, Kapahulu, Pearlridge, Kailua, and the new DFS Galleria on Kalakaua Ave. (© **808/ 926-4944**). The ubiquitous **Boston's North End Pizza Bakery** chain claims an enthusiastic following with its reasonable prices and generous toppings. Boston's can be found in Kaimuki, Kailua, Kaneohe, Pearlridge, and Makakilo.

In Waikiki, the local **Hard Rock Cafe** is at 1837 Kapiolani Blvd. (© **808/955-7383**), while at the Ala Moana end of Waikiki, **Outback Steakhouse,** 1765 Ala Moana Blvd (© **808/951-6274**), serves great steaks and is always full. In downtown's Restaurant Row, beef eaters can also chow down at **Ruth's Chris Steak House,** 500 Ala Moana Blvd. (© **808/599-3860**).

Yohei Sushi ★ *Finds* JAPANESE/SUSHI BAR   Yohei is difficult to find; it's tucked away in a small, nondescript complex just before Dillingham Blvd. crosses the bridge into Kalihi, Honolulu's industrial area. But it's well worth the hunt, especially for lovers of authentic Tokyo-style sushi. Try the sweet shrimp (amaebi), surf clam (akagai), yellowtail tuna (hamachi), butterfly tuna (negi toro temaki), bluefish (kohada gari chiso temaki), and wonderful assortment of seafood, fresh as can be. An evening at Yohei is like a trip to a Tokyo sushi bar, where regulars know the chef, and even familiar gastronomic territory can be a grand adventure.

1111 Dillingham Blvd., across from Honolulu Community College. (©) **808/841-3773.** Reservations recommended. Lunch entrees $6–$15; complete dinners $15–$26. DC, MC, V. Mon–Sat 11am–1:45pm and 5–9:30pm.

MANOA VALLEY/MOILIILI/MAKIKI
VERY EXPENSIVE
Chef Mavro Restaurant ★★★ PROVENÇAL/HAWAII REGIONAL Chef/owner George Mavrothalassitis, a native of Provence, has fans all over the world who have admired his creativity since his days at Halekulani's La Mer and Seasons at the Four Seasons Resort Wailea. His restaurant is the only independently operated AAA Four-Diamond restaurant in Hawaii, located in a conveniently accessible, untouristy neighborhood in McCully where you can order prix fixe or a la carte, with or without wine pairings. And they are dazzling pairings. To his list of signature items (filet of moi with crisp scales, sautéed mushrooms, and saffron coulis; award-winning onaga baked in Hawaiian-salt crust), he's added new favorites: Hudson Valley foie gras terrine, Keahole lobster in vanilla-coconut sauce, and a coriander-crusted beef entrecôte that was featured in *Wine Spectator*. Hints of Tahitian vanilla, lemongrass, ogo, rosemary, and Madras curry add exotic flavors to the French-inspired cooking and fresh island ingredients. The desserts are extraordinary, especially the lilikoi malassadas with guava coulis. The split-level room is quietly cordial, and the menu changes monthly to highlight seasonal ingredients.

1969 S. King St. (©) **808/944-4714.** Reservations recommended. Main courses $27–$38; prix fixe $48–$85. AE, DC, DISC, MC, V. Daily 6–9:30pm.

EXPENSIVE
Alan Wong's Restaurant ★★ HAWAII REGIONAL CUISINE   Alan Wong is one of Hawaii's most popular chefs, but the service at his bustling eatery has often suffered because of his popularity. Long waits in front of the elevator have angered many. But the worshipful foodies come from all over the state, drawn by the food—which is brilliant—and a menu that is irresistible. The 90-seat room has a glassed-in terrace and open kitchen. Sensitive lighting and curly koa wall panels accent an unobstrusively pleasing environment—casual but not too. The menu's cutting-edge offerings sizzle with the Asian flavors of lemongrass, sweet-and-sour, garlic, and wasabi, deftly melded with the fresh seafood and produce of the islands. The California roll is a triumph, made with salmon roe, wasabi, and Kona lobster instead of rice, and served warm. We love the opihi shooters, day-boat scallops, and fresh-fish preparations. But don't get attached to any one item, as the menu changes daily.

1857 S. King St., 3rd floor. (©) **808/949-2526.** Reservations recommended. Main courses $15–$30; chef's tasting menu $85. AE, DC, MC, V. Daily 5–10pm.

MODERATE

Contemporary Museum Cafe ⊛ HEALTHFUL GOURMET   The surroundings are an integral part of the dining experience at this tiny lunchtime
cafe, part of an art museum nestled on the slopes of Tantalus amid carefully cultivated Asian gardens, with a breathtaking view of Diamond Head and priceless
contemporary artwork displayed indoors and out. The menu is limited to sandwiches, soups, salads, and appetizers, but you won't leave disappointed: They're
the perfect lunchtime fare, especially in this environment. Before crowning the
meal with flourless chocolate cake, consider the grilled vegetable bruschetta,
Gorgonzola-walnut spread, garden burger, black-bean pita wrap, or fresh-fish
specials. If Noreen Lam's fresh-baked chocolate chip cookies are hiding in the
kitchen, snatch 'em.

In the Contemporary Museum, 2411 Makiki Heights Dr. ☎ 808/523-3362. Reservations recommended.
Main courses $8–$12. AE, MC, V. Tues–Sat 11am–3pm; Sun noon–3pm.

Donato's ⊛ SOUTHERN ITALIAN   The new kid on the block, Donato's
has settled in comfortably, upstairs in Manoa Marketplace where two windowed
sides and an intimate loft complement the fine Italian fare that appears from the
open kitchen. Donato Loperfido, a native of Alberobello in Puglia, Italy, is cooking up a storm, turning out dishes like risotto with mushrooms and truffle oil;
spaghetti al cartoccio (spaghetti with seafood, garlic, white wine, and spicy
tomato sauce, cooked in parchment); and a superb orecchiette (ear-shaped
pasta) with luscious fresh tomatoes, arugula, Parmesan and romano cheeses and
a lusty dose of garlic. It's fantastic—clean and crisp, pleasing to the eye, a symphony of tingling flavors. Another fave: the fresh mussels and manila clams with
cannellini beans, cooked in a white wine broth with generous slivers of garlic—
a taste sensation. The wine list is reasonable and the desserts (Gianduia chocolate soufflé, lemon-lime sorbet with Italian lemon liqueur), are legendary. If you
love Italian fare, it's worth a drive to Manoa Valley.

In Manoa Marketplace, 2756 Woodlawn Dr. ☎ 808/988-2000. Reservations recommended. Main courses
$13.95–$25.95. AE, DISC, MC, V. Sun–Thurs 5:30–10pm; Fri–Sat 5:30–10:30pm.

Maple Garden SZECHUAN   It hums like a top and rarely disappoints.
Maple Garden is known for its garlic eggplant, Peking duck, and Chinaman's
Hat, a version of mu shu pork, available in a vegetarian version as well. The crisp
green beans are out of this world. Other hits: braised scallops with Chinese
mushrooms, sautéed spinach, and prawns in chile sauce. There are ample vegetarian selections and dozens of seafood entrees—everything from sea cucumbers
and braised salmon to lobster with black-bean sauce. An ever-expanding visual
feast adorns the dining-room walls, covered with noted artist John Young's original drawings, sketches, and murals.

909 Isenberg St. ☎ 808/941-6641. Main courses $5–$29.50 (most $8–$9). AE, DISC, MC, V. Daily
11am–2pm and 5:30–10pm.

Sushi King ⟨Value⟩ JAPANESE   This is a top value for lovers of Japanese food.
Brusque service can't deter the throngs that arrive for the excellent lunch specials. At arrestingly low prices, the jumbo platters come with soup, pickles, California roll sushi, and your choice of chicken teriyaki, beef teriyaki, shrimp and
vegetable tempura, or calamari and vegetable tempura. Other combination
lunches offer generous choices that include sashimi, tempura, butterfish, fried
oysters, and noodles hot and cold. Early bird specials are offered daily from 5:30
to 6:30pm.

2700 S. King St. ✆ **808/947-2836.** Reservations recommended. Main courses $11.50–$25. AE, DC, DISC, MC, V. Wed–Mon 11:30am–2pm and 5:30pm–2am; Tues 5:30–10pm.

Willows LOCAL   Food is not the headliner here; the ambience is. Willows will never reachieve the charm and nostalgia of its early kamaaina days, but it has been beautifully restored and the food is more than adequate, with some of the Hawaiian dishes (laulau, lomi salmon, poke) quite good. There just aren't many places in Hawaii anymore with this kind of tropical setting. Shoes click on hardwood floors in rooms surrounded by lush foliage and fountains fed by the natural springs of the area. The dining rooms are open-air, with private umbrella tables scattered about. While the restaurant is buffet only, the upstairs dining room, called Top of the Willows, offers sit-down service and a pricier a la carte menu.

817 Hausten St. ✆ **808/952-9200.** Reservations recommended. Lunch buffet $14.95; dinner buffet $24.95; Sun brunch $24.95; upstairs a la carte main dishes $18.25–$24.95. AE, DC, DISC, MC, V. Daily 11am–2pm and 5:30–9pm. Upstairs dining room daily 5:30–9:30pm.

INEXPENSIVE

Andy's Sandwiches & Smoothies GOURMET HEALTH FOOD   It started as a health-food restaurant, expanded into a juice bar, and today is a neighborhood fixture for fresh baked bread, healthy breakfasts and lunches (its mango muffins are famous), and vegetarian fare. Andy's roadside stops always carry fresh papayas, sandwiches, and healthy snacks for folks on the run. The ahi deluxe sandwich is tops, but the fresh roasted turkey sandwiches are the acclaimed favorite.

2904 E. Manoa Rd., opposite Manoa Marketplace. ✆ **808/988-6161.** Also at 745 Keeaumoku St. near Ala Moana Center. ✆ **808/946-6161.** Most items less than $5. MC, V. Mon–Thurs 7am–6pm; Fri 7am–5pm; Sun 7am–2pm.

Chiang Mai Thai Cuisine THAI   Chiang Mai made sticky rice famous in Honolulu, serving it in bamboo steamers with fish and exotic curries that have retained a following. Menu items include toothsome red, green, and yellow curries; the signature Cornish game hen in lemongrass and spices; and a garlic-infused green papaya salad marinated in tamarind sauce. Spicy shrimp soup, eggplant with basil and tofu, and the vegetarian green curry are favorites.

2239 S. King St. ✆ **808/941-1151.** Reservations recommended for dinner. Main courses $7.50–$13.50. AE, DC, DISC, MC, V. Mon–Fri 11am–2pm; daily 5:30–10pm.

Jimbo's Restaurant ✿✿ Value JAPANESE   Jimbo's is the quintessential neighborhood restaurant—small, a line of regulars outside, fantastic house-made noodles and broths, everything good and affordable. A must for any noodle lover, Jimbo's serves homemade udon in a flawless broth with a subtly smoky flavor, then tops the works with shrimp tempura, chicken, eggs, vegetables, seaweed, roasted mochi, and a variety of accompaniments of your choice. Cold noodles (the Tanuki salad is wonderful!), stir-fried noodles, donburi rice dishes with assorted toppings, and combination dinners are other delights. The earthenware pot of noodles, with shiitake mushrooms, vegetables, and udon, plus a platter of tempura on the side, is the top-of-the-line combo. But our fave is the *nabeyaki* (an earthenware pot of udon with tempura on top). Owner Jimbo Motojima, a perfectionist, uses only the finest ingredients from Japan.

1936 S. King St. ✆ **808/947-2211.** Main courses $5–$10.75. MC, V. Daily 11am–3pm; Sun–Thurs 5–10pm; Fri–Sat 5–10:30pm.

Well Bento GOURMET HEALTH/ORGANIC PLATE LUNCHES   We wondered whether such healthy organic food, without the use of eggs, refined sugar, or dairy products, would be satisfying. Countless plate lunches later, we can report that Well Bento will make a guiltless gourmet out of even the fussiest palate. Each plate is aesthetically pleasing, wholesome, and tasty. Louisiana tempeh, salmon grilled over lava rocks or poached with shiitake mushrooms, Cajun-style chicken, and creative vegetarian selections ("plant-based plates") make this a place worth trying. Bean salad, cabbage and seaweed salads, and organic brown rice accompany each plate and are as decorative as they are delicious. This is a good picnic choice, as it's mostly takeout, and only a few seats are provided.

2570 S. Beretania St., 2nd floor. ✆ **808/941-5261.** Plate lunches $5.95–$8.50. No credit cards. Mon–Sat 10:30am–6pm.

KAIMUKI/KAPAHULU
EXPENSIVE

3660 On the Rise ✦ EURO-ISLAND   In his 200-seat restaurant, chef Russell Siu adds an Asian or local touch to the basics: rack of lamb with macadamia nuts, filets of catfish in ponzu sauce, and seared ahi salad with grilled shiitake mushrooms, a local favorite. The ahi katsu, wrapped in nori and fried medium-rare, is a main attraction in the appetizer department, and for dessert, Lisa Siu's warm chocolate cake is one of many raves.

3660 Waialae Ave. ✆ **808/737-1177.** Reservations suggested. Main courses $17–$31; prix fixe $36.60. AE, DC, DISC, MC, V. Tues–Thurs and Sun 5:30–9pm; Fri–Sat 5:30–10pm.

Ninniku-Ya Garlic Restaurant ✦ EURO-ASIAN   This is a great garlic restaurant, a paean to the stinking rose. Ninniku-Ya is located in a cozy old home, with tables in a split-level dining room and outdoors under venerable trees. The menu titillates with many garlic surprises and specials. Seasonal specialties (winter pumpkin in garlic potatoes, opah in winter, beet-colored sauces for Valentine's Day) are fine but not necessary, as the staples are quite wonderful. The three-mushroom pasta is sublime, the hot-stone filet mignon tender and tasty, and the garlic rice a meal in itself. Every garlic lover should experience the garlic toast and the roasted garlic with blue cheese. Everything contains garlic, even the house-made garlic gelato, but it doesn't overpower. Yes, that's garlic gelato—and it gets high marks from us. Look for the festive fairy lights lining the building.

3196 Waialae Ave. ✆ **808/735-0784.** Reservations recommended. Main dishes $12–$28. DC, DISC, MC, V. Tues–Sat 5:30–10:30pm; Sun 5:30–9pm.

Sam Choy's Diamond Head Restaurant ✦ HAWAII REGIONAL   You'll know you're in the right place if you see a parade of exiting diners clutching their Styrofoam bundles, for leftovers are de rigueur at any Sam Choy operation. The servings here are gargantuan, verging on off-putting. Choy has won over a sizable chunk of Hawaii's dining population with his noisy, informal, and gourmet-cum-local style of cooking. Now his kitchen is also the set for his cooking show. The master of poke, Choy serves several of the best versions to be had, and the best way to try them is in the $12.95 poke sampler (which could even include a tofu poke). Recommended: the fried Brie wontons, the seafood laulau, and seared ahi. All dinners include soup and a salad.

449 Kapahulu Ave. ✆ **808/732-8645.** Reservations required. Main courses $20.50–$34.95; Sun brunch buffet $24.95 adults, $14.95 children. AE, DC, DISC, MC, V. Mon–Thurs 5:30–9:30pm; Fri–Sun 5–10pm; Sun brunch 9:30am–2pm.

MODERATE

C & C Pasta ★★ *Finds* ITALIAN   Once primarily a takeout place, and now Honolulu's best Italian eatery (still with great sauces and homemade pasta to go), this tiny neighborhood gem really sizzles. Be sure to make a reservation, because there's always a line for dinner. Oenophiles gather regularly to uncork their best bottles of red, while an eclectic crowd of pasta lovers tucks into tongue-tingling feasts: a *sublime* mushroom risotto with truffle butter, excellent bruschetta and raviolis, and my perpetual favorites, linguine with clams and spaghetti puttanesca. Other excellent choices include the lasagna (meat and vegetarian) or penne with roasted eggplant. If that's not enough, try one of the specials on the blackboard, like the linguine I had recently that was generously flavored with spinach and roasted garlic. Owner Carla Magziar recently added pizza to the menu (with garlic, Gorgonzola, and other such tasty toppings) and a heroic salad of mixed greens, Gorgonzola, hazelnuts, roasted onions and peppers, with fig balsamic dressing. The quality is tops at C & C, the atmosphere is casual, and even the pickiest palates should find something to rave about. *Tip:* If the bread pudding or tiramisu are on the menu, they're a must-have. And if you're in a rush, there's always a pot of puttanesca sauce simmering, and it's great to go. Although service can lag when it's busy, the food is hard to beat.

3605 Waialae Ave. ✆ 808/732-5999. Reservations required for dinner. Main courses $12.50–$22.50. MC, V. Daily 11am–3pm and 5–10pm.

Genki Sushi ★ *Kids* SUSHI   Take your place in line for a seat at one of the U-shaped counters. Conveyor belts parade by with freshly made sushi, usually two pieces per color-coded plate, priced inexpensively. The possibilities are dizzying: spicy tuna topped with scallions, ahi, scallops with mayonnaise, Canadian roll (like California roll, except with salmon), sea urchin, flavored octopus, sweet shrimp, surf clam, corn, tuna salad, and so on. Genki starts with a Japanese culinary tradition and takes liberties with it, so don't be a purist. By the end of the meal, the piled-high plates are tallied up by color, and presto, your bill appears, much smaller than the pleasure. Brilliant combination platters are available for takeout.

900 Kapahulu Ave. ✆ 808/735-8889. A la carte sushi from $1.20 for two pieces; combination platters $7.40–$38.65. AE, DC, DISC, MC, V. Sun–Thurs 11am–9pm; Fri–Sat 11am–10pm; takeout available daily 11am–9pm.

INEXPENSIVE

Bueno Nalo Diamond Head MEXICAN/SOUTHWESTERN   Bravo for Bueno Nalo and its sizzling fajitas, hearty combination platters, and famous chimichangas. Hearty new additions include the *grande* chicken chimichanga with heaps of sour cream, big and daring and delicious. There are a couple of tables outside, six tables indoors, and a brisk takeout business as well. The adjoining juice bar serves terrific smoothies.

3045 Monsarrat Ave. ✆ 808/735-8818. Most items less than $9.95. No credit cards. Daily 11am–9pm.

Cafe Laufer ★ BAKERY/SANDWICH SHOP   This small, cheerful cafe features frilly decor and sublime pastries—from apple scones and linzer tortes to fruit flan, decadent chocolate mousse, and carrot cake—to accompany the latte and espresso. Fans drop in for simple soups and deli sandwiches on fresh-baked breads; biscotti during coffee break; or a hearty loaf of seven-grain, rye, pumpernickel, or French. The place is a solid hit for lunch; the small but satisfying menu includes soup-salad-sandwich specials for a song, a fabulous spinach salad with dried cranberries and Gorgonzola, and gourmet greens with mango-infused honey-mustard dressing. The orange-seared shrimp salad and the Chinese chicken salad are hits for the light eater, and the smoked Atlantic salmon with fresh pumpernickel bread and cream cheese, Maui onions, and capers is excellent. The special Saturday-night desserts draw a brisk postmovie business.

3565 Waialae Ave. (C) 808/735-7717. Most items less than $8. AE, DC, DISC, MC, V. Sun–Mon and Wed–Thurs 8am–10pm; Fri–Sat 8am–11pm.

Hale Vietnam VIETNAMESE   Duck into this house of pho and brave the no-frills service for the steaming noodle soups, the house specialty. The stock is simmered and skimmed for many hours and is accompanied by noodles, beef, chicken, and a platter of bean sprouts and fresh herbs. Approach the green chiles with caution. We love the chicken soup and shrimp vermicelli, as well as the seafood pho and spicy chicken with eggplant. Sautéed green beans, a seasonal offering, is not to be missed if available, nor is the *bun,* cold noodles heaped with sliced veggies and herbs, a fabulous sauce, and spring rolls. Be advised that this restaurant, like most other Vietnamese eateries, uses MSG, and that the pho, although respectable, does not equal that of To Chau in Chinatown, the ne plus ultra of pho in Honolulu.

1140 12th Ave. (C) 808/735-7581. Reservations recommended for groups. Main courses $4.50–$16. AE, DISC, MC, V. Daily 11am–10pm.

3 East of Waikiki: Kahala

EXPENSIVE

Hoku's ★★★ PACIFIC/EUROPEAN   Elegant without being stuffy, creative without being overwrought, the fine-dining room of the Kahala Mandarin offers elegant lunches and dinners combining European finesse with an island touch. This is fusion that really works. The ocean view, open kitchen, and astonishing bamboo floor are stellar features. Reflecting the restaurant's cross-cultural influences, the kitchen is equipped with a *kiawe* grill; an Indian tandoori oven for its chicken and nan bread; and Szechuan woks for the prawn, lobster, tofu, and other stir-fried specialties. The steamed Hong Kong–style whole fresh fish is an occasion, and at lunch, the warm Caesar salad, with kiawe-grilled tiger prawns, is smashing. (It's hard to order anything else once you've tried it.) Hoku's Sampler, the chef's daily selection of appetizers, could include sashimi, dim sum, and other dainty tastings, and is a good choice for the curious. Rack of lamb, peppered ahi steak, and the full range of East-West specialties appeal to many tastes.

In the Kahala Mandarin Oriental Hotel, 5000 Kahala Ave. (C) 808/739-8780. Reservations recommended. Main courses $18–$35; prix fixe dinner $65. AE, DC, DISC, MC, V. Mon–Fri 11:30am–2:30pm; daily 5:30–10pm; Sun brunch 10:30am–2:30pm.

INEXPENSIVE

The Patisserie GERMAN/AUSTRIAN   The complete dinners are a pleasant surprise, more elegant than the casual mall surroundings would indicate and surprisingly kind to the pocketbook, too. In its bakery setting with eight tables and a gleaming deli counter, The Patisserie sells everything from deluxe wedding cakes and European breads to inexpensive deli sandwiches (tuna, egg salad, pastrami, Black Forest ham), and nearly a dozen types of complete dinners. The dinners include sauerbraten, osso buco, veal ribs, baked pork tenderloin, braised lamb shank, and a particularly memorable sautéed chicken breast in a Marsala mushroom sauce and linguine. The German dinners are popular among those longing for Wiener schnitzel, pepper schnitzel, and potato pancakes with sour cream and applesauce. Served with garden salad and rolls, the dinners are a good value.

4211 Waialae Ave., Kahala Mall. © **808/735-4402.** Deli sandwiches $3.75–$4.75; complete dinners $13.50–$17. MC, V. Dinner service Mon–Sat 5:30–8:30pm; deli service Mon–Sat 7am–9pm and Sun 7am–5pm.

Olive Tree Cafe ⭐ *(Finds* GREEK/EASTERN MEDITERRANEAN   Delectables at bargain prices stream out of the tiny open kitchen here. Recently voted "best restaurant in Hawaii under $20" in a local survey, Olive Tree is every neighborhood's dream—a totally hip restaurant with divine Greek fare and friendly prices. There are umbrella tables outside and a few seats indoors, and you order and pay at the counter. Larger parties now have an awning over the sturdy wooden tables on the Koko Head side. The mussel ceviche is broke-the-mouth fabulous, with lemon, lime, capers, herbs, and olive oil—a perfect blend of flavors. The creamy, tender chicken saffron, a frequent special, always elicits groans of pleasure, as does the robust and generous Greek salad, another Olive Tree attraction. We also love the souvlaki, ranging from fresh fish to chicken and lamb, spruced up with the chef's homemade yogurt-dill sauce. A large group can dine here like sultans without breaking the bank, and take in a movie next door, too. BYOB.

4614 Kilauea Ave., next to Kahala Mall. © **808/737-0303.** Main courses $5–$10. No credit cards; checks accepted. Mon–Fri 5–10pm; Sat–Sun 11am–10pm.

4 East Oahu

NIU VALLEY

Swiss Haus *(Kids* CONTINENTAL   Although the former Swiss Inn has been renamed and is under new ownership, little has changed at this friendly neighborhood haunt. The new owners know a good thing when they see one, and they've wisely retained the quality, menu and service that have made this a multi-generational Honolulu favorite for nearly 2 decades. Swiss Haus is known for its Wiener schnitzel, New York steak, baked chicken, Swiss onion soup, and cheese fondue, and there are two to four daily specials, including fresh fish. The complete dinners include soup, salad, vegetables, and coffee or tea; light dinners range from $5.75 to $7.75. This restaurant has kept its quality up without raising its prices for several years. Families have always been welcome at Swiss Inn, and when the kids grow up, they bring their friends and families, too. Specialties include the veal dishes and the fresh fish, usually mahimahi or onaga in a lemon-butter-caper sauce, and at Thanksgiving and holidays, the home-cooked turkey dinner is just the way mom made it.

In the Niu Valley Shopping Center, 5730 Kalanianaole Hwy. © **808/377-5447.** Reservations recommended. Complete dinners $14.50–$22. AE, DC, DISC, MC, V. Wed–Sun 6pm–closing; Sunday brunch 10:30am–1pm.

HAWAII KAI

Roy's Restaurant ⭐⭐ EUROPEAN/ASIAN   This is the first of Roy Yamaguchi's six signature restaurants in Hawaii (he has two dozen all over the world). It is still the flagship and many people's favorite, true to its Euro-Asian roots and Yamaguchi's winning formula: open kitchen, fresh ingredients, ethnic touches, and a good dose of nostalgia mingled with European techniques. The menu changes nightly, but you can generally count on individual pizzas, a varied appetizer menu (summer rolls, blackened ahi, hibachi-style salmon), a small pasta selection, and entrees such as lemongrass-roasted chicken, garlic-mustard short ribs, hibachi-style salmon in ponzu sauce, and several types of fresh catch. One of Hawaii's most popular restaurants, Roy's is lit up at night with tiki torches outside; the view from within is of scenic Maunalua Bay. Roy's is also renowned for its high-decibel style of dining—it's always full and noisy. Other Roy's restaurants in Hawaii appear in Poipu, Kauai; Waikoloa, Big Island; Kihei, Maui; and Napili, Maui, where there are two. Live music Friday and Saturday evenings from 7:30 to 10:30pm and Sunday 6:30 to 9:30pm.

6600 Kalanianaole Hwy. ✆ 808/396-7697. Reservations recommended. Main courses $13.95–$28.95. AE, DC, DISC, MC, V. Mon–Thurs 5:30–9pm; Fri 5:30–9:30pm; Sat 5–9:30pm; Sun 5–9pm.

5 The Windward Coast

MODERATE

Assaggio ✪ ITALIAN   This was the mother ship of the Assaggio empire before the Ala Moana branch opened in 1999 (see p. 118). The affordable prices, attentive service, and winning menu items have attracted loyal fans throughout the years. The best-selling homemade hot antipasto has jumbo shrimp, fresh clams, mussels, and calamari in a sauce of cayenne pepper, white wine, and garlic. You can choose linguine, fettuccine, or ziti with 10 different sauces in small or regular portions, or any of nine chicken pastas (the chicken Assaggio, with garlic, peppers, and mushrooms, is especially flavorful). Equally impressive is the extensive list of seafood pastas, including the garlic/olive oil sauté. A plus: servings in two sizes and prices.

354 Ulunui St., Kailua. ✆ 808/261-2772. Reservations recommended. Main courses $10–$20. AE, DC, DISC, MC, V. Mon–Fri 11:30am–2:30pm; Sun–Thurs 5–9:30pm; Fri–Sat 5–10pm.

Buzz's Original Steak House STEAK/SEAFOOD   A Lanikai fixture for 40 years, Buzz's is a few feet from Kailua Beach (windsurfing central), just past the bridge that leads into Lanikai. (Though it's on the beach, shirt and shoes are required.) A small deck, varnished koa bar, rattan furniture, and wood walls covered with snapshots and surf pictures will put you immediately at ease. Buzz's has the perfect Gauguinesque tropical ambience to go with its offerings: great burgers at lunch (including a terrific mushroom garden burger), fresh catch, superb artichoke appetizer, and steak-and-lobster combos, all much loved by fans. Dinner offerings are pricier, but include Alaskan King crab legs (market price), prime rib, fresh fish, and wonderful items at the soup and salad bar.

413 Kawailoa Rd., Lanikai. ✆ 808/261-4661. Reservations required. Lunch main courses $6.95–$12.95; dinner main courses $10.95–$28.95. No credit cards. Daily 11am–3pm and 5–10pm.

Casablanca MOROCCAN   You can't miss the striking blue-and-yellow entrance with a Moorish arch over a tiny concrete pathway painted in brilliant primary colors. This gets our vote for the most cheerful ambience in Kailua. One section features traditional Moroccan dining on the floor, without utensils, though there are regular tables and silverware in the front section. Couscous with vegetables, chicken, lamb; lamb in brochettes, braised; with eggplant and with prunes, are among the savory offerings of this charming eatery. Large shrimp sautéed with Pernod and finished with sweet anise are a tasty treat, while some swear by the Cornish hen in Moroccan spices, cinnamon prunes, and honey.

19 Hoolai St., Kailua. ✆ 808/262-8196. Reservations recommended. Prix fixe $29.75. MC, V. Mon–Sat 6–9:30pm.

Jarons on Hamakua ITALIAN/ECLECTIC   The newly renovated Jarons offers a little of everything, from calamari and crab cakes to blackened ahi and vegetable lasagna. At lunch, the offerings range from a macadamia-nut mahimahi sandwich and grilled chicken tostadas to walnut artichoke fettuccine. For dinner, Wanda's shrimp scampi is a rich and carefree favorite, a steal at $14.95. (All entrees come with soup and a choice of Caesar or garden green salad.) Jarons is an old Kailua favorite, with live music on Thursdays from 8:30 to 11:30pm; and on Fridays and Saturdays, from 10:30pm to 1:30am, a dance floor emerges for disco and dancing.

201A Hamakua Dr., Kailua. ℂ 808/261-4600. Main courses $9.95–$18.95. AE, DC, DISC, MC, V. Daily Mon–Sat 11am–10pm; Sun 9am–10pm.

INEXPENSIVE

Ahi's Restaurant 𝒜 AMERICAN/LOCAL   There's no place like Ahi's in Hawaii: beautiful rural setting, tasty local fare, and the generous aloha of Ahi Logan and his three-generation family business. Their restaurant is nothing fancy, a lush roadside oasis with split-level indoor dining and an airy, screened-in room (for larger parties), a charming throwback to pre-resort, pre-plastic Hawaii. A rolling green lawn and towering shade trees surround the wooden structure; it's casual and rural. The shrimp—the menu highlight—comes four ways: steamed, scampi-style, tempura, and spicy, in Ahi's special Hawaiian spicy sauce. The mahimahi and fresh-fish specials are simple but good. On Saturdays, the generous Hawaiian lunch plate includes laulau, grilled fish, shrimp, and *pipikaula* (dried, salted beef). Ask about their Hawaiian Jamborees, with Hawaiian music and hula. Come here when you're hungry for the taste of real Hawaii that resorts long ago abandoned.

53146 Kamehameha Hwy., Punaluu. ℂ 808/293-5650. Reservations accepted for parties of 8 or more. Main courses $6–$12. No credit cards. Mon–Sat 11am–9pm.

Brent's Restaurant & Delicatessen DELI   Finally, a kosher deli with real cheese blintzes, cream-cheese and shrimp omelets, and some spirited cultural digressions, such as pesto poached eggs and an artichoke-laced frittata. And bagels galore, with baked salmon, sturgeon and cream cheese, or any number of accompaniments to compete with the New York–style pastrami and hot corned-beef sandwiches on Brent's abundant menu.

629-A Kailua Rd. ℂ 808/262-8588. Most items under $15. MC, V. Tues–Sun 7am–8pm; Fri–Sat 7am–9pm.

Bueno Nalo MEXICAN/SOUTHWESTERN   From its early days in Waimanalo, Bueno Nalo has built a solid following with its hearty plates of homemade Mex, including several types of chimichangas and burritos: shredded beef, shredded chicken, and a "wet" burrito, enchilada style, topped with homemade enchilada sauce and melted cheese. The seven different combination platters feature beans and rice and combos such as two tacos and an enchilada (a lot!) and the triple whammy: a taco, tamale, and enchilada. The same menu is offered at both the Kailua and Diamond Head locations in colorful, upbeat, casual surroundings—local color meets Tex-Mex.

20 Kainehe St., Kailua. ℂ 808/263-1999. Most items under $9.95. MC, V. Daily 11am–10pm.

Kimoz LOCAL/KOREAN   After working up an appetite in the waves at Waimanalo Beach, there's nothing like tucking into the huli huli chicken at Kimoz. Kimoz is doing a brisk business with its popular plates and generous *kal bi*, the spicy marinated Korean meat. Lovers of local food will find no stone unturned, from generous Portuguese sausage and seafood omelets to sandwiches, huli huli chicken (recommended!) to made-from-scratch mandoo, beef stew, and a killer Hawaiian plate. Groups enjoy Kimoz's "pupu platter," an assortment of vegetables, chicken, and poke. A recent expansion has added a new full bar; there's live Hawaiian and contemporary music on weekends. Karaoke and dart machines explain the late hours.

41–1537 Kalanianaole Hwy., Waimanalo. ✆ **808/259-8800.** Plate lunches $5.25–$13.95; sandwiches $4.95–$6.75. AE, DC, DISC, MC, V. Mon–Thurs 9am–midnight; Fri–Sat 9am–2am; Sun 9am–9pm.

6 The North Shore

MODERATE

Haleiwa Joe's ⭐ AMERICAN/SEAFOOD   Next to the Haleiwa bridge, with a great harbor and sunset view, Haleiwa Joe's is serving up fresh local seafood such as whole Hawaiian moi, opakapaka, ahi, and whatever comes in fresh that day. This is a steak-and-seafood harborside restaurant with indoor-outdoor seating and a surf-and-turf menu that could include Parker Ranch New York steak, coconut shrimp, black-and-blue sashimi, and smoked Hawaiian ono. With sandwiches and salads, it's a great lunch stop too. There are only two Haleiwa restaurants close to the ocean, and this is one of them.

66–0011 Kamehameha Hwy., Haleiwa. ✆ **808/637-8005.** Main courses $12.75–$19.95. V. Mon–Thurs 11:30am–9:30pm (limited menu 4:15–5:30pm); Fri–Sat 11:30am–10:30pm (limited menu 4:15–5:30pm; bar until midnight); Sun 11:30am–9:30pm (limited menu 3:45–5pm).

Jameson's by the Sea SEAFOOD   Duck into this roadside watering hole across the street from the ocean for cocktails, sashimi, and its celebrated salmon paté, or for other hot and cold appetizers, salads, and sandwiches. The grilled crab-and-shrimp sandwich (pardon the mayonnaise) on sourdough bread is a perennial, and it's hard to go wrong with the fresh-fish sandwich of the day, grilled plain and simple. Upstairs, the much pricier dining room opens its doors 5 nights a week for the usual surf-and-turf choices: fresh opakapaka, ulua (Hawaiian jackfish), and mahimahi; scallops in lemon butter and capers; and lobster tail, New York steak, and filet mignon.

62–540 Kamehameha Hwy., Haleiwa. ✆ **808/637-4336.** Reservations recommended. Main courses $13–$39 in upstairs dining room; downstairs lunch menu $7–$14. AE, DC, DISC, MC, V. Downstairs, daily 11am–5pm; pub menu Mon–Tues 5–9pm, Sat–Sun 11am–9pm. Upstairs, Wed–Sun 5–9pm.

INEXPENSIVE

Cafe Haleiwa BREAKFAST/LUNCH/MEXICAN   Haleiwa's legendary breakfast joint is a big hit with surfers, urban gentry with weekend country homes, reclusive artists, and anyone who loves mahimahi plate lunches and heroic sandwiches. It's a wake-up-and-hit-the-beach kind of place, serving generous omelets with names like Off the Wall, Off the Lip, and Breakfast in a Barrel. Surf pictures line the walls, and the ambience is Formica-style casual. And what could be better than an espresso bar for a java launch to the day?

66–460 Kamehameha Hwy., Haleiwa. ✆ **808/637-5516.** Main courses $5.50–$10.50. AE, MC, V. Daily 7am–2pm.

Cholos Homestyle Mexican II *(Value)* MEXICAN   There's usually a wait at this popular North Shore eatery, where some of the tables have leather stools without backs and the excellent spinach quesadillas and roasted veggie combination plate are presented with so-so service. Still, this is the unhurried North

Shore, and the biggest rush for most folks is getting to and from the beach. We recommend the above-mentioned spinach quesadilla, a generous serving filled with black beans, cheese, and fresh vegetables; the chicken fajita plate, a winner; and the fish taco plate, a steal at $5.75. There are tables and stools outdoors; indoors, it's dark and cavelike, with loud music, Mexican handicrafts all over the place, and great home-style Mexican, down to the last drop of fresh-tomato salsa.

North Shore Marketplace, 66–250 Kamehameha Hwy. 𝒞 808/637-3059. Combination plates $4.95–$13.95. No credit cards. Daily 8am–9pm; breakfast served until 11am.

Kua Aina 𝄞 AMERICAN   "What's the name of that sandwich shop on the North Shore?" We hear that often. Although this North Shore staple has expanded to the Ward Centre area in Kakaako, you'd never know it by the lines here. It's busy as ever, and because there are never enough tables, many diners get their burgers to go and head for the beach. Kua Aina's thin and spindly french fries are renowned islandwide and are the perfect accompaniment to its legendary burgers. Fat, moist, and homemade, the burgers can be ordered with avocado, bacon, and many other accompaniments, including ortega chiles and cheese. The tuna/avocado, roast turkey, and mahimahi sandwiches are excellent alternatives to the burgers. Kua Aina is unparalleled on the island and is a North Shore must, eclipsing its fancier competitors at lunch. Plans call for a move to a larger location just a few hundred feet away on Kamehameha Highway by the fall of 2001, so call ahead to check.

66–214 Kamehameha Hwy., Haleiwa. 𝒞 808/637-6067. Most items less than $6. No credit cards. Daily 11am–8pm.

Paradise Found Cafe VEGETARIAN   A tiny cafe behind Celestial Natural Foods, Paradise Found is a bit of a hunt, but stick with it. For more than a few townies, the North Shore sojourn begins at Paradise, the only pure vegetarian restaurant in these parts. Their smoothies (especially the Waimea Shorebreak!) are legendary, and their organic soups, fresh pressed vegetable juices, sandwiches and healthy plate lunches are a great launch to a Haleiwa day. Surf movies are played throughout the day, and vegan substitutes are willingly made in place of dairy products, and to accommodate dietary needs.

66–443 Kamehameha Hwy., Haleiwa. 𝒞 808/637-4540. All items less than $7. No credit cards. Mon–Sat 9am–5pm.

6

Fun in the Surf & Sun

by Jeanette Foster

Pictures of hotels lining the shores of Waikiki Beach and canyons of tall buildings in downtown Honolulu have given Oahu a bad rap. The island is much more than an urban concrete jungle or a tropical Disneyland blighted by overdevelopment; it's also a haven for the nature lover and outdoor enthusiast. With year-round temperatures in the upper 70s, and miles of verdant and unspoiled landscape, Oahu is perfect for outdoor activities of all kinds, including hiking, golf, tennis, biking, and horseback riding.

But the island's waters, which also enjoy year-round temperatures in the upper 70s, are where the majority of both residents and visitors head for relaxation, rejuvenation, and recreation. Locals don't think of their island or state boundaries as ending at land's edge—rather, they extend beyond the reefs, well out into the ocean.

For camping information, see section 6, "Oahu's Campgrounds & Wilderness Cabins," at the end of chapter 4.

1 Beaches

Oahu has more than 130 beaches of every conceivable description, from legendary white-sand stretches to secluded rocky bays. Waikiki, of course, is the best known, but there are many others—some more beautiful, all less crowded. What follows is a selection of Oahu's finest beaches, carefully selected to suit every need, taste, and interest, from the sunbather in repose to the most ardent diver.

THE WAIKIKI COAST
ALA MOANA BEACH PARK ★★
Quite possibly America's best urban beach, gold-sand Ala Moana ("by the sea"), on sunny Mamala Bay, stretches for more than a mile along Honolulu's coast between downtown and Waikiki. This 76-acre midtown beach park, with spreading lawns shaded by banyans and palms, is one of the island's most popular playgrounds. It has a man-made beach, created in the 1930s by filling a coral reef with Waianae Coast sand, as well as its own lagoon, yacht harbor, tennis courts, music pavilion, bathhouses, picnic tables, and enough wide-open green spaces to accommodate 4 million visitors a year. The water is calm almost year-round, protected by black lava rocks set offshore. There's a large parking lot as well as metered street parking.

WAIKIKI BEACH ★★★
No beach anywhere is so widely known or so universally sought after as this narrow, 1½-mile-long crescent of imported sand (from Molokai) at the foot of a string of high-rise hotels. Home to the world's longest-running beach party,

Beaches & Outdoor Pursuits on Oahu

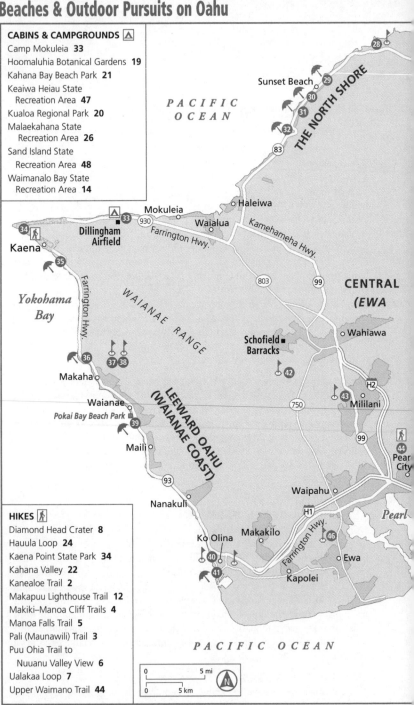

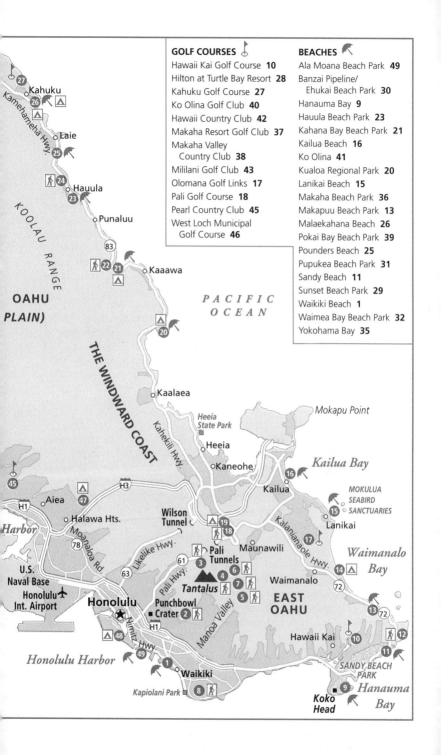

GOLF COURSES ⛳

Hawaii Kai Golf Course **10**
Hilton at Turtle Bay Resort **28**
Kahuku Golf Course **27**
Ko Olina Golf Club **40**
Hawaii Country Club **42**
Makaha Resort Golf Club **37**
Makaha Valley
  Country Club **38**
Mililani Golf Club **43**
Olomana Golf Links **17**
Pali Golf Course **18**
Pearl Country Club **45**
West Loch Municipal
  Golf Course **46**

BEACHES 🏖

Ala Moana Beach Park **49**
Banzai Pipeline/
  Ehukai Beach Park **30**
Hanauma Bay **9**
Hauula Beach Park **23**
Kahana Bay Beach Park **21**
Kailua Beach **16**
Ko Olina **41**
Kualoa Regional Park **20**
Lanikai Beach **15**
Makaha Beach Park **36**
Makapuu Beach Park **13**
Malaekahana Beach **26**
Pokai Bay Beach Park **39**
Pounders Beach **25**
Pupukea Beach Park **31**
Sandy Beach **11**
Sunset Beach Park **29**
Waikiki Beach **1**
Waimea Bay Beach Park **32**
Yokohama Bay **35**

Kahuku
Laie
Hauula
Punaluu
Kaaawa

KOOLAU RANGE

OAHU
PLAIN)

PACIFIC
OCEAN

Kaalaea

Mokapu Point

Heeia
State Park

Heeia
Kaneohe
Kailua

Kailua Bay

THE WINDWARD COAST

MOKULUA
SEABIRD
SANCTUARIES

Lanikai

Aiea
Halawa Hts.

Wilson
Tunnel

Kahekili Hwy.

Pali
Tunnels
Maunawili

Waimanalo
Bay

Likelike Hwy.

Pali Hwy.

Tantalus
Waimanalo

EAST
OAHU

Manoa Valley

U.S.
Naval Base
Honolulu ✈
Int. Airport

Honolulu

Punchbowl
Crater

Harbor

Moanalua Rd.

Nimitz Hwy.

Hawaii Kai

Honolulu Harbor

Waikiki

Kapiolani Park

SANDY BEACH
PARK

Koko
Head

Hanauma
Bay

Kalanianaole Hwy.

⌐Tips **A Word of Warning**

Wherever you are on Oahu, remember that you're in an urban area. Never leave valuables in your car. Thefts do occur at Oahu's beaches, and locked cars are not a deterrent.

Waikiki attracts nearly five million visitors a year from every corner of the planet. First-timers are always amazed to discover how small Waikiki Beach actually is, but there's always a place for them under the tropical sun here.

Waikiki is actually a string of beaches that extends between **Sans Souci State Recreational Area,** near Diamond Head to the east, and **Duke Kahanamoku Beach,** in front of the Hilton Hawaiian Village Beach Resort & Spa, to the west. Great stretches along Waikiki include **Kuhio Beach,** next to the Sheraton Moana Surfrider, which provides the quickest access to the Waikiki shoreline; the stretch in front of the Royal Hawaiian Hotel known as **Grey's Beach,** which is canted so it catches the rays perfectly; and **Sans Souci,** the small, popular beach in front of the New Otani Kaimana Beach Hotel that's locally known as "Dig Me" Beach because of all the gorgeous bods who strut their stuff here.

Waikiki is fabulous for swimming, board- and bodysurfing, outrigger canoeing, diving, sailing, snorkeling, and pole fishing. Every imaginable type of marine equipment is available for rent here. Facilities include showers, lifeguards, restrooms, grills, picnic tables, and pavilions at the **Queen's Surf** end of the beach (at Kapiolani Park, between the zoo and the aquarium). The best place to park is at Kapiolani Park, near Sans Souci.

EAST OAHU
HANAUMA BAY ★★

Oahu's most popular snorkeling spot is this volcanic crater with a broken sea wall; its small, curved, 2,000-foot gold-sand beach is packed elbow-to-elbow with people year-round. The bay's shallow shoreline water and abundant marine life are the main attractions, but this good-looking beach is also popular for sunbathing and people-watching. Serious divers shoot "the slot" (a passage through the reef) to gain Witch's Brew, a turbulent cove, then brave strong currents in 70-foot depths at the bay mouth to see coral gardens, turtles, and—that's right—sharks. (Divers: Beware the Molokai Express, a strong current.) Snorkelers hug the safe, shallow (10 ft.) inner bay that, depending on when you go, is like either swimming in a fish-feeding frenzy or bathing with 300,000 honeymooners. Because Hanauma Bay is a conservation district, you may look at but not touch or take any marine life here. Feeding the fish is also prohibited.

Facilities include parking, restrooms, a pavilion, a grass volleyball court, lifeguards, barbecues, picnic tables, and food concessions. Alcohol is prohibited in the park; there is no smoking past the visitor center. Expect to pay $1 per vehicle to park and a $3 per person entrance fee (children 12 and under are free). If you're driving, take Kalanianaole Highway to Koko Head Regional Park. Avoid the crowds by going early, about 8am, on a weekday morning; once the parking lot's full, you're out of luck. Or, take TheBus to escape the parking problem: The Hanauma Bay Shuttle runs from Waikiki to Hanauma Bay every half hour from 8:45am to 1pm; you can catch it at the Ala Moana Hotel, the Ilikai Hotel, or any city bus stop. It returns every hour from noon to 4:30pm. Hanauma Bay is closed on Tuesdays so the fish can have a day off.

SANDY BEACH ⊛

Sandy Beach is one of the best bodysurfing beaches on Oahu; it's also one of the most dangerous. It's better to just stand and watch the daredevils literally risk their necks at this 1,200-foot-long gold-sand beach that's pounded by wild waves and haunted by a dangerous shore break and strong backwash. Weak swimmers and children should definitely stay out of the water here; Sandy Beach's heroic lifeguards make more rescues in a year than those at any other beach. Visitors, easily fooled by experienced bodysurfers who make wave-riding look easy, often fall victim to the bone-crunching waves. Lifeguards post flags to alert beachgoers to the day's surf: Green means safe, yellow caution, and red indicates very dangerous water conditions; always check the flags before you dive in.

Facilities include restrooms and parking. Go weekdays to avoid the crowds, weekends to catch the bodysurfers in action. From Waikiki, drive east on the H-1, which becomes Kalanianaole Highway; proceed past Hawaii Kai, up the hill to Hanauma Bay, past the Halona Blow Hole, and along the coast. The next big, gold, sandy beach you see ahead on the right is Sandy Beach. TheBus no. 22 will also get you here.

MAKAPUU BEACH PARK ⊛

Makapuu Beach, the most famous bodysurfing beach in Hawaii, is a beautiful 1,000-foot-long gold-sand beach cupped in the stark black Koolau cliffs on Oahu's easternmost point. Even if you never venture into the water, it's worth a visit just to enjoy the great natural beauty of this classic Hawaiian beach. You've probably already seen it in countless TV shows, from *Hawaii Five-O* to *Magnum, P.I.*

In summer, the ocean here is as gentle as a Jacuzzi, and swimming and diving are perfect; come winter, however, Makapuu is hit with big, pounding waves that are ideal for expert bodysurfers, but too dangerous for regular swimmers. Small boards—3 feet or less with no skeg (bottom fin)—are permitted; regular board surfing is banned by state law.

Facilities include restrooms, lifeguards, barbecue grills, picnic tables, and parking. To get here, follow Kalanianaole Highway toward Waimanalo, or take TheBus no. 57 or 58.

THE WINDWARD COAST
LANIKAI BEACH ⊛⊛

One of Hawaii's best spots for swimming, gold-sand Lanikai's crystal-clear lagoon is like a giant saltwater swimming pool that you're lucky enough to be able to share with the resident tropical fish and sea turtles. Too gorgeous to be real, this is one of Hawaii's postcard-perfect beaches: It's a mile long and thin in places, but the sand's as soft as talcum powder. Prevailing onshore trade winds make this an excellent place for sailing and windsurfing. Kayakers often paddle out to the two tiny offshore Mokulua islands, which are seabird sanctuaries. Because Lanikai is in a residential neighborhood, it's less crowded than other Oahu beaches; it's the perfect place to enjoy a quiet day. Sun worshipers should arrive in the morning, though, as the Koolau Range blocks the afternoon rays.

There are no facilities here, just off-street parking. From Waikiki, take the H-1 to the Pali Highway (Hwy. 61) through the Nuuanu Pali Tunnel to Kailua, where the Pali Highway becomes Kailua Road as it proceeds through town. At Kalaheo Avenue, turn right and follow the coast about 2 miles to Kailua Beach Park; just past it, turn left at the T intersection and drive uphill on Aalapapa Drive, a one-way street that loops back as Mokulua Drive. Park on Mokulua

Frommer's Favorite Oahu Experiences

Getting a Tan on Waikiki Beach. The best spot for catching the rays on the world-famous beach is in front of the big, pink Royal Hawaiian Hotel—the beach here is set at the perfect angle for sunning. It's also a great spot for people-watching. Get here early; by midday (when the rays are at their peak), it's towel-to-towel out there.

Exploring Oahu's Rain Forests. In the misty sunbeams, colorful birds flit among giant ferns and hanging vines, while towering tropical trees form a thick canopy that shelters all below in cool shadows. This emerald world is a true Eden. For the full experience, try Manoa Falls Trail, a walk of less than a mile that ends at a freshwater pool and waterfall.

Snorkeling the Glistening Waters of Hanauma Bay. This underwater park, once a volcanic crater, is teeming with a rainbow of tropical fish. Bordered by a 2,000-foot gold-sand beach, the bay's shallow water (10 ft. in places) is perfect for neophyte snorkelers. Arrive early to beat the crowds—and don't forget that the bay is closed on Tuesday. **Aloha Dive Shop,** Koko Marina Shopping Center (© 808/395-5922), can set you up with fins, mask, and snorkel for just $7 a day.

Hiking to the Top of Diamond Head Crater. Almost everyone can make this easy hike to the top of Hawaii's most famous landmark. The 1.4-mile round-trip goes up to the top of the 750-foot volcanic cone, where you have a 360° view of Oahu. Allow an hour for the trip up and back, and don't forget your camera.

Heading to Waimea Bay When the Surf's Up. From November to March, monstrous waves—some 30 feet tall—roll into Waimea. When they break on the shore, the ground actually shakes and everyone on the beach is covered with salt spray mist. The best surfers in the world paddle out to challenge these freight trains. It's amazing to see how small they appear in the lip of the giant waves. This is an experience you'll never forget—and the show won't cost you a dime.

Watching the Ancient Hawaiian Sport of Canoe Paddling. On weekday evenings and weekend days from February to September, hundreds of paddlers gather at Ala Wai Canal and practice taking traditional Hawaiian canoes out to sea. Find a comfortable spot at Ala Wai Park, next to the canal, and watch the canoe paddlers re-create this centuries-old sport.

Finding a Bargain at the Aloha Flea Market. Just 50¢ will get you into this all-day show at the Aloha Stadium parking lot, where more than 1,000 vendors sell everything from junk to jewels. Go early for the best deals. Open Wednesday, Saturday, and Sunday from 6am to 3pm.

Drive and walk down any of the eight public-access lanes to the shore. Or, take TheBus no. 56 or 57 (Kailua), then transfer to the shuttle.

KAILUA BEACH 🐠🐠🐠

Windward Oahu's premier beach is a 2-mile-long, wide golden strand with dunes, palm trees, panoramic views, and offshore islets that are home to

Attending a Hawaiian-Language Church Service. Built in 1842, Kawaia-hao Church, 957 Punchbowl St. (near King St.), is the Westminster Abbey of Hawaii; the vestibule is lined with portraits of the Hawaiian monarchy, many of whom were coronated in this very building. The coral church is a perfect setting to experience an all-Hawaiian service, complete with Hawaiian song. Hawaiian-language services are held every Sunday at 10:30am and admission is free—let your conscience be your guide as to a donation.

Visiting the Lei Sellers in Chinatown. There's a host of cultural sights and experiences to be had in Honolulu's Chinatown. Wander through this several-square-block area with its jumble of exotic shops offering herbs, Chinese groceries, and acupuncture services. Be sure to check out the lei sellers on Maunakea Street (near N. Hotel St.), where Hawaii's finest leis go for as little as $2.50.

Experiencing a Turning Point in America's History: The Bombing of Pearl Harbor. Standing on the deck of the USS *Arizona* Memorial at Pearl Harbor, with the ship underneath, is an unforgettable experience. On that fateful day—December 7, 1941—the 608-foot *Arizona* sank in just 9 minutes after being bombed during the Japanese air raid. The 1,177 men on board plunged to a fiery death—and the United States went to war. Go early; you'll wait 2 to 3 hours if you visit at midday. You must wear closed-toed shoes, no slippers.

Watching the Sun Sink into the Pacific from a 1,048-Foot Hill Named After a Sweet Potato. Actually, it's more romantic than it sounds. Puu Ualakaa State Park, at the end of Round Hill Drive, translates into "rolling sweet potato hill" (which was how the early Hawaiians harvested the crop). This majestic view of the sunset is not to be missed.

Ordering a Shave Ice in a Tropical Flavor You Can Hardly Pronounce. In Haleiwa, stop at Matsumoto Shave Ice, 66-087 Kamehameha Hwy., for a snow cone with an exotic flavor poured over the top, such as the local favorite, *li hing mui,* or with sweet Japanese adzuki beans hidden inside. This taste of tropical paradise goes for just $1.

Listening to the Soothing Sounds of Hawaiian Music. Sit under the huge banyan tree at the Sheraton Moana Surfrider's Banyan Veranda in Waikiki, order a cocktail, and sway to live Hawaiian music any night of the week. Another quintessential sunset oasis is the Halekulani's House Without a Key, a sophisticated oceanfront lounge with wonderful hula and steel-guitar music, a great view of Diamond Head, and the best mai tais on the island.

seabirds. The swimming is excellent, and the azure waters are usually decorated with bright sails; this is Oahu's premier windsurfing beach as well. It's also a favorite spot to sail catamarans, bodysurf the gentle waves, or paddle a kayak. Water conditions are quite safe, especially at the mouth of Kaelepulu Stream, where toddlers play in the freshwater shallows at the middle of the beach park.

The water's usually about 78°F, the views are spectacular, and the setting, at the foot of the sheer, green Koolaus, is idyllic. Best of all, the crowds haven't found it yet.

The 35-acre beach park is intersected by a freshwater stream and watched over by lifeguards. Facilities include picnic tables, barbecues, restrooms, a volleyball court, a public boat ramp, free parking, and an open-air cafe. Kailua's new bike path weaves through the park, and Windsurfer and kayak rentals are available as well. To get here, take Pali Highway (Hwy. 61) to Kailua, drive through town, turn right on Kalaheo Avenue, and go a mile until you see the beach on your left. Or, take TheBus no. 56 or 57 into Kailua, then the no. 70 shuttle.

KUALOA REGIONAL PARK ★★

This 150-acre coco palm–fringed peninsula is the biggest beach park on the windward side and one of Hawaii's most scenic. It's located on Kaneohe Bay's north shore, at the foot of the spiky Koolau Ridge. The park has a broad, grassy lawn and a long, narrow, white-sand beach ideal for swimming, walking, beach-combing, kite-flying, or just sunbathing. Picnic and camping areas are available too. In ancient Hawaii, this was a very sacred spot where Hawaiian chiefs brought their infant children here to be raised and trained as rulers. Today the park is listed on the National Register of Historic Places. It's easy to see why this was place was so revered: The curtain of the Koolau Mountains provides a spectacular backdrop in one direction. The waters are shallow and safe for swimming year-round, and at low tide, you can swim or wade out to the islet of Mokolii (popularly known as Chinaman's Hat), which has a small sandy beach and is a bird preserve—so don't spook the red-footed boobies. Lifeguards are on duty.

Since both residents and visitors frequent this huge beach park, it's better to go on a weekday. The park is located on Kamehameha Highway (Hwy. 83) in Kualoa; you can get here via TheBus no. 55.

KAHANA BAY BEACH PARK ★★

This white-sand, crescent-shaped beach is backed by a huge, jungle-cloaked valley with dramatic, jagged cliffs, and is protected by ironwood and kamani trees. The bay's calm water and shallow, sandy bottom make it a safe swimming area for children. The bay is famous for the *akule* (big-eyed scad), which come in seasonally; papio and goatfish are also found here. The surrounding park has picnic areas, camping, and hiking trails. The wide sand-bottom channel that runs through the park and out to Kahana Bay is one of the largest on Oahu—it's perfect for kayakers. Locals come here on weekends, so weekdays are less crowded. The beach park is located on Kamehameha Highway in Kahana; take TheBus no. 55 (Circle Island) to get here.

HAUULA BEACH PARK

The town of Hauula and nearby Hauula Beach Park were named after the *hau* trees that were once abundant. Although less plentiful now, the trees continue to blossom here every July and August. The blossoms begin as a bright yellow flower in the morning, changing color as the day progresses, until they are reddish gold by dusk and dark red by night, when they fall to the ground. The cycle is repeated the next day.

Hauula Beach Park fronts Kamehameha Highway, is straight and narrow (about 1,000 ft. long), and is shaded by kamani and ironwood trees. An offshore reef protects the waters off the beach, but the shallow and rocky bottom make the area unsafe for swimming. Snorkeling is good along the edge of the coral reef, and fishing for papio and goatfish can be fruitful. There are picnic and camping facilities. Weekends tend to be more crowded here, too. TheBus no. 55 (Circle Island) will get you to Hauula Beach.

POUNDERS BEACH

Because of its easy access and its great bodysurfing waves, Pounders is a popular weekend beach. The beach used to be called Pahumoa, after a local fisherman who arranged the local *hukilau* (the catching of fish in a net) and made sure that the elderly living in the area received a portion of the catch. The name change occurred in the 1950s, when a group of students at the Church College of the Pacific (now Brigham Young University–Hawaii) called the beach "Pounders" after the crushing shorebreak that provided brief but spectacular bodysurfing rides; the nickname stuck.

Pounders is a wide beach, extending a quarter mile between two points. At the west end of the beach, next to the old landing, the waters usually are calm and safe for swimming; at the opposite end, near the limestone cliffs, there's a shorebreak that can be dangerous for inexperienced bodysurfers. The bottom here drops off abruptly, causing strong rip currents. The weekends and after-school hours are the busiest time for this beach; weekday mornings are the quietest. Park on Kamehameha Highway in Kailua, or take TheBus no. 55 (Circle Island) to get here.

THE NORTH SHORE
BANZAI PIPELINE/EHUKAI BEACH PARK ⭐

These are actually three separate areas, but since the sandy beach is continuous with only one sign, EHUKAI BEACH PARK, most people think of it as one beach park. Located near Pupukea, the actual Ehukai Beach Park is 1 acre of grass with a parking lot. The long, broad, white-sand beach is known for its winter surfing action. Swimming is good during the spring and summer months, but currents and waves prohibit safe swimming in the winter. The surf in front of Ehukai Beach Park is excellent for body and board surfers.

The park also provides access to Pipeline and Banzai. **Pipeline** is actually about 100 yards to the left of Ehukai Beach Park. When the winter surf rolls in and hits the shallow coral shelf, the waves that quickly form are steep—so steep, in fact, that the crest of the wave falls forward, forming a near-perfect tube, or "pipeline." Surfers have tried for years to master Pipeline; many have wiped out, suffering lacerations and broken bones on the shallow reef. The first surfer to ride Pipeline successfully was Phil Edwards in the early 1960s. Even today, Pipeline still causes injuries and a few fatalities.

Just west of Pipeline is the area surfers call **"Banzai Beach."** The Japanese word *banzai* means "10,000 years"; it's given as a toast or as a battle charge, meaning "go for it." In the late 1950s, filmmaker Bruce Brown was shooting one of the first surf movies ever made, *Surf Safari,* when he saw a bodysurfer ride a huge wave. Brown yelled: "Banzai!" and the name stuck. In the winter, this is a very popular beach with surfers, surf fans, curious residents, and visitors; it's less

---

Impressions

The boldness and address with which we saw them perform these difficult and dangerous maneuvers was altogether astonishing.
—Capt. James Cook's observations of Hawaiian surfers

crowded in the summer months. Again, access is via Ehukai Beach Park, located off Kamehameha Highway on Ke Nui Road in Pupukea. TheBus no. 52 (Circle Island) will drop you on the highway.

PUPUKEA BEACH PARK 🐾

This 80-acre beach park is a Marine Life Conservation District; as such, it has strict rules about taking marine life, sand, coral, shells, and rocks. There are two major swimming areas in the Marine Life Conservation District: **Shark's Cove** and **Three Tables.** Don't worry: Shark's Cove, near the northern end, is *not* named for an abundance of sharks that call this home (in fact, it's relatively uncommon to see a shark here); rather, it's a popular snorkeling and dive site. Diving is best outside the cove, where caves promise interesting night diving. During the calm summer months, this is a popular dive site both day and night.

At the southern end of the Marine Life Conservation District is Three Tables, which is named for the three flat sections of reef visible at low tide. Snorkeling is good around the tables where the water is about 15 feet deep. Diving outside the tables, where the water is 30 to 45 feet deep, is excellent—there are many ledges, arches, lava tubes, and a variety of marine life. Swimming, diving, and snorkeling are best from May to October, when the water is calm; nevertheless, watch out for surges. In the winter, when currents form and waves roll in, this area is very dangerous, even in the tide pools; there is no lifeguard present. Summers find this Marine Life Conservation District brimming with visitors weekdays and weekends; it's a popular site for local dive operators to take their clients. In the winter, it's nearly empty during the week. It's right on Kamehameha Highway in Pupukea; there's a small parking lot. TheBus no. 52 (Circle Island) stops at the park.

MALAEKAHANA BAY STATE RECREATION AREA 🐾🐾🐾

This almost mile-long white-sand crescent lives up to just about everyone's image of the perfect Hawaii beach. It's excellent for swimming. On a weekday, you may be the only one here; but should some net fisherman—or kindred soul—intrude upon your delicious privacy, you can swim out to Goat Island (or wade across at low tide) and play Robinson Crusoe. (The islet is a sanctuary for seabirds and turtles, so no chase 'em, brah.) Facilities include restrooms, barbecue grills, picnic tables, outdoor showers, and parking.

To get here, take Kamehameha Highway (Hwy. 83) 2 miles north of the Polynesian Cultural Center; as you enter the main gate, you'll come upon the wooded beach park. Or, you can take TheBus no. 52.

SUNSET BEACH PARK 🐾🐾

Surfers around the world know this famous site for its spectacular winter surf—the waves can be huge thundering peaks reaching 15 to 20 feet. Oddly enough, this surfing site wasn't really "discovered" until the 1940s; before that, surfers preferred Makaha on the leeward side of the island. During the winter surf season (Sept–Apr) swimming is very dangerous here, due to the alongshore currents and powerful rip currents. The "Sunset rip" has been the site of many rescues and has carried numerous surfboards out to sea. The only safe time to swim at Sunset is during the calm summer months. Sunset also features a huge sandy beach adjacent to the street. This is a great place to people-watch, but don't go too near the water when the lifeguards have posted the red warning flags. One of the most popular beaches on the island, Sunset attracts local surfers, sunbathing beauties, and visitors wanting to get a glimpse of this world-famous surf spot. To avoid the crowds, go during midweek. Located right on Kamehameha

Highway in Paumalu, TheBus no. 52 (Circle Island) will get you there if you'd rather not drive.

WAIMEA BEACH PARK 👁👁

This deep, sandy bowl has gentle summer waves that are excellent for swimming, snorkeling, and bodysurfing. To one side of the bay is a huge rock that local kids like to climb up and dive from. In this placid scene, the only clues of what's to come in winter are those evacuation whistles on poles beside the road. But what a difference a season makes: Winter waves pound the narrow bay, sometimes rising to 50 feet high. When the surf's really up, very strong currents and shore breaks sweep the bay—and it seems like everyone on Oahu drives out to Waimea to get a look at the monster waves and those who ride them. Weekends are great for watching the surfers; to avoid the crowds, go on weekdays. *A safety tip:* Don't get too distracted by the waves and forget to pay attention when parking or crossing the road.

Facilities include lifeguards, restrooms, showers, parking, and nearby restaurants and shops in Haleiwa town. The beach is located on Kamehameha Highway (Hwy. 83); from Waikiki, you can take TheBus no. 52.

LEEWARD OAHU/THE WAIANAE COAST
KO OLINA

The developer of the 640-acre Ko Olina Resort has created four white-sand lagoons to make the rocky shoreline more attractive and accessible. Only two of these man-made lagoons are currently open. The northernmost lagoon, next to the Ihilani Resort and Spa, is the best. The nearly circular lagoon, with calm, shallow waters and a powdery white-sand beach bordered by a broad, grassy lawn, is the most attractive of the four lagoons. Lifeguards and restrooms are on the site, and the amenities and restaurants of the hotel are steps away. The other lagoon that's open right now is three lagoons away from the Ihilani Hotel. There's plenty of public parking, a lifeguard station, and restrooms. This scenic, calm lagoon is used mainly by local residents, but it doesn't have quite the ambience of the lagoon next to the hotel (only part of which is used by hotel guests). Located off H-1 in Kapolei. There is no local bus service to Ko Olina; the closest bus stop is on Farrington Highway, more than 4 miles away.

MAKAHA BEACH PARK

When surf's up here, it's spectacular: Monstrous waves pound the beach from October through April. This is the original home of Hawaii's big-wave surfing championship; surfers today know it as the home of Buffalo's Big Board Surf Classic, where surfers ride the waves on 10-foot-long wooden boards in the old Hawaiian style of surfing. Nearly a mile long, this half-moon gold-sand beach is tucked between 231-foot Lahilahi Point, which locals call Black Rock, and Kepuhi Point, a toe of the Waianae mountain range. Summer is the best time to hit this beach—the waves are small, the sand abundant, and the water safe for swimming. Children hug the shore on the north side of the beach, near the lifeguard stand, while surfers dodge the rocks and divers seek an offshore channel full of big fish. *A caveat:* This is a "local" beach; you are welcome, of course, but you can expect "stink eye" (mild approbation) if you are not respectful of the beach and the local residents who use the facility all the time.

Facilities include restrooms, lifeguards, and parking. To get here, take the H-1 freeway to the end of the line, where it becomes Farrington Highway (Hwy. 93), and follow it to the beach; or you can take TheBus no. 51.

YOKOHAMA BAY 𝒜

Where Farrington Highway (Hwy. 93) ends, the wilderness of Kaena Point State Park begins. It's a remote 853-acre coastline park of empty beaches, sand dunes, cliffs, and deep-blue water. This is the last sandy stretch of shore on the northwest coast of Oahu. Sometimes, it's known as Keawalua Beach or Puau Beach, but everybody here calls it Yokohama, after the Japanese immigrants who came from that port city to work the cane fields and fished along this shoreline. When the surf's calm—mainly in summer—this is a good area for snorkeling, diving, swimming, shore fishing, and picnicking. When surf's up, board and body-surfers are out in droves; don't go in the water then unless you're an expert. There are no lifeguards or facilities, except at the park entrance, where there's a restroom and lifeguard stand. No bus service.

POKAI BAY BEACH PARK 𝒜

This wonderful beach, off the beaten path for most visitors, offers excellent swimming year-round, even when the rest of the Waianae shoreline is getting battered by heavy surf. The waters inside this protected bay are calm enough for children and offer excellent snorkeling. The swimming area is marked by buoys. Waianae-area residents have a bit of a reputation for being xenophobic; however, they want the same things most people want. So go with respect for local customs, be a good steward of the land, and appreciate the local resources. Do what the locals do: pick up your garbage, don't play loud music, and be courteous and friendly. On weekdays, you can practically have the area to yourself. The beach park is located on Waianae Valley Road, off Farrington Highway. TheBus no. 51 will drop you off on the highway, and you can walk the block to the park.

2 Watersports

Oahu has a wealth of watersports opportunities, whether you're a professional surfer braving giant winter waves on the North Shore, or a recreational water-skier enjoying the calm waters of Hawaii Kai. You can kayak from Lanikai Beach to the Mokulua Islands or float above Waikiki on a parasail as a speedboat tows you blissfully through the air. If you have something of an adventurous spirit, you might scuba dive the walls of the Kahuna Canyon, swim with clouds of *ta'ape* (butterflyfish), or view an occasional shark from the comfort of a passenger submarine. No matter what your aquatic interests are, whether you're a beginner or an expert, you can find it on Oahu.

If you want to rent beach toys (such as masks, snorkels, fins; Boogie boards; surfboards; kayaks; and more), check out the following Waikiki rental shops: **Snorkel Bob's,** on the way to Hanauma Bay at 700 Kapahulu Ave. (at Date St.), Honolulu (© **808/735-7944;** www.snorkelbob.com); **Aloha Beach Service,** in the Sheraton Moana Surfrider Hotel, 2365 Kalakaua Ave. (© **808/922-3111,** ext. 2341), and at **Blue Sky Rentals,** in the Inn on the Park, 1920 Ala Moana Blvd. (© **877/947-0101** or 808/947-0101), in Waikiki. On Oahu's windward side, try **Kailua Sailboards & Kayaks,** 130 Kailua Rd., a couple blocks from the Kailua Beach Park (© **808/262-2555**). On the North Shore, get equipment from **Surf-N-Sea,** 62–595 Kamehameha Hwy., Haleiwa (© **808/637-9887**).

BOATING

A funny thing happens to people when they come to Hawaii: Maybe it's the salt air, the warm tropical nights, or the blue Hawaiian moonlight, but otherwise-rational people who have never set foot on a boat in their life suddenly want to go out to sea. You can opt for a "booze cruise" with a thousand loud, rum-soaked strangers, or you can sail on one of these special yachts, all of which will take you out **whale-watching** in season (roughly Dec–Apr).

For fishing charters, see "Sportfishing," below.

Captain Bob's Adventure Cruises ⚡ See the majestic Windward Coast the way it should be seen—from a boat. Captain Bob will take you on a 4-hour, lazy-day sail of Kaneohe Bay aboard his 42-foot catamaran, which skims across the almost-always calm water above the shallow coral reef, lands at the disappearing sandbar Ahu o Laka, and takes you past two small islands to snorkel spots full of tropical fish and, sometimes, turtles. The color of the water alone is worth the price. This is an all-day affair, but hey, getting out on the water is the reason you came to Hawaii, right? A shuttle will pick you up at your Waikiki hotel between 9 and 9:30am and bring you back at about 4pm—it's a lot quicker than taking TheBus (no. 55 or 56).

Kaneohe Bay. ✆ 808/942-5077. $69 adults, $59 children 13–17, $49 children 12 and under. Rates include all-you-can-eat barbecue lunch and transportation from Waikiki hotels. No cruises Sun and holidays. TheBus: 55 or 56.

Dream Cruises ⚡ If you aren't lucky enough to be in Hawaii during humpback-whale season (roughly Jan–Apr), you can go **dolphin-watching** instead. Dream Cruises offers year-round dolphin-watching cruises that check out friendly pods of bottle-nosed and spinner dolphins near Yokahama Bay on the northern end of Oahu. This might be your only chance to get "up-close and personal" with these protected marine mammals. During whale season, the company guarantees that if you don't see whales, you can sail again for free. Departing from the Kewalo Basin is a range of cruises, including a snorkel/splash tour that anchors off Waikiki for snorkeling, swimming, and lunch; a 3-hour Pearl Harbor coastal cruise; and a 2-hour sunset dinner-and-dancing cruise with views of the Waikiki skyline.

Kewalo Basin and Waianae Small Boat Harbor. ✆ 800/400-7300 or 808/592-5200. www.dream-cruises. com. $25.50–$69.10 adults, $18.05–$36.10 children 4–12. Rates include hotel pickup and drop-off, plus some meals.

Honolulu Sailing Co. This company has been in business for 2 decades, offering a variety of sailing activities. Our favorite is the Diamond Head snorkel-picnic sail on the waves. During whale season (roughly Jan–Apr), check out the half- and full-day adventures to see whales, dolphins, flyingfish, and sea turtles.

Pier 2, Honolulu Harbor (across from Restaurant Row). ✆ 800/829-0114 or 808/239-3900. www.honsail. com. $98 adults for full-day cruises, $49 for children 12 and under; $68 adults for half day, $34 for children. For all-day cruises, park at Restaurant Row, 500 Ala Moana Blvd. (entrance on Pohukaina St., between South and Punchbowl sts.), for $6 all day; for half-day cruises, park in metered spaces in front of Pier 2, for 50¢ per hour. TheBus: 19, 20, or 47.

Navatek I ⚡⚡ You've never been on a boat, you don't want to be on a boat, but here you are being dragged aboard one. Why are you boarding this weird-looking vessel? It guarantees that you'll be "seasick-free," that's why. The 140-foot-long *Navatek I* isn't even called a boat; it's actually a SWATH (Small Waterplane Area Twin Hull) vessel. That means the ship's superstructure—the part you ride on—rests on twin torpedo-like hulls that cut through the water so you don't bob like a cork and spill your mai tai. It's the smoothest ride on Mamala Bay. In fact, *Navatek I* is the only dinner cruise ship to receive U.S. Coast Guard certification to travel beyond Diamond Head.

Sunset dinner cruises leave Pier 6 (across from the Hawaii Maritime Museum) nightly. If you have your heart set on seeing the city lights, take the royal Sunset Dinner Cruise (four courses for $120, $72 for children 2–11), which runs from 5:15 to 7:15pm. The best deal is the noon-to-2pm **lunch cruise,** with full buffet lunch, live Hawaiian music, and a great view of Oahu offshore ($47 adults, $28.50 kids 2–11). In **whale season** (roughly Jan–Apr), morning whale-watching cruises depart at 8:30am and return at 10:30am. The cost ($45 adults, $26.50 kids 2–11) includes a continental breakfast and commentary by a naturalist. The lunch cruise lasts from noon to 2pm and costs $47 for adults and $28.50 for children 2 to 11.

Aloha Tower Marketplace, Pier 6. c/o Hawaiian Cruises Ltd. (*C* 808/973-1311. www.go-atlantis.com. Rates vary depending on cruise. Validated parking $3. TheBus: 8, 19, 20, 55, 56, or 57; or the Waikiki Trolley to stop no. 7.

BODYBOARDING (BOOGIE BOARDING) & BODYSURFING

Good places to learn to bodyboard are in the small waves of **Waikiki Beach** and **Kailua Beach,** and **Bellows Field Beach Park,** off Kalanianaole Highway (Hwy. 72) in Waimanalo, which is open to the public on weekends (from noon on Fri to midnight on Sun and holidays). To get here, turn toward the ocean on Hughs Road, then right on Tinker Road, which takes you right to the park.

See above for a list of rental shops where you can get a Boogie board.

OCEAN KAYAKING

For a wonderful adventure, rent a kayak, arrive at Lanikai Beach just as the sun is appearing, and paddle across the emerald lagoon to the pyramid-shaped islands off the beach called Mokulua—it's an experience you won't forget. Kayak equipment rental starts at $10 an hour, or $37 for a day.

First-timers should go to **Kailua Sailboards & Kayaks,** 130 Kailua Rd., in Kailua, (*C* **808/262-2655;** www.kailuasailboards.com), where the company offers a guided tour with the novice in mind in safe, protected environment. Included in the tour are lunch, all equipment, and transportation from Waikiki hotels for $79.

In addition to the rental shops listed above, you can rent a kayak from **Prime Time Sports,** Fort DeRussy Beach (*C* **808/949-8952**). On the North Shore, contact **Waimea Falls Park,** 59–864 Kamehameha Hwy., Haleiwa (*C* **888/ 973-9200** or 808/638-8511).

SCUBA DIVING

Oahu is a wonderful place to scuba dive, especially for those interested in wreck diving. One of the more famous wrecks in Hawaii is the *Mahi,* a 185-foot former minesweeper easily accessible just south of Waianae. Abundant marine life makes this a great place to shoot photos—schools of lemon butterflyfish and taape are so comfortable with divers and photographers that they practically pose. Eagle rays, green sea turtles, manta rays, and white-tipped sharks occasionally cruise by as well, and eels peer out from the wreck.

For nonwreck diving, one of the best dive spots in summer is **Kahuna Canyon.** In Hawaiian, *kahuna* means priest, wise man, or sorcerer; this massive amphitheater, located near Mokuleia, is a perfect example of something a sorcerer might conjure up. Walls rising from the ocean floor create the illusion of an underwater Grand Canyon. Inside the amphitheater, crabs, octopi, slippers, and spiny lobsters abound (be aware that taking them in summer is illegal), and

Impressions

Thousands have daily lined the wharves to witness the carpenter, Mr. Dibble, in his novel suit of India-rubber with a glass helmet disappear beneath the surface of the water . . .

—1840 Honolulu newspaper article

giant trevally, parrotfish, and unicorn fish congregate as well. Outside the amphitheater, you're likely to see an occasional shark in the distance.

Since Oahu's best dives are offshore, your best bet is to book a two-tank dive from a dive boat. Hawaii's oldest and largest outfitter is **Aaron's Dive Shop,** 307 Hahani Street, Kailua (✆ **808/262-2333;** www.hawaii-scuba.com), which offers boat and beach dive excursions off the coast. The boat dives cost from $90 per person, including two tanks and transportation from the Kailua shop. The beach dive off the North Shore in summer or the Waianae Coast in winter is the same price as a boat dive, including all gear and transportation, so Aaron's recommends the boat dive.

In Waikiki, **South Sea Aquatics,** 2155 Kalakaua, Suite 112 (next to Planet Hollywood; ✆ **808/922-0852**), features two-tank boat dives for $75 to $89 (plus $16 if you need equipment), with transportation to and from Waikiki hotels. On the North Shore, **Surf-N-Sea,** 62–595 Kamehameha Hwy., Haleiwa (✆ **808/637-9887;** fax 808/637-3008), has dive tours from the shore (starting at $65), from a boat (starting at $110), and at night ($80). Surf-N-Sea also rents equipment and can point you to the best dive sites in the area.

Another great resource for diving on your own is the University of Hawaii Sea Grant's *Dive Hawaii Guide,* which describes 44 dive sites on the various Hawaiian islands, including Oahu. Send $2 to UH/SGES, Attn: Dive Guide, 2525 Correa Rd., HIG 237, Honolulu, HI 96822.

SNORKELING

Some of the best snorkeling in Oahu is at the underwater park at **Hanauma Bay** ★★. It's crowded—sometimes it seems there are more people than fish, but Hanauma has clear, warm, protected waters and an abundance of friendly reef fish—including Moorish idols, scores of butterflyfish, damselfish, and wrasses. Hanauma Bay has two reefs, an inner and an outer—the first for novices, the other for experts. The inner reef is calm and shallow (less than 10 ft.); in some places, you can just wade and put your face in the water. Go early: It's packed by 10am and closed on Tuesdays. For details, see p. 142.

Braver snorkelers may want to head to **Shark's Cove,** on the North Shore just off Kamehameha Highway, between Haleiwa and Pupukea. Sounds risky, we know, but we've never seen or heard of any sharks in this cove, and in summer, this big, lava-edged pool is one of Oahu's best snorkel spots. Waves splash over the natural lava grotto and cascade like waterfalls into the pool full of tropical fish. To the right of the cove are deep-sea caves to explore.

The uninitiated might feel better after a lesson and a snorkel tour. **Surf-N-Sea,** 62–595 Kamehameha Hwy., Haleiwa (✆ **808/637-9887**), has 2-hour tours, with equipment, starting at $45. On the North Shore, **Haleiwa Surf Center,** 66–167 Haleiwa Rd., Haleiwa (✆ **808/637-5051**) teaches snorkeling and offers guided snorkel tours. **Aloha Dive Shop,** Koko Marina Shopping Center (✆ **808/395-5922**), is the closest dive shop to the underwater park at Hanauma Bay.

SPORTFISHING

Kewalo Basin, located between the Honolulu International Airport and Waikiki, is the main location for charter fishing boats on Oahu. From Waikiki, take Kalakaua Ewa (west) beyond Ala Moana Center; Kewalo Basin is on the left, across from Ward Centre. Look for charter boats all in a row in their slips; on lucky days, the captains display the catch of the day in the afternoon. You can also take TheBus no. 19 or 20 (Airport).

The best way to book a sportfishing charter is through the experts; the best booking desk in the state is **Sportfish Hawaii** ⚓ (✆ **877/388-1376** or 808/396-2607; www.sportfishhawaii.com), which not only books boats on Oahu, but on all islands. These fishing vessels have been inspected and must meet rigorous criteria to guarantee that you will have a great time. Prices range from $500 to $1,000 for a full-day exclusive charter (you, plus five friends, get the entire boat to yourself), $325 to $700 for a half-day exclusive, or from $165 for a full-day share charter (you share the boat with five other people).

SUBMARINE DIVES

Here's your chance to play Jules Verne and experience the underwater world from the comfort of a submarine, which will take you on an adventure below the surface in high-tech comfort. The entire trip is narrated as you watch tropical fish and sunken ships just outside the sub; if swimming's not your thing, this is a great way to see Hawaii's spectacular sea life. Shuttle boats to the sub leave from Hilton Hawaiian Village Pier. The cost is $80 to $100 for adults, $30 to $40 for kids 12 and under (children must be at least 36 in. tall); call **Atlantis Submarines** ⚓ (✆ **800/548-6262** or 808/973-9811; www.go-atlantis.com) to reserve. To save money, ask about advance purchase for the shorter "Discovery Adventure," which is only $50 for adults ($30 for children). *A word of warning:* The ride is safe for everyone, but skip it if you suffer from claustrophobia.

SURFING

In summer, when the water's warm and there's a soft breeze in the air, the south swell comes up. It's surf season in Waikiki, the best place to learn how to surf on Oahu. For lessons, go early to **Aloha Beach Service,** next to the Sheraton Moana Surfrider, 2365 Kalakaua Ave., Waikiki (✆ **808/922-3111**). The beach boys offer surfing lessons for $25 an hour; board rentals are $8 for 1 hour and $12 for 2 hours. You must know how to swim.

Surfboards are also available for rent at **Local Motion,** 1958 Kalakaua Ave., Honolulu (✆ **808/979-7873**), and **Surf-N-Sea,** 62–595 Kamehameha Hwy., Haleiwa (✆ **808/637-9887**), which offers lessons as well. For the best surf shops, where you can soak in the culture as well as pick up gear, also see p. 231, p. 234, and p. 235.

More experienced surfers should drop in on any surf shop around Oahu, or call the **Surf News Network Surfline** (✆ **808/596-SURF**) to get the latest surf conditions. **The Cliffs,** at the base of Diamond Head, is a good spot for advanced surfers; 4- to 6-foot waves churn here, allowing high-performance surfing.

If you're in Hawaii in winter and want to see the serious surfers catch the really big waves, bring your binoculars and grab a front-row seat on the beach near **Kalalua Point.** To get here from Waikiki, take the H-1 toward the North Shore, veering off at H-2, which becomes Kamehameha Highway (Hwy. 83). Keep going to the funky surf town of Haleiwa and Waimea Bay; the big waves will be on your left, just past Pupukea Beach Park.

SWIMMING

For a quiet, peaceful place to swim, **Malaekahana Bay** ⋆, near Kahuku, is one of the best Oahu beaches. This mile-long, white-sand, crescent-shaped beach is about a 90-minute drive and a million miles from the crowds at Waikiki. To get there, take Kamehameha Highway past Laie and follow the signs to Malaekahana State Recreational Area. Or take TheBus no. 52 (Circle Island). Another good swimming beach is **Lanikai;** secluded and calm, this beach is great for families. From Waikiki, take TheBus no. 56 or 57 (Kailua), and then transfer to the shuttle.

See also section 1 of this chapter, "Beaches"; each description mentions the relative calmness of the waters.

WATER-SKIING

To learn to water-ski, or to just go out and have a good time, call the oldest water-ski company in Hawaii, **Hawaii Sports,** at Koko Marina Shopping Center (© **808/395-3773;** TheBus: 58). Lessons and boat rental are $69 for a first time lesson of two 15-minute runs, if you do not need lessons, then prices are $49 for a 20-minute ride and $59 for a 30-minute ride, including the boat and all equipment rental (maximum of five people).

WHALE-WATCHING

From December to April, 45-foot humpback whales—Hawaii's most impressive visitors—come to spend the winter. They make the journey from Alaska to calve and mate in Hawaii's calm, warm waters. Once nearly hunted to extinction, humpback whales are now protected by federal law. The mammals may not be approached by any individual or watercraft within 100 yards.

Whales can frequently be seen off the island on calm days. If you spot the familiar spout of water—a sign the mammal is exhaling—there's a good chance you'll see the whale on the surface. If you're in a car, please pull over, as many accidents have occurred when visitors try to spot whales and drive at the same time.

For whale-watching cruises, see "Boating," earlier in this section.

WINDSURFING

Windward Oahu's **Kailua Beach** is the home of champion and pioneer windsurfer Robbie Naish; it's also the best place to learn to windsurf. The oldest and most established windsurfing business in Hawaii is **Naish Hawaii/Naish Windsurfing Hawaii,** 155-A Hamakua Dr., Kailua (© **800/767-6068** or 808/ 262-6068; www.naish.com). The company offers everything: sales, rentals, instruction, repair, and free advice on where to go when the wind and waves are happening. Private lessons start at $55 for one, $75 for two; beginner equipment rental is $25 for a half day and $30 for a full day. Kite surfing lessons are also available. **Kailua Sailboards & Kayaks,** 130 Kailua Rd., a couple of blocks from the Kailua Beach Park (© **808/262-2555;** www.kailuasailboards.com), offers 3-hour small-group lessons ($69 per person, including all gear) and rentals of windsurfing equipment, surfboards, snorkel gear, and ocean kayaks.

Windsurfer wannabes on the North Shore can contact **North Shore Windsurfing School,** 59–452 Makana Rd. (Kamehameha Hwy.), Haleiwa (© **808/ 638-8198**). Experts give 2½-hour lessons in a protected area for $40. Owner Jack Lauer says the school specializes in making confident windsurfers out of nervous beginners within one lesson. Unfortunately, this school does not rent equipment. Also on the North Shore, **Surf-N-Sea,** 62–595 Kamehameha Hwy., Haleiwa (© **808/637-9887**), offers equipment rental as well as private lessons (beginning at $65 for 2 hr.).

3 Nature Hikes

People think Oahu is just one big urban island, so they're always surprised to discover that the great outdoors is less than an hour away from downtown Honolulu. Highlights of the island's 33 major hiking trails include razor-thin ridge backs and deep waterfall valleys.

Check out Stuart Ball's *The Hikers Guide to Oahu* (University of Hawaii Press, 1993) before you go. Another good source of hiking information on Oahu is the state's **Na Ala Hele** (Trails to Go On) Program (© **808/973-9782** or 808/587-0058).

For a free Oahu recreation map listing all 33 trails, write to the **Department of Land and Natural Resources,** 1151 Punchbowl St., Room 131, Honolulu, HI 96813 (© **808/587-0300**). The department will also send free topographic trail maps on request and issue camping permits.

Another good source of information is the *Hiking/Camping Information Packet,* which costs $7 (postage included); to order, contact **Hawaii Geographic Maps and Books,** 49 S. Hotel St., Honolulu, HI 96813 (© **800/538-3950** or 808/538-3952). This store also carries a full line of United States Geographic Survey topographic maps, very handy for hikers.

Also be sure to get a copy of *Hiking on Oahu: The Official Guide,* a hiking safety brochure that includes instructions on hiking preparation, safety procedures, emergency phone numbers, and necessary equipment; for a copy, contact Erin Lau, Trails and Access Manager, **City and County of Honolulu** (© **808/973-9782**); the **Hawaii Nature Center,** 2131 Makiki Heights Dr. (© **808/955-0100**); or **The Bike Shop,** 1149 S. King St. (© **808/596-0588**).

The **Hawaiian Trail and Mountain Club,** P.O. Box 2238, Honolulu, HI 96804, offers regular hikes on Oahu. You bring your own lunch and drinking water and meet up with the club at the Iolani Palace to join them on a hike. The club also has an information packet on hiking and camping in Hawaii, as well as a schedule of all upcoming hikes; send $2 plus a legal-sized, self-addressed, stamped envelope to the address above.

Other organizations that offer regularly scheduled hikes are the **Sierra Club,** P.O. Box 2577, Honolulu, HI 96803 (www.hi.sierraclub.org); the **Nature Conservancy,** 1116 Smith St., Suite 201, Honolulu, HI 96817 (© **808/537-4508,** ext. 220); and the **Hawaii Nature Center,** 2131 Makiki Heights Dr. (© **808/955-0100**).

Casual hikers and walkers will enjoy the maps put out by the Hawaii Department of Health on great places to walk. The two brochures are *The Honolulu Walking Map,* with 16 routes in Honolulu ranging from 1½ miles to 3.6 miles, and *The Fun Fitness Map,* with 12 walking adventures all over Oahu. To get a free copy of each, send a self-addressed, stamped envelope (with four 34¢ stamps) to Angela Wagner, Health, Promotions and Education Branch, Room 217, 1250 Punchbowl St., Honolulu, HI 96813. For more information, call © **808/586-4661.**

For camping information, see section 6, "Oahu's Campgrounds & Wilderness Cabins," at the end of chapter 4.

HONOLULU AREA HIKES
DIAMOND HEAD CRATER ⟨★★★⟩

This is a moderate, but steep, walk to the summit of Hawaii's most famous landmark. Kids love to look out from the top of the 750-foot volcanic cone, where

Fun Fact **Fly Away**

Amelia Earhart was the first woman to fly solo from Hawaii to the U.S. mainland in 1935. A plaque on Diamond Head Road memorializes her 12-hour, 50-minute flight from Honolulu to Oakland, California.

they have 360-degree views of Oahu up the leeward coast from Waikiki. The 1.4-mile round-trip takes about 1½ hours.

Diamond Head was created by a volcanic explosion about half a million years ago. The Hawaiians called the crater *Leahi* (meaning the brow of the ahi, or tuna, referring to the shape of the crater). Diamond Head was considered a sacred spot; King Kamehameha offered human sacrifices at a *heiau* (temple) on the western slope. It wasn't until the 19th century that Mount Leahi got its current name: A group of sailors found what they thought were diamonds in the crater; it turned out they were just worthless calcite crystals, but the Diamond Head moniker stuck.

Before you begin your journey to the top of the crater, put on some decent shoes (rubber-soled tennies are fine) and gather a flashlight (you'll walk through several dark tunnels), binoculars (for better viewing at the top), water (very important), a hat to protect you from the sun, and a camera. You might want to put all your gear in a pack to leave your hands free for the climb. If you don't have a flashlight or your hotel can't lend you one, you can buy a small one for a few dollars as part of a Diamond Head climbers' "kit" at the gift shop at the **New Otani Kaimana Beach Hotel,** on the Diamond Head end of Kalakaua Avenue, just past the Waikiki Aquarium and across from Kapiolani Park.

Go early, preferably just after the 6:30am opening, before the midday sun starts beating down. The hike to the summit of Diamond Head starts at Monsarrat and 18th avenues on the crater's inland (or mauka) side. To get here, take TheBus no. 58 from the Ala Moana Shopping Center or drive to the intersection of Diamond Head Road and 18th Avenue. Follow the road through the tunnel (which is closed 6pm–6am) and park in the lot. The trailhead starts in the parking lot and proceeds along a paved walkway (with handrails) as it climbs up the slope. You'll pass old World War I and II pillboxes, gun emplacements, and tunnels built as part of the Pacific defense network. Several steps take you up to the top observation post on Point Leahi. The views are indescribable.

If you want to go with a guide, the Clean Air Team leads a free guided hike to the top of Diamond Head every Saturday. The group gathers at 9am, near the front entrance to the Honolulu Zoo (look for the rainbow windsock). Hikers should bring a flashlight. Each person will be given a bag and asked to help keep the trail clean by picking up litter. For more information, call © **808/948-3299.**

KANEALOLE TRAIL

This is the starting place for some of Oahu's best hiking trails; miles of trails converge through the Makiki Valley–Tantalus–Round Top–Nuuanu Valley area. To get a general feel for the hikes in the region, take this 1½-mile round-trip moderate hike, which climbs some 500 feet and takes less than an hour. If you're interested, stop at the **Hawaii Nature Center,** located by the trailhead at 2131 Makiki Heights Dr. (© **808/955-0100;** open Mon–Fri, 8am–4:30pm), where you can find information on the environmental and conservation needs of Hawaii, displays of plants and animals, hands-on exhibits, and numerous maps and pamphlets about this hiking area. They also sponsor organized hikes on weekends.

To get here, take McCully Avenue north out of Waikiki; cross over the H-1 Freeway and turn left on Wilder Avenue. Make a right turn on Makiki Street and continue until the road forks at the park. Take the left fork past the Makiki Pumping Station; the road is now called Makiki Heights Drive. Follow it up to the hairpin turn and make a right onto the small spur road that goes into Makiki Valley; park just beyond the green trailers that house the Hawaii Nature Center. If you are taking the bus, it's a little trickier: From Waikiki, take TheBus no. 8, 19, 20, or 58 to the Ala Moana Shopping Center and transfer to TheBus no. 17. Tell your driver where you're going, and he'll let you off near the spur road just off Makiki Heights Drive; you'll have to walk the rest of the way.

After stopping at the Hawaii Nature Center, continue up the path, which wanders under the protection of kukui trees and lush vines. The road gets smaller and smaller until it's just a footpath. Along this narrow path, look for the tall, bushy grasslike plant called Job's tears. It's considered a weed in Hawaii, but this is no ordinary grass; it can grow up to 5 feet high and produces a gray, tear-shaped seed. The trail continues through an abandoned valley where there once was a thriving Hawaiian community. Occasionally you'll spot the remains of stone walls and even a few coffee plants—Makiki Valley supported a coffee plantation in the 19th century. When you meet the Makiki Valley Trail, you can retrace your steps or choose from the dozens of trails in the area.

MAKIKI–MANOA CLIFFS &&

From rain forests to ridge-top views, this somewhat strenuous loop trail is one you'll never forget. The hike is just over 6 miles, gains 1,260 feet in elevation, and takes about 3 hours. This trail is part of the labyrinth of trails found in this area (see "Kanealole Trail," above). To get to these trails, follow the directions for the Kanealole Trail (see above).

The trail starts by the restrooms of the Hawaii Nature Center. Look for the paved path that crosses Kanealole Stream via a footbridge (Maunalaha Trail). Stay on the trail, following it up the hill into the forest, where you'll pass bananas, Norfolk and Cook Island pines, ti plants, and even a few taro patches. Cross over Moleka Stream and look for the four-way junction with the Makiki Valley and Ualakaa trails; turn right on the **Makiki Valley Trail.** This takes you through a dense forest, past a giant banyan tree, and then joins with the Moleka Trail. Turn left on the **Moleka Trail**—now you're in the rain forest: Ancient guava trees reach overhead, maidenhair ferns cling to rocks, and tiny white-flowered begonias crop up.

Further on, the kukui and koa give way to a bamboo-filled forest, which opens up to a parking lot on Round Top Drive at the end of the Moleka Trail. Cross Round Top Drive to the **Manoa Cliffs Trail,** which emerges on Tantalus Drive. Turn right on Tantalus and walk about 100 yards down the street to the **Nahuina Trail** on the left side of Tantalus. As you walk downhill, you'll have breathtaking views of downtown Honolulu. At the junction of Kanealole Trail, turn right and continue back to where you started.

MANOA FALLS TRAIL &&

This easy, eight-tenths of a mile (one-way) hike is terrific for families; it takes less than an hour to reach idyllic Manoa Falls. The trailhead, marked by a foot-bridge, is at the end of Manoa Road, past Lyon Arboretum. The staff at the arboretum prefers that hikers do not park in their lot, so the best place to park is in the residential area below Paradise Park; you can also get to the arboretum via TheBus no. 5. The often-muddy trail follows Waihi Stream and meanders

---

Tips **Outdoor Etiquette**

Carry out what you carry in. Find a rubbish container for all your litter (including cigarette butts—it's very bad form to throw them out your car window). Observe kapu and no trespassing signs. Don't climb on ancient Hawaiian heiau walls and temples or carry home rocks, all of which belong to the Hawaiian volcano goddess Pele. Some say it's just a silly superstition or coincidence, but each year the U.S. Park Service gets boxes of lava rocks sent back to Hawaii by visitors who've experienced unusually bad luck.

---

through the forest reserve past guavas, mountain apples, and wild ginger. The forest is moist and humid and is inhabited by giant bloodthirsty mosquitoes, so bring repellent.

PUU OHIA TRAIL TO NUUANU VALLEY VIEW 🅐

This moderate hike takes you through a rain forest, up to the top of Tantalus (Puu Ohia) cinder cone, and down through Pauoa Flats to view Nuuanu Valley. Plan about 2 hours for this 3½-mile round-trip hike, which gains about 1,200 feet in altitude.

To get here, follow the directions for the Kanealole Trail, above, but turn to the right at the park fork in Makiki Street. The fork to the right is Round Top Drive. Drive to the top and park in the turnout on the ocean side of the street. Unfortunately, bus service is not available.

The Puu Ohia trailhead is across the street from where you parked. As you head up (a series of switchbacks and, at the steepest part, hand-cut stairs in the dirt), you pass night-blooming jasmine, ginger, Christmas berry, and avocado trees. After dense guava trees and bamboo, the vegetation parts for a magnificent view of Honolulu and Diamond Head. Just as quickly, as you continue along the trail, the bamboo once again obstructs the view. At the next junction, stay on the main trail by bearing to the left; you'll pass through ginger, koa, and bamboo. At the next junction, bear left again, and climb up the steps around the trunk of an old koa tree. At the top is a paved road; turn right and walk downhill. The road leads to an old telephone relay station, and then turns into a footpath. Passing through bamboo, koa, ti, and strawberry guava, turn left onto the Manoa Cliffs Trail. At the next junction, turn right on the Puu Ohia Trail, which leads to the Pauoa Flats and to the view of the Nuuanu Valley. Retrace your steps for your return.

UALAKAA LOOP 🅐

The same series of volcanic eruptions that produced Diamond Head and Koko Crater also produced the cinder cones of Round Top (Puu Ualakaa), Sugarloaf (Puu Kakea), and Tantalus (Puu Ohia). *Puu,* as you may have already guessed, means "hill"; these three hills overlook Honolulu and offer spectacular views. The easy Ualakaa Loop Trail is a half-hour hike of about a mile that traverses through woods, offering occasional panoramic views of Honolulu.

There's no bus service to this trailhead. Follow the directions for the Puu Ohia hike, above, but instead of driving to the top of Round Top Drive, turn off on the fourth major hairpin turn (look for it after a long stretch of panoramic straightaway). The turn will go through the gate of the **Puu Ualakaa State Wayside Park.** Continue a little more than 4 miles inside the park; look for a stand of Norfolk pine trees and park there. The trailhead is on the right side of the Norfolk pines. The park is open 7am to 7:45pm from April 1 to Labor Day; in winter, the park closes at 6:45pm.

The loop trail, lined with impatiens, passes through Norfolk pines, palm trees, ironwoods, and Christmas berry trees. The once-native forest now has many foreign intrusions—including all of the foregoing—as well as ti, banana, banyan, guava, and mountain apple. At two points along the trail, you emerge on Round Top Drive; just walk about 100 feet to continue on the trail on the opposite side of the road. The loop will bring you back to where you started.

PEARL CITY

UPPER WAIMANO TRAIL

This is a strenuous, 14-mile round-trip with an altitude gain of nearly 2,000 feet. The rewards are worth the effort: magnificent views from the top of windward Oahu's Koolau Mountains and a chance to see rare native Hawaiian plants. Plan a full day for this 8-hour hike.

To get here from Waikiki, take H-1 to the Pearl City exit (Exit 10) on Moanalua Road; head north and turn right on Waimano Home Road; follow it to the end, just over 22 miles. Park on the road. Or take TheBus no. 8, 19, 20, or 58 from Waikiki to the Ala Moana Shopping Center and transfer to TheBus no. 53. Tell your driver where you are going and he will take you as far as he can on Waimano Home Road; you'll have to walk the rest of the way to the trailhead (about 1½ miles).

You'll pick up the trailhead at the dirt path to the left of the gate, outside the fence surrounding the Waimano Home. Follow the trail through swamp mahogany trees to the first junction; turn right at the junction to stay on the upper Waimano Trail. At the second junction, turn right again to stay on the upper trail. The Christmas berry becomes denser, but as you move up the mountain, koa, kukui, hau, mango, guava, mountain apple, and ginger start to appear. You'll know you are getting closer to the streambed when the mosquitoes begin buzzing. Cross the streambed and climb the switchbacks on the eucalyptus-covered ridge. More native plants will appear: ohia, uluhe, and koa. Just before you reach the crest of the next ridge, look for rarely seen plants like yellow-flowered *ohia lehua, kanawao* (a relative of the hydrangea), and mountain *naupaka.* The trail ends on the sometimes rainy—and nearly always windy—peak of the Koolaus, where you'll have views of Waihee Valley and the entire windward side from Kahaluu to Kaneohe Bay. It's very clear that this is the end of the trail; retrace your steps to the trailhead.

EAST OAHU

MAKAPUU LIGHTHOUSE TRAIL ★

You've seen this famous old lighthouse on episodes of *Magnum, P.I.* and *Hawaii Five-O.* No longer manned by the Coast Guard (it's fully automated now), the lighthouse is the goal of hikers who challenge a precipitous cliff trail to gain an airy perch over the Windward Coast, Manana (Rabbit) Island, and the azure Pacific. It's about a 45-minute, mile-long hike from Kalanianaole Highway (Hwy. 72), along a paved road that begins across from Hawaii Kai Executive Golf Course and winds around the 646-foot-high sea bluff to the lighthouse lookout.

To get to the trailhead from Waikiki, take Kalanianaole Highway (Hwy. 72) past Hanauma Bay and Sandy Beach to Makapuu Head, the southeastern tip of the island; you can also take TheBus no. 57 or 58. Look for a sign that says NO

VEHICLES ALLOWED on a gate to the right, a few hundred yards past the entrance to the golf course. The trail isn't marked, but it's fairly obvious: Just follow the abandoned road that leads gradually uphill to a trail that wraps around Makapuu Point. It's a little precarious, but anyone in reasonably good shape can handle it.

Blowhole alert: When the south swell is running, usually in summer, there are a couple of blowholes on the south side of Makapuu Head that put the famous Halona blowhole to shame.

WINDWARD OAHU
HAUULA LOOP 👁

For one of the best views of the coast and the ocean, follow the Hauula Loop Trail on the windward side of the island. It's an easy, 2½-mile loop on a well-maintained path that passes through a whispering ironwood forest and a grove of tall Norfolk pines. The trip takes about 3 hours and gains some 600 feet in elevation.

To get to the trail, take TheBus no. 55 or follow Highway 83 to Hauula Beach Park. Turn toward the mountains on Hauula Homestead Road; when it forks to the left at Maakua Road, park on the side of the road. Walk along Maakua Road to the wide, grassy trail that begins the hike into the mountains. The climb is fairly steep for about 300 yards, but continues to easier-on-the-calves switchbacks as you go up the ridge. Look down as you climb: You'll spot wildflowers and mushrooms among the matted needles. The trail continues up, crossing Waipilopilo Gulch, where you'll see several forms of native plant life. Eventually, you reach the top of the ridge, where the views are spectacular.

Camping is permitted along the trail, but it's difficult to find a place to pitch a tent on the steep slopes and in the dense forest growth. There are a few places along the ridge, however, that are wide enough for a tent. Contact the **Division of Forestry and Wildlife,** 1151 Punchbowl St., Honolulu, HI 96813 (© **808/ 587-0166**), for information on camping permits.

KAHANA VALLEY

Spectacular views of this verdant valley and some clear swimming holes are the rewards of this 4.5-mile loop trial. The down side to this 2-3 hour, somewhat ardent adventure are mosquitoes (clouds of them) and some thrashing about in dense forest with a bit of navigation along the not-always marked trail.

The trail starts behind the Visitor's Center at the Kahana Valley State Park. To get there, take H-1 to the Pali Highway over to the Windward side of Kailua-Kaneohe. Turn left onto Highway 83 (Kamehameha Hwy.) to Kahana Valley State Park. You can also take TheBus no. 55 and get off at the park entrance.

After checking in at the Visitor's Center for the latest trail conditions and any warnings about stream flooding, continue down the paved road, past homes, farm lots, and lots of birds until you get to the Y junction, where you bear right past abandoned World War II structures. At the next fork go left. Be sure to sign in at the hunter's and hiker's check-in station after forging a stream. Now you are on the loop, if you are just interested in jumping in the pools at the Gaging Station, you can turn left at the dam. If you are up for the hike, continue on. Sweeping views of the valley are at about a mile into the loop. A half mile past the views, the road ends at the fenced water take and you'll have to make your way up a steep, but somewhat terraced side of the tank, be alert for the tagged narrow trail that continues down into the forest.

The only caution is when it has been raining and the streams are swollen. If you check with the Visitor's Center, they will let you know if it is safe to cross the streams. The trail meanders through dense forest, past meadows and makes its way back to the Gaging Station, where big, cool mountain stream pools (great for swimming) are your reward. From the Gaging Station, retrace your steps back to the Visitor's Center.

PALI (MAUNAWILI) TRAIL 𝄞

For a million-dollar view of the Windward Coast, take this easy 11-mile (one-way) foothill trail. The trailhead is about 6 miles from downtown Honolulu, on the windward side of the Nuuanu Pali Tunnel, at the scenic lookout just beyond the hairpin turn of the Pali Highway (Hwy. 61). Just as you begin the turn, look for the scenic overlook sign, slow down, and pull off the highway into the parking lot (sorry, no bus service available).

The mostly flat, well-marked, easy-to-moderate trail goes through the forest on the lower slopes of the 3,000-foot Koolau Mountain range and ends up in the backyard of the coastal Hawaiian village of Waimanalo. Go halfway to get the view and return to your car, or have someone meet you in 'Nalo.

LEEWARD OAHU

KAENA POINT 𝄞

At the very western tip of Oahu lie the dry, barren lands of Kaena Point State Park; 853 acres consisting of a remote, wild coastline of jagged sea cliffs, deep gulches, sand dunes, endangered plant life, and a wind- and surf-battered coastline. *Kaena* means "red-hot" or "glowing" in Hawaiian; the name refers to the brilliant sunsets visible from the point.

Kaena is steeped in numerous legends. A popular one concerns the demigod Maui: Maui had a famous hook that he used to raise islands from the sea. He decided that he wanted to bring the islands of Oahu and Kauai closer together, so one day he threw his hook across the Kauai Channel and snagged Kauai (which is actually visible from Kaena Point on clear days). Using all his might, Maui was able to pull loose a huge boulder, which fell into the waters very close to the present lighthouse at Kaena. The rock is still called Pohaku o Kauai (the rock from Kauai). Like Black Rock in Kaanapali on Maui, Kaena is thought of as the point on Oahu from which souls depart.

To hike out to the departing place, take the clearly marked trail from the parking lot of Kaena Point State Park. The moderate, 5-mile round-trip to the point will take a couple of hours. The trail along the cliff passes tide pools abundant in marine life and rugged protrusions of lava reaching out to the turbulent sea; seabirds circle overhead. There are no sandy beaches, and the water is nearly always turbulent. In winter, when a big north swell is running, the waves at Kaena are the biggest in the state, averaging heights of 30 to 40 feet. Even when the water appears calm, offshore currents are powerful, so don't plan to swim. Go early in the morning to see the schools of porpoises that frequent the area just offshore.

To get to the trailhead from Honolulu or Waikiki, take the H-1 west to its end; continue on Highway 93 past Makaha and follow Highway 930 to the end of the road. There's no bus service.

4 Great Golf

It *is* possible to play some top-notch golf in Hawaii without having to take out a second mortgage on your home. Oahu has nearly three dozen golf courses, ranging from bare-bones municipal courses to exclusive country clubs with annual membership fees in the six figures. Golfers unfamiliar with Hawaii's

---

Tips **Avoiding the Crowds & Saving Money**

Oahu's golf courses tend to be crowded, so we suggest that you go during midweek. Also, most island courses have twilight rates with substantial discounts if you're willing to tee off in the afternoon, usually between 1 and 3pm. Look for this feature in the golf listings that follow.

---

courses will be dazzled by some of the spectacular views—the shimmering ocean and majestic mountains, to name a few.

Golfers will also come to know that the windward golf courses play much differently than the leeward courses. On the windward side, the prevailing winds blow from the ocean to shore and the grain direction of the greens tends to run the same way—from the ocean to the mountains. Leeward golf courses have the opposite tendency; the winds usually blow from the mountains to the ocean, and the grain direction on the greens matches. Below are a variety of courses, with greens fees (cart costs included) and notes on scenic views, challenges, and a taste of what golfing in paradise is like.

For last-minute and discount tee times, call **Stand-by Golf** (from Hawaii, call ✆ **888/645-BOOK**), which offers discounted and guaranteed tee times for same-day or next-day golfing. You can call between 7am and 11pm Hawaii Standard Time, to book one of the seven semiprivate and resort courses they handle and get a guaranteed tee time for the next day at a 10% to 40% discount.

TheBus does not allow golf bags onboard. If you don't have another means of transportation, you're going to have to rent clubs at the course.

EAST OAHU

Hawaii Kai Golf Course This is actually two golf courses in one. The par-72, 6,222-yard **Hawaii Kai Championship Golf Course** is moderately challenging, with scenic vistas. The course is forgiving to high-handicap golfers, although it does have a few surprises. The par-3 **Hawaii Kai Executive Golf Course** is fun for beginners and those just getting back in the game after a few years. The course has lots of hills and valleys, with no water hazards and only a few sand traps. Lockers are available.

8902 Kalanianaole Hwy., Honolulu. ✆ 808/395-2358. Greens fees: $90 Mon–Fri.; $100 Sat.–Sun, with twilight rates (after 1pm) $60. Take H-1 east past Hawaii Kai; it's immediately past Sandy Beach on the left. TheBus: 58.

THE WINDWARD COAST

Olomana Golf Links Low-handicap golfers may not find this gorgeous course difficult, but the striking views of the craggy Koolau mountain ridge are worth the fees alone. The par-72, 6,326-yard course is popular with locals and visitors alike. The course starts off a bit hilly on the front nine, but flattens out by the back nine. The back nine have their own surprises, including tricky water hazards. The first hole, a 384-yard, par-4 that tees downhill and approaches uphill, is definitely a warm-up. The next hole is a 160-yard, par-3 that starts from an elevated tee to an elevated green over a severely banked, V-shaped gully. Shoot long here—it's longer than you think—as short shots tend to roll all the way back down the fairway to the base of the gully. This course is very, very green; the rain gods bless it regularly with brief passing showers. You can spot the regular players here—they all carry umbrellas and wait patiently for the squalls to pass, then resume play. Reservations are a must. Facilities include a driving range, practice greens, club rental, pro shop, and restaurant.

41–1801 Kalanianaole Hwy., Waimanalo. ℭ 808/259-7926. Greens fees $65, including cart; after 2:30pm, it's $24 with cart or $14 without ($2 more on weekends). Take H-1 to the Pali Hwy. (Hwy. 61); turn right on Kalanianaole Hwy.; after 5 miles, it will be on the left. TheBus: 57.

Pali Golf Course *Value*   This beautiful municipal course sits near Kaneohe, just below the historic spot where King Kamehameha the Great won the battle that united the islands of Hawaii. The par-72, 6,494-yard course, designed by Willard G. Wilkinson and built in 1953, makes use of the natural terrain (hills and valleys make up the majority of the 250 acres). The course does not have man-made traps, but a small stream meanders through it. If you're off line on the ninth, you'll get to know the stream quite well. The challenge here is the weather—whipping winds and frequent rainsqualls. Because of the potential for rain, you might want to pay for nine holes, and then assess the weather before signing up for the back nine. The views include Kaneohe Bay, the towns of Kailua and Kaneohe, and the verdant cliffs of the Koolau Mountains. Facilities include practice greens, club rental, locker rooms, and a restaurant.

45–050 Kamehameha Hwy., Kaneohe, HI 96744. ℭ 808/296-2000. Fees: $42 ($16 extra for an optional cart, which carries 2 golfers); $21 twilight rate after 4pm (walking only, no carts). From Waikiki, take the H-1 freeway to the Pali Hwy. (Hwy. 61). Turn left at Kamehameha Hwy. at the first traffic light after you are through the Pali Tunnels. The course is immediately on your left after you turn on Kamehameha Hwy. TheBus: 55.

THE NORTH SHORE

Kahuku Golf Course *Finds*   This nine-hole budget golf course is a bit funky. There are no club rentals, no clubhouse, and no facilities other than a few pull carts that disappear with the first handful of golfers. But a round at this scenic oceanside course amidst the tranquillity of the North Shore is quite an experience nonetheless. Duffers will love the ease of this recreational course, and weight watchers will be happy to walk the gently sloping greens. Don't forget to bring your camera for the views (especially at holes 3, 4, 7, and 8, which are right on the ocean). No reservations are taken; tee times are first-come, first-served—with plenty of retirees happy to sit and wait, the competition is fierce for early tee times. Bring your own clubs and call ahead to check the weather. The cost for this experience? Ten bucks!

ℭ 808/293-5842. Greens fees: $10 for 9 holes. Take H-1 west to H-2; follow H-2 through Wahiawa to Kamehameha Hwy. (Hwy. 99, then Hwy. 83); follow it to Kahuku.

Hilton at Turtle Bay Resort *☆*   This North Shore resort is home to two of Hawaii's top golf courses. The 18-hole **Arnold Palmer Course** (formerly the Links at Kuilima) was designed by Arnold Palmer and Ed Seay. Turtle Bay used to be labeled a "wind tunnel"; it still is one, though the casuarina (ironwood) trees have matured and dampened the wind somewhat. But Palmer and Seay never meant for golfers to get off too easy; this is a challenging course. The front nine, with rolling terrain, only a few trees, and lots of wind, play like a British Isles course. The back nine have narrower, tree-lined fairways and water. The course circles Punahoolapa Marsh, a protected wetland for endangered Hawaiian waterfowl.

The budget option is the **George Fazio–designed nine-hole course**—the only one Fazio designed in Hawaii—which can be played twice for a regulation par-71, 6,200-yard course. The course has two sets of tees, one designed for men and one for women, so you get a slightly different play if you decide to tackle 18 holes. Larry Keil, pro at Turtle Bay, says that people like the Fazio course because it's more of a forgiving resort course, without the water hazards and bunkers of the more challenging Links course. The sixth hole has two greens so you can play the hole as a par-3 or a par-4. The toughest hole has to be the par-3, 176-yard second hole, where you tee off across a lake with the trade winds creating a mean crosswind. The most scenic hole is the seventh, where the ocean is on your left; if you're lucky, you'll see whales cavorting in the winter months. Facilities include a pro shop, driving range, putting and chipping green, and snack bar. Weekdays are best for tee times.

57–091 Kamehameha Hwy., Kahuku. © 808/293-8811. Greens fees at the Links: $135 (Turtle Bay guests pay $90); twilight fees are $75 ($55 for guests). Greens fees at the Fazio: $55 for 9 holes, $90 for 18 holes (guests pay $45 for 9, $75 for 18).Take H-1 west past Pearl City; when the freeway splits, take H-2 and follow the signs to Haleiwa; at Haleiwa, take Hwy. 83 to Turtle Bay Resort. TheBus: 52 or 55.

LEEWARD OAHU: THE WAIANAE COAST

Ko Olina Golf Club 𝘈𝘈𝘈   *Golf Digest* named this 6,867-yard, par-72 course one of "America's Top 75 Resort Courses" in 1992. The Ted Robinson–designed course has rolling fairways and elevated tee and water features. The signature hole—the 12th, a par-3—has an elevated tee that sits on a rock garden with a cascading waterfall. Wait until you get to the 18th hole, where you'll see and hear water all around you—seven pools begin on the right side of the fairway and slope down to a lake. A waterfall is on your left off the elevated green. You'll have no choice but to play the left and approach the green over the water. Book in advance; this course is crowded all the time. Facilities include a driving range, locker rooms, Jacuzzi, steam rooms, and a restaurant and bar. Lessons are available.

92–1220 Aliinui Dr., Kapolei © 808/676-5300. Greens fees: $145 ($115 for Ihilani Resort guests); twilight rates (after 2pm in winter and 2:30pm in summer) are $75. Men are asked to wear a collared shirt. Take H-1 west until it becomes Hwy. 93 (Farrington Hwy.); turn off at the Ko Olina exit; take the exit road (Aliinui Dr.) into Ko Olina Resort; turn left into the clubhouse. No bus service.

Makaha Resort Golf Club 𝘈𝘈   This challenging course—recently named "The Best Golf Course on Oahu" by *Honolulu* magazine—sits some 45 miles west of Honolulu, in Makaha Valley. Designed by William Bell, the par-72, 7,091-yard course meanders toward the ocean before turning and heading into the valley. Sheer volcanic walls tower 1,500 feet above the course, which is surrounded by swaying palm trees and neon-bright bougainvillea; an occasional peacock will even strut across the fairways. The beauty here could make it difficult to keep your mind on the game if it weren't for the course's many challenges: 8 water hazards, 107 bunkers, and frequent brisk winds. This course is packed on weekends, so it's best to try weekdays. Facilities include a pro shop, bag storage, and snack shop.

84–626 Makaha Valley Rd., Waianae. © 800/757-8060 or 808/695-9544. Greens fees: guests of Waikiki's Sheraton resorts (Sheraton Moana Surfrider, Royal Hawaiian, Sheraton Waikiki, and Princess Kaiulani): $90, $80 after noon; for non-Sheraton guests, $100, $85 after noon. Twilight rates are $50 for both guests and visitors. Take H-1 west until it turns into Hwy. 93, which winds through the coastal towns of Nanakuli, Waianae, and Makaha. Turn right on Makaha Valley Rd. and follow it to the fork; the course is on the left. TheBus: 51 and Shuttle: 75.

Makaha Valley Country Club   This beautiful public course offers three tees to choose from. You can probably play your handicap from the middle tee, so for a challenge, you might want to go for the back tee, still a sporting par-69 for the 6,369 yards. The course presents a few challenges along the way: numerous trees and an abundance of water (especially on the third hole, which has a couple of small lakes right at a 90° dogleg, followed by a stand of trees). You might want to get an early tee time, as the afternoons in Makaha Valley can get windy. The last hole is a doozie, a 494-yard, par-5 with two 90-degree turns to get up to the green. Facilities include driving range, practice greens, club rental, and clubhouse with restaurant.

84–627 Makaha Valley Rd., Waianae, HI 96792. ✆ **808/695-9578.** Fees (with cart): $55 weekdays; $65 weekends. From Waikiki, take H-1 west until it turns into Hi. 93, which winds through the coastal towns of Nanakuli, Waianae, and Makaha. Turn right on Makaha Valley Rd. and follow it to the fork; turn right. TheBus: 51 and Shuttle: 75.

West Loch Municipal Golf Course (Value) This par-72, 6,615-yard course located just 30 minutes from Waikiki, in Ewa Beach, offers golfers a challenge at bargain rates. The difficulties on this municipal course are water (lots of hazards), wind (constant trade winds), and narrow fairways. To help you out, the course features a "water" driving range (with a lake) to practice your drives. After a few practice swings on the driving range, you'll be ready to take on this unusual course, designed by Robin Nelson and Rodney Wright. In addition to the driving range, West Loch has practice greens, a pro shop, and a restaurant.

91–1126 Olepekeupe Loop, Ewa Beach. ✆ **808/296-2000.** Greens fees: $50; twilight rates between 1–3 pm $25 for 9 holes. Booking a week in advance is recommended. Take H-1 west to the Hwy. 76 exit; stay in the left lane and turn left at West Loch Estates, just opposite St. Francis Medical Center. To park, take two immediate right turns. TheBus: 50.

CENTRAL OAHU

Hawaii Country Club This public course, located in Wahiawa, is a modest course where golfers usually have no trouble getting a tee time. The 5,861-yard, par-71 course is not manicured like the resort courses, but it does offer fair play, with relatively inexpensive greens fees. Located in the middle of former sugarcane and pineapple fields, the greens and fairways tend to be a bit bumpy and there are a number of tall monkeypod and pine trees to shoot around, but the views of Pearl Harbor and Waikiki in the distance are spectacular. There are a few challenging holes, like the seventh (a 252-yd., par-4), which has a lake in the middle of the fairway and slim pickings on either side. With the wind usually blowing in your face, most golfers choose an iron to lay up short of the water and then pitch it over for par. Facilities include a driving range, practice greens, club rental pro shop, and restaurant.

98–1211 Kunia Rd., Wahiawa, HI 96786. ✆ **808/621-5654.** Fees: $45 weekdays, $55 weekends (cart included); $15 twilight rate weekdays after 3pm, $21 weekends. From Waikiki, take the H-1 freeway west for about 20 min. Turn off at the Kunia exit (Exit 5B) and follow it to the course. No bus service.

Mililani Golf Club This par-72, 6,455-yard public course is home to the Sports Shinko Rainbow Open, where Hawaii's top professionals compete. Located between the Koolau and Waianae mountain ranges on the Leilehua Plateau, this is one of Oahu's most scenic courses, with views of mountains from every hole. Unfortunately, there are also lots of views of trees, especially eucalyptus, Norfolk pine, and coconut palm; it's a lesson in patience to stay on the fairways and away from the trees. The two signature holes, the par-4 number 4 (a classic middle hole with water, flowers, and bunkers) and the par-3 number 12 (a comfortable tee shot over a ravine filled with tropical flowers that jumps to the undulating green with bunkers on each side) are so scenic, you'll forgive the challenges they pose.

95–176 Kuahelani Ave., Mililani. ✆ **808/623-2222.** Greens fees: $89 Mon–Fri. ($65 after 11am); $95 Sat–Sun, and holidays. Take H-1 west past Pearl City; when the freeway splits, take H-2. Exit at Mililani (exit

5B) onto Meheula Pkwy.; go to the third stoplight (about 2 miles from the exit) and turn right onto Kuahe-lani Ave. TheBus: 52.

Pearl Country Club   Looking for a challenge? You'll find one at this popular public course, located just above Pearl City in Aiea. Sure, the 6,230-yard, par-72 looks harmless enough, and the views of Pearl Harbor and the USS *Arizona* Memorial are gorgeous, but around the fifth hole, you'll start to see what you're in for. That par-5, a blind 472-yard hole, doglegs seriously to the left (with a small margin of error between the tee and the steep out-of-bounds hillside on the entire left side of the fairway). A water hazard and a forest await your next two shots. Suddenly, this nice public course becomes not so nice. Oahu residents can't get enough of it, so don't even try to get a tee time on weekends. Stick to weekdays—Mondays are usually the best bet. Facilities include a driving range, practice greens, club rental, pro shop, and restaurant.

98–535 Kaonohi St., Aiea. ✆ 808/487-3802. Greens fees: $65 Mon–Fri.; $70 Sat–Sun. After 4pm, 9 holes are $20; on Wed after 3pm, 18 holes are $30. Call for a tee time at least a week in advance. Take H-1 past Pearl Harbor to the Hwy. 78 (Moanalua Freeway) exit; stay in the left lane where Hwy. 78 becomes Hwy. 99 (Kamehameha Hwy.); turn right on Kaonohi St. TheBus: 32 (stops at Pearlridge Shopping Center at Kaonohi and Moanalua sts.; you'll have to walk about a half mile uphill from here).

5 Other Outdoor Activities

BICYCLING

Bicycling is a great way to see Oahu. Most streets here have bike lanes. For information on biking trails, races, and tours, check out **www.bikehawaii.com**. For information on bikeways and maps, contact the **Honolulu City and County Bike Coordinator** (✆ 808/527-5044).

If you're in Waikiki, you can rent a bike for as little as $15 for a half day and $20 for 24 hours at **Blue Sky Rentals,** Inn on the Park, 1920 Ala Moana Blvd. (✆ 808/947-0101); or **Wiki Wiki Wheels,** 1827 Ala Moana, Suite 201 (✆ 808/951-5787). On the North Shore, try **Raging Isle,** 66–250 Kamehameha Hwy., Haleiwa (✆ 808/637-7707; www.ragingisle.com). If you're interested in taking a bicycling tour, **The Parks at Waimea,** 59–864 Kamehameha Hwy., Haleiwa (✆ 888/973-9200 or 808/638-5300), has mountain bikes, for advanced and expert riders, starting at $35 for an hour and 45 minutes.

If you'd like to join some club rides, contact the **Hawaii Bicycle League** (✆ 808/735-5756), which offers rides every weekend, as well as several annual events. The league can also provide a schedule of upcoming rides, races, and outings.

GLIDER RIDES

Imagine soaring through silence on gossamer-like wings, a panoramic view of Oahu below you. A glider ride is an unforgettable experience, and it's available at Dillingham Air Field, in Mokuleia, on Oahu's North Shore. The glider is towed behind a plane; at the proper altitude, the tow is dropped and you (and the glider pilot) are left to soar in the thermals. You can get the best deal if you go with another person—the price drops: a 15-minute ride is $50 for two, a 20-minute ride is $70 for two and a 30-minute ride is $90 for two. We recommend Mr. Bill at **Glider Rides** 🛪 (✆ 808/677-3404); he's been offering piloted glider rides since 1970. If Mr. Bill is booked, try **Soar Hawaii** (✆ 808/637-3147), which offers rides at the same price.

HANG GLIDING
See things from a bird's-eye view (literally) as you and your instructor float high above Oahu on a tandem hang glider. **North Shore Hang/Para Gliding,** at the Dillingham Air Field (© **808/637-3178**), offers you an opportunity to try out this daredevil sport. A tandem lesson of 45 minutes to an hour in the air costs $150.

HORSEBACK RIDING
You can gallop on the beach at the **Hilton at Turtle Bay Resort,** 57–091 Kamehameha Hwy., Kahuku (© **808/293-8811;** TheBus: 52 or 55), where 45-minute rides along sandy beaches with spectacular ocean views and through a forest of ironwood trees cost $35 for adults and $22 for children 9 to 12 (they must be at least 54 in. tall). Romantic evening rides take place on Friday, Saturday, and Sunday from 5 to 6:30pm ($65 per person). Advanced riders can sign up for a 40-minute trot-and-canter ride along Kawela Bay ($50).

For guided horseback tours of lush Waimea Valley on the North Shore, contact **The Parks at Waimea,** 59–864 Kamehameha Hwy., Haleiwa (© **888/ 973-9200** or 808/638-5300), which offers a range of tours starting at $35 for 1 hour.

If you've dreamed of learning how to ride, the **Hilltop Equestrian Center,** 41–430 Waikupanaha St., Waimanalo (© **808/259-8463;** TheBus: 57 or 58), can teach you. British Horse Society–accredited instructors offer lessons in either British or Western style riding for $40 per lesson, minimum of three lessons.

SKYDIVING
Everything you need to leap from a plane and float to earth can be obtained from **Blue Sky Rentals and Sports Center,** 1920 Ala Moana Blvd. (on the ground floor of Inn on the Park, in Waikiki, on the corner of Ala Moana Blvd. and Ena Rd.), Honolulu (© **808/947-0101**). The cost is $175 per jump (including suit, parachute, goggles, plane rental, lesson, and so on). For instructions, call **SkyDive Hawaii,** 68–760 Farrington Hwy., Waiawa (© **808/ 637-9700**). They offer a tandem jump (where you're strapped to an expert who wears a chute big enough for the both of you) for $225. There's no doubt about it—this is the thrill of a lifetime.

TENNIS
Oahu has 181 free public tennis courts. To get a complete list of all facilities or information on upcoming tournaments, send a self-addressed, stamped envelope to **Department of Parks and Recreation,** Tennis Unit, 650 S. King St., Honolulu, HI 96813. In Waikiki, if you want to check on the Diamond Head courts, 3908 Paki Ave., across from the Kapiolani Park, call (© **808/971-7150**). The courts are available on a first-come, first-served basis; playing time is limited to 45 minutes if others are waiting.

If you're staying in Waikiki, try the **Ilikai Tennis Center** at the Ilikai Hotel, 1777 Ala Moana Blvd., at Hobron Lane (© **800/367-8434** or 808/949-3811; TheBus: 19 or 20), which has six courts, equipment rental, lessons, and repair service. Courts cost $5 per person per hour; private lessons are $44 per hour.

If you're on the North Shore, the **Hilton at Turtle Bay Resort,** 57–091 Kamehameha Hwy., Kahuku (© **808/293-8811,** ext. 24; TheBus: 52 or 55), has 10 courts, four of which are lit for night play. You must reserve the night courts in advance, as they're very popular. Nonguests pay $12 per person for singles and $10 per person for doubles. *Budget tip:* Book a court between noon and 4pm for 50% off. Equipment rental and lessons are available.

6 From the Sidelines: Spectator Sports

Although there aren't any major league sports teams in Hawaii, there are college teams and a handful of professional exposition games played in Hawaii, many of them immensely popular among the local residents. Check the schedule at the 50,000-seat **Aloha Stadium,** located near Pearl Harbor, 99–500 Salt Lake Blvd. (© **808/486-9300**), where high school and University of Hawaii football games are also held from September to November, (© **808/944-BOWS** or www. uhathletics.hawaii.edu). There are usually express buses that take you to the stadium on game nights; they depart from Ala Moana Shopping Center (TheBus no. 47–50 and 52), or from Monsarrat Avenue near Kapiolani Park (TheBus no. 20). Call TheBus at © **808/848-5555** for times and fares.

The **Neal Blaisdell Center,** at Kapiolani Boulevard and Ward Avenue (© **808/521-2911;** www.co.honolulu.hi.us/Depts/aud/blaisd), features a variety of sporting events, such as professional boxing and Japanese sumo wrestling. In December, the Annual **Rainbow Classic,** a collegiate basketball invitational tournament, takes place at the Blaisdell. For bus information, call TheBus at © **808/848-5555.**

At the University of Hawaii, the **Rainbow Stadium,** 1337 Lower Campus Rd, and the **Rainbow Wahine Softball Stadium,** next door, are hosts to college baseball and softball from January through May. Information is at © **808/ 944-BOWS;** www.uhathletics.hawaii.edu. Collegiate volleyball, which is extremely popular in Hawaii, takes place at the Stan Sheriff Center, also on the UH campus, 1355 Lower Campus Rd., from November through May. Information at same phone number and website above.

With Hawaii's cowboy history, **polo** is a popular sport, played every Sunday from March through August in Mokuleia or Waimanalo. Bring a picnic lunch and enjoy the game. Call © **808/637-7656** for details on times and admission charges.

A sport you might not be familiar with is Hawaiian **outrigger canoe racing,** which is very big locally. Every weekend from Memorial Day to Labor Day, canoe races are held around Oahu. The races are free and draw huge crowds. Check the local papers for information on race schedules.

Motor-racing fans can enjoy their sport at **Hawaii Raceway Park,** 91–201 Malakole, in Campbell Industrial Park, in Ewa Beach next to the Barbers Point Naval Air Station (© **808/841-3724**), on Friday and Saturday nights. No bus service.

Some of the other spectator sports scheduled during the year, such as the NFL Pro Bowl, the Rainbow Classic, and major golf and surfing tournaments, are listed in the "Oahu Calendar of Events" on p. 33.

Exploring Oahu

by Jeanette Foster

Honolulu is packed with sights and activities. While the rest of the Hawaiian islands are sleepier, Oahu is loaded with diversions. There's historic Honolulu to explore—from the Queen's Summer Palace to the USS *Arizona* Memorial in Pearl Harbor. You can wander through exotic gardens, come face-to-face with brilliantly colored tropical fish, stand on the deck of a four-masted schooner that sailed 100 years ago, venture into haunted places where ghosts are said to roam, take in the spicy smells and sights of Chinatown, and participate in a host of cultural activities from flower lei making to hula dancing.

You don't need a huge budget to experience Honolulu's best activities, and you don't really need a car. The-Bus can get you where you need to go for a $1.50, or you can hop on a moderately priced tour or trolley. Your only obstacle to enjoying all the activities in Honolulu and Oahu might be fitting in everything you want to do.

See chapter 6 for complete coverage of Oahu's best beaches and all kinds of outdoor activities.

SUGGESTED ITINERARIES

If You Have 1 Day

No question—drive around the island of Oahu. If you don't have a car, take TheBus 52 or 55 (see the "By Bus" section, below). If you do have a car, take off across the middle of Oahu and go to Haleiwa for breakfast. Spend the morning stopping at as many beaches as you have time for. Wander into the Polynesian Cultural Center in the early afternoon. Drive along the windward side for a late afternoon dip at Lanikai Beach. Head back to Honolulu and Waikiki as the sun is setting, and plan on dinner at Roy's in Hawaii Kai to finish your perfect day.

If You Have 2 Days

Spend the first day driving around the island (see above). On the second day, get up early and go to the USS *Arizona* Memorial at Pearl Harbor (get there early, as the lines get longer as the day goes on); be sure to check out the USS *Bowfin* submarine next door. In the afternoon, hit either Waikiki Beach or Hanauma Bay for snorkeling and swimming. Head for Waikiki at sunset for sweet Hawaiian music and a night on the town.

If You Have 3 Days

See above for the first 2 days. On day 3, put on your walking shoes and explore Honolulu: downtown (take in the cultural sites from the Iolani Palace to the Mission Museum House), Chinatown (where the smells will compel you to stop for lunch), and the waterfront area. In the afternoon, check out the Waikiki Aquarium. Take in a luau in the evening.

If You Have 4 Days

See above for the first 3 days. On day 4, you might want to consider driving to Southeast Oahu and going to Sea Life Park in the morning, with a quick swim at one of the many beaches lining the coast. In the afternoon, explore Kailua and Kaneohe: Wander through Heeia State Park, check out the replica of the 900-year-old Byodo-In in the Valley of the Temples, bike or horseback ride in Senator Fong's Plantation and Gardens, or take windsurfing lessons at Kailua Beach.

If You Have 5 Days

Allow yourself a great day in the sun on the sands of Waikiki, or else drive to the North Shore, stopping to watch the surfers during the winter, or snorkeling the incredible reefs in the summer.

1 Guided Tours

GUIDED ISLAND TOURS

If your time is limited, you might want to consider a guided tour. These tours are informative and surprisingly entertaining.

E Noa Tours (© **800/824-8804** or 808/591-2561; www.enoa.com) offers a range of tours, from island loops to explorations of historic Honolulu. These narrated tours are on air-conditioned 27-passenger minibuses. The Royal Circle Island tour ($47.50 for adults, $37.50 for children 6–11, $31.50 for children under 6), stops at Diamond Head Crater, Hanauma Bay, Byodo-In Temple, Sunset Beach, Waimea Valley (admission included), and various beach sites along the way. Other tours go to Pearl Harbor/USS *Arizona* Memorial and the Polynesian Cultural Center.

Waikiki Trolley Tours ★ (© **800/824-8804** or 808/596-2199; www.enoa. com) offers three fun tours of sightseeing, entertainment, and dining/shopping. These tours are a great way to get the lay of the land. You can get on and off the trolley as needed (trolleys come along every 2–20 min.). An all-day pass (8:30am–11:35pm) is $18 for adults and $8 for children under 11; a 4-day pass is $30 for adults, $10 for kids. For the same price, you can experience the new 2-hour narrated Ocean Coastline tour of the southeast side of Oahu, an easy way to see the stunning views.

Polynesian Adventure Tours (© **808/833-3000;** www.polyad.com) also offers a range of guided excursions. The all-day island tour starts at $49.50 for adults, $20 for children 6 to 12, and $15 for children 5 and under; the half-day scenic shore and rain-forest tour is $22 for adults, $18 for children 3 to 11; the half-day *Arizona* Memorial Excursion is $22 for adults, $18 for children ages 3 to 11.

WAIKIKI & HONOLULU WALKING TOURS

Honolulu TimeWalk ★, 2634 S. King St., Suite 3, Honolulu (© **808/943-0371;** www.chicken-skin.com), features Glen Grant and his storytelling guides leading a variety of lively 2- to 3-hour walks through Waikiki and other areas of Honolulu. Much of what they "show" you doesn't exist anymore, so they need to be clever—and you need to have some imagination—to get the picture. Guides appear in turn-of-the-century togs and tell it like it was through lively anecdotes about King Kalakaua, Prince Kuhio, Robert Louis Stevenson, and Mark Twain. The **Ghost Walk through Old Honolulu,** which takes place two Wednesdays a month from 7 to 9:30pm, includes the strange and unexplainable happenings around the capitol district; the cost is $10. Another walk on the "chicken-skin" side (a local word referring to the texture of your skin

Moments   A Bird's-Eye View

To understand why Oahu was the island of kings, you need to see it from the air. **Island Seaplane Service** ★★ (© **808/836-6273**) operates flights departing from a floating dock in the protected waters of Keehi Lagoon (parallel to Honolulu International Airport's runway) in either a six-passenger DeHavilland Beaver or a four-passenger Cessna 206. There's nothing quite like feeling the slap of the waves as the plane skims across the water and then effortlessly lifts into the air.

Your tour will give you aerial views of Waikiki Beach, Diamond Head Crater, Kahala's luxury estates, and the sparkling waters of Hanauma and Kaneohe bays. The half-hour tour ($89) ends here, while the 1-hour tour ($139) continues on to Chinaman's Hat, the Polynesian Cultural Center, and the rolling surf of the North Shore. The flight returns across the island, flying over Hawaii's historic wartime sites: Schofield Barracks and the USS *Arizona* and *Missouri* memorials in Pearl Harbor.

Captain Pat Magie, company president and chief pilot, has logged more than 32,000 hours of flight time without an accident (26,000 hr. in seaplanes in Alaska, Canada, the Arctic, and the Caribbean). Any day now, he'll break the world record for seaplane hours.

---

when "goose bumps" appear) is the **Mysteries of Moiliili,** a walk into the supernatural forces of a Honolulu neighborhood, which takes place on Fridays, from 7 to 9:30pm, also $10. History buffs will love the historical tours of Honolulu's cemeteries, which are morning tours and cost $10. Honolulu TimeWalks also offers a variety of storytelling and historical theater programs, as well as excursions around the island. Call for complete information and scheduling.

DOWNTOWN HONOLULU

The **Mission Houses Museum,** 553 S. King St., at Kawaiahao Street (© **808/531-0481;** TheBus: 2), offers a guided walking tour of historic downtown Honolulu, on Thursday and Saturday, from 9:30am to 12:45pm. The fee is $15 for adults, $13 for seniors, $11 for ages 13 to 18, and $10 for kids 4 to 12; rates includes the regular Mission Houses tour (see "Historic Honolulu," later in this chapter). The tour includes the capitol district, making stops at sites such as Iolani Place, the Kamehameha Statue, the Royal Tomb, and James Kekela's grave. Reserve a day ahead in person or by phone.

Kapiolani Community College has a unique series of walking tours into Hawaii's past, including visits to Honolulu's famous cemeteries, the almost-vanished "Little Tokyo" neighborhood, and many more fascinating destinations. Tours, which generally cost about $5, are for groups only, but you may be able to tag along. For information and reservations, call © **808/734-9234.**

The **Hawaii Geographic Society** (© **808/538-3952**) presents numerous interesting and unusual tours, such as "A Temple Tour," which includes Chinese, Japanese, Christian, and Jewish houses of worship; an archaeology tour in and around downtown Honolulu; and others. Each is guided by an expert from the Hawaii Geographic Society and must have a minimum of three people; the cost is $10 per person. The society's brochure, *Historic Downtown Honolulu Walking Tour,* is a fascinating self-guided tour of the 200-year-old city center. If you'd like a copy, send $3 to **Hawaii Geographic Maps and Books,** 49 S. Hotel St. (P.O. Box 1698), Honolulu, HI 96808.

CHINATOWN HISTORIC DISTRICT

Two 3-hour guided tours of Chinatown are offered Tuesdays at 9:30am by the **Chinese Chamber of Commerce** ✵, 42 N. King St., at Smith Street (℃ 808/533-3181; TheBus: 2). The cost is $5 per person; call to reserve. The **Hawaii Heritage Center** (℃ 808/521-2749) also conducts 2-hour walking tours that focus on the history, culture, and multicultural aspects of Chinatown. Tours begin Fridays at 9:30am at the Ramsay Gallery, 1128 Smith St., at N. King Street (TheBus: 2 or 13, get off on Hotel and Smith sts.); the cost is $5 per person.

For a self-guided tour of the neighborhood, see "Walking Tour 1: Historic Chinatown," on p. 187.

GUIDED ECOTOURS

If you want to explore a hidden, ancient Hawaii that most lifelong residents have never seen, book a tour with **Mauka Makai Excursions** ✵, 350 Ward Ave., Honolulu (℃ 808/593-3525), a Hawaiian-owned and -operated ecotour company specializing in field trips to off-the-beaten-path (and sometimes hidden in the jungle) ancient temples, sea caves, sacred stones, petroglyphs, and other cultural treasures. Tours range from a half day ($47 adult, $32 children 6–17 years) to a full day ($78 adult, $63 children). They provide bottled water, insect repellent, fresh fruit snacks, rain gear, beach gear, fishing tackle, and hotel pickup; you bring your imagination.

2 Historic Honolulu

The Waikiki you see today bears no resemblance to the Waikiki of yesteryear, when vast taro fields extended from the ocean into Manoa Valley, and the area was dotted with numerous fishponds and gardens tended by thousands of people. This picture of old Waikiki can be recaptured by following the **Waikiki Historic Trail** ✵, a meandering 2-mile walk with 20 bronze surfboard markers (standing 6 ft., 5 in. tall, you can't miss 'em), complete with descriptions and archive photos of the historic sites. The markers note everything from Waikiki's ancient fishponds to the history of the Ala Wai Canal. Free walking tours are given Monday to Friday from 9 to 10:30am and Saturdays from 4:30 to 6 pm; meet at the beachside surfboard marker at the entrance to Kapiolani Park, on Kalakaua Avenue, across from the Honolulu Zoo. For more information, call ℃ 808/841-6442 or point your browser to www.waikikihistoricaltrail.com.

A hula performance is a popular way for visitors to get a taste of traditional Hawaiian culture. For just about as long as anyone can remember, the Eastman Kodak Company has been hosting the **Kodak Hula Show** ✵, at the Waikiki Band Shell at Kapiolani Park (TheBus: 4, 8, 19, or 20). It's really more 1950s nostalgia than ancient culture, but it's a good bit of fun any way you slice it. Shows run from 10 to 11:15am every Tuesday, Wednesday, and Thursday. Admission is free. The area seats 1,500, and you'll have a good view no matter where you sit; however, if you want to be front and center (the best spot for photo ops), Kodak suggests that you arrive around 9:15am. For more information, call ℃ 808/627-3300.

For a more genuine Hawaiian hula experience, catch the hula *halau* performed Monday through Friday at 1pm at the **Bishop Museum** (see below).

Honolulu Attractions

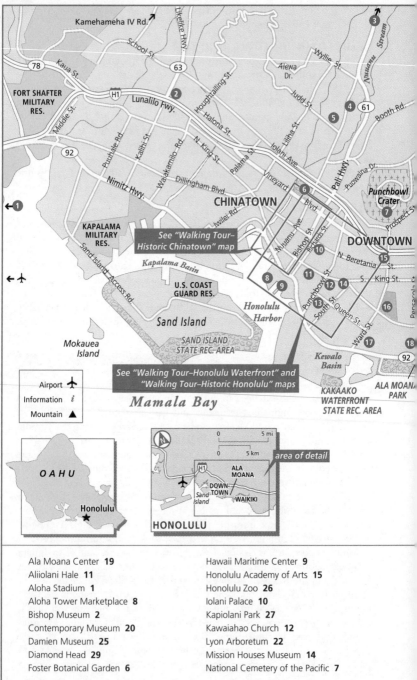

Kamehameha IV Rd.
Likelike Hwy.
School St.
78
Kaua St.
63
Houghtailing St.
H1
Lunalilo Fwy.
2
Halona St.
N. King St.
Palama St.
Alewa Dr.
Wyllie St.
Judd St.
5
Liliha St.
Iolani Ave.
4 **61**
Booth Rd.
Pali Hwy.
Puowaina Dr.
Prospect St.
FORT SHAFTER MILITARY RES.
Middle St.
Puuhale Rd.
Kalihi St.
Waiakamilo Rd.
92
Nimitz Hwy.
Dillingham Blvd.
Vineyard
6
Blvd.
Nuuanu Ave.
Bishop St.
Richards St.
3
Nuuanu Stream
Punchbowl Crater
7
←1
KAPALAMA MILITARY RES.
Iwilei Rd.
CHINATOWN
See "Walking Tour– Historic Chinatown" map
10
N. Beretania St.
DOWNTOWN
15
←✈
Sand Island Access Rd.
Kapalama Basin
U.S. COAST GUARD RES.
8
9
11
Punchbowl St.
12 **14**
S. King St.
Honolulu Harbor
13
South St.
Queen St.
16
Pensacola St.
Mokauea Island
Sand Island
SAND ISLAND STATE REC. AREA
See "Walking Tour–Honolulu Waterfront" and "Walking Tour–Historic Honolulu" maps
Kewalo Basin
17
18
Ward St.
92
Airport ✈
Information *i*
Mountain ▲
Mamala Bay
KAKAAKO WATERFRONT STATE REC. AREA
ALA MOANA PARK

OAHU
★ Honolulu

0 — 5 mi
0 — 5 km
area of detail
H1
ALA MOANA
DOWN-TOWN
Sand Island
✈
WAIKIKI
HONOLULU

Ala Moana Center **19**
Aliiolani Hale **11**
Aloha Stadium **1**
Aloha Tower Marketplace **8**
Bishop Museum **2**
Contemporary Museum **20**
Damien Museum **25**
Diamond Head **29**
Foster Botanical Garden **6**

Hawaii Maritime Center **9**
Honolulu Academy of Arts **15**
Honolulu Zoo **26**
Iolani Palace **10**
Kapiolani Park **27**
Kawaiahao Church **12**
Lyon Arboretum **22**
Mission Houses Museum **14**
National Cemetery of the Pacific **7**

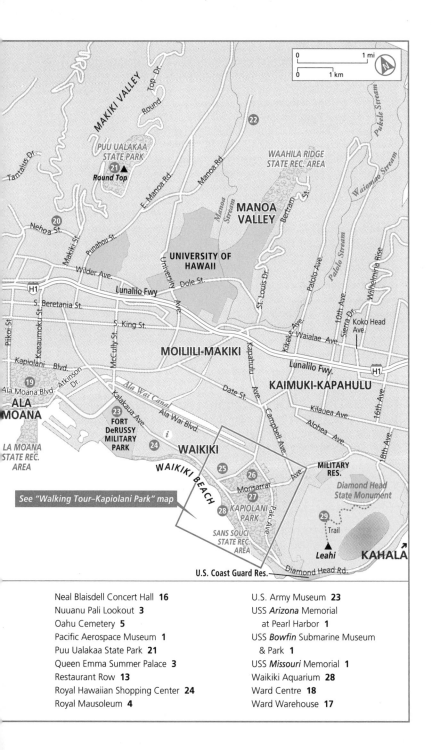

Bishop Museum ★★ *Kids* This forbidding, four-story Romanesque lava-rock structure (it looks like something out of a Charles Addams cartoon) holds safe the world's greatest collection of natural and cultural artifacts from Hawaii and the Pacific. It's a great rainy-day diversion; plan to spend about half a day here. The museum was founded by a Hawaiian princess, Bernice Pauahi, who collected priceless artifacts and in her will instructed her husband, Charles Reed Bishop, to establish a Hawaiian museum "to enrich and delight" the people of Hawaii. The institution is now home to Dr. Yosihiko Sinoto, the last in a proud line of adventuring archaeologists who explored more of the Pacific than Captain Cook and traced Hawaii's history and culture through its fishhooks.

Plan to spend a day here. The Bishop is jam-packed with acquisitions—from insect specimens and ceremonial spears to calabashes and old photos of topless hula dancers. A visit here will give you a good basis for understanding Hawaiian life and culture. You'll see the great feathered capes of kings, the last grass shack in Hawaii, preindustrial Polynesian art, even the skeleton of a 50-foot sperm whale. There are also seashells, koa-wood bowls, nose flutes, and Dr. Sinoto's major collection of fishhooks.

Hula performances ★ take place daily at 11am and 2pm, and various Hawaiian crafts, such as feather-working and quilting, are demonstrated. This daily cultural event is worth making time for. For a look at spectacular artifacts such as the ancient feather cloak of King Kamehameha and other items not shown to the general public, take the "Behind the Scenes Tour," offered weekdays at 1:30pm for an additional fee of $15.

1525 Bernice St., just off Kalihi St. (also known as Likelike Hwy.). ℂ 808/847-3511. www.bishopmuseum. org. Admission $14.95 adults, $11.95 children 4–12 and seniors. Daily 9am–5pm. TheBus: 2.

Hawaii Maritime Center ★ *Finds* You can easily spend a couple of hours here, wandering around and learning the story of Hawaii's rich maritime past, from the ancient journey of Polynesian voyagers to the nostalgic days of the *Lurline*, which once brought tourists from San Francisco on 4-day cruises. Inside the Hawaii Maritime Center's Kalakaua Boat House, patterned after His Majesty King David Kalakaua's own canoe house, are more than 30 exhibits, including Matson cruise ships (which brought the first tourists to Waikiki), flying boats that delivered the mail, and the skeleton of a Pacific humpback

---

Moments **Cultural Activities**

The best place to learn about and participate in ancient Hawaiian culture is the Hawaiian Hall of the **Bishop Museum,** 1525 Bernice St., Honolulu (ℂ 808/847-3511; www.bishopmuseum.org; TheBus: 2). The museum offers a series of free classes in Hawaiian quilt making (Mon and Fri, 9am–2pm) and feather lei making (Thurs, 9am–2pm). They also have hula performances daily at 11am and 2pm, as well as dramatic presentations of Hawaiian legends, Monday through Friday at 1pm.

Hawaiian quilt making is also taught at **Kwilts 'n Koa,** 1126 12th Ave. (between Harding and Waialae aves. in Kaimuki), Honolulu (ℂ 808/735-2300). Call for class information and times.

If you've ever wanted to learn the hula, the **Waikiki Community Center,** 310 Paoakalani Ave. (ewa side of the street between Ala Wai Blvd. and Kuhio Ave.), Honolulu (ℂ 808/923-1802), offers "drop-in" beginner hula classes every Monday at 9am; the cost is $3.

whale that beached on Kahoolawe. Outside, the *Hokulea,* a double-hulled sailing canoe that in 1976 reenacted the Polynesian voyage of discovery, is moored next to the *Falls of Clyde,* a four-masted schooner that once ran tea from China to the West Coast.

Pier 7 (next to Aloha Tower), Honolulu Harbor. © **808/536-6373.** Admission $7.50 adults, $4.50 children 6–17. Daily 8:30am–8pm. TheBus: 19, 20, 55, 56, or 57.

Iolani Palace ⚸   If you want to really "understand" Hawaii, this 45-minute tour is well worth the time. The Iolani Palace was built by King David Kalakaua, who spared no expense. The 4-year project, completed in 1882, cost $360,000—and nearly bankrupted the Hawaiian kingdom. This four-story Italian Renaissance palace was the first electrified building in Honolulu (it had electricity before the White House and Buckingham Palace). Royals lived here for 11 years, until Queen Liliuokalani was deposed and the Hawaiian monarchy fell forever, in a palace coup led by U.S. Marines on January 17, 1893, at the demand of sugar planters and missionary descendants.

Cherished by latter-day royalists, the 10-room palace stands as an architectural statement of the monarchy period. Iolani attracts 100,000 visitors a year in groups of 20; everyone must don denim booties to scoot across the royal floors.

At S. King and Richards sts. © **808/522-0832.** Admission $15 adults, $5 children 5–13. Guided tours Tues–Sat 9am–2:15pm; call ahead to reserve. You must be booked on a guided tour to enter the palace. Children under 5 not permitted. TheBus: 2.

Kawaiahao Church ⚸   In 1842, Kawaiahao Church stood complete at last, the crowning achievement of missionaries and Hawaiians working together for the first time on a common project. Designed by Rev. Hiram Bingham and supervised by Kamehameha III, who ordered his people to help build it, the project took 5 years. Workers quarried 14,000 thousand-pound coral blocks from the offshore reefs and cut timber in the forests for the beams.

This proud stone church, complete with bell tower and colonial colonnade, was the first permanent Western house of worship in the islands. It became the church of the Hawaiian royalty and remains in use today by Hawaiians who conduct services in the Hawaiian language (which probably sets old Rev. Bingham spinning in his grave). Some fine portraits of Hawaiian royalty hang inside. We'd recommend the best time to see this edifice is at the **Hawaiian-language services** ⚸⚸, conducted on Sundays at 10:30am.

957 Punchbowl St. (at King St.). © **808/522-1333.** Free admission (small donations appreciated). Mon–Fri 9am–3pm; Sun services 10:30am. TheBus: 2.

Mission Houses Museum   This museum tells the dramatic story of cultural change in 19th-century Hawaii. American Protestant missionaries established their headquarters here in 1820. Included in the complex are a visitor center and three historic mission buildings, which have been restored and refurnished to reflect the daily life and work of the missionaries.

Insider's tip: The best way to see the museum is as part of a walking tour of historic downtown buildings, offered on Thursday and Friday mornings (museum admission is included in the tour price); for details, see p. 199.

553 S. King St. (at Kawaiahao St.). © **808/531-0481.** www.lava.net/~mhm/. Admission $8 adults, $7 military personnel, $6 seniors, $4 college students and youths 13–18, $3 children 4–12. Tues–Sat 9am–4pm. TheBus: 2.

Queen Emma Summer Palace   Hanaiakamalama, the name of the country estate of Kamehameha IV and Queen Emma, was once in the secluded uplands of Nuuanu Valley. These days, it's adjacent to a six-lane highway full of speeding cars that sound remarkably like surf as they zip by. This simple, seven-room New England–style house, built in 1848 and restored by the Daughters of Hawaii, is worth about an hour of your time to see the interesting blend of Victorian furniture and hallmarks of Hawaiian royalty, including feather cloaks and *kahili,* the feathered standards that mark the presence of *alii* (royalty). Other royal treasures include a canoe-shaped cradle for Queen Emma's baby, Prince Albert, who died at the age of 4. (Kauai's ultra-ritzy Princeville Resort is named for the little prince.)

2913 Pali Hwy. (at Old Pali Rd.). ℂ **808/595-3167.** Admission $5 adults, $4 seniors, $1 children 11 and under. Daily 9am–4pm. TheBus: 4, 55, 56, 57, 65.

Royal Mausoleum   In the cool uplands of Nuuanu, on a 3.7-acre patch of sacred land dedicated in 1865—and never surrendered to the United States—stands the Royal Mausoleum, the final resting place of King Kalakaua, Queen Kapiolani, and 16 other Hawaiian royals. Only the Hawaiian flag flies over this grave, a remnant of the kingdom.

2261 Nuuanu Ave. (between Wyllie and Judd sts.). ℂ **808/536-7602.** Free admission. Mon–Fri 8am–4:30pm. TheBus: 4.

WARTIME HONOLULU

USS *Arizona* Memorial at Pearl Harbor ★★★   On December 7, 1941, the USS *Arizona,* while moored here in Pearl Harbor, was bombed in a Japanese air raid. The 608-foot battleship sank in 9 minutes without firing a shot, taking 1,177 sailors and Marines to their deaths—and catapulting the United States into World War II.

Nobody who visits the memorial will ever forget it. The deck of the ship lies 6 feet below the surface of the sea. Oil still oozes slowly up from the *Arizona*'s engine room to stain the harbor's calm, blue water; some say the ship still weeps for its lost crew. The memorial is a stark white 184-foot rectangle that spans the sunken hull of the ship; it was designed by Alfred Pries, a German architect interned on Sand Island during the war. It contains the ship's bell, recovered from the wreckage, and a shrine room with the names of the dead carved in stone.

Today, free U.S. Navy launches take visitors to the *Arizona.* Try to arrive early at the visitor center (no later than 1:30pm), operated jointly by the National Park Service and the U.S. Navy, to avoid the huge crowds; waits of 1 to 3 hours are common, and they don't take reservations. While you're waiting for the shuttle to take you out to the ship—you'll be issued a number and time of departure, which you must pick up yourself—you can explore the interesting museum's personal mementos, photographs, and historic documents. A moving 20-minute film precedes your trip to the ship. Allow a total of at least 4 hours for your visit.

Parents, note that baby strollers, baby carriages, and baby backpacks are not allowed in the theater, on the boat, or on the USS *Arizona* Memorial. All babies must be carried.

One last note: Most unfortunately, the USS *Arizona* Memorial is a high-theft area—leave your valuables at the hotel.

Pearl Harbor. ℂ **808/422-0561** (recorded info) or 808/422-2771. www.nps.gov/usar. Daily 7:30am–5pm (programs run 8am–3pm). Free admission. Children under 12 should be accompanied by an adult. Shirts and shoes required; no swimsuits or flip-flops allowed (shorts are okay). Wheelchairs gladly accommodated. Drive west on H-1 past the airport; take the USS *Arizona* Memorial exit and follow the green-and-white signs;

there's ample free parking. TheBus: 20 and 47; or Arizona Memorial Shuttle Bus ((C) **808/839-0911**), which picks up at Waikiki hotels 6:50am–1pm ($6 round-trip).

USS *Bowfin* Submarine Museum & Park ✪   The USS *Bowfin* is one of only 15 World War II submarines still in existence today. You can go below deck of this famous submarine—nicknamed the "Pearl Harbor Avenger" for its successful attacks on the Japanese—and see how the 80-man crew lived during wartime. The *Bowfin* Museum has an impressive collection of submarine-related artifacts. The Waterfront Memorial honors submariners lost during World War II.

11 Arizona Memorial Dr. (next to the USS *Arizona* Memorial Visitor Center). (C) **808/423-1341**. www.aloha.net/~bowfin. Admission $8 adults, $6 active-duty military personnel, $3 children 4–12. Daily 8am–5pm. See USS *Arizona* Memorial, above, for driving, bus, and shuttle directions.

USS *Missouri* Memorial ✪   On the deck of this 58,000-ton battleship (the last one the Navy built), World War II came to an end with the signing of the Japanese surrender on September 2, 1945. The *Missouri* was part of the force that carried out bombing raids over Tokyo and provided firepower in the battles of Iwo Jima and Okinawa. In 1955, the Navy decommissioned the ship and placed it in mothballs at the Puget Sound Naval Shipyard, in Washington State. But the *Missouri* was modernized and called back into action in 1986, eventually being deployed in the Persian Gulf War, before retiring once again in 1992. Here it sat until another battle ensued, this time over who would get the right to keep this living legend. Hawaii won that battle and brought the ship to Pearl Harbor in 1998. The next year, the 887-foot ship, like a phoenix, rose again into the public spotlight; it's now open to visitors as a museum memorial.

If you have the time, take the tour, which begins at the visitor center. Guests are shuttled to Ford Island on military-style buses while listening to a 1940s-style radio program (complete with news clips, wartime commercials, and music). Once on the ship, guests watch an informational film and are then free to explore on their own or take a guided tour. Highlights of this massive (more than 200 ft. tall) battleship include the forecastle (or *foc'sle*, in Navy talk), where the 30,000-pound anchors are "dropped" on 1,080 feet of anchor chain; the 16-inch guns (each 65 ft. long and weighing 116 tons), which can accurately fire a 2,700-pound shell some 23 miles in 50 seconds; and the spot where the Instrument of Surrender was signed as Douglas MacArthur, Chester Nimitz, and "Bull" Halsey looked on.

Battleship Row, Pearl Harbor. (C) **808/423-2263**. www.ussmissouri.com. Daily 9am–5pm. Admission $10 adults, $6 children 4–12 (hour-long guided tours, available 9:30am–4:30pm, cost an additional $4 per person). Check in at the visitor center of the USS *Bowfin* Memorial, next to the USS *Arizona* Memorial. Drive west on H-1 past the airport, take the USS *Arizona* Memorial exit, and follow the green-and-white signs; there's ample free parking. TheBus: 20 and 47.

National Cemetery of the Pacific   The National Cemetery of the Pacific (also known as "the Punchbowl") is an ash-and-lava tuff cone that exploded about 150,000 years ago—like Diamond Head, only smaller. Early Hawaiians called it Puowaina, or "hill of sacrifice." The old crater is a burial ground for 35,000 victims of three American wars in Asia and the Pacific: World War II, Korea, and Vietnam. Among the graves, you'll find many unmarked ones with the date December 7, 1941, carved in stone. Some will be unknown forever; others are famous, like that of war correspondent Ernie Pyle, killed by a Japanese sniper in April 1945 on Okinawa; still others buried here are remembered only by family and surviving buddies. The white stone tablets known as the Courts of the Missing bear the names of 28,788 Americans missing in action in World War II.

Survivors come here often to reflect on the meaning of war and to remember those, like themselves, who stood in harm's way to win peace a half-century ago. Some fight back tears, remembering lost buddies, lost missions, and the sacrifices of those who died.

Punchbowl Crater, 2177 Puowaina Dr. (at the end of the road). ✆ 808/541-1434. Free admission. Daily 8am–5:30pm (Mar–Sept to 6:30pm). TheBus: 15.

JUST BEYOND PEARL HARBOR

Hawaiian Railway *(Kids)* All aboard! This is a train ride back into history. Between 1890 and 1947, the chief mode of transportation for Oahu's sugar mills was the Oahu Railway and Land Co.'s narrow-gauge trains. The line carried not only equipment, raw sugar, and supplies, but also passengers from one side of the island to the other. You can relive those days every Sunday with a 1½-hour narrated ride through Ko Olina Resort and out to Makaha. As an added attraction, on the second Sunday of the month, you can ride on the nearly-100-year-old, custom-built parlor-observation car belonging to Benjamin F. Dillingham, founder of the Oahu Railway and Land Co.; the fare is $15 (no kids under 13), you must reserve in advance.

Ewa Station, Ewa Beach. ✆ 808/681-5461. http://members.aol.com/hawaiianrr/index.html. Admission $8 adults, $5 seniors and children 2–12. Departures Sun 12:30 and 2:30pm. Take H-1 west to exit 5A; take Hwy. 76 south for 2½ miles to Tesoro Gas; turn right on Renton Rd. and drive 1½ miles to end of paved section. The station is on the left. TheBus: 49, 50, 51, 52, 53, or 55 to the State Capitol, then transfer to TheBus no. 48 (Ewa Mill).

Hawaiian Waters Adventure Park *(Kids)* If you have kids, you have to take them here! This 29-acre water-theme amusement park opened in spring 1999 with some $14 million in attractions. Plan to spend the day. Highlights are a football field–sized wave pool for bodysurfing, two 65-foot-high free-fall slides, two water-toboggan bullet slides, inner-tube slides, body flume slides, a continuous river for floating inner tubes, and separate pools for adults, teens, and children. In addition, there are restaurants, food carts, Hawaiian performances, and shops.

400 Farrington Hwy., Kapolei. ✆ 808/674-9283. www.hawaiianwaters.com. Admission $29.99 adults, $19.99 children 4–11, free for children under 3. Daily 10:30am–6pm. Take H-1 west to Exit 1 (Campbell Industrial Park). Make an immediate left turn to Farrington Hwy and you will see the park on your left.

Hawaii's Plantation Village The hour-long tour of this restored 50-acre village offers a glimpse back in time to when sugar planters from America shaped the land, economy, and culture of territorial Hawaii. From 1852, when the first contract laborers arrived here from China, to 1947, when the plantation era ended, more than 400,000 men, women, and children from China, Japan, Portugal, Puerto Rico, Korea, and the Philippines came to work the sugarcane fields. The "talk story" tour brings the old village alive with 30 faithfully restored camp houses, Chinese and Japanese temples, the Plantation Store, and even a sumo-wrestling ring.

Waipahu Cultural Garden Park, 94–695 Waipahu St. (at Waipahu Depot Rd.), Waipahu. ✆ 808/677-0110. Admission (including escorted tour) $7 adults, $5 military personnel, $4 seniors, $3 children 5–12. Mon–Fri 9am–3pm; Sat 10am–3pm. Take H-1 west to Waikele-Waipahu exit (exit 7); get in the left lane on exit and turn left on Paiwa St.; at the fifth light, turn right onto Waipahu St.; after the second light, turn left. TheBus: 47.

3 Fish, Flora & Fauna

Foster Botanical Garden ★★ *Finds*   You could spend days in this unique and historic garden, a leafy oasis amid the high-rises of downtown Honolulu, but your schedule will probably only allow a couple of hours. Combine a tour of the Garden with a trip to Chinatown (just across the street) to maximize your time. The giant trees that tower over the main terrace were planted in the 1850s by William Hillebrand, a German physician and botanist, on royal land leased from Queen Emma. Today, this 14-acre public garden, on the north side of Chinatown, is a living museum of plants, some rare and endangered, collected from the tropical regions of the world. Of special interest are 26 "Exceptional Trees" protected by state law, a large palm collection, a primitive cycad garden, and a hybrid orchid collection.

50 N. Vineyard Blvd. (at Nuuanu Ave.). © 808/522-7066. www.co.honolulu.hi.us/park/hbg/. Admission $5 adults, $1 children 6–12. Daily 9am–4pm; guided tours Mon–Fri at 1pm (reservations recommended). TheBus: 2, 4, or 13.

Honolulu Zoo ★ *Kids*   Nobody comes to Hawaii to see an Indian elephant, or African lions and zebras. Right? Wrong. This 43-acre municipal zoo in Waikiki attracts visitors in droves. If you've got kids, allot at least half a day or more. The highlight is the new African Savannah, a 10-acre wild preserve exhibit with more than 40 uncapped African critters roaming around in the open. The zoo also has a rare Hawaiian nene goose, a Hawaiian pig, and mouflon sheep. (Only the goose, an evolved version of the Canadian honker, is considered to be truly Hawaiian; the others are imported from Polynesia, India, and elsewhere.)

For a real treat, take the Zoo by Moonlight tour, which offers a rare behind-the-scenes look into the lives of the zoo's nocturnal residents. Tours are offered 2 days before, during, and 2 days after the full moon, from 7 to 9pm; the cost is $7 for adults and $5 for children.

151 Kapahulu Ave. (between Paki and Kalakaua aves.), at entrance to Kapiolani Park. © 808/971-7171. www.honoluluzoo.org. Admission $6 adults, $1 children 6–12. Daily 9am–4:30pm. TheBus: 2, 8, 19, 20, or 47.

Kapiolani Park ★ *Kids*   In 1877 King David Kalakaua gave 130 acres of land to the people of Hawaii and named it after his beloved wife, Queen Kapiolani. This truly royal park has something for just about everyone: tennis courts, soccer and rugby fields, archery, picnic areas, wide-open spaces for kite flying and Frisbee throwing, and a jogging path with aerobic exercise stations. On Sundays in the summer, the Royal Hawaiian Band plays in the bandstand, just as they did during Kalakaua's reign. The Waikiki Shell, located in the park, is host to a variety of musical events, from old Hawaiian songs to rock and roll.

Bordered by Kalakaua Ave. on the ocean side, Monsarrat Ave. on the Ewa side, and Paki Ave. on the mountain side. TheBus: 2.

Lyon Arboretum ★   Six-story-tall breadfruit trees . . . yellow orchids no bigger than a bus token . . . ferns with fuzzy buds as big as a human head: Lyon Arboretum is 194 budding acres of botanical wonders. A whole different world opens up to you along the self-guided 20-minute hike through the arboretum to Inspiration Point. You'll pass more than 5,000 exotic tropical plants full of birdsong in this cultivated rain forest (a University of Hawaii research facility) at the head of Manoa Valley. Guided tours for serious plant lovers are offered the first Friday and the third Wednesday of the month at 1pm and the third Saturday at 10am; call © **808/988-3177** for schedule and reservations.

3860 Manoa Rd. (near the top of the road). © 808/988-0464. $1 donation requested. Mon–Sat 9am–3pm. TheBus: 5.

Kids Especially for Kids

Shop the Aloha Flea Market *(see p. 144)*   Most kids hate to shop, but the Aloha Flea Market, a giant outdoor bazaar at the Aloha Stadium on Wednesday, Saturday, and Sunday, is more than shopping. It's an experience akin to a carnival, full of interesting food, odd goods, and bold barkers. Nobody ever leaves this place empty-handed—or without having had lots of fun.

Splash Down at Hawaiian Waters Adventure Park *(see p. 180)*   This 29-acre water-theme amusement park features a wave pool for bodysurfing, two 65-foot-high free-fall slides, two water-toboggan bullet slides, inner-tube slides, body flume slides, a continuous river for floating inner tubes, and separate pools for adults, teens, and children.

Explore the Bishop Museum *(see p. 176)*   There are some 1,180,000 Polynesian artifacts; 13,500,000 different insect specimens; 6,000,000 marine and land shells; 490,000 plant specimens; 130,000 fish specimens; and 85,000 birds and mammals, all in the Bishop Museum. Kids can explore interactive exhibits, see a 50-foot sperm whale skeleton, and check out a Hawaii grass hut. There's something for everyone here.

Walk Through a Submarine *(see p. 179)*   At the USS *Bowfin* Submarine Museum Park, an interactive museum offers kids the chance to experience a real submarine—one that served in some of the fiercest naval battles in World War II. Kids can explore the interior of the tightly packed submarine that housed some 90 to 100 men and see the stacked shelves where they slept, the radar and electronics in the command center, and the storage place of the torpedoes.

Dream at the Hawaii Maritime Center *(see p. 176)*   Kids will love the Kalakaua Boathouse, the two-story museum of the Maritime Center. Exhibits include such topics as the development of surfing, the art of tattooing, and artifacts from the whaling industry. Next door you'll find the fully-rigged, four-masted *Falls of Clyde*. Built in 1878, this vessel served as a cargo and passenger liner and a sailing tanker before being declared a National Historic Landmark; it is permanently docked as a museum. If it's not out sailing, you'll find the *Hokule'a*

Waikiki Aquarium ★★★ *Kids*   Do not miss this! Half of Hawaii is its underwater world; plan to spend at least two hours discovering it. Behold the chambered nautilus, nature's submarine and inspiration for Jules Verne's *20,000 Leagues Under the Sea*. You may see this tropical spiral-shelled cephalopod mollusk—the only living one born in captivity—any day of the week here. Its natural habitat is the deep waters of Micronesia, but aquarium director Bruce Carlson not only succeeded in trapping the pearly shell in 1,500 feet of water (by dangling chunks of raw tuna), but also managed to breed this ancient relative of the octopus. There are also plenty of other fish in this small but first-class aquarium, located on a live coral reef. The Hawaiian reef habitat moored next to the *Falls of Clyde*. The *Hokule'a* is a re-creation of a traditional double-hulled sailing canoe, which in 1976 made the 6,000-mile round-trip voyage to Tahiti using only ancient navigation techniques—the stars, the wind, and the sea.

Watch the Fish and Sharks at the Waikiki Aquarium *(see p. 182)* Much more than just a big fish tank, the Waikiki Aquarium will astound and educate your youngsters. They can probably sit for hours staring at the sharks, turtles, eels, rays, and fish swimming in the main tank. For a few laughs, wander out to the monk seal area and watch the antics of these seagoing clowns.

Snorkel in Hanauma Bay *(see p. 142)* Kids will be enthralled with the teeming tropical fish and the underwater world at this marine park. The shallow waters near the beach are perfect for neophyte snorkelers to learn in, and the long (2,000-ft.) beach has plenty of frolicking room for kids. Get there early; it can get very crowded.

Hike to the top of Diamond Head Crater *(see p. 156)* The entire family can make this easy 1.4-mile round-trip walk to the top of the 750-foot volcanic cone with its rewarding view of Oahu. Bring a flashlight for the entry tunnel and a camera for the view.

Explore the Depths in a Submarine Dive *(see p. 154)* Better than a movie, more exciting than a video game, the *Atlantis* or *Voyager* submarines journey down 100 feet below the water's surface to explore the Neptunian world of tropical reef fish and even an occasional shark or two.

See Sea Creatures at Sea Life Park *(see p. 183)* Kids will love this 62-acre ocean theme park that features orca whales, dolphins, seals, and penguins going through their hoops to the delight of kids of all ages. There's a Hawaiian reef tank full of native tropical fish, a "touch" pool where you can grab a real sea cucumber (commonly found in tide pools), and a bird sanctuary where you can see birds such as the red-footed booby and the Frigate bird that are usually seen overhead. The chief curiosity, though, is the world's only "wolphin"—a cross between a false killer whale and an Atlantic bottle-nosed dolphin.

features sharks, eels, a touch tank, and habitats for the endangered Hawaiian monk seal and green sea turtle. Recently added: a rotating biodiversity exhibit and interactive displays focusing on corals and coral reefs.

2777 Kalakaua Ave. (across from Kapiolani Park). (*) **808/923-9741**. www.waquarium.org. Admission $7 adults, $5 military personnel, $4 seniors and students, $2.50 children 13–17. Daily 9am–5pm. TheBus: 19 or 20.

IN NEARBY EAST OAHU

Sea Life Park (*) (*Kids*)   This 62-acre ocean theme park, located in East Oahu, is one of the island's top attractions. It features whales from Puget Sound,

Atlantic bottle-nosed dolphins, California sea lions, and penguins going through their hoops to the delight of kids of all ages. If you have kids, allow all day to take in the sights. There's also a Hawaiian reef tank full of tropical fish; a "touch" pool, where you can touch a real sea cucumber (commonly found in tide pools); and a bird sanctuary, where you can see birds like the red-footed booby and the frigate bird. The chief curiosity, though, is the world's only "wholphin"—a cross between a false killer whale and an Atlantic bottle-nosed dolphin. On-site, marine biologists operate a recovery center for endangered marine life; during your visit, you'll be able to see rehabilitated Hawaiian monk seals and seabirds.

41–202 Kalanianaole Hwy. (at Makapuu Point), Honolulu. ℂ 808/259-7933. Admission $24 adults, $12 children 4–12. Daily 9:30am–5pm. Parking $3. Shuttle buses from Waikiki $5. TheBus: 22 or 58.

4 Spectacular Views

Diamond Head 🅰🅰🅰 *Kids* *Moments*   The 360-degree view from atop Diamond Head Crater is worth the 560-foot ascent and is not to be missed. You can see all the way from the Koko Crater to Barbers Point and the Waianae Mountains. The 750-foot-tall volcano, which has become the symbol for Hawaii, is about 350,000 years old. The trail to the summit was built in 1910 to service the military installation along the crater; it's about a 30-minute hike to the top, but it's quite manageable by anyone of any age. (For additional details, see p. 156.)

Diamond Head has always been considered a "sacred sight" by Hawaiians. According to legend, Hi'iaka, the sister to the volcano goddess Pele, named the mountain Leahi (meaning the "brow of the ahi") when she saw the resemblance to the yellowfin tuna (called "ahi" in Hawaiian). Kamehameha the Great built a "luakini heiau" on the top where human sacrifices were made to the god of war, Ku.

The name *Diamond Head* came into use around 1825 when a group of British sailors (some say they were slightly inebriated) found some rocks sparkling in the sun. Absolutely sure they had struck it rich, the sailors brought these "diamonds" back into Honolulu. Alas, the "diamonds" turned out to be calcite crystals. The sailors didn't become fabulously rich, but the name Diamond Head stuck.

Diamond Head Rd. Daily 6am–6pm. To get here from Waikiki, take Kalakaua Ave. toward Kapiolani Park. Turn left onto Monsarrat Ave. at the Park. Monsarrat Ave. becomes Diamond Head Rd. after Campbell Ave. Continue on Diamond Head Rd. to turnoff to crater. Turn right into turnoff, follow to parking lot. TheBus: 22 or 58.

Lanikai Beach 🅰🅰   This is one of the best places on Oahu to greet the sunrise. Watch the sky slowly move from pitch black to wisps of gray to burnt orange as the sun begins to rise over the two tiny offshore islands of Mokulua. Use your five senses for this experience: hear the birds sing, feel the gentle breezes on your face, taste the salt in the air, smell the ocean, and see the kaleidoscope of colors as another day dawns.

Mokulua Dr., Kailua. To get here from Honolulu, take Hi. 61 (Pali Hwy.) into Kailua. Follow the street (which becomes Kailua Rd., then becomes Kuulei Rd.) until it ends. Turn right on Kalaheo Ave. (which will become Kawailoa Rd. in a few blocks). Follow the road over the canal. At the stop sign, turn left on Kaneapu Place. At the fork in the road, bear left on the one-way Aalapapa Dr. Turn right at any cross street onto Mokulua Dr. No bus service.

Nuuanu Pali Lookout 🅰 *Moments*   Gale-force winds sometimes howl through the mountain pass at this 1,186-foot-high perch guarded by 3,000-foot peaks, so hold on to your hat—and small children. But if you walk up from the parking lot to the precipice, you'll be rewarded with a view that'll blow you away. At the edge, the dizzying panorama of Oahu's windward side is breathtaking: Clouds low enough to pinch scoot by on trade winds; pinnacles of the *pali* (cliffs), green with ferns, often disappear in the mist, the vertical slopes of the Koolaus end in lush green valleys that become the town of Kaneohe; and the Pacific, a magnificent blue, dotted with whitecaps, beckons in the distance. Definitely take a jacket with you; it can be quite misty at the lookout. On very windy days, you'll notice that the waterfalls look as though they are flowing up rather than down.

In 1898, John Wilson built the road up to the lookout using 200 laborers. Even before the road existed, the Nuuanu Pali (which translates as "cool heights") was infamous because legend claims it was the location of Kamehameha the Great's last battle. Although some academic scholars scoff at this, the story alleges that in 1795, Kamehameha pursued Oahu's warriors up Nuuanu to these cliffs and waged a battle in his attempt to unite the Hawaiian islands. Supposedly, the Oahu warriors were driven over the cliffs by Kamehameha's men. Some say the battle never happened, some say it happened but there were only a few men fighting, and some say thousands were forced over the cliff, plunging to their deaths. Others say at night you can still hear the cries of these long-dead warriors coming from the valley below.

From on high, the tropical palette of green and blue runs down to the sea. Combine this 10-minute stop with a trip over the Pali to the windward side.

Near the summit of Pali Hwy. (Hwy. 61); take the Nuuanu Pali Lookout turnoff.

Nuuanu Valley Rain Forest *Finds*   It's not the same as a peaceful nature walk, but if time is short and hiking isn't your thing, Honolulu has a rain forest you can drive through. It's only a few minutes from downtown Honolulu in verdant Nuuanu Valley, where it rains nearly 300 inches a year. And it's easy to reach: As the Pali Highway leaves residential Nuuanu and begins its climb though the forest, the last stoplight is the Nuuanu Pali Road turnoff; turn right for a jungly detour of about 2 miles under a thick canopy strung with liana vines, past giant bamboo that creaks in the wind, Norfolk pines, and wild shell ginger. The road rises and the vegetation clears as you drive, blinking in the bright light of day, past a small mountain reservoir.

Soon the road rejoins the Pali Highway. Kailua is to the right and Honolulu to the left—but it can be a hair-raising turn. Instead, turn right, go a half mile to the Nuuanu Pali Lookout (see above), stop for a panoramic view of Oahu's windward side, and return to the town-bound highway on the other side.

Take the Old Nuuanu Pali Rd. exit off Pali Hwy. (Hwy. 61).

Puu o Mahuka Heiau *Moments*   Go around sundown to feel the *mana* (sacred spirit) of this Hawaiian place. The largest sacrificial temple on Oahu, it's associated with the great Kaopulupulu, who sought peace between Oahu and Kauai. This prescient *kahuna* predicted that the island would be overrun by strangers from a distant land. In 1794, three of Captain George Vancouver's men of the *Daedalus* were sacrificed here. In 1819, the year before New England missionaries landed in Hawaii, King Kamehameha II ordered all idols here to be destroyed.

A national historic landmark, this 18th-century heiau, known as the "hill of escape," sits on a 5-acre, 300-foot bluff overlooking Waimea Bay and 25 miles of Oahu's wave-lashed North Coast—all the way to Kaena Point, where the

Waianae Range ends in a spirit leap to the other world. The heiau appears as a huge rectangle of rocks twice as big as a football field (170 ft. by 575 ft.), with an altar often covered by the flower and fruit offerings left by native Hawaiians.

1 mile past Waimea Bay. Take Pupukea Rd. mauka (inland) off Kamehameha Hwy. at Foodland, and drive 0.7 miles up a switchback road. TheBus: 52, then walk up Pupukea Rd.

Puu Ualakaa State Park *(Moments*   The best **sunset view** of Honolulu is from a 1,048-foot-high hill named for sweet potatoes. Actually, the poetic Hawaiian name means "rolling sweet potato hill," which is how early planters used gravity to harvest their crop. The panorama is sweeping and majestic. On a clear day—which is almost always—you can see from Diamond Head to the Waianae Range, almost the length of Oahu. At night, several scenic overlooks provide romantic spots for young lovers who like to smooch under the stars with the city lights at their feet. It's a top-of-the-world experience—the view, that is.

At the end of Round Hill Dr. Daily 7am–6:45pm (to 7:45pm in summer). From Waikiki, take Ala Wai Blvd. to McCully St., turn right, and drive mauka (inland) beyond the H-1 on-ramps to Wilder St.; turn left and go to Makiki St.; turn right, and continue onward and upward about 3 miles.

5 More Museums

Aliiolani Hale   Don't be surprised if this place looks familiar; you probably saw it on *Magnum, P.I.* This gingerbread Italianate building, designed by Australian Thomas Rowe in Renaissance revival style, was built in 1874 and was originally intended to be a palace. Instead, Aliiolani Hale ("chief unto heavens") became the Supreme Court and Parliament government office building. Inside, there's a **Judiciary History Center**, which features a multimedia presentation, a restored historic courtroom, and exhibits tracing Hawaii's transition from precontact Hawaiian law to Western law.

417 S. King St. (between Mililani and Punchbowl sts.). 808/539-4999. Fax 808/539-4996. www. jhchawaii.org. Free admission. Mon–Fri 9am–4pm; reservations for group tours only. TheBus: 1, 2, 3, 4, 8, 11, or 12. Limited meter parking on street.

Contemporary Museum   Set up on the slopes of Tantalus, one of Honolulu's upscale residential communities, the Contemporary Museum is renowned for its 3 acres of Asian gardens (with reflecting pools, sun-drenched terraces, views of Diamond Head, and stone benches for quiet contemplation). Its Cades Pavilion houses David Hockney's *L'Enfant et les Sortileges,* an environmental installation of his sets and costumes for Ravel's 1925 opera, and six galleries display significant works from the last 4 decades. Equally prominent is the presence of contemporary Hawaii artists in the museum's programs and exhibitions. Ask about the daily docent-led tours, and look for an excellent cafe and shop.

2411 Makiki Heights Dr. 808/526-0232. www.tcmhi.org. Admission $5 adults, $3 seniors and students, free for children; free to all third Thurs of each month. Tues–Sat 10am–4pm; Sun noon–4pm.

Damien Museum   This is a tiny museum about a large subject in Hawaii's history: Father Damien's work with leprosy victims on the island of Molokai. The museum contains prayer books used by Father Damien in his ministry as well as his personal items. Don't miss the award-winning video on Damien's story.

130 Ohua St. (between Kuhio and Kalakaua aves., behind St. Augustine's Catholic Church). 808/923-2690. Donations accepted. Mon–Fri 9am–3pm. TheBus: 8, 19, or 20.

Honolulu Academy of Arts ★★   This acclaimed museum unveiled its new $28-million Henry R. Luce Pavilion Complex in May 2001, and wowed the state with its new exhibition space, courtyard, expanded outdoor cafe, and gift shop. A magnificent facility got even better, as two 4,000-square-foot galleries were added to the existing 30, and the John Dominis and Patches Damon Holt Gallery displayed the museum's Hawaii regional collection in one space for the first time. Considered Hawaii's premier example of *kamaaina-* (old-timer-) style architecture, the Academy is the state's only general fine-arts museum and has expanded steadily over the last decade. It boasts one of the top Asian art collections in the country, including James Michener's collection of Hiroshige's *Ukiyo-e* prints. Also on exhibit are American and European masters and prehistoric works of Maya, Greek, and Hawaiian art. The museum's award-winning architecture is a paragon of graciousness, featuring magnificent court-yards, lily ponds, and sensitively designed galleries.

900 S. Beretania St. ✆ 808/532-8700, or 808/532-8701 for a recording. www.honoluluacademy.org. Admission $7 adults; $4 students, seniors, and military personnel; free for children under age 12. Tues–Sat 10am–4:30pm; Sun 1–5pm.

Pacific Aerospace Museum   While you're waiting for your plane to depart, check out the history of flight in the Pacific at this shrine to flying. You can trace elapsed time and distance of all direct flights from Honolulu on a 6-foot globe using fiber optics, watch old film clips of NASA astronauts splashing down in Hawaiian waters after landing on the moon, see models of early planes and flying boats (including a life-sized replica of the flight deck of the space shuttle *Challenger*), and hear the heroic stories of the aviators who pioneered sky routes to the islands and beyond.

In the Central Waiting Lobby, Honolulu International Airport, 300 Rodgers Blvd., Honolulu. ✆ 808/839-0777. Admission $3 adults, $2.50 military personnel and students; $1 children 6–12. Mon–Wed 8am–6pm; Thurs–Sun 8am–10pm. TheBus: 19 or 20.

U.S. Army Museum   This museum, built in 1909 and used in defense of Honolulu and Pearl Harbor, houses military memorabilia ranging from ancient Hawaiian warfare items to modern-day high-tech munitions. On the upper deck, the Corps of Engineers Pacific Regional Visitors Center shows how the corps works with the civilian community to manage water resources in an island environment.

Fort DeRussy Park, Waikiki. ✆ 808/438-2822. Free admission. Tues–Sun 10am–4:30pm. TheBus: 8.

WALKING TOUR 1   HISTORIC CHINATOWN

Getting There	From Waikiki, take TheBus no. 2 or 20 toward downtown; get off on North Hotel Street (after Maunakea St.). If you're driving, take Ala Moana Boulevard and turn right on Smith Street; make a left on Beretania Street and a left again at Maunakea. The city parking garage (50¢ per hr.) is on the Ewa (west) side of Maunakea Street, between North Hotel and North King streets.
Start and Finish	North Hotel and Maunakea streets.
Time	1 to 2 hours, depending on how much time you spend browsing.
Best Times	Daylight hours.

Chinese laborers from the Guangdong Province first came to work on Hawaii's sugarcane and pineapple plantations in the 1850s. They quickly figured out that they would never get rich working in the fields; once their contracts were up, a few of the ambitious started up small shops and restaurants in the area around River Street.

Chinatown was twice devastated by fire, once in 1886 and again in 1900. The second fire still intrigues historians. In December 1899, bubonic plague broke out in the area, and the Board of Health immediately quarantined its 7,000 Chinese and Japanese residents. But the plague continued to spread. On January 20, 1900, the board decided to burn down plague-infected homes, starting at the corner of Beretania Street and Nuuanu Avenue. But the fire department wasn't quite ready; a sudden wind quickly spread the flames from one wooden building to another in the densely built area, and soon Chinatown's entire 40 acres were leveled. Many historians believe that the "out-of-control" fire may have been purposely set to drive the Chinese merchants—who were becoming economically powerful and controlled prime real estate—out of Honolulu. If this was indeed the case, it didn't work: The determined merchants built a new Chinatown in the same spot.

Chinatown reached its peak in the 1930s. In the days before air travel, visitors arrived here by cruise ship. Just a block up the street was the pier where they disembarked—and they often headed straight for the shops and restaurants of Chinatown, which mainlanders considered an exotic treat. In the 1940s, military personnel on leave flocked here looking for different kinds of exotic treats—in the form of pool halls, tattoo joints, and brothels.

Today, Chinatown is again rising from the ashes. After deteriorating over the years into a tawdry district of seedy bars, drug dealing, and homeless squatters, the neighborhood recently underwent extensive urban renewal. There's still just enough sleaze on the fringes (a few peep shows and a couple of topless bars) to keep it from being some theme park–style tourist attraction, but Chinatown is poised to relive its glory days.

It's not exactly a microcosm of China, however. What you'll find is a mix of Asian cultures, all packed into a small area where tangy spices rule the cuisine, open-air markets have kept out the minimalls, and the way to good health is through acupuncture and herbalists. The jumble of streets comes alive every day with bustling residents and visitors from all over the world; a cacophony of sounds, from the high-pitched bleating of vendors in the market to the lyrical dialects of the retired men "talking story" over a game of mahjong; and brilliant reds, blues, and greens trimming buildings and goods everywhere you look. No trip to Honolulu is complete without a visit to this exotic, historic district.

Start your walk on the Ewa (west) side of Maunakea Street at:

❶ Hotel Street
During World War II, Hotel Street was synonymous with good times. Pool halls and beer parlors lined the blocks, and prostitutes were plentiful. Nowadays, the more nefarious establishments have been replaced with small shops, from art galleries to specialty boutiques, and urban professionals and recent immigrants look for

bargains where the sailors once roamed.

Once you're done wandering through the shops, head to the intersection with Smith Street. On the Diamond Head (east) side of Smith, you'll notice stones in the sidewalk; they were taken from the sandalwood ships, which came to Hawaii empty of cargo except for these stones, which were used as ballast on the trip over. The stones were removed and the

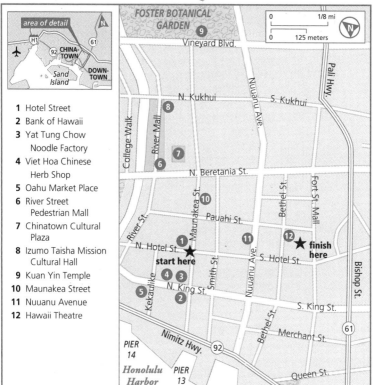

area of detail

CHINA-TOWN
Sand Island
DOWN-TOWN

FOSTER BOTANICAL GARDEN

Vineyard Blvd.

N. Kukhui   S. Kukhui

Nuuanu Ave.

Pali Hwy.

College Walk

River Mall

N. Beretania St.

Bethel St.

Fort St. Mall

Maunakea St.

Pauahi St.

River St.

N. Hotel St.   S. Hotel St.   finish here

start here

Smith St.

Kekaulike

N. King St.

Nuuanu Ave.

Bishop St.

S. King St.

Bethel St.

Merchant St.

Nimitz Hwy.

PIER 14

Honolulu Harbor   PIER 13

Queen St.

1 Hotel Street
2 Bank of Hawaii
3 Yat Tung Chow Noodle Factory
4 Viet Hoa Chinese Herb Shop
5 Oahu Market Place
6 River Street Pedestrian Mall
7 Chinatown Cultural Plaza
8 Izumo Taisha Mission Cultural Hall
9 Kuan Yin Temple
10 Maunakea Street
11 Nuuanu Avenue
12 Hawaii Theatre

ships' hulls were filled with sandalwood for the return to the mainland.

From Hotel Street, turn left on Maunakea and proceed to the corner of King Street to the:

➋ Bank of Hawaii

This unusual-looking bank is not the conservative edifice you'd expect—it's guarded by two fire-breathing dragon statues.

Turn right onto King Street, where you'll pass the shops of various Chinese herbalists, such as the:

➌ Yat Tung Chow Noodle Factory

150 N. King St. The delicious, delicate noodles that star in numerous Asian dishes are made here, ranging from threadlike noodles (literally no thicker than embroidery thread) to fat udon noodles. There aren't any tours of the factory, but you can look through the window, past the white cloud of flour that hangs in the air, and watch as dough is fed into rollers at one end of the noodle machines; perfectly cut noodles emerge at the other end.

Another interesting shop on North King Street is the:

➍ Viet Hoa Chinese Herb Shop

162 N. King St., where Chinese herbalists act as both doctors and dispensers of herbs. Patients come in and tell the herbalist what ails them; the herbalist then decides which of the myriad herbs to mix together. Usually, there's a wall of tiny drawers all labeled in Chinese characters; the herbalist quickly pulls from the drawers various objects that range from dried flowers and ground-up roots to such exotics as mashed antelope antler. The patient

Bargaining: A Way of Life in Chinatown

In Chinatown, nearly every purchase—from haggling over the price of chicken's feet to buying an 18-carat gold necklace—is made by bargaining. It's the way of life for most Asian countries—and part of the fun and charm of shopping in Chinatown.

The main rule of thumb when negotiating a price is **respect.** The customer must have respect for the merchant and understand that he's in business to make money. This respect is coupled with the understanding that the customer does not want to be taken advantage of and would like the best deal possible.

Keep in mind two rules when bargaining: **cash** and **volume.** Don't even begin haggling if you're not planning to pay cash. The second you pull out a credit card (if the merchant or vendor will even accept it), all deals are off. And remember, the more you buy, the better the deal the merchant will extend to you.

Significant savings can be realized for high-ticket items like jewelry. The price of gold in Chinatown is based on the posted price of the tael (a unit of weight, slightly more than an ounce), which is listed for 14-, 18-, and 24-carat gold, plus the value of the labor. There's no negotiating on the tael price, but the cost of the labor is where the bargaining begins.

---

then takes the concoction home to brew into a strong tea.

Cross to the south side of King Street, where, just west of Kekaulike Street, you'll come to the most visited part of Chinatown, the open-air market known as:

➎ Oahu Market Place

Those interested in Asian cooking will find all the necessary ingredients here, including pig's heads, poultry (some still squawking), fresh octopi, salted jellyfish, pungent fish sauce, fresh herbs, and thousand-year-old eggs. The friendly vendors are happy to explain their wares and give instructions on how to prepare these exotic treats. The market, which has been at this spot since 1904, is divided into meats, poultry, fish, vegetables, and fruits. Past the open market are several grocery stores with fresh produce on display on the sidewalk. You're bound to spot some varieties here that you're not used to seeing at your local supermarket.

Follow King down to River Street and turn right toward the mountains. A range of inexpensive restaurants lines River Street from King to Beretania. You can get the best Vietnamese and Filipino food in town in these blocks, but go early—lines for lunch start at 11:15am. Beyond Beretania Street is the:

➏ River Street Pedestrian Mall

Here, River Street ends and the pedestrian mall begins with the **statue of Chinese revolutionary leader Sun Yat-sen.** The wide mall, which borders the Nuuanu Stream, is lined with shade trees, park benches, and tables where seniors gather to pay mahjong and checkers. There are plenty of takeout restaurants nearby if you'd like to eat lunch outdoors. If you're up early (5:30am in summer and 6am in winter), you'll see senior citizens practicing tai chi.

Along the River Street Mall, extending nearly a block over to Maunakea Street, is the:

➐ Chinatown Cultural Plaza

This modern complex is filled with shops featuring everything from tailors to calligraphers (most somewhat more expensive than their street-side counterparts), as well as numerous restaurants—a great idea, but in reality, people seem to prefer wandering Chinatown's crowded streets to venturing into a modern mall. A couple of interesting shops here specialize in Asian magazines; there's also a small post office tucked away in a corner of the plaza, for those who want to mail cards home with the "Chinatown" postmark. The best feature of the plaza is the **Moongate Stage** in the center, the site of many cultural presentations, especially around the Chinese New Year.

Continue up the River Street Mall and cross the Nuuanu Stream via the bridge at Kukui Street, which will bring you to the:

8 Izumo Taisha Mission Cultural Hall

This small, wooden Shinto shrine, built in 1923, houses a male deity (look for the X-shaped crosses on the top). Members of the faith ring the bell out front as an act of purification when they come to pray. Inside the temple is a 100-pound sack of rice, symbolizing good health. During World War II, the shrine was confiscated by the city of Honolulu and wasn't returned to the congregation until 1962.

If temples interest you, walk a block toward the mountains to Vineyard Boulevard; cross back over Nuuanu Stream, past the entrance of Foster Botanical Gardens, to:

9 Kuan Yin Temple

This Buddhist temple, painted in a brilliant red with a green ceramic-tiled roof, is dedicated to Kuan Yin Bodhisattva, the goddess of mercy, whose statue towers in the prayer hall. The aroma of burning incense is your clue that the temple is still a house of worship, not an exhibit, so enter with respect and leave your shoes outside. You may see people burning paper "money" for prosperity and good luck, or leaving flowers and fruits at the altar (gifts to the goddess). A common offering is the pomelo, a grapefruit-like fruit that's a fertility symbol as

well as a gift, indicating a request for the blessing of children.

Continue down Vineyard and then turn right (toward the ocean) on:

10 Maunakea Street

Between Beretania and King streets are numerous **lei shops** (with lei-makers working away right on the premises). The air is heavy with the aroma of flowers being woven into beautiful treasures. Not only is this the best place in all of Hawaii to get a deal on leis, but the size, color, and design of the leis made here are also exceptional. Wander through the shops before you decide which lei you want.

> **TAKE A BREAK**
> If you have a sweet tooth, stop in at **Shung Chong Yuein** (★), 1027 Maunakea St. (near Hotel St.), for delicious Asian pastries like moon cakes and almond cookies, all at very reasonable prices. The shop also has a wide selection of dried and sugared candies (like ginger, pineapple, and lotus root) that you can eat as you stroll or give as an exotic gift to friends back home.

Turn left on Hotel Street and walk in the Diamond Head (east) direction to:

11 Nuuanu Avenue

You may notice that the sidewalks on Nuuanu are made of granite blocks; they came from the ballasts of ships that brought tea from China to Hawaii in the 1800s. On the corner of Nuuanu Avenue and Hotel Street is **Lai Fong Department Store,** a classic Chinatown store owned by the same family for more than 75 years. Walking into Lai Fong is like stepping back in time. The old store sells everything from precious antiques to god-awful knickknacks to rare turn-of-the-century Hawaiian postcards—but it has built its reputation on its fabulous selection of Chinese silks, brocades, and custom dresses.

Between Hotel and Pauahi streets is the **Pegge Hopper Gallery,** 1164 Nuuanu Ave., where you can admire Pegge's well-known paintings of beautiful Hawaiian women.

At Pauahi Street, turn right (toward Diamond Head) and walk up to Bethel Street and the:

⓬ **Hawaii Theatre**
This restored 1920 Art-Deco theater is a work of art in itself. It hosts a

variety of programs, from the Hawaii International Film Festival to beauty pageants (see chapter 9, "Oahu After Dark," for how to find out what's on).

Turn right onto Bethel and walk toward the ocean. Turn right again onto Hotel Street, which will lead you back to where you started.

WALKING TOUR 2 | **HONOLULU WATERFRONT**

Getting There   From Waikiki, take Ala Moana Boulevard in the Ewa direction. When Ala Moana ends, turn left on Nimitz Highway. There is parking on the ocean side of Nimitz at Bishop Street. TheBus: 19 or 20.

Start   Aloha Tower, ocean end of Fort Street Mall at Pier 9.

Finish   Waterfront Plaza and Restaurant Row, Punchbowl Street/Ala Moana Boulevard.

Time   About 1 to 2 hours, depending on how long you linger in museums and shops.

Best Time   Daylight, when the Hawaii Maritime Museum is open (8:30am–5pm daily).

For a walk into Honolulu's past when Polynesians first came to Hawaii, take this leisurely stroll along the waterfront and the surrounding environs.

Until about 1800, the area around Honolulu Harbor (from Nuuanu Ave. to Alakea St. and from Hotel St. to the ocean) was known as *Koa.* Some scholars say it was named after a dedicated officer to Chief Kakuhihewa of Oahu; others say it comes from the koa tree, which flourishes in this area. In 1793, Captain William Brown, on the British frigate *Butterworth,* sailed the first foreign ship into Honolulu harbor. Like most British explorers, he didn't bother to ask about the name of the harbor; instead, he just called it Fair Haven. Other ships that followed started to call the harbor "Brown's Harbor." Luckily, the name the Hawaiians gave the harbor, Honolulu, which translates into "sheltered bay," became the popular name.

The waterfront area played a vital role in the history of Honolulu. King Kamehameha I moved his royal court here in 1809 to keep an eye on the burgeoning trade from the numerous ships that were coming here. The royal residence was at the makai end of Bethel Street, just 1 block from the start of our tour at the Aloha Tower.

Park in the parking lot on Bishop Street and Nimitz Highway and walk over to Pier 9 to:

❶ **Aloha Tower**
One of the reasons that the word *aloha* is synonymous with Hawaii is because of the Aloha Tower. Built in 1926 (for the then-outrageous sum of

$160,000), this 184-foot, 10-story tower (until 1959, the tallest structure in Hawaii) has clocks on all four of its sides with the word *aloha* under each clock. Aloha, which has come to mean both "hello" and "farewell," was the first thing steamship passengers saw

1 Aloha Tower
2 Aloha Tower Marketplace
3 Hawaii Maritime Center
4 *Falls of Clyde*
5 *Hokule'a*
6 *Navatek I*
7 Waterfront Plaza and Restaurant Row

† Church
⊠ Post Office

✝ St. Andrew's
■ Cathedral

area of detail

DOWN-TOWN   ALA MOANA

Sand Island

WAIKIKI

HONOLULU

0   5 mi
0   5 km

S. Beretania St.
Alapai St.

State Office Building

N. Beretania St.
Smith St.
Nuuanu Ave.
Bethel St.
Fort Street
Bishop St.
Hotel St.
Mall

State Capitol

Library   City Hall

Kapiolani Blvd.

Richards St.

S. King St.

Cooke St.

CHINATOWN

N. King St.

Alakea St.

Iolani Palace

Kawaiahao St.

Kawaiahao Cemetery

Mission Lane

South St.

Fish Market

Merchant St.

⊠

Kamehameha Statue

Queen St.

← To Airport

Halekauwila St.

Punchbowl St.

0   1/5 mi
0   0.2 km

Federal Bldg.

Pohukaina St.

Aloha Tower

5

finish here
7 ★

start here ★

1   **2** **4** **3**

Ala Moana Blvd.

Auahi St.

6

---

when they entered Honolulu Harbor. In the days when tourists arrived by steamer, "boat days" were a very big occasion. The Royal Hawaiian band would be on hand to play, crowds would gather, flower leis were freely given, and Honolulu came to a standstill to greet the visitors.

Go up the elevator inside the Aloha Tower to the **10th floor observation deck** for a bird's-eye view that encompasses Diamond Head and Waikiki, the downtown and Chinatown areas, and the harbor coastline to the airport. On the ocean side you can see the harbor mouth, Sand Island, the Honolulu reef runway, and the Pearl Harbor entrance channel. No charge to see the view; the Aloha Tower is open Sunday through Wednesday,

9am to 6pm, and Thursday through Saturday, 9am to 10pm.

Next to the Tower is the:

2 Aloha Tower Marketplace

In the early 1990s, city officials came up with the idea to renovate and restore the waterfront with shops, restaurants, and bars to bring back the feeling of "boat days." The shops, restaurants, and bars inside the two-story Aloha Tower Marketplace offer an array of cuisines, one-of-a-kind shops, and even a microbrewery. Most shops open at 9am daily and the restaurants and bars don't shut down until the wee hours of the morning.

From the Aloha Tower Marketplace, walk in the Diamond Head direction along the waterfront to Pier 7, where you'll find the:

③ Hawaii Maritime Center

The center is composed of three entities: the museum, which is in the **Kalakaua Boathouse;** the *Falls of Clyde,* the four-masted ship moored next door; and the *Hokule'a,* the 60-foot Polynesian sailing canoe, also moored at Pier 7.

When you enter the two-story Boathouse, stop to look at the glass case of trophies and artifacts from the days when the boathouse really did belong to King David Kalakaua. The museum has great exhibits on Hawaii's maritime history, whaling, the history of surfing in the islands, and the cultural art of tattooing. There's also an auditorium with videos of Hawaii's seagoing culture, and a reproduction of a Matson Liner stateroom.

Moored next door is the:

④ Falls of Clyde

The world's only remaining fully rigged, four-masted ship is on display as a National Historic Landmark. Still afloat, the 266-foot, iron-hulled ship was built in 1878 in Glasgow, Scotland. Matson Navigation bought the ship in 1899 to carry sugar and passengers between Hilo and San Francisco. When that became economically unfeasible, in 1906 the boat was converted into a sail-driven oil tanker. After 1920, it was dismantled and became a floating oil depot for fishing boats in Alaska.

She was headed for the scrap pile when a group of Hawaii residents raised the money to bring her back to Hawaii in 1963. Since then she has been totally restored, and now visitors can wander across her decks and through the cargo area below.

After viewing the *Falls of Clyde,* wander over to the:

⑤ Hokule'a

If you're lucky, the 60-foot Polynesian canoe will be docked, but it's often out on jaunts. In 1976, this reproduction of the traditional double-hulled sailing canoe proved to the world that the Polynesians could have made the 6,000-mile round-trip from Tahiti to Hawaii, navigating only by the stars and the wave patterns. Living on an open deck (9 ft. wide by 40 ft. long), the crew of a dozen, along with a traditional navigator from an island in the Northern Pacific, made the successful voyage. Since then there has been a renaissance in the Pacific among native islanders to relearn this art of navigation.

Next door, at Pier 6, you'll find the:

⑥ Navatek I

From ancient Polynesian sailing canoes to today's high-tech, *Navatek I* is the latest specimen in naval engineering. The 140-foot-long vessel isn't even called a boat; it's actually a SWATH (Small Waterplane Area Twin Hull) vessel. That means the ship's superstructure—the part you ride on—rests on twin torpedolike hulls that cut through the water so you don't bob like a cork. It's the smoothest ride in town and guarantees you will not get seasick or spill your mai tai.

From Pier 6, walk down Ala Moana Boulevard and turn mauka at Punchbowl, where you'll come to:

⑦ Waterfront Plaza and Restaurant Row

Eateries serving an array of cuisines from gourmet Hawaii regional to burgers, shops, and theaters fill this block-long complex. This is a great place to stop for lunch or dinner, or for a cool drink at the end of your walk.

Getting There: From Waikiki, take Ala Moana Boulevard in the Ewa direction. Ala Moana
                  Boulevard ends at Nimitz Highway. Turn right on the next street on your
                  right (Alakea St.). Park in the parking garage across from St. Andrews
                  Church after you cross Beretania Street. TheBus: 1, 2, 3, 4, 11, 12, or 50.
Start: St. Andrew's Church, Beretania and Alakea streets.
Finish: Same place.
Time: 2 to 3 hours, depending on how long you linger in museums.
Best Times: Wednesday through Saturday, daytime, when the Iolani Palace has tours.

The 1800s were a turbulent time in Hawaii. By the end of the 1790s, Kamehameha the Great had united all the islands. Foreigners then began arriving by ship—first explorers, then merchants, and in 1820, missionaries. The rulers of Hawaii were hard-pressed to keep up. By 1840 it was clear that the capital had shifted from Lahaina, where the Kingdom of Hawaii was actually centered, to Honolulu where the majority of commerce and trade was taking place. In 1848 the Great Mahele (division) enabled commoners and eventually foreigners to own crown land, and in two generations, more than 80% of all private lands had shifted to foreign ownership. With the introduction of sugar as a crop, the foreigners prospered, and in time they put more and more pressures on the government.

By 1872, the monarchy had run through the Kamehameha line and in 1873 David Kalakaua was elected to the throne. Known as the "Merrie Monarch," Kalakaua redefined the monarchy by going on a world tour, building Iolani Palace, having a European-style coronation, and throwing extravagant parties. By the end of the 1800s, however, the foreign sugar growers and merchants had become extremely powerful in Hawaii. With the assistance of the U.S. Marines, they orchestrated the overthrow of Queen Liliuokalani, Hawaii's last reigning monarch, in 1893. The United States declared Hawaii a territory in 1898.

You can witness the remnants of these turbulent years in just a few short blocks.

Cross the street from the church parking lot and venture back to 1858 when you enter:

❶ St. Andrew's Church

The Hawaiian monarchs were greatly influenced by the royals in Europe. When King Kamehameha IV saw the grandeur of the Church of England, he decided to build his own cathedral. He and Queen Emma founded the Anglican Church of Hawaii in 1858. The king, however, didn't live to see the church completed; he died on St. Andrew's Day, 4 years before King Kamehameha V oversaw the laying of the cornerstone in 1867. The church was named St. Andrew's in honor of King Kamehameha IV's death. This French-Gothic structure was shipped in pieces from England and reassembled here. Even if you aren't fond of visiting churches, you have to see the floor-to-eaves hand-blown stained-glass window that faces the setting sun. In the glass is a mural of Reverend Thomas Staley, the first bishop in Hawaii; King Kamehameha IV; and Queen Emma. There's also an excellent thrift shop on the grounds with some real bargains that's open Monday, Wednesday, and Friday 9:30am to 4pm and Saturday 9am to 1pm.

Next, walk down Beretania Street in the Diamond Head direction to the gates of:

❷ Washington Place

Today this is the residence of the Governor of Hawaii (sorry, no tours; just peek through the iron fence), but it occupies a distinguished place in Hawaii's history. Originally the colonial-style home was built by a U.S. sea captain named John Dominis. The sea captain's son, also named John, married a beautiful Hawaiian princess, Lydia Kapaakea, who later became Hawaii's last queen, Liliuokalani. When the queen was overthrown by U.S. businessmen in 1893, she moved out of Iolani Palace and into her husband's inherited home, Washington Place, where she lived until her death in 1917. On the left side of the building, near the sidewalk, is a plaque inscribed with the words to one of the most popular songs written by Queen Liliuokalani, "Aloha Oe" ("Farewell to Thee").

Cross the street and walk to the front of the Hawaii State Capitol, where you'll find the:

❸ Father Damien Statue

The people of Hawaii have never forgotten the sacrifice this Belgian priest made to help the sufferers of leprosy when he volunteered to work with them in exile on the Kalaupapa Peninsula on the island of Molokai. After 16 years of service, Father Damien died of leprosy, at the age of 49. The statue is frequently draped in leis in recognition of Father Damien's humanitarian work.

Behind Father Damien's statue is the:

❹ Hawaii State Capitol

Here's where Hawaii's state legislators work from mid-January to the end of April every year. This is not your typical white dome structure, but a building symbolic of Hawaii. Unfortunately, it symbolizes more of Hawaii than the architect and the state legislature probably bargained for. The building's unusual design has palm tree–shaped pillars, two cone-shaped chambers (representing volcanoes) for the legislative bodies, and in the inner courtyard, a 600,000-tile mosaic of the sea (Aquarius) created by a local artist. A reflecting pool (representing the sea) surrounds the entire structure. Like a lot of things in Hawaii, it was a great idea, but no one considered the logistics. The reflecting pond also draws brackish water, which rusts the hardware; when it rains, water pours into the rotunda, dampening government business; and the Aquarius floor mosaic became so damaged by the elements that it became a hazard. In the 1990s, the entire building (built in 1969) was closed for a couple of years for renovations, forcing the legislature to set up temporary quarters in several buildings. It's open again, and you are welcome to go into the rotunda and see the woven hangings and murals at the entrance, or take the elevator up to the fifth floor for a spectacular view of the city's historical center.

Walk down Richards Street toward the ocean and stop at:

❺ Iolani Palace

Hawaii is the only state in the U.S. to have not one, but two royal palaces; one in Kona, where the royals went during the summer, and Iolani Palace (*Iolani* means "royal hawk"). Don't miss the opportunity to see this grande dame of historic buildings. Tours are limited. Admission is $15 for adults, $5 for children ages 5 to 13. Guided tours are offered Tuesday through Saturday 9am to 2:15pm; call ahead to reserve at ✆ **808/522-0832.**

In ancient times a heiau stood in this area. When it became clear to

Map legend:

✝ Church
✉ Post Office

area of detail

DOWNTOWN ALA MOANA

Sand Island

WAIKIKI

HONOLULU

start here ★

finish here ★

CHINATOWN

1 St. Andrew's Church
2 Washington Place
3 Father Damien Statue
4 Hawaii State Capitol
5 Iolani Palace
6 Iolani Palace Grounds
7 King Kamehameha Statue
8 Aliiolani Hale
9 Kawaiahao Church
10 Mission Houses and Museums
11 Honolulu Hale
12 State Library
13 Kalanimoku

King Kamehameha III that the capital should be transferred from Lahaina to Honolulu, he moved to a modest building here in 1845. The construction of the palace was undertaken by King David Kalakaua and was begun in 1879; it was finished 3 years later at a cost of $350,000. The king spared no expense: You can still see the glass and iron work imported from San Francisco. The palace had all the modern conveniences for its time: Electric lights were installed 4 years before the White House had them; every bedroom had its own full bath with hot and cold running water and copper-lined tubs, a flush toilet, and a bidet. The king had a telephone line from the palace to his boathouse on the water a year after Alexander Graham Bell introduced it to the world.

It was also in this palace that Queen Liliuokalani was overthrown and placed under house arrest for 9 months. Later, the territorial and then the state government used the palace until it outgrew it. When the legislature left in 1968, the palace was in shambles and has since undergone a $7 million overhaul to restore it to its former glory.

After you visit the palace, spend some time on the:

6 Iolani Palace Grounds

You can wander around the grounds at no charge. The ticket window to the palace and the gift shop are in the former barracks of the Royal Household Guards. The domed pavilion on the grounds was originally built as a Coronation Stand by King Kalakaua (9 years after he took the throne, he decided to have a formal European-style coronation ceremony where he crowned himself and his queen, Kapiolani). Later he used it as a **Royal Bandstand** for concerts (King Kalakaua, along with Herni Berger, the first Royal Hawaiian Bandmaster, wrote "Hawaii Pono'i," the state anthem). Today the Royal Bandstand is still used for concerts by the Royal Hawaiian Band. The more modern building on the grounds is the **State Archives,** built in 1953, which hold records, documents, and photos of Hawaii's people and its history.

From the palace grounds, walk makai to King Street, and cross the street to the:

❼ King Kamehameha Statue

At the juncture of King, Merchant, and Mililani streets stands a replica of the man who united the Hawaiian Islands. The striking black and gold bronze statue is magnificent. The best day to see the statue is on June 11 (King Kamehameha Day), when it is covered with leis in honor of Hawaii's favorite son.

The statue of Kamehameha I was cast by Thomas Gould in 1880 in Paris. However, it was lost at sea somewhere near the Falkland Islands. Subsequently, the insurance money was used to pay for a second statue, but in the meantime, the original statue was recovered. The original was eventually sent to the town of Kapaau on the Big Island, the birthplace of Kamehameha, and the second statue was placed in Honolulu in 1883, as part of King David Kalakaua's coronation ceremony. A third statue (all three are very different, but they were supposedly all cast from the same mold) was sent to Washington, D.C., when Hawaii became a state in 1959.

Right behind King Kamehameha's statue is:

❽ Aliiolani Hale

The name translates to "House of Heavenly Kings." This distinctive building, with a clock tower, now houses the State Judiciary Building. King Kamehameha V originally wanted to build a palace here and commissioned the Australian architect Thomas Rowe in 1872. However, it ended up as the first major government building for the Hawaiian monarchy. Kamehameha V didn't live to see it completed, and King David Kalakaua dedicated the building in 1874. Ironically, less than 20 years later, on January 17, 1893, Stanford Dole, backed by other prominent sugar planters, stood on the steps to this building and proclaimed the overthrow of the Hawaiian monarchy and the establishment of a provisional government. Tours are conducted on Tuesday through Thursday, 10am to 3pm, no charge.

Walk toward Diamond Head on King Street; at the corner of King and Punchbowl, stop in at:

❾ Kawaiahao Church

When the missionaries came to Hawaii, the first thing they did was build churches. Four thatched grass churches (one measured 54 ft. by 22 ft. and could seat 300 people on lauhala mats; the last thatched church held 4,500 people) had been built on this site through 1837 before Rev. Hiram Bingham began building what he considered a "real" church—a New England–style congregational structure with Gothic influences. Between 1837 and 1842, the building of the church required some 14,000 giant coral slabs (some weighing more than 1,000 lbs.). Hawaiian divers literally raped the reefs, digging out huge chunks of coral and causing irreparable environmental damage.

Kawaiahao is Hawaii's oldest church, and it has been the site of numerous historical events, such as a speech made by King Kamehameha III in 1843, an excerpt from which became Hawaii's state motto (*"Ua mau ke ea o ka aina i ka pono,"* which translates as "The life of the land is preserved in righteousness").

The clock tower in the church, which was donated by King Kamehameha III and installed in 1850, continues to tick today. The church is open Monday through Saturday, from 8am to 4pm; you'll find it to be very cool in temperature. Don't sit in the pews in the back, marked with kahili feathers and velvet cushions; they are still reserved for the descendants of royalty. Sunday service (in Hawaiian) at 10:30am.

Cross the street, and you'll see the:

⓿ **Mission Houses and Museums**
On the corner of King and Kawaiahao streets stand the original buildings of the Sandwich Islands Mission Headquarters: the **Frame House** (built in 1821), the **Chamberlain House** (1831), and the **Printing Office** (1841). The complex is open Tuesday through Saturday from 9am to 4pm; admission is $8 for adults, $7 for military personnel, $6 for seniors, $4 for college students and ages 13 to 18, and $3 for children ages 4 to 12. The tours are often led by descendants of the original missionaries to Hawaii.

Believe it or not, the missionaries brought their own prefab house along with them when they came around Cape Horn from Boston in 1819. The Frame House was designed for New England winters and had small windows (it must have been stifling hot inside). Finished in 1921 (the interior frame was left behind and didn't arrive until Christmas 1920), it is Hawaii's oldest wooden structure.

The Chamberlain House, built in 1931, was used by the missionaries as a storehouse.

The missionaries believed that the best way to spread the Lord's message to the Hawaiians was to learn their language, and then to print literature for them to read. So it was the missionaries who gave the Hawaiians a written language. The Printing House on the grounds was where the lead-type Ramage press (brought from New England, of course) printed the Hawaiian Bible.

Cross King Street and walk in the Ewa direction to the corner of Punchbowl and King to:

⓫ **Honolulu Hale**
The **Honolulu City Hall,** built in 1927, was designed by Honolulu's most famous architect, C. W. Dickey. His Spanish mission–style building has an open-air courtyard, which is used for art exhibits and concerts. Open weekdays.

Cross Punchbowl Street and walk mauka to the:

⓬ **State Library**
Anything you want to know about Hawaii and the Pacific can be found here, the main branch of the state's library system. Located in a restored historic building, there is an open garden courtyard in the middle of the building, great for stopping for a rest on your walk.

Head mauka up Punchbowl to the corner of Punchbowl and Beretania streets to:

⓭ **Kalanimoku**
This beautiful name, "Ship of Heaven," has been given to this dour state office building. Here you can get information on hiking and camping (from the Department of Land and Natural Resources) in state parks.

Retrace your steps in the Ewa direction down Beretania to Alakea back to the parking garage.

WALKING TOUR 4   KAPIOLANI PARK

Getting There	From Waikiki, walk toward Diamond Head on Kalakaua Avenue. If you are coming by car, the cheapest parking is metered street parking on Kalakaua Avenue adjacent to the park. TheBus: 19 or 20.
Start	Waikiki Beach Center, Kalakaua Avenue, Diamond Head side of the Sheraton Moana Hotel, across the street from the Hyatt Regency and Uluniu Avenue.
Finish	Kapiolani Beach Park.
Time	4 to 5 hours. Allow at least an hour each for walking around the park, wandering around the zoo, exploring the aquarium, and snapping photos at the Kodak Hula Show, plus all the time you want for the beach.
Best Time	Tuesday to Thursday mornings if you want to catch the Kodak Hula Show.

On June 11, 1877, King Kamehameha Day, then-King David Kalakaua donated some 140 acres of land to the people of Hawaii for Hawaii's first park. He asked that the park be named after his beloved wife, Queen Kapiolani, and he celebrated the opening of this vast grassy area with a free concert and "high stakes" horse races (the king loved gambling) on the new horse-racing oval he had built below Diamond Head.

The horse races, and the gambling that accompanied it, were eventually outlawed, but the park—and the free concerts—live on. Just a coconut's throw from the high-rise concrete jungle of Waikiki lies this 133-acre grassy park (the Paki playground and a fire station make up the remaining acreage) dotted with spreading banyans, huge monkeypod trees, blooming royal poincianas, and swaying ironwoods. Throughout the open spaces are jogging paths, tennis courts, soccer and cricket fields, and even an archery range. People come to the park to listen to music, watch ethnic dancing, exercise, enjoy team sports, take long meditative walks, picnic, buy art, smell the roses, and just relax. The park is the site of international kite-flying contests, the finishing line for the Honolulu marathon, and the home of yearly Scottish highland games, Hawaiian cultural festivals, and about a zillion barbecues and picnics every year.

Start at the:

❶ Waikiki Beach Center

On the ocean side of Kalakaua Avenue, next to the Sheraton Moana Hotel, is a complex of restrooms, showers, surfboard lockers, rental concessions, and the Waikiki police substation.

On the Diamond Head side of the police substation are the:

❷ Wizard Stones or Healing Stones

These four basalt boulders, which weigh several tons apiece and sit on a lava rock platform, are held sacred by the Hawaiian people.

The story goes that sometime before the 15th century, four powerful healers from Moaulanuiakea, in the Society Islands, named Kapaemahu, Kahaloa, Kapuni, and Kihohi, lived in the Ulukoa area of Waikiki. After years of healing the people and the alii of Oahu, they wished to return home. They asked the people to erect four monuments made of bell stone, a basalt rock that was found in a Kaimuki quarry and that produced a bell-like ringing when struck. The healers spent a ceremonious month transferring their spiritual healing power, or *mana,* to the stones. The great mystery is how the boulders were transported from Kaimuki to the marshland near Kuhio Beach in Waikiki! Over time a bowling alley was built on the spot,

1 Waikiki Beach Center
2 Wizard Stones or Healing Stones
3 Duke Kahanamoku Statue
4 Kuhio Beach Park
5 Father Damien Museum
6 Kapiolani Park Kiosk
7 Honolulu Zoo
8 Kapiolani Park Bandstand
9 Art Mart
10 Waikiki Shell
11 Queen Kapiolani Garden
12 People's Open Market
13 Diamond Head Tennis Courts
14 San Souci Beach
15 Natatorium
16 Waikiki Aquarium
17 Kapiolani Beach Park

and the stones got buried beneath the structure. After the bowling alley was torn down in the 1960s, tourists used the stones to eat lunch on or to drape their wet towels over. In 1997 the stones were once again given a place of prominence with the construction of a $75,000 shrine that includes the platform and a wrought-iron fence. Since then the stones have become something of a mecca for students and patients of traditional healing.

Just west of the stones you'll find the:

❸ Duke Kahanamoku Statue

Here, cast in bronze, is Hawaii's most famous athlete, also known as the father of modern surfing. Duke (1890–1968) won Olympic swimming medals in 1912, 1920, 1924, and 1928. He was enshrined in both the Swimming Hall of Fame and the Surfing Hall of Fame. He also traveled around the world promoting surfing. Interestingly, when the city of Honolulu first erected the statue of this lifelong ocean athlete, they placed it with his back to the water. There was public outcry, because no one familiar with the ocean would ever stand with his back to it. To quell the outcry, the city moved the statue closer to the sidewalk.

Continuing in the Diamond Head direction, you'll come to:

④ Kuhio Beach Park

The two small swimming holes here are great, but heed the warning sign: watch out for holes. There actually are deep holes in the sandy bottom, and you may suddenly find yourself in very deep water. The best pool for swimming is the one on the Diamond Head end, but the water circulation is questionable—there sometimes appears to be a layer of suntan lotion floating on the surface. If the waves are up, watch the Boogie boarders surf by the seawall. They ride toward the wall and at the last minute veer away with a swoosh.

After watching the surfers, cross Kalakaua Avenue and walk mauka down Ohua Avenue; behind St. Augustine's Church you'll find the:

⑤ Father Damien Museum

This small museum is a tribute to the priest who worked with the sufferers of leprosy on Molokai. A video of Father Damien and the leprosy colony is available for viewing here. The museum is open Monday through Friday from 9am to 3pm, and Saturday from 9am to noon; admission is free.

Go back to Kalakaua Avenue and walk towards Diamond Head to the entrance of Kapiolani Park, where you'll see the:

⑥ Kapiolani Park Kiosk

On the corner of Kalakaua and Kapahulu avenues, this small display stand contains brochures and actual photos of the park's history. It also carries information on upcoming events at the various sites within the park (Aquarium, Zoo, Waikiki Shell, Kodak Hula Show, and Kapiolani Bandstand). An informative map will help to orient you to the park grounds.

Continue up Kapahulu Avenue to the entrance of the:

⑦ Honolulu Zoo

The city's 42-acre zoo is open every day from 9am to 4:30pm, but the best time to go is as soon as the gates open—the animals seem to be more active and it is a lot cooler than walking around at midday in the hot sun.

You can walk or ride the tram to view the animals from around the world, stopping at the new African Savannah exhibit, a 10-acre wild preserve with more than 40 African critters (including lions, cheetahs, white rhinos, giraffes, zebras, hippos, and monkeys) roaming around in the open. There's also a petting zoo of farm animals, an aviary for Hawaii's rapidly disappearing native birds, and an interesting collection of Hawaii's native plants. Admission is $6 adults, $1 children 6 to 12 when accompanied by an adult (if a child isn't with an adult, he or she pays the adult fee; children under 6 are not allowed in without an adult).

For a real treat, take the **"Zoo by Moonlight"** tour, which allows you a rare behind-the-scenes look into the lives of the zoo's nocturnal creatures. Tours are offered 2 days before, during, and 2 days after the full moon from 7 to 9pm; the cost is $7 for adults and $5 for children.

Trace your steps back to Kapahulu and Kalakaua avenues and head mauka down Monsarrat Avenue to the:

⑧ Kapiolani Park Bandstand

On the mauka side of the bandstand, the **Kodak Hula Show** has been presenting the hula to visitors since 1937 (and a few of the senior ladies in the show have been dancing since the show started). Some 3,000 people fit into the bleachers around a grassy stage area (with the sun to your back for perfect picture-taking). If you forget your camera or run out of film,

Kodak has cameras for rent and plenty of film for sale. For a good seat, get there by 8am; to get into the show, be there no later than 9am. Once the show starts, they admit people only between acts. The show is nonstop entertainment with hula dancers, bedecked in ti-leaf skirts and flower leis, swaying to an assortment of rhythms. Be sure to save some film to photograph the grand finale, which consists of all the dancers lining up on the stage and spelling out A-L-O-H-A and H-A-W-A-I-I with placards. The performances are Tuesday through Thursday, 10 to 11:15am, and are free.

Back on Monsarrat Avenue, on the fence facing the zoo, you'll find the:

⑨ Art Mart
The Artists of Oahu Exhibit is the new official name of this display. Here, local artisans hang their artwork on a fence for the public to view and buy. Not only do you get to meet the artists, but you also have an opportunity to purchase their work at a considerable discount from the prices you'll see in galleries. Exhibits are Saturday, Sunday, and Wednesday, 10am to 4pm.

Cross Monsarrat Avenue, and you'll see the:

⑩ Waikiki Shell
Just mauka of the Kodak Hula Show is the open-air amphitheater that hosts numerous musical shows, from the Honolulu Symphony to traditional Hawaiian music.

Continue walking down to the end of the block to the corner of Monsarrat and Paki avenues to the:

⑪ Queen Kapiolani Garden
You'll see a range of hibiscus plants and dozens of varieties of roses, including the somewhat rare Hawaiian rose. The tranquil gardens are always open and are a great place to wander and relax.

Across the street on a Wednesday morning, you'll find the:

⑫ People's Open Market
Open from 10 to 11am on Wednesdays, the farmer's market with its open stalls is an excellent spot to buy fresh produce and flowers.

After you make your purchases, continue in the Diamond Head direction down Paki Avenue to the:

⑬ Diamond Head Tennis Courts
Located on the mauka side of Paki Avenue, the free City and County tennis courts are open for play during daylight hours 7 days a week. Tennis etiquette suggests that if someone is waiting for a court, limit your play to 45 minutes.

After watching or playing, turn onto Kalakaua Avenue, and begin walking back toward Waikiki to:

⑭ San Souci Beach
Located next to the New Otani Kaimana Beach Hotel, this is one of the best swimming beaches in Waikiki. The shallow reef, which is close to shore, keeps the waters calm. Farther out there is good snorkeling in the coral reef by the Kapua Channel. Facilities include outdoor showers and a lifeguard.

After a brief swim, keep walking toward Waikiki until you come to the:

⑮ Natatorium
This huge concrete structure next to the beach is both a memorial to the soldiers of World War I and a 100-meter saltwater swimming pool. Opened in 1927, when Honolulu had hopes of hosting the Olympics, the ornate swimming pool fell into disuse and disrepair after World War II, and was finally closed in 1979. The City and County of Honolulu just finished the first phase of renovation, a $4.4 million restoration of the outside arches to the building, construction of modern restrooms and showers and refurbishment of the bleacher seating. The next phase is an $11.5 million renovation of the salt-water swimming pool.

After a brief stop here, continue on to the:

⑯ Waikiki Aquarium

The Aquarium is located at 2777 Kalakaua Ave. Try not to miss this stop—the tropical aquarium is worth a peek if only to see the only living **chambered nautilus** born in captivity. Its natural habitat is the deep waters of Micronesia, but Bruce Carlson, director of the aquarium, succeeded not only in trapping the pearly shell in 1,500 feet of water by dangling chunks of raw tuna, but also managed to breed this ancient relative of the octopus. The aquarium was also the first to successfully display the cuttlefish and Hawaii's favorite eating fish, the mahimahi. There are plenty of other fish in this small but first-class aquarium, located at the edge of a live coral reef. Owned and operated by the University of Hawaii, the aquarium, after a $3 million upgrade, now features a Hawaiian reef habitat with sharks, eels, a touch tank, and habitats for the endangered Hawaiian monk seal and green sea turtles. Recently added: a rotating Biodiversity Special Exhibit, which features a look at the diversity of sea life and interactive exhibits focusing on corals and coral reefs. Admission is $7 for adults, $5 for members of the military, $4 for seniors and students, $2.50 for children ages 13 to 17. Open daily 9am to 5pm; closed Christmas Day.

Your final stop is:

⑰ Kapiolani Beach Park

Relax on the stretch of grassy lawn alongside the sandy beach, one of the best-kept secrets of Waikiki. This beach park is much less crowded than the beaches of Waikiki, plus it has adjacent grassy lawns, barbecue areas, picnic tables, restrooms, and showers. The swimming is good here year-round, a surfing spot known as "Public's" is offshore, and there's always a game going at the volleyball courts. The middle section of the beach park, in front of the pavilion, is known as Queen's Beach or Queen's Surf, and is popular with the gay community.

6 Beyond Honolulu: Exploring the Island

The moment always arrives—usually after a couple of days at the beach, snorkeling in the warm, blue-green waters of Hanauma Bay, enjoying sundown mai tais—when a certain curiosity kicks in about the rest of Oahu, largely unknown to most visitors. It's time to find the rental car in the hotel garage and set out around the island. You can also explore Oahu using **TheBus** (see p. 53 for details on the transit system).

For great places to stop for a bite to eat while you're exploring, see chapter 5, "Dining." You also might want to check out chapter 8, "Shopping." Beaches, nature hikes, camping, and other outdoor activities outside of Honolulu are covered in chapter 6.

OAHU'S SOUTHEAST COAST

From the high-rises of Waikiki, venture down Kalakaua Avenue through tree-lined Kapiolani Park to take a look at a different side of Oahu, the arid south shore. The landscape here is more moonscape, with prickly cacti onshore and, in winter, spouting whales cavorting in the water. Some call it the South Shore, others Sandy's (after the mile-long beach here), but Hawaiians call it **Ka Iwi,** which means "the bone"—no doubt because of all the bone-cracking shore breaks along this popular bodyboarding coastline. The beaches here are long, wide, and popular with local daredevils.

Eastern Oahu & the Windward Coast

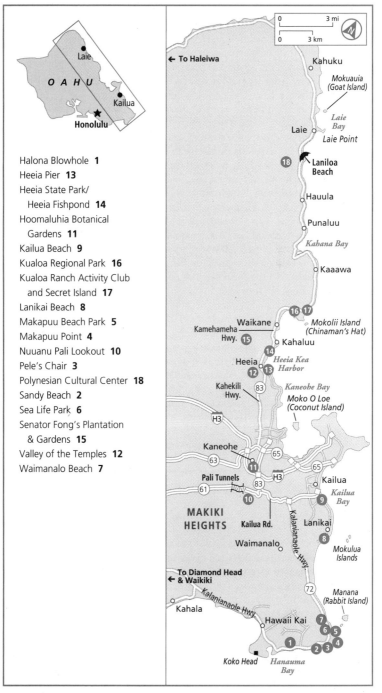

Halona Blowhole **1**
Heeia Pier **13**
Heeia State Park/
  Heeia Fishpond **14**
Hoomaluhia Botanical
  Gardens **11**
Kailua Beach **9**
Kualoa Regional Park **16**
Kualoa Ranch Activity Club
  and Secret Island **17**
Lanikai Beach **8**
Makapuu Beach Park **5**
Makapuu Point **4**
Nuuanu Pali Lookout **10**
Pele's Chair **3**
Polynesian Cultural Center **18**
Sandy Beach **2**
Sea Life Park **6**
Senator Fong's Plantation
  & Gardens **15**
Valley of the Temples **12**
Waimanalo Beach **7**

This open, scenic coast is the best place on Oahu to watch sea, shore, and even land birds. It's also a good whale-watching spot in season, and the night sky is ideal for amateur astronomers on the lookout for meteors, comets, and stars.

To get to this coast, follow Kalakaua Avenue past the multitiered Dillingham Fountain and around the bend in the road, which now becomes Poni Moi Road. Make a right on Diamond Head Road and begin the climb up the side of the old crater. At the top are several lookout points, so if the official Diamond Head Lookout is jammed with cars, try one of the other lookouts just down the road. The view of the rolling waves is spectacular; take the time to pull over.

Diamond Head Road rolls downhill now into the ritzy community of **Kahala.** At the V in the road at the triangular Fort Ruger Park, veer to your right and continue on the palm-tree-lined Kahala Avenue. Make a left on Hunakai Street, then a right on Kilauea Avenue, and look for the sign: H-1 WEST—WAIMANALO. Turn right at the sign, although you won't get on the H-1 Freeway; get on the Kalanianaole Highway, a four-lane highway interrupted every few blocks by a stoplight. This is the suburban bedroom community to Honolulu, marked by malls on the left and beach parks on the right.

About a half hour outside of Waikiki, you'll see the turnoff to **Hanauma Bay** (see p. 142) on the right. This marine preserve is a great place to stop for a swim; you'll find the friendliest fish on the island here. *A reminder:* The beach park is closed on Tuesdays.

Around mile marker 11, the jagged lava coast itself spouts sea foam at the **Halona Blowhole.** Look out to sea from Halona over Sandy Beach and across the 26-mile gulf to neighboring Molokai and the faint triangular shadow of Lanai on the far horizon. **Sandy Beach** (see p. 143) is Oahu's most dangerous beach; it's the only one with an ambulance always standing by to whisk injured wave catchers to the hospital. Bodyboarders just love it.

The coast looks raw and empty along this stretch, but the road weaves past old Hawaiian fishponds and the famous formation known as **Pele's Chair,** just off Kalanianaole Highway (Hwy. 72) above Queen's Beach. From a distance, the lava-rock outcropping looks like a mighty throne; it's believed to be the fire goddess's last resting place on Oahu before she flew off to continue her work on other islands.

Ahead lies 647-foot-high **Makapuu Point,** with a lighthouse that once signaled safe passage for steamship passengers arriving from San Francisco. The automated light now brightens Oahu's south coast for passing tankers, fishing boats, and sailors. You can take a short hike up here for a spectacular vista (see p. 160).

If you're with the kids, you may want to spend the day at **Sea Life Park**, a marine amusement park described earlier in this chapter (see p. 183).

Turn the corner at Makapuu, and you're on Oahu's windward side, where cooling trade winds propel windsurfers across turquoise bays; the waves at **Makapuu Beach Park** are perfect for bodysurfing (see p. 143).

Ahead, the coastal vista is a profusion of fluted green mountains and strange peaks, edged by golden beaches and the blue, blue Pacific. The 3,000-foot-high sheer green Koolau Mountains plunge almost straight down, presenting an irresistible jumping-off spot for hang-glider pilots, who catch the thermals on hours-long rides.

Winding up the coast, Kalanianaole Highway (Hwy. 72) leads through rural **Waimanalo,** a country beach town of nurseries and stables, fresh-fruit stands, and some of the island's best conch and triton shell specimens at roadside stands.

Nearly 4 miles long, **Waimanalo Beach** is Oahu's longest beach and the most popular for bodysurfing. Take a swim here or head on to **Kailua Beach** ⋆⋆⋆, one of Hawaii's best (see p. 144).

If it's still early in the day, you can head up the lush, green Windward Coast by turning right at the Castle Junction, Highway 72, and Highway 61 (which is also Kailua Rd. on the makai, or seaward, side of the junction, and Kalanianaole Hwy. on the mauka, or inland, side of the junction), and continuing down Kailua Road (Hwy. 61). After Kailua Road crosses the Kaelepulu Stream, the name of the road changes to Kuulei Road. When Kuulei Road ends, turn left onto Kalaheo Avenue, which becomes Kaneohe Bay Drive after it crosses the Kawainui Channel. Follow this scenic drive around the peninsula until it crosses Kamehameha Highway (Hwy. 83); turn right and continue on Kamehameha Highway for a scenic drive along the ocean.

If you're in a hurry to get back to Waikiki, turn left at Castle Junction and head over the Pali Highway (Hwy. 61), which becomes Bishop Street in Honolulu and ends at Ala Moana. Turn left for Waikiki; it's the second beach on the right.

THE WINDWARD COAST

From the **Nuuanu Pali Lookout** ⋆, near the summit of the Pali Highway (Hwy. 61), you get the first hint of the other side of Oahu, a region so green and lovely that it could be an island sibling of Tahiti. With its many beaches and bays, the scenic 30-mile Windward Coast parallels the corduroy-ridged, nearly perpendicular cliffs of the Koolau Range, which separates the windward side of the island from Honolulu and the rest of Oahu. As you descend on the serpentine Pali Highway beneath often gushing waterfalls, you'll see the nearly 1,000-foot spike of **Olomana,** the bold pinnacle that always reminds us of Devil's Tower National Monument in Wyoming, and beyond, the Hawaiian village of **Waimanalo.**

From the Pali Highway, to the right is **Kailua,** Hawaii's biggest beach town, with more than 50,000 residents and two special beaches, Kailua and Lanikai, begging for visitors. Funky little Kailua is lined with million-dollar houses next to tarpaper shacks, antiques shops, and bed-and-breakfasts. Although the Pali Highway (Hwy. 61) proceeds directly to the coast, it undergoes two name changes, becoming first Kalanianaole Highway—from the intersection of Kamehameha Highway (Hwy. 83)—and then Kailua Road as it heads into Kailua town; but the road remains Highway 61 the whole way. Kailua Road ends at the T intersection at Kalaheo Drive, which follows the coast in a northerly and southerly direction. Turn right on South Kalaheo Drive to get to Kailua Beach Park and Lanikai Beach. No signs point the way, but you can't miss them.

If you spend a day at the beach here, stick around for sunset, when the sun sinks behind the Koolau Range and tints the clouds pink and orange. After a hard day at the beach, you'll work up an appetite, and Kailua has several great, inexpensive restaurants (see chapter 5, "Dining").

If you want to skip the beaches this time, turn left on North Kalaheo Drive, which becomes Kaneohe Bay Drive as it skirts Kaneohe Bay and leads back to Kamehameha Highway (Hwy. 83), which then passes through Kaneohe. The suburban maze of Kaneohe is one giant strip mall of retail excess that mars one of the Pacific's most picturesque bays. After clearing this obstacle, the place begins to look like Hawaii again.

Incredibly scenic Kaneohe Bay is spiked with islets and lined with gold-sand beach parks like **Kualoa,** a favorite picnic spot (see p. 146). The bay has a barrier reef and four tiny islets, one of which is known as Moku o loe, or Coconut Island. Don't be surprised if it looks familiar—it appeared in *Gilligan's Island.*

At Heeia State Park is **Heeia Fish Pond,** which ancient Hawaiians built by enclosing natural bays with rocks to trap fish on the incoming tide. The 88-acre fishpond, which is made of lava rock and had four watchtowers to observe fish movement and several sluice gates along the 5,000-foot-long wall, is now in the process of being restored.

Stop by the **Heeia Pier,** which juts onto Kaneohe Bay. You can take a snorkel cruise here, or sail out to a sandbar in the middle of the bay for an incredible view of Oahu that most people, even those who live here, never see. If it's Tuesday through Sunday between 7am and 6pm, stop in and see Ernie Choy at the **Deli on Heeia Kea Pier** (✆ **808/235-2192**). He has served fishermen, sailors, and kayakers the beach town's best omelettes and plate lunches at reasonable prices since 1979.

Everyone calls it **Chinaman's Hat,** but the tiny island off the eastern shore of Kualoa Regional Park is really named **Mokolii.** It's a sacred *puu honua,* or place of refuge, like the restored Puu Honua Honaunau on the Big Island of Hawaii. Excavations have unearthed evidence that this area was the home of ancient *alii* (royalty). Early Hawaiians believed that Mokolii ("fin of the lizard") is all that remains of a *mo'o,* or lizard, slain by Pele's sister, Hiiaka, and hurled into the sea. At low tide, you can swim out to the island, but keep watch on the changing tide, which can sweep you out to sea. The islet has a small, sandy beach and is a bird preserve, so don't spook the red-footed boobies.

Little poly voweled beach towns like **Kaaawa, Hauula, Punaluu,** and **Kahaluu** pop up along the coast, offering passersby shell shops and art galleries to explore. Famed hula photographer **Kim Taylor Reece** lives on this coast; his gallery at 53–866 Kamehameha Hwy., near Sacred Falls (✆ **808/293-2000**), is open daily from noon to 6pm. You'll also see working cattle ranches, fishermen's wharves, and roadside fruit and flower stands vending ice-cold coconuts (to drink) and tree-ripened mangoes, papayas, and apple bananas.

Sugar, once the sole industry of this region, is gone. But **Kahuku,** the former sugar-plantation town, has found new life as a small aquaculture community with prawn farms that supply island restaurants.

From here, continue along Kamehameha Highway (Hwy. 83) to the North Shore.

ATTRACTIONS ALONG THE WINDWARD COAST

The attractions below are arranged geographically as you drive up the coast from south to north.

Hoomaluhia Botanical Gardens 👯 This 400-acre botanical garden at the foot of the steepled Koolau Mountains is the perfect place for a picnic. Its name means "a peaceful refuge" and that's exactly what the Army Corps of Engineers created when they installed a flood-control project here, which resulted in a 32-acre freshwater lake and garden. Just unfold a beach mat, lie back, and watch the clouds race across the rippled cliffs of the majestic Koolau Range. This is one of the few public places on Oahu that provides a close-up view of the steepled cliffs. The park has hiking trails and—best of all—the island's only free inland campground (see p. 104). If you like hiking and nature, plan to spend at least a half a day here.

45–680 Luluku Rd., Kaneohe. (✆) **808/233-7323.** Free admission. Daily 9am–4pm. Guided nature hikes Sat 10am and Sun 1pm. Take H-1 to the Pali Hwy. (Hwy. 61); turn left on Kamehameha Hwy. (Hwy. 83); at the fourth light, turn left onto Luluku Rd. TheBus: 55 or 56 will stop on Kamehameha Hwy.; it's a 2-mile walk to the visitor center.

Valley of the Temples   This famous cemetery in a cleft of the pali is stalked by wild peacocks and about 700 curious people a day, who pay to see the 9-foot meditation Buddha, 2 acres of ponds full of more than 10,000 Japanese koi carp, and a replica of Japan's 900-year-old Byodo-in Temple of Equality. The original, made of wood, stands in Uji, on the outskirts of Kyoto; the Hawaiian version, made of concrete, was erected in 1968 to commemorate the 100th anniversary of the arrival of the first Japanese immigrants to Hawaii. It's not the same as seeing the original, but it's worth a detour. A 3-ton brass temple bell brings good luck to those who can ring it—although the gongs do jar the Zen-like serenity of this little bit of Japan. If you are in a rush, you can sail through here in an hour, but you'll want to stay longer.

47–200 Kahekili Hwy. (across the street from Temple Valley Shopping Center), Kaneohe. (✆) **808/239-8811.** Admission $2 adults, $1 children under 12 and seniors 65 and over. Daily 8:30am–4:30pm. Take the H-1 to the Likelike Hwy. (Hwy. 63); after the Wilson Tunnel, get in the right lane and take the Kahekili Hwy. (Hwy. 63); at the sixth traffic light is the entrance to the cemetery (on the left). TheBus: 65.

Senator Fong's Plantation & Gardens   Senator Hiram Fong, the first Chinese American elected to the U.S. Senate, served 17 years before retiring to tropical gardening years ago. Now you can ride an open-air tram through five gardens named for the American presidents he served. His 725-acre private estate includes 75 edible nuts and fruits. It's definitely worth an hour—if you haven't already seen enough botanics to last a lifetime.

47–285 Pulama Rd., Kaneohe. (✆) **808/239-6775.** www.fonggarden.net. Admission $10 adults, $8 seniors, $6 children 5–12. Daily 9am–4pm; 45-min. narrated tram tours daily from 10:30am, last tour 3pm. Take the H-1 to the Likelike Hwy. (Hwy. 63); turn left at Kahekili Hwy. (Hwy. 83); continue to Kaneohe and turn left on Pulama Rd. TheBus: 55; it's a mile walk uphill from the stop.

Kualoa Ranch and Activity Club   This once-working ranch now has five different adventure packages covering two dozen activities on its 4,000 acres. Activities include horseback riding, mountain-bike riding, shooting a rifle or a .22-caliber handgun, hiking, dune cycling, jet skiing, canoeing, kayaking, snorkeling, freshwater fishing, and more. We highly recommend the beach activities. You'll be shuttled to Molii fishpond's outermost bank, which is decked out like a country club: hammocks on the beach, volleyball courts, horseshoe pits, Ping-Pong tables, and beach pavilions. From here, you can take a 45-foot catamaran to Kaneohe Bay for snorkeling.

49–560 Kamehameha Hwy., Kaaawa. (✆) **800/231-7321** or 808/237-7321. www.kualoa.com. Daily 9:30am–3pm. Various activity packages $50–$139 adults, $35–$89 children 3–11. Reservations required. Take H-1 to the Likelike Hwy. (Hwy. 63), turn left at Kahekili Hwy. (Hwy. 83), and continue to Kaaawa. TheBus: 52.

Polynesian Cultural Center (✺) (Kids)   Even if you never leave Hawaii, you can still experience the natural beauty and culture of the vast Pacific in a single day at the Polynesian Cultural Center, a kind of living museum of Polynesia. Here, you can see first-hand the lifestyles, songs, dance, costumes, and architecture of seven Pacific islands—Fiji, New Zealand, Marquesas, Samoa, Tahiti, Tonga, and Hawaii—in the re-created villages scattered throughout the 42-acre lagoon park.

You "travel" through this museum by foot or in a canoe on a man-made freshwater lagoon. Each village is "inhabited" by native students from Polynesia who attend Hawaii's Brigham Young University. The park, which is operated by the Mormon Church, also features a variety of stage shows celebrating the music, dance, history, and culture of Polynesia. There's a luau every evening. Because a visit can take up to 8 hours, it's a good idea to arrive before 2pm.

Just beyond the center is the **Hawaii Temple** of the Church of Jesus Christ of Latter-Day Saints, which is built of volcanic rock and concrete in the form of a Greek cross and includes reflecting pools, formal gardens, and royal palms. Completed in 1919, it was the first Mormon temple built outside the continental United States. An optional tour of the Temple Visitors Center, as well as neighboring Brigham Young University, Hawaii, is included in the package admission prices.

55–370 Kamehameha Hwy., Laie. ℂ 800/367-7060, 808/293-3333, or 808/923-2911. www.polynesia.com. Admission only, $27 adults, $16 children 5–11. Admission, buffet, and nightly show $47 adults, $30 children. Admission, IMAX, luau, and nightly show $64 adults, $43 children. Ambassador VIP (deluxe) tour $95 adults, $63 children. Mon–Sat 12:30–9:30pm. Take H-1 to Pali Hwy. (Hwy. 61) and turn left on Kamehameha Hwy. (Hwy. 83). TheBus: 55. Polynesian Cultural Center coaches $15 round-trip; call numbers above to book.

CENTRAL OAHU & THE NORTH SHORE

If you can afford the splurge, rent a bright, shiny convertible—the perfect car for Oahu, since you can tan as you go—and head for the North Shore and Hawaii's surf city: **Haleiwa** ⚡, a quaint turn-of-the-20th-century sugarcane-plantation town designated a historic site. A collection of faded clapboard stores with a picturesque harbor, Haleiwa has evolved into a surfer outpost and major roadside attraction with art galleries, restaurants, and shops that sell hand-decorated clothing, jewelry, and sports gear (see chapter 8, "Shopping").

Getting here is half the fun. You have two choices: The first is to meander north along the lush Windward Coast, through country hamlets with roadside stands selling mangoes, bright tropical pareus, fresh corn, and pond-raised prawns. Attractions along that route are discussed in the previous section.

The second choice is to cruise up the H-2 through Oahu's broad and fertile central valley, past Pearl Harbor and the Schofield Barracks of *From Here to Eternity* fame, and on through the red-earthed heart of the island, where pineapple and sugarcane fields stretch from the Koolau to the Waianae mountains, until the sea reappears on the horizon. If you take this route, the tough part is getting on and off the H-1 freeway from Waikiki, which is done by way of convoluted routing on neighborhood streets. Try McCully Street off Ala Wai Boulevard, which is always crowded but usually the most direct route.

Once you're on H-1, stay to the right side; the freeway tends to divide abruptly. Keep following the signs for the H-1 (it separates off to Hwy. 78 at the airport and reunites later on; either way will get you there), then the H-1/H-2. Leave the H-1 where the two "interstates" divide; take the H-2 up the middle of the island, heading north toward the town of Wahiawa. That's what the sign will say—not North Shore or Haleiwa, but Wahiawa.

The H-2 runs out and becomes a two-lane country road about 18 miles outside downtown Honolulu, near Schofield Barracks (see below). The highway becomes Kamehameha Highway (Hwy. 99 and later Hwy. 83) at Wahiawa. Just past Wahiawa, about a half hour out of Honolulu, the **Dole Pineapple Plantation,** 64–1550 Kamehameha Hwy. (ℂ **808/621-8408;** TheBus: 52), offers a rest stop with pineapples, pineapple history, pineapple trinkets, and pineapple juice. Its latest feature is a maze you can wander through. Open daily

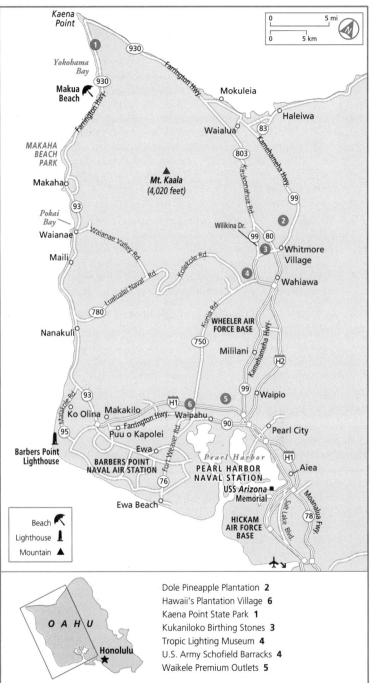

0   5 mi
0   5 km

Kaena
Point

1

930

*Yokohama
Bay*

930

**Makua
Beach**

930

Farrington Hwy.

Mokuleia

Waialua

Haleiwa

83

Kamehameha Hwy.

*MAKAHA
BEACH
PARK*

803

Makaha

▲ *Mt. Kaala
(4,020 feet)*

*Pokai
Bay*

93

99

Waianae

Waianae Valley Rd.

Wilikina Dr.

2

Maili

Kolekole Rd.

99   80

3

Whitmore
Village

Lualualei Naval Rd.

4

Wahiawa

780

*WHEELER AIR
FORCE BASE*

Kunia Rd.

Nanakuli

750

Mililani

Kamehameha Hwy.

H2

Malakole Rd.

93

Ko Olina

Makakilo

H1

6

Farrington Hwy.

Waipahu

5

99

Waipio

Fort Weaver Rd.

Puu o Kapolei

90

Pearl City

95

Ewa

Pearl Harbor

H1

Aiea

**Barbers Point
Lighthouse**

*BARBERS POINT
NAVAL AIR STATION*

*PEARL HARBOR
NAVAL STATION*

76

Salt Lake Blvd.

Moanalua Hwy.

78

Ewa Beach

USS *Arizona*
Memorial ■

*HICKAM
AIR FORCE
BASE*

Beach ☂
Lighthouse ♁
Mountain ▲

O A H U

★ **Honolulu**

Dole Pineapple Plantation **2**
Hawaii's Plantation Village **6**
Kaena Point State Park **1**
Kukaniloko Birthing Stones **3**
Tropic Lighting Museum **4**
U.S. Army Schofield Barracks **4**
Waikele Premium Outlets **5**

from 9am to 6pm; admission is $4.50 for adults and $2.50 for children 4 to 12. "Kam" Highway, as everyone calls it, will be your road for most of the rest of the trip to Haleiwa.

CENTRAL OAHU ATTRACTIONS

On the central plains of Oahu, tract homes and malls with factory-outlet stores are now spreading across abandoned sugarcane fields, where sandalwood forests used to stand at the foot of Mount Kaala, the mighty summit of Oahu. Hawaiian chiefs once sent commoners into thick sandalwood forests to cut down trees, which were then sold to China traders for small fortunes. The scantily clad natives caught cold in the cool uplands, and many died.

On these plains in 1908, the U.S. Army pitched a tent that later become a fort. And on December 7, 1941, Japanese pilots came screaming through Kolekole Pass to shoot up the Art-Deco barracks at Schofield, sending soldiers running for cover, and then flew on to sink ships at Pearl Harbor.

U.S. Army Schofield Barracks   James Jones, author of *From Here to Eternity*, called Schofield Barracks "the most beautiful army post the U.S. has or ever had." The *Honolulu Star Bulletin* called it a country club. More than a million soldiers called Schofield Barracks home. With its broad, palm-lined boulevards and Art-Deco buildings, this old army cavalry post is still the largest operated by the U.S. Army outside the continental United States. And it's still one of the best places to be a soldier.

The history of Schofield Barracks and the 25th Infantry Division is told in the small **Tropic Lightning Museum,** Schofield Barracks, Bldg. 361, Waianae Ave. (📞 **808/655-0438;** troplight1@juno.com). Displays range from a 1917 bunker exhibit to a replica of Vietnam's infamous Cu Chi tunnels. Open Tuesday through Saturday from 10am to 4pm; free admission.

TheBus: 52 to Wahiawa; transfer at California Ave. to no. 72, Schofield Barracks Shuttle.

Kukaniloko Birthing Stones   This is the most sacred site in central Oahu. Two rows of 18 lava rocks once flanked a central birthing stone, where women of ancient Hawaii gave birth to potential *alii* (royalty). The rocks, according to Hawaiian belief, held the power to ease the labor pains of childbirth. Birth rituals involved 48 chiefs who pounded drums to announce the arrival of newborns likely to become chiefs. Children born here were taken to the now-destroyed Holonopahu Heiau in the pineapple field, where chiefs ceremoniously cut the umbilical cord.

Used by Oahu's *alii* for generations of births, the *pohaku* (rocks), many in bowl-like shapes, now lie strewn in a grove of trees that stands in a pineapple field here. Some think the site also may have served ancient astronomers—like a Hawaiian Stonehenge. Petroglyphs of human forms and circles appear on some of the stones. The Wahiawa Hawaiian Civic Club recently erected two interpretive signs, one explaining why this was chosen as a birth site and the other telling how the stones were used to aid in the birth process.

Off Kamehameha Hwy. between Wahiawa and Haleiwa, on Plantation Rd. opposite the road to Whitmore Village.

SURF CITY: HALEIWA

Only 28 miles from Waikiki is Haleiwa, the funky ex-sugar-plantation town that's the world capital of big-wave surfing. This beach town really comes alive in winter, when waves rise up, light rain falls, and temperatures dip into the 70s; then, it seems, every surfer in the world is here to see and be seen.

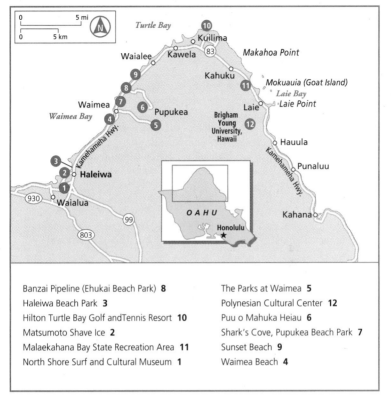

Banzai Pipeline (Ehukai Beach Park) **8**

Haleiwa Beach Park **3**

Hilton Turtle Bay Golf andTennis Resort **10**

Matsumoto Shave Ice **2**

Malaekahana Bay State Recreation Area **11**

North Shore Surf and Cultural Museum **1**

The Parks at Waimea **5**

Polynesian Cultural Center **12**

Puu o Mahuka Heiau **6**

Shark's Cove, Pupukea Beach Park **7**

Sunset Beach **9**

Waimea Beach **4**

Officially designated a historic cultural and scenic district, Haleiwa thrives in a time warp recalling the turn of the 20th century, when it was founded by sugar baron Benjamin Dillingham, who built a 30-mile railroad to link his Honolulu and North Shore plantations in 1899. He opened a Victorian hotel overlooking Kaiaka Bay and named it Haleiwa, or "house of the Iwa," the tropical seabird often seen here. The hotel and railroad are gone, but Haleiwa, which was rediscovered in the late 1960s by hippies, resonates with rare rustic charm. Tofu, not taro, is a staple in the local diet. Arts and crafts, boutiques, and burger stands line both sides of the town. There's also a busy fishing harbor full of charter boats and captains who hunt the Kauai Channel daily for tuna, mahimahi, and marlin. The bartenders at **Jameson's** ⍟, 62–540 Kamehameha Hwy. (© **808/ 637-6272**), make the best mai tais on the North Shore; they use the original recipe by Trader Vic Bergeron.

Once in Haleiwa, the hot and thirsty traveler should report directly to the nearest shave-ice stand, usually **Matsumoto Shave Ice** ⍟⍟, 66–087 Kamehameha Hwy. (© **808/637-4827**). For 40 years, this small, humble shop operated by the Matsumoto family has served a popular rendition of the Hawaii-style snow cone flavored with tropical tastes. The cooling treat is also available at neighboring stores, some of which still shave the ice with a hand-crank device.

Just down the road are some of the fabled shrines of surfing—**Waimea Beach, Banzai Pipeline, Sunset Beach**—where some of the world's largest waves, reaching 20 feet and more, rise up between November and January. They draw professional surfers as well as reckless daredevils and hordes of onlookers, who jump in their cars and head north when word goes out that "surf's up." Don't forget your binoculars. (For more details on North Shore beaches, see chapter 6.)

North Shore Surf and Cultural Museum   Even if you've never set foot on a surfboard, you'll want to visit Oahu's only surf museum to learn the history of this Hawaiian sport of kings. This collection of memorabilia traces the evolution of surfboards from an enormous, weathered redwood board made in the 1930s for Turkey Love, one of Waikiki's legendary beach boys, to the modern-day equivalent—a light, sleek, racy, foam-and-fiberglass board made for big-wave surfer Mark Foo, who drowned while surfing in California in 1994. Other items include classic 1950s surf-meet posters, 1960s surf-music album covers, old beach movie posters with Frankie Avalon and Sandra Dee, the early black-and-white photos by legendary surf photographer LeRoy Grannis, and trophies won by surfing's greatest. Curator Steve Gould is working on a new exhibit of surfing in the ancient Hawaiian culture, complete with Hawaiian artifacts.

North Shore Marketplace, 66–250 Kamehameha Hwy. (behind Kentucky Fried Chicken), Haleiwa. ℂ 808/637-8888. Free admission. Tues–Sun noon–5pm.

MORE NORTH SHORE ATTRACTIONS

The Parks at Waimea 🛪 *Kids*   If you have only a day to spend on Oahu and want to see an ancient hula, sniff tropical flowers, go kayaking along the shore or hiking to archaeological sites and a waterfall, and play the games of ancient Hawaii (such as spear-throwing and lawn bowling), there's only one place to be: Waimea Falls Park. This is the perfect family place. You can also explore remnants of the old Hawaiian settlements in a scenic 1,800-acre river valley that's full of tropical blooms; watch authentic demonstrations of the ancient hula by the park's own *halau* (school); and see cliff divers swan-dive into a pool fed by a 45-foot waterfall. Other activities include riding a mountain bike, paddling a kayak, and walking along the Elehaha River into the jungle.

59–864 Kamehameha Hwy. ℂ 808/638-8511. www.atlantisadventures.com Admission $24 adults, $12 children 4–12. Various packages available, including camping, kayaking, horseback riding, and more. Daily 10am–5:30pm. Parking $3. TheBus: 52. Shuttle service from some Waikiki hotels $5 round-trip.

Puu o Mahuka Heiau 🛪 *Moments*   Go around sundown to feel the *mana* (sacred spirit) of this Hawaiian place. The largest sacrificial temple on Oahu, it's associated with the great Kaopulupulu, who sought peace between Oahu and Kauai. This prescient *kahuna* predicted that the island would be overrun by strangers from a distant land. In 1794, three of Capt. George Vancouver's men of the *Daedalus* were sacrificed here. In 1819, the year before New England missionaries landed in Hawaii, King Kamehameha II ordered all idols here to be destroyed.

A national historic landmark, this 18th-century heiau, known as the "hill of escape," sits on a 5-acre, 300-foot bluff overlooking Waimea Bay and 25 miles of Oahu's wave-lashed North Coast—all the way to Kaena Point, where the Waianae Range ends in a spirit leap to the other world. The heiau appears as a huge rectangle of rocks twice as big as a football field (170 ft. by 575 ft.), with an altar often covered by the flower and fruit offerings left by native Hawaiians.

1 mile past Waimea Bay. Take Pupukea Rd. mauka (inland) off Kamehameha Hwy. at Foodland, and drive 0.7 miles up a switchback road. TheBus: 52, then walk up Pupukea Rd.

Shopping

by Jocelyn Fujii

I t's a no-brainer: Honolulu is a shopping destination. Shopping competes with golf, surfing, and sightseeing as a bona fide Honolulu attraction. And why not? The proliferation of top-notch made-in-Hawaii products, the vitality of the local crafts scene, and the unquenchable thirst for mementos of the islands lend respectability to shopping here. More than 1,000 stores occupy the 11 major shopping centers on this island.

From T-shirts to Versace, posh European to down-home local, avant-garde to unspeakably tacky, Oahu's offerings are wide-ranging indeed. But you must sometimes wade through oceans of schlock to arrive at the mother lode. Nestled amid the Louis Vuitton, Chanel, and Tiffany boutiques on Waikiki's Kalakaua Avenue are plenty of tacky booths hawking airbrushed T-shirts, gold by the inch, and tasteless aloha shirts.

The chapter that follows is not about finding cheap souvenirs or tony items from designer fashion chains; you can find these on your own. Rather, we offer a guide to finding those special treasures that lie somewhere in between.

1 In & Around Honolulu & Waikiki

ALOHA WEAR

One of Hawaii's lasting afflictions is the penchant visitors have for wearing loud, matching aloha shirts and muumuus. We applaud such visitors' good intentions (to act local), but no local resident would be caught dead in such a get-up. Muumuus and aloha shirts are wonderful, but the real thing is what island folks wear on Aloha Friday (every Fri), to the Brothers Cazimero Lei Day Concert (every May 1), or to work (where allowed). It's what they wear at home and to special parties where the invitation reads "Aloha Attire."

Aside from the vintage Hawaiian wear (1930s–1950s) found in collectibles shops and at swap meets, our favorite contemporary aloha-wear designer is Hawaii's **Tori Richards. Tommy Bahama,** which never calls its shirts "aloha shirts" but claims instead a Caribbean influence, is another shirt icon, and so is the up-and-coming **Tiki** brand, quirky and distinctive, with fabulous fabric prints and retro elements that hark back to 1950s bowling shirts and Jimmy Dean charisma. (Bahama and Tiki are not Hawaii companies, but have jumped on the bandwagon and are riding the aloha shirt wave.)

Unless you score at a garage sale or swap meet, the best aloha shirts are pricey these days, going for $60 to $90 (and some, especially in places like Kapaa, Kauai, for $110!). For the vintage look, **Avanti** has a corner on the market with its line of silk shirts and dresses in authentic 1930s to 1950s patterns. The $60-and-up shirts boast all the qualities of a vintage silky but without the high price or the web-thin fragility of an authentic antique. Women's dresses, tea timers from the 1940s, pant sets, and many other styles are the epitome of island chic, comfort and nostalgic good looks. The line is distributed in better boutiques and department stores throughout Hawaii. In Waikiki, the major retail outlet is **Avanti Fashion,** at 2229 Kuhio Ave. (© **808/924-1668**); Waikiki Shopping Plaza, 2250 Kalakaua Ave. (© **808/922-2828**); 307 Lewers St. (© **808/ 926-6886**); and 2160 Kalakaua Ave. (© **808/924-3232**).

The surf lines have hopped on the aloha shirtmobile, too, with some viable styles put out by **Quicksilver's Silver Edition** line. Also popular is **Kahala Sportswear,** a well-known local company established in 1936. Kahala has faithfully reproduced, with astounding success, the linoleum-block prints of noted Maui artist Avi Kiriaty and the designs of other contemporary artists, including the popular Yvonne Cheng and surfer John Severson. Kahala is sold in department stores (from Liberty House to Nordstrom), surf shops, and stylish boutiques throughout Hawaii and the mainland.

For the most culturally correct aloha wear, and for a graphic identity that is rare in the aloha shirt realm, check out the shirts, dresses, and pareus of **Sig Zane Designs,** available at his Hilo (Big Island) and Wailuku (Maui) stores. Zane, an accomplished hula dancer married to one of Hawaii's most revered hula masters, has an unmistakable visual style and a profound knowledge of Hawaiian culture that brings depth and meaning to his boldly styled renditions. Each Sig Zane aloha shirt, in pure cotton, tells a story. Connoisseurs also buy his fabrics by the yard for cushions, curtains, and interior accents.

Another name to watch for is **Tutuvi,** whose T-shirts, dresses, and pareus are distinctive for their brilliant color combinations and witty juxtaposition of design motifs. Tutuvi can be found in various shops throughout Hawaii (such as **Native Books & Beautiful Things;** see below), or by appointment at **Tutuvi,** 2850 S. King St. (© **808/947-5950**).

Reyn Spooner is another source of attractive aloha shirts and muumuus in traditional and contemporary styles, with stores in Ala Moana Center, Kahala Mall, and the Sheraton Waikiki. Reyn years ago popularized the reverse-print aloha shirt—the uniform of downtown boardrooms—and has also jumped aboard the vintage-look bandwagon with old-Hawaii cotton and rayon prints, some of them in attractive two-color pareu patterns.

Well-known muumuu labels in Hawaii include **Mamo Howell,** with a boutique in Ward Warehouse, and **Princess Kaiulani** and **Bete** for the dressier muus, sold along with many other lines at Liberty House and other department stores.

See also "Fashion," later in this chapter.

Avanti Fashion   This is the leading retro aloha shirt label, turning out stunning silk shirts and dresses in authentic 1930s to 1950s fabric patterns. The shirts, though made of thin silk, are hip and nostalgic, without the web-thin fragility of authentic antique shirts. The line is distributed in better boutiques and department stores throughout Hawaii, but the best selections are at its Waikiki retail stores. 2229 Kuhio Ave. (© **808/924-1668**); 2250 Kalakaua Ave., Waikiki Shopping Plaza (© **808/922-2828**); 307 Lewers St. (© **808/926-6886**); and 2160 Kalakaua Ave. (© **808/924-3232**).

Bailey's Antiques & Aloha Shirts *Finds*   A large selection (thousands) of vintage, secondhand, and nearly new aloha shirts and other collectibles fills this eclectic emporium. It looks as though the owners regularly scour Hollywood movie costume departments for odd ballgowns, feather boas, fur stoles, leather jackets, 1930s dresses, and scads of other garments from periods past. Bailey's has one of the largest vintage aloha-shirt collections in Honolulu, with prices ranging from inexpensive to sky-high. Old Levi's jeans, mandarin jackets, vintage vases, household items, shawls, purses, and an eye-popping assortment of bark-cloth fabrics (the real thing, not repros) are among the mementos in this monumental collection. 517 Kapahulu Ave. © 808/734-7628.

Hilo Hattie *Value*   Hilo Hattie, the largest manufacturer of Hawaiian fashions, attracts more than a million visitors to its ever-expanding empire throughout the state. Its Ala Moana store is a leap in image, quality, range of merchandise, and overall shopping options. You can find great gifts here, from coconut utensils to food products and aloha shirts in all price ranges and motifs. There are some inexpensive silk aloha shirts as well as brand-name aloha shirts like Tommy Bahama and the store's own Hilo Hattie label. 1450 Ala Moana Blvd., Ala Moana Center. © 808/973-3266. Also at 700 N. Nimitz Hwy., © 808/544-3500.

J.C. Penney   If you're a fashion snob, you're in for a surprise when you see the J.C. Penney aloha shirt selection. It's wide-ranging and commendable. Although not known for its taste, this chain department store has put a high priority on aloha shirts, with a selection that includes all the name brands, and more. Racks and racks of aloha shirts fill the floor with vintage looks, Hawaiian heritage designs, and the usual surf-oriented motifs. You'll find great Tori Richard and Kahala selections here. 1450 Ala Moana Blvd., Ala Moana Center. © 808/946-8068; and other locations throughout Hawaii.

Kamehameha Garment Co.   This Ward Centre shop carries dresses and aloha shirts by the time-honored Kamehameha label. Aloha shirts and dresses, many of them with a vintage look, fill the cordial room with a sense of nostalgia. Wide variety, good styling, and striking fabric patterns make this a must for those in search of the perfect aloha shirt. In Ward Centre, 1200 Ala Moana Blvd. © 808/597-1503.

Liberty House   If it's aloha wear, Liberty House has it. The extensive aloha shirt and muumuu departments of Liberty House stores feature every label you can conjure, with a selection that changes with the times, and in all price ranges. 1450 Ala Moana Blvd., Ala Moana Center. © 808/941-2345.

Reyn's   Reyn's used to be a prosaic line but has stepped up its selection of women's and men's aloha wear with contemporary fabric prints and stylings, appealing to a hipper clientele. 1450 Ala Moana Blvd., Ala Moana Center. © 808/949-5929. Also at 4211 Waialae Ave., Kahala Mall. © 808/737-8313.

ANTIQUES & COLLECTIBLES

For the best in collectible aloha wear, see "Aloha Wear," above (especially the listing for **Bailey's Antiques & Aloha Shirts**).

Aloha Antiques and Collectables   This is arguably the largest antiques mall in Hawaii, with shops strung together in a mind-boggling labyrinth of treasures waiting to be found. This is not for the weak-kneed: the chockablock, multilevel stores can put you in sensory overload. But if the shopping gods are good to you, you may find rare Japanese plates or a priceless Lalique among the tchotchkes that fill every square inch of this dizzying mini-emporium, where the items literally spill out onto the sidewalk. You'll have to look hard, but it's worth it—the prices are good and the rewards substantial. Jewelry, vintage aloha shirts, vases, silver, Asian lacquer, Hawaiian collectibles, and countless eclectic items make up this collection of junk, treasures, and nostalgia. 930 Maunakea St. (at the harbor end of the street). © 808/536-6187.

Oahu's Vibrant Gallery Scene

Like restaurants, galleries come and go in Chinatown, where efforts to revitalize the area have moved in fits and spurts. Two exceptions are the **Ramsay Galleries,** Tan Sing Building, 1128 Smith St. (℗ **808/ 537-2787**), and the **Pegge Hopper Gallery,** 1164 Nuuanu Ave. (℗ **808/ 524-1160**). Both are housed in historic Chinatown buildings that have been renovated and transformed into stunning showplaces. Nationally known quill-and-ink artist Ramsay, who has drawn everything from the Plaza in New York to most of Honolulu's historic buildings, maintains a vital monthly show schedule featuring her own work, as well as shows of her fellow Hawaii artists. The finest names in contemporary crafts and art appear here, ranging in media from photography and sculpture to glass, clay, and, yes, computer art. A consummate preservationist, Ramsay has added a courtyard garden with an oval pond and exotic varieties of bamboo.

Pegge Hopper, one of Hawaii's most popular artists, displays her widely collected paintings (usually of Hawaiian women with broad, strong features) in her attractive gallery, which has become quite the gathering place for exhibits ranging from Tibetan sand-painting by saffron-robed monks to the most avant-garde printmaking in the islands.

Newcomer **Bibelot,** 1130 Koko Head Ave., Suite 2, in Kaimuki (℗ **808/738-0368**), is small and smart, with an impressive selection of works from new and emerging artists, as well as those well established. More than 30 artists, almost all from Hawaii, are represented, including Charles Higa, Margaret Ezekiel, Doug Britt, Ron Lee, and Kenny Kicklighter. Jewelry, ceramics, glass, and Japanese tansu and antiques are among the treasures here.

The **Gallery at Ward Centre** in Ward Centre, 1200 Ala Moana Blvd. (℗ **808/597-8034**), a cooperative gallery of Oahu artists, features fine works in all media, including paper, clay, scratchboard, oils, watercolors, collages, woodblocks, lithographs, glass, jewelry, and more.

Hawaii's most unusual gallery, listed on the Hawaii Register of Historic Places, is perched on the slopes of Punchbowl. The **Tennent Art Foundation Gallery,** 203 Prospect St. (℗ **808/531-1987**), is devoted to the oeuvre of artist Madge Tennent, whose paintings hang in the National Museum of Women alongside the work of Georgia O'Keeffe. Tennent's much-imitated style depicts Polynesians from the 1920s to the 1940s in bold, modernist strokes that left an indelible influence on Hawaii art. Open limited hours and by appointment, so call before you go.

Art lovers now have a wonderful new resource: a 34-page brochure offering an overview of the music, theater, history, music, and visual arts of Oahu. The free brochure, which includes a map, phone numbers, websites, and more information, is put out by Arts with Aloha, representing 11 major Honolulu cultural organizations. Send a legal-sized, self-addressed, stamped (55¢) envelope to **Arts with Aloha,** c/o Honolulu Academy of Arts, 900 S. Beretania St., Honolulu, HI 96814, or call the 24-hour hot line at ℗ **808/532-8713.**

Anchor House Antiques   This highly eclectic collection of Hawaiian, Asian, and European pieces sprawls over thousands of square feet. You'll find wooden calabashes, camphor chests, paintings, Hawaiian artifacts, and trinkets, priced from $10 to $2,000. 471 Kapahulu Ave. ℂ 808/732-3884.

Antique Alley   This narrow shop is chockablock with the passionate collections of several vendors under one roof. With its expanded collection of old Hawaiian artifacts and surfing and hula nostalgia, it's a sure winner for eclectic tastes. The showcases include estate jewelry, antique silver, Hawaiian bottles, collectible toys, pottery, cameras, Depression glass, linens, plantation photos and ephemera, and a wide selection of nostalgic items from Hawaii and across America. At the rear is a small, attractive selection of Soiree clothing, made by Julie Lauster of antique kimonos and obis. 1347 Kapiolani Blvd. ℂ 808/941-8551.

Antique House   Small but tasteful, the low-profile Antique House is hidden below the lobby level of the illustrious Royal Hawaiian Hotel. Come here for small items, such as Asian antiques, Chinese and Japanese porcelains, and a stunning selection of snuff bottles, bronzes, vases, and china. In the Royal Hawaiian Hotel, 2259 Kalakaua Ave. ℂ 808/923-5101.

Garakuta-Do   This huge warehouse/store at the gateway to Waikiki has a sublime collection of Japanese antiques. In its expanded space on the Ala Wai Canal, across from the Convention Center, it offers ample free parking. It's worth finding for its late-Edo period (1800s–early 1900s) antiques, collected and sold by cheerful owner Wataru Harada. The selection of gorgeous tansus, mingei folk art, Japanese screens, scrolls, Imari plates, bronze sculptures, kimonos, obis, modern woodblock prints, and stone objects makes shopping here a treasure hunt. Noritake lovers, listen up: The shop now carries a sizable collection of old Noritake china from 1891 to the 1940s. Yum. 1833 Kalakaua Ave., Suite 100. ℂ 808/955-2099.

Kilohana Square   If we had to recommend only one destination for antiques, we'd pick this tiny square in Kapahulu. Kilohana's antiques shops cover a rich range of Asian art, Japanese and European objects, and high-quality collectibles. Many have loyal clients across the country. Our favorites include **T. Fujii Japanese Antiques** (ℂ 808/732-7860), a long-standing icon in Hawaii's antiques world and an impeccable source for ukiyo-e prints, scrolls, obis, Imari porcelain, tansus, tea-ceremony bowls, and screens, as well as contemporary ceramics from Mashiko and Kasama, with prices from $25 to five digits. The owners close their shop on their buying trips to Japan, so call ahead to be sure the store is open. Also in Kilohana Square, **Miko Oriental Art Gallery** (ℂ 808/735-4503) recently moved to a bigger space within Kilohana Square and houses an even larger repository of Chinese, Japanese, Korean, and Southeast Asian ceramics, bronzes, and furniture, ranging in price from $50 to $22,000. **Silk Winds** (ℂ 808/735-6599), with a wonderful selection of Asian antiques and beads, continues to draw loyal collectors. Each shop has its own hours; call for details. 1016 Kapahulu Ave.

Robyn Buntin   Robyn Buntin's 5,000-square-foot gallery and picture-framing department, called Robyn Buntin's Picture Framing and Oceania Gallery, and his gallery for Hawaiian art, at 820 S. Beretania St., are among the features of this burgeoning art resource, located three doors from the Honolulu Academy of Art. This is Honolulu's stellar source of museum-quality Asian art and contemporary and traditional Hawaiian art. The gracious and authoritative Robyn Buntin is an expert in netsuke and a highly esteemed resource in Asian art. As much a gallery as an antiques store, Robyn Buntin radiates a tasteful serenity. The offerings include jade; scholar's table items; Buddhist sculpture; Japanese prints; contemporary Chinese, Japanese, and Korean pictorial (graphic) art; and a large and magnificent collection of Hawaiiana. Some pieces are 5,000 years old, while many others are hot off the presses from Tokyo, Seoul, and Beijing. The brilliant selection of netsuke and Japanese carvings is complemented with Hawaiian works by Isami Doi, Avi Kiriaty, Guy Buffet, Mark Kadota, and others. Few people know that John Kelly's legacy includes Asian works; they're here, along with rare etchings and prints that move swiftly to waiting collectors. 848 S. Beretania St. © **808/523-5913**.

BOOKSTORES
In addition to the local stores below, Honolulu is home to the major chains. **Barnes & Noble** is located at Kahala Mall, 4211 Waialae Ave. (© **808/737-3323**). **Borders** is located at Ward Centre, 1200 Ala Moana Blvd. (© **808/591-8995**) and at Waikele Center, 94-821 Lumiaina St. (© **808/676-6699**). **Waldenbooks** has six branches on Oahu, including Kahala Mall, 4211 Waialae Ave. (© **808/737-9550**); Ala Moana Center, 1450 Ala Moana Blvd. (© **808/942-1605**); and Waikiki Shopping Plaza, 2250 Kalakaua Ave. (© **808/922-4154**).

Pacific Book House Denis Perron, connoisseur of rare books, continues to build and expand his rare and out-of-print book inventory. He has also expanded into paintings, antiques, and estate jewelry, even offering appraisals of rare books and paintings and handling restorations others are afraid to touch. When you tire of book browsing, look into the selection of antique silver and china. Literati still come here for finds in Hawaiiana, rare prints, collectible books, and other out-of-print treasures. 1249 S. Beretania St. © 808/591-1599.

Rainbow Books and Records A little weird but totally lovable, especially among students and eccentrics (and insatiable readers), Rainbow Books is notable for its selection of popular fiction, records, and Hawaii-themed books, second-hand and reduced. Because it's located in the university area, it's always bulging with textbooks, Hawaiiana, and popular music. It's about the size of a large closet, but you'll be surprised by what you'll find. 1010 University Ave. © 808/ 955-7994.

CONSIGNMENT SHOPS
comme ci comme ca Great finds abound here, especially if your timing is good. Brand-new Prada bags, old Hermès jackets and dresses in pristine condition, an occasional Ferragamo purse, Armani suits, and vintage fur-collared sweaters straight out of 1940s Hollywood are some of the pleasures that await you. Timing is paramount here; finds—such as a made-in-Italy, brand-new, mostly cashmere Donna Karan for Men jacket—disappear to the early birds, but you can always count on great finds in designer clothes, bags, shoes, jewelry, and stylish vintage treasures. 3464 Waialae Ave., Kaimuki. © 808/734-8869.

Consignment Closet *Value* Manoa's neighborhood consignment store is cheaper (much) and funkier than most, with a promising selection of shoes, dresses, and separates. Many treasures lurk among the racks and stacks of merchandise. Recently moved from Manoa to its new Kapahulu location, it's still got the magic touch with its racks and racks of secondhand goodies—silk blouses, blazers, separates, sweaters. An entire wall is lined with dresses. Call before you go for directions, though, because the location is tricky. The good news: there's parking aplenty. 1113-B Kapahulu Ave. © 808/737-2002.

The Ultimate You   At this resale boutique, the clothes are relatively current (fashion of the last 2 years) and not always cheap, but they're always 50% to 90% off retail. This means designer suits and dresses, often new or barely worn, from such names as Escada, Chanel, Prada, Gianfranco Ferre, Donna Karan, Yves St. Laurent, Armani, Ralph Lauren, Laura Ashley, and Ann Taylor. You'll also find aisles of separates, cashmere sweaters, dresses, shoes, scarves, and purses. When a red star appears on the tag, it means another big chunk off the bill. In its new Ward Centre location, it's spiffier than ever. In the Ward Centre, 1200 Ala Moana Blvd. ✆ 808/591-8388.

EDIBLES

In addition to the stores listed below, we also recommend **Executive Chef,** in the Ward Warehouse, and **Islands' Best,** in the Ala Moana Center. Both shops contain wide-ranging selections that include Hawaii's specialty food items.

Asian Grocery   Asian Grocery supplies many of Honolulu's Thai, Vietnamese, Chinese, Indonesian, and Filipino restaurants with authentic spices, rice, noodles, produce, sauces, herbs, and adventurous ingredients. Browse among the kaffir lime leaves, tamarind and fish pastes, red and green chilies, curries, chutneys, lotus leaves, gingko nuts, jasmine and basmati rice, and shelf upon shelf of medium to hot chili sauces. The chefs for most of Honolulu's Asian and ethnic restaurants shop here. 1319 S. Beretania St. ✆ 808/593-8440.

Daiei   Stands offering takeout sushi, Korean *kal bi*, pizza, Chinese food, flowers, Mrs. Fields cookies, and other items for self and home surround this huge emporium. Inside, you'll find household products, a pharmacy, and inexpensive clothing, but it's the prepared foods and produce that excel. The fresh-seafood section is one of Honolulu's best, not far from where regulars line up for the bento lunches and individually wrapped sushi. When Kau navel oranges, macadamia nuts, Kona coffee, Chinese taro, and other Hawaii products are on sale, savvy locals arrive in droves to take advantage of the high quality and good value. 801 Kaheka St. ✆ 808/973-4800.

Fujioka's Wine Merchants   This Kapahulu shop has a mouthwatering selection of wines, single malt Scotches, excellent Italian wines, and affordable, farm-raised caviar—food and libations for all occasions. Everyday wines, special-occasion wines, and esoteric wines are priced lower here than at most places, especially the crates and rows of excellent, affordable finds from Italy. Scotch lovers will find a selection of rare single malts in all price ranges—like the service, friendly all the way. The wine-tasting bar at the rear of the store is a new attraction. In the Market City Shopping Center, 2919 Kapiolani Blvd., lower level. ✆ 808/739-9463.

Honolulu Chocolate Co.   Life's greatest pleasures are dispensed here with abandon: expensive gourmet chocolates made in Honolulu, Italian and Hawaiian biscotti, boulder-size turtles (caramel and pecans covered with chocolate), truffles, chocolate-covered coffee beans, jumbo apricots in white and dark chocolate. There are also tinned biscuits, European candies, and sweets in a million disguises. *Hint:* You pay dearly for them, but the dark-chocolate-dipped macadamia-nut clusters are beyond compare. In the Ward Centre, 1200 Ala Moana Blvd. ✆ 808/591-2997.

It's Chili in Hawaii   This is *the* oasis for chileheads, a house of heat with endorphins aplenty and good food to accompany the hot sauces from around the world, including a fabulous selection of made-in-Hawaii products. Scoville units (measurements of heat in food) are the topic of the day in this shop, lined with thousands of bottles of hot sauces, salsas, and other chile-based food products. Not everything is scorching, however; some products, like Dave's Soyabi and the limu-habañero sauce called Makai, are everyday flavor enhancers that can be used on rice, salads, meats, and pasta. If you're eating in, the fresh frozen tamales, in several varieties (including meatless), are now in regular supply. Every Saturday, free samples of green-chile stew are dished up to go with the generous hot-sauce tastings. 2080 S. King St., Suite 105. ℭ **808/945-7070.**

Mauna Kea Marketplace Food Court   Hungry patrons line up in front of these no-nonsense food booths that sell everything from pizza and plate lunches to quick, authentic, and inexpensive Vietnamese, Thai, Italian, Chinese, Japanese, and Filipino dishes. The best seafood fried rice comes from the woks of **Malee Thai/Vietnamese Cuisine,** at the mauka (inland) end of the marketplace—perfectly flavored with morsels of fish, squid, and shrimp. The booth next to it, **Masa's,** serves bento and Japanese dishes, such as excellent miso eggplant, that are famous. A few stalls makai, at **Pho Lau,** haupia (coconut pudding), tapioca and taro are served in individual baskets made of pandanus—it's the best dessert around. Walk the few steps down to the produce stalls (pungent odors, fish heads, and chicken feet on counters—not for the squeamish) and join in the spirit of discovery. Vendors sell everything from fresh ahi and whole snapper to yams and taro, seaweed, and fresh fruits and vegetables of every shape and size, including durian in season and jackfruit as big as a steer's head. 1120 Maunakea St., Chinatown. ℭ **808/ 524-3409.**

Padovani's Chocolate Boutique   Chef extraordinaire Philippe Padovani has opened his own elegant chocolate boutique, a full expression of his way with sweets. Refrigerated display cases showcase the handmade truffles, macadamia-nut chocolates, chocolate-covered candied orange peel, and silky lilikoi in chocolate—ambrosia to the last lick. Padovani uses top-of-the-line chocolate, such as Valrhona from France. In their elegant green-and-gold packaging, the chocolates make excellent, lavish gifts to go. In the Royal Hawaiian Shopping Center, McInerny Galleria, 2301 Kalakaua Ave. ℭ **808/971-4207.**

Paradise Produce Co.   Neat rows of mangoes, top-quality papayas, and reasonably priced and very fresh produce make this a paradise for food lovers. When mangoes are in season, you'll find Yee's Orchard Haydens set apart from the less desirable Mexican mangoes and, if you're lucky, a stash of ambrosial Piries that will sell out quickly. Chinese taro, litchis and asparagus in season, local eggplant, and dozens of fruits and vegetables are offered up fresh, neat, and colorful. 83 N. King St., Chinatown. ℭ **808/533-2125.**

People's Open Markets   Truck farmers from all over the island bring their produce to Oahu's neighborhoods in regularly scheduled, city-sponsored open markets, held Monday through Saturday at various locations. Among the tables of ong choy, choi sum, Okinawan spinach, opal basil, papayas, mangoes, seaweed, and fresh fish, you'll find homemade banana bread, Chinese pomelo (like large grapefruit), fresh fiddleheads (fern shoots) when available, and colorful, bountiful harvests from land and sea. Various sites around town. ℭ **808/527-5167.** Call to find the open market nearest you.

R. Field Wine Co.   Foodland has won countless new converts since Richard Field—oenophile, gourmet, and cigar aficionado—moved his shop from Ward Centre to this location in lower Makiki. The thriving gourmet store offers gemlike vine-ripened tomatoes and juicy clementines, sparkling bags of Nalo gourmet greens, designer cheeses, caviar, Langenstein Farms coffee and macadamia nuts, vegetarian and salmon mousses, truffle/cognac patés, designer vinegars, and all manner of epicurean delights, including wines and single malt Scotches. A huge hit: the warm, just-baked breads (rosemary–olive oil, whole wheat, organic wheat, and others) baked on the premises with dough flown in from Los Angeles's famous La Brea Bakery. Field has a talent for finding great gourmet products from Hawaii and around the world, including Hawaii. In Foodland Super Market, 1460 S. Beretania St. ✆ 808/596-9463.

Shirokiya   Shirokiya's upstairs food department is well-known throughout Honolulu as *the* marketplace for Japanese treats and a place to discover the best new made-in-Hawaii products, from exotic fern-shoot noodles from the Big Island to the latest in cookies and macadamia nuts. Food samples hot off the grill or out of the oven are offered from the counters: Fish, mochi, pickled vegetables, and black beans fill the air with briny, smoky scents. A separate take-out food department sells sushi, udon and noodle soups, and many varieties of boxed bento lunches. Tables are available, or you can order the food to go. In the surrounding retail food department, exotic assortments, from deluxe dried shiitake mushrooms to Japanese teas and rice crackers, call out for your attention. In the Ala Moana Center, 1450 Ala Moana Blvd. ✆ **808/973-9111.**

Strawberry Connection of Hawaii   If you love food, this is your place. It's an ever-growing showcase of Hawaii's gourmet food products and many more prepared foods to go. Strawberry Connection has always been the saving grace of busy hostesses and gourmet-minded working folks who love foie gras and fancy sauces but are too busy to make them. Jackets are loaned to the unprepared for entry into the large walk-in "chill box" containing exquisite asparagus, mushrooms, strawberries, greens, and designer produce from across the state. Non-perishable food items, from olive oils to condiments to upscale curds, chocolates, pasta, spices and teas, line the shelves and aisles. The staff will also pack and ship produce to the mainland. In the Dole Cannery, 735 Iwilei Rd. ✆ **808/ 521-9777.**

Sushi Company   It's not easy to find premium-grade hamachi, ahi, ikura (salmon roe), ika (cuttlefish), and other top-grade fresh ingredients in anything but a bona-fide sit-down sushi bar. But here it is, a small, sparkling gem of a sushi maker that sells fast-food sushi of non-fast-food quality, at great prices. Order ahead or wait while they make it. The combinations range from mini sets (27 pieces) to large variety sets (43–51 pieces), ideal for picnics and potlucks. Individual hand rolls range from 99¢ to $1.55, and the nigiri comes in orders of two and more. An expanded menu now offers excellent miso soup, salmon skin sushi to go, scallop, sea urchin, and spicy tuna. A newcomer to the neighborhood and already a mainstay, Sushi Company has one four-person table; most of the business is take-out. Hint: The miso soup is excellent. 1111 McCully St., McCully. ✆ **808/947-5411.**

BAKERIES

If you're looking for a bakery, **Saint-Germain,** in Shirokiya at Ala Moana Shopping Center (✆ **808/955-1711**), and near Times Supermarket, 1296 S. Beretania St. (✆ **808/593-8711**), sells baguettes, country loaves, and oddball delicacies such as mini mushroom-and-spinach pizzas. The reigning queen of bakers, though, is **Cafe Laufer,** 3565 Waialae Ave. (✆ **808/735-7717**); see p. 132. Nearby, old-timers still line up at **Sconees,** 1117 12th Ave. (✆ **808/ 734-4024**), formerly Bea's

Pies. Sconees has fantastic scones, pumpkin-custard pies, and danishes. For warm bread, nothing can beat **Foodland,** 1460 S. Beretania St. (© **808/949-4365** for the bakery department), where R. Field is located. The Foodland bakery flies in dough from Los Angeles's famous La Brea bakery and bakes it fresh at this location, so you can pick up fresh-from-the-oven organic wheat, rosemary-olive oil, roasted garlic, potato-dill, and other spectacular breads.

Mary Catherine's Bakery   This topnotch European bakery sells everything from lavishly tiered wedding cakes to killer carrot cakes and chocolate decadence cake that is moist, rich, and extravagant. Cookies, cakes, scones, pastries, tortes, and all manner of baked sweets line the counters. Long a favorite of locals. 2820 S. King St., across from the Hawaiian Humane Society. © **808/946-4333.**

FISH MARKETS

Safeway on Beretania Street has a seafood counter with fresh choices and a staff that takes pride in its deftness with prepared foods. (Don't be shy about asking for a taste.) The prepared foods (fresh ahi poke, seaweed salad, marinated crab) are popular among busy working folks heading home. **Foodland** on Beretania Street occasionally offers good buys on live lobster and Dungeness crab, fresh ahi and aku poke, ahi sashimi and steaks, and a wide variety of fresh fish and shellfish, including whole snappers and oysters when available.

Tamashiro Market   This is the granddaddy of fish markets and the ace in the hole for home chefs with bouillabaisse or paella in mind. A separate counter sells seaweed salad, prepared poke, Filipino and Puerto Rican ti-wrapped steamed rice, and dozens of other ethnic foods. You'll think you're in a Fellini movie amid the tanks of live lobsters and crabs, and the dizzying array of counters glistening with fresh slabs of ahi, opakapaka whole and in filets, onaga, and ehu. Point and ask if you don't know what you're looking at, and one of the fish cutters will explain, then clean and fillet your selection. Good service and the most extensive selection in Honolulu make Tamashiro a Honolulu treasure. 802 N. King St., Kalihi. © **808/841-8047.**

Yama's Fish Market   Neighbor islanders have been known to drive directly from the airport to Yama's for one of the best plate lunches in Honolulu. Robust Hawaiian plates with pork or chicken *lau lau* (20 combinations!), baked ahi, chili, beef stew, shoyu chicken, and dozens of other varieties stream out to those who line up at the counter. Many Honolulu businesses order by the dozen for their offices. But Yama's is also known for its inexpensive fresh fish (mahimahi is always less expensive here than in the supermarkets), tasty poke (ahi, aku, Hawaiian-style, Oriental-style, with seaweed), lomi salmon, and many varieties of prepared seafood. Chilled beer, boiled peanuts, and fresh ahi they'll slice into sashimi are popular for local-style gatherings, sunset beach parties, and festive *pau hana* (end of work) celebrations. At its new, larger location just a few hundred feet away, Yama's is offering more prepared foods and bakery items than ever before, and let me tell you, their chocolate-chip/mac nut cookies are peerless. 2332 Young St., Moiliili. © **808/941-9994.**

HEALTH FOOD

Down to Earth   This university district shop sells organic vegetables and bulk foods, with a strong selection of supplements, herbs, and cosmetic products. Everything here is vegetarian, down to the last drop of tincture. Cereals, bulk grains and nuts, breads, many varieties of honey, nonalcoholic beer, teas, snacks, environment-friendly paper and household products, and a vegetarian juice and sandwich bar are among the reasons shoppers of all ages come here. 2525 S. King St., Moiliili. (✆ 808/947-7678.

Hou Ola   Tiny, with a loyal clientele that has stuck by it through management and name changes and a hefty dose of parking problems, Hou Ola has competitive prices and a wide and user-friendly selection of health-food supplements. The supplements are good enough reason to shop here. No produce, but there are frozen vegetarian foods, cosmetics, bulk grains, and healthy snacks. 1541 S. Beretania St. (✆ 808/955-6168.

Huckleberry Farms   Located in Nuuanu across town from the university area, Huckleberry Farms has two locations in the same shopping plaza. One houses a wide selection of vitamins, nutritional supplements, beauty creams and cosmetics, books, and nonperishable health products. A few feet away, the other store offers prepared health foods, fresh produce, and food products for the health-conscious. The selection at both stores is good. 1613 Nuuanu Ave., Nuuanu. (✆ 808/524-7960.

Kokua Market   Kokua is Honolulu's best source of healthy grinds in all categories but vitamin supplements. They are trying, however: the vitamin selection is expanding noticeably. Voluminous, leafy organic vegetables; an excellent variety of cheeses; pastas and bulk grains; sandwiches, salads, and prepared foods; poi as fresh as can be; organic coffee beans; breads and pastries; and a solid selection of organic wines give Kokua a special place in the hearts of health-minded shoppers. There's ample parking behind the store. 2643 S. King St., Moiliili. (✆ 808/ 941-1922.

FLOWERS & LEI

At most lei shops, simple leis sell for $3 and up, deluxe leis for $10 and up. For a special-occasion designer bouquet or lei, you can't do better than Michael Miyashiro of **Rainforest Plantes et Fleurs** (✆ 808/942-1550, or 808/ 591-5999). He's an ecologically aware, highly gifted lei-maker—his leis are pricey, but worth it. He is the consummate lei designer who custom-creates the lei for the person, occasion, and even destination. (Many of his original designs have been adopted by the Chinatown lei makers.) Order by phone or stop by the Ward Warehouse, where his tiny shop is an oasis of green and beauty. Upon request, Miyashiro's leis will come in ti-leaf bundles, called *pu'olo;* custom gift baskets (in woven green coconut baskets), and special arrangements. You can even request the card sentiments in Hawaiian, with English translations.

The other primary sources for flowers and leis are the shops lining the streets of Moiliili and Chinatown. Moiliili favorites include **Rudy's Flowers,** 2722 S. King St. (✆ 808/944-8844), a local institution with the best prices on roses, Micronesian ginger lei, and a variety of cut blooms. Across the street, **Flowers for a Friend,** 2739 S. King St. (✆ 808/955-4227), has good prices on leis, floral arrangements, and cut flowers. Nearby, **Flowers by Jr. and Lou,** 2652 S. King St. (✆ 808/941-2022), offers calla lilies, Gerber daisies, a riot of potted orchids, and the full range of cut flowers along with its lei selection.

In Chinatown, lei vendors line Beretania and Maunakea streets, and the fragrances of their wares mix with the earthy scents of incense and ethnic foods. Our top picks are **Lita's Leis,** 59 N. Beretania St. (✆ 808/521-9065), which has fresh puakenikeni, gardenias that last, and a supply of fresh and reasonable leis; **Sweetheart's Leis,** 69 N. Beretania St. (✆ 808/537-3011), with a worthy selection of the classics at fair prices; **Lin's Lei Shop,** 1017-A Maunakea St.

(✆ **808/537-4112**), with creatively fashioned, unusual leis; and **Cindy's Lei Shoppe,** 1034 Maunakea St. (✆ **808/536-6538**), with terrific sources for unusual leis such as feather dendrobiums, firecracker combinations, and everyday favorites like ginger, tuberose, orchid, and pikake. Ask Cindy's about its unique "curb service," available with phone orders. Just give them your car's color and model, and you can pick up your lei curbside—a great convenience on this busy street.

HAWAIIANA & GIFT ITEMS
Our top recommendations are the fabulous, newly expanded **Academy Shop,** at the Honolulu Academy of Arts, 900 S. Beretania St. (✆ **808/523-8703**), and the **Contemporary Museum Gift Shop,** 2411 Makiki Heights Rd. (✆ **808/523-3447**), two of the finest shopping stops on Oahu—worth a special trip whether or not you want to see the museums themselves. (And you will want to see the museums, especially the recently expanded Honolulu Academy of Arts.) The Academy Shop offers a brilliant selection of art books, jewelry, basketry, ethnic fabrics and native crafts from all over the world, posters and books, and fiber vessels and accessories. The Contemporary Museum shop focuses on arts and crafts such as avant-garde jewelry, cards and stationery, books, home accessories, and gift items made by artists from Hawaii and across the country. We love the glammy selection of jewelry and novelties, such as the twisted-wire wall hangings. (For details on the collections at both museums, see p. 186–187.)

Other good sources for quality gift items are the **Little Hawaiian Craft Shop,** in the Royal Hawaiian Shopping Center, and **Martin and MacArthur,** in the Aloha Tower Marketplace.

Following Sea   The buyers scour the country for the best representations of fine American craftsmanship in everything from candles and bath products to fine arts and crafts. Incense and candles scent the air, amid the soothing bubbling of indoor water fountains. Hawaii is well represented in the collection, with handsome hand-turned bowls and accessories made of native and introduced woods, jewelry, ceramics, handmade paper, and hand-bound books. Local artists have crafted a noteworthy selection of koa boxes and Hawaii-inspired jewelry in gold and silver. The Terrain candles, scented with ginger and tea, are intoxicating. 4211 Waialae Ave. ✆ 808/734-4425.

Hula Supply Center   Hawaiiana meets kitsch in this shop's marvelous selection of Day-Glo cellophane skirts, bamboo nose flutes, T-shirts, hula drums, shell leis, feathered rattle gourds, lauhala accessories, fiber mats, and a wide assortment of pareu fabrics. Although hula dancers shop here for their dance accoutrements, it's not all serious shopping. This is fertile ground for souvenirs and memorabilia of Hawaii, rooted somewhere between irreverent humor and cultural integrity. A great stop for Hawaiian and Polynesian gift items. Hawaiian Traders, its new adjoining store, is a showcase for made-in-Hawaii products. 2346 S. King St., Moiliili. ✆ 808/941-5379.

Liberty House, Ku'u Home Island Gifts   The fourth-floor island lifestyle department, called Ku'u Home ("my home") Island Gifts, is the best thing this department store has done in recent memory. Cultural/retail wizards Donna Burns and Maile Meyer of the enormously successful Native Books & Beautiful Things (see below) contacted 65 Hawaii artists and created a department of more than 600 unique, made-in-Hawaii products, skillfully displayed in a warm, real-life setting. Furniture, lamps, books, cushions, baskets, Hawaiian implements, quilts, lauhala and coconut home accessories, glassware, fabrics, gifts, personal adornments—the selection is eclectic and wonderful, capturing a distinctive Hawaii flavor that has its own strong identity within the store. The "Hawaii Artist of the Month" series brings the artists into the store to talk about their works. More than a shopping must, Ku'u Home is a cultural and aesthetic eye-opener. In the Ala Moana Center, 1450 Ala Moana Blvd. ℂ 808/945-5636.

Native Books & Beautiful Things *(Finds)*   Come to either of the two locations of this *hui* (association) of artists and craftspeople and you'll be enveloped in a love of things Hawaiian, from musical instruments to calabashes, jewelry, lei, books, and items of woven fibers—beautiful things of Hawaii. You'll find contemporary Hawaiian clothing, handmade koa journals, Hawaii-themed home accessories, lauhala handbags and accessories, jams and jellies and food products, etched glass, hand-painted fabrics and clothing, stone poi pounders, and other high-quality gift items. Some of Hawaii's finest artists in all craft media have their works available here on a regular basis, and the Hawaiian-book selection is tops. The 5,000-square-foot emporium at Ward Warehouse is a browser's paradise and features new artists every month. 222 Merchant St., downtown. ℂ 808/599-5511. Also at the Ward Warehouse, 1050 Ala Moana Blvd. ((ℂ 808/596-8885).

Nohea Gallery   A fine showcase for contemporary Hawaii art, Nohea celebrates the islands with thoughtful, attractive selections in all media, from pit-fired raku and finely turned wood vessels to jewelry, hand-blown glass, paintings, prints, fabrics (including Hawaiian quilt cushions), and furniture. Nohea's selection is always evolving and growing, with 90% of the works by Hawaii artists and a thoughtful selection of works representing Hawaii's best in all media. This is a terrific source of art and unique gift items from Hawaii. In the Ward Warehouse, 1050 Ala Moana Blvd. ℂ 808/596-0074. Also at Kahala Mandarin Oriental Hawaii, 5000 Kahala Ave. ((ℂ 808/737-8688); and two Waikiki locations, in Ohana Reef Towers Hotel, 227 Lewers St. ((ℂ 808/926-2224), and Sheraton Moana Surfrider Hotel, 2365 Kalakaua Ave. ((ℂ 808/923-6644).

Nui Mono   We love this tiny shop's kimono, clothing and accessories and the contemporary clothes made from ethnic fabrics. Other items include handbags made of patchwork vintage fabrics and priceless kimono silks, drapery Asian shapes and ikat fabrics, and richly textured vests and skirts. Warm, rich colors are the Nui Mono signature—and everything's moderately priced. 2745 S. King St., Moiliili. ℂ 808/946-7407.

Shop Pacifica   Local crafts, lauhala and Cook Island woven coconut, Hawaiian music tapes and CDs, pareos, and a vast selection of Hawaii-themed books anchor this gift shop. Hawaiian quilt cushion kits, jewelry, glassware, seed and Niihau shell leis, cookbooks, and many other gift possibilities will keep you occupied between stargazing in the planetarium and pondering the shells and antiquities of the esteemed historical museum. In the Bishop Museum, 1525 Bernice St. ℂ 808/848-4158.

Vagabond House   Home accessories, gift items, one-of-a-kind island crafts, and multicultural treasures are displayed in this attractive 1,700-square-foot space. Gleaming woods, fine porcelain and pottery, children's books, bath products, unique pillows, bamboo accessories, and Asian and Indonesian imports highlight this shop of wonders. Leave time to browse, because shopping here is like a journey through an island-style kamaaina home. In the Ward Centre, 1200 Ala Moana Blvd. ℂ 808/593-0288.

SHOPPING CENTERS

Ala Moana Center   The new third level is abuzz with eateries and shops, while the ponds on the mall level are thriving with taro and Hawaiian plants, even hapu'u ferns and koa trees. At press time, the finishing touches were being applied to the parking areas, but most of the shops are in, and many of them are the familiar names of mainland chains, such as **DKNY, Old Navy,** and **Eddie Bauer.**

The three-story, super-luxe Neiman Marcus, which opened in September 1998, was a bold move in Hawaii's troubled economy and has retained its position as the shrine of the fashionistas. But there are practical touches in the center, too, such as banks and airline ticket counters (in **Sears**), a foreign-exchange service (**Thomas Cook**), a U.S. Post Office, several optical companies (including 1-hr. service by **LensCrafters**), **Foodland Supermarket, Longs Drugs,** and a handful of photo-processing services. The smaller, locally owned stores (alas, fewer by the year) are scattered among the behemoths, mostly on the ground floor. Approximately 250 shops and services sprawl over several blocks (and 1.8 million sq. ft. of store space) on this 50-acre site, catering to every imaginable need, from over-the-top upscale (**Tiffany, Chanel, Versace, Escada, Gucci**) to mainland chains such as the **Gap, Banana Republic, Body Shop, Sharper Image, Ann Taylor,** and **Polo/Ralph Lauren.** Department stores such as **Liberty House** sell fashion, food, cosmetics, shoes, and household needs.

Shoes? They're a kick at **Nordstrom,** and newcomer **Walking Co.** has first-rate comfort styles by Mephisto, Ecco, and Naot. **Sephora,** the cosmetics emporium to top all, neighbors **Williams-Sonoma,** which will appeal to anyone who loves food, or even the smell of it.

A good stop for gifts is **Islands' Best,** which spills over with Hawaiian-made foodstuffs, ceramics, fragrances, and more. **Splash! Hawaii** is a good source for women's swimwear; for aloha shirts and men's swimwear, try **Liberty House, Town & Country Surf, Reyn's,** or the terminally hip **Hawaiian Island Creations.** Lovers of Polynesian wear and pareus shouldn't miss **Tahiti Imports.** The **food court** is abuzz with dozens of stalls purveying Cajun food, ramen, pizza, plate lunches, vegetarian fare, green tea and fruit freezes (like frozen yogurt), panini, and countless other treats. 1450 Ala Moana Blvd. ✆ **808/955-9517.** Bus: 8, 19, or 20. Ala Moana Shuttle runs daily every 15 minutes from 7 stops in Waikiki; Waikiki Trolley also stops at Ala Moana.

Aloha Tower Marketplace   The valet parking is *such* a relief! It takes some of the pressure out of the grim parking shortage (take the trolley if you can). Once you get to the new harborfront complex, however, a sense of nostalgia, of what it must have been like in the "Boat Days" of the 1920s to 1940s, will inevitably take over. Sleek ocean liners (as well as malodorous fishing boats) still tie up across the harbor, and the refurbished Aloha Tower stands high over the complex, as it did in the days when it was the tallest structure in Honolulu.

Hawaiian House is a hit with its island-style interiors and home accents. Dining and shopping prospects abound: **Martin & MacArthur** gift shop, **Hawaiian Ukulele Company, Sunglass Hut, Don Ho's Island Grill, Chai's Island Bistro,** and **Gordon Biersch Brewery** (see chapter 5, "Dining," for reviews of the restaurants). 1 Aloha Tower Dr., on the waterfront between piers 8 and 11, Honolulu Harbor. ✆ **808/ 528-5700.** Aloha Tower Entertainment Hotline. ✆ 808/566-2333. Various Honolulu trolleys stop here; if you want a direct ride from Waikiki, take the free Hilo Hattie's trolley or the Waikiki Red Line trolley, which continues on to Hilo Hattie's in Iwilei.

DFS Galleria   "Boat days" is the theme at this newly renovated (to the tune of $65 million) Waikiki emporium, a three-floor extravaganza of shops ranging from the chi-chi (**Givenchy, Coach, Polo/Ralph Lauren,** and many more) to the very touristy. There are elements of this complex that are tacky, but there are some great Hawaii food products, ranging from the incomparable Big Island Candies shortbread cookies to a spate of coffees and preserves. Servers bearing warm, fresh-from-the-oven cookies are a nice touch. **The Tube,** a walk-through aquarium complete with spotted and sting rays, is a big attraction, visible from indoors and on the sidewalk at the corner of Kalakaua and Royal Hawaiiian Avenues. There are multitudes of aloha shirts and T-shirts, a virtual golf course, surf and skate equipment, a terrific Hawaiian music department, and a labyrinth of boutiques once you get past the Waikiki Walk. Fragrances and cosmetics make a big splash at **DFS**—they're a big part of the upper floors. **Starbucks** and **Jamba Juice** are always buzzing with coffee and smoothies, and **Kalia Grill,** with rotisserie and deli items for casual dining. *Caveat:* Some sections are restricted to international travelers only. Free live Hawaiian entertainment, featuring hula styles from the 1920s to the 1940s, takes place nightly at 7pm. 330 Royal Hawaiian Ave., at the corner of Kalakaua Ave. ℂ 808/931-2655.

Kahala Mall   Chic, manageable, and unfrenzied, Kahala Mall is home to some of Honolulu's best shops. Located east of Waikiki in the posh neighborhood of Kahala, the mall has everything from a small **Liberty House** to chain stores, such as **Banana Republic** and **Gap**—nearly 100 specialty shops (including dozens of eateries and eight movie theaters) in an enclosed, air-conditioned area. **Starbucks** is a java magnet, a stone's throw from the **Gourmet Express** with its fast, healthy salads, tortilla wraps, and fresh juices and smoothies. **Jamba Juice** is the hot spot of the mall, with lines of smoothie lovers waiting for their Citrus Squeeze or Kiwi-Berry Burner. For gift, fashion, and specialty stores, our picks of the mall's best and brightest are the **Following Sea** (see "Hawaiiana & Gift Items," above); **Riches,** a tiny kiosk with a big, bold selection of jewelry; the **Compleat Kitchen;** the **Paperie,** with an impressive selection of everything you'll need in stationery, cards, napkins, and paper goods; and the sprawling **Hawaiian House.** Anchoring the mall are stalwarts **Longs Drugs, Liberty House, Star Market,** and **Barnes & Noble** with its books, coffee bar, and inviting nooks. Look also for the **Liberty House Men's Store** at the mauka (inland) corner of the mall, under a separate roof from the main store. 4211 Waialae Ave., Kahala. ℂ 808/732-7736.

Royal Hawaiian Shopping Center   Upscale is the operative word here. Although there are drugstores, lei stands, restaurants, and food kiosks, the most conspicuous stores are the European designer boutiques (**Chanel, Cartier, Hermès,** and more) that cater largely to visitors from Japan. One of our favorite stops is the **Little Hawaiian Craft Shop,** which features a distinctive collection of Niihau shell leis, museum replicas of Hawaiian artifacts, and works by Hawaii artists, as well as South Pacific crafts. **Beretania Florist,** located in the hut under the large banyan tree, will ship cut tropical flowers anywhere in the United States. A favorite fashion stop is **McInerny Galleria,** a cluster of boutiques under one roof, with such big names as **DKNY, Ralph Lauren, Coach,** and **Armani.** Chocolate lovers, take note: the new **Padovani Chocolate Boutique,** selling the finest handmade designer chocolates in Hawaii, recently opened in the Galleria. 2201 Kalakaua Ave. ℂ 808/922-0588.

Waikele Premium Outlets   Just say the word "Waikele" and our eyes glaze over. So many shops, so little time! And so much money to be saved while spending for what you don't need. There are two sections to this sprawling discount shopping mecca: the **Waikele Premium Outlets,** some 51 retailers offering designer and name-brand merchandise; and the **Waikele Value Center** across the street, with another 25 stores more practical than fashion-oriented (**Eagle Hardware, Sports Authority, Borders**). The 64-acre complex has made discount shopping a major activity and a travel pursuit in itself, with shopping tours for visitor groups and carloads of neighbor islanders and Oahu residents making pilgrimages from all corners of the state. They come to hunt down bargains on everything from perfumes, luggage, and hardware to sporting goods, fashions, vitamins, and china. Examples: **Geoffrey Beene, Donna Karan, Saks Fifth Avenue, Anne Klein, Max Studio, Levi's, Converse, Vitamin World, Mikasa, Kenneth Cole, Banana Republic,** and dozens of other name brands at a fraction of retail. The ultra-chic **Barneys** has added new cachet to this shopping haven. 94–790 Lumiaina St., Waikele (about 20 miles from Waikiki). © **808/676-5656.** Take H-1 west toward Waianae and turn off at exit 7. Bus: no. 42 from Waikiki to Waipahu Transit Center, then 433 from Transit Center to Waikele. To find out which companies offer shopping tours with Waikiki pickups, call the Information Center at © 808/678-0786.

Ward Centre   Although it has a high turnover and a changeable profile, Ward Centre is a standout for its concentration of restaurants and shops. The surrounding construction points to many more changes ahead. **Ryan's** and **Kakaako Kitchen** are as popular as ever, the former looking out over Ala Moana Park and the latter with lanai views of the sprawling **Pier 1 Imports** across the street. Across from **Pier 1, Nordstrom Rack,** and **Office Depot** have sprouted in a new development area that will also include a 16-theater movie megaplex now being built. All these establishments are part of developer Victoria Ward's Kakaako projects, which take up several blocks in this area: Ward Centre, Ward Farmers Market, Ward Village Shops, Ward Gateway Center, and Ward Warehouse.

Ward Centre's gift shops and galleries include **Kamehameha Garment Company** for aloha shirts, **Vagabond House** (see "Hawaiiana & Gift Items," above), **Paper Roses** for wonderful paper products, **Honolulu Chocolate Company** (see "Edibles," earlier in this chapter), and the very attractive **Gallery at Ward Centre. Handblock** proffers wonderful table linens, clothing, and household accents, while **Borders** is action central, bustling with browsers. 1200 Ala Moana Blvd. © **808/591-8411.**

Ward Warehouse   Older than its sister property, Ward Centre, and endowed with an endearing patina, Ward Warehouse remains a popular stop for dining and shopping. **Native Books & Beautiful Things** and the **Nohea Gallery** (see "Hawaiiana & Gift Items" for both) are excellent sources for quality Hawaii-made arts and crafts.

Other recommended stops in the low-rise wooden structure include the ever-colorful **C. June Shoes,** with flamboyant designer women's shoes and handbags (tony, expensive, and oh-so-entertaining!); **Executive Chef,** for gourmet Hawaii food items and household accessories; **Out of Africa,** for pottery, beads, and interior accents; **Mamo Howell,** for distinctive aloha wear; and **Private World,** for delicate sachets, linens, and fragrances. Other great stops are **Paradise Walking Co.,** with Arche, Mephisto, and all manner of cloud-comfort footwear; and **Bambini,** brimming with tasteful gifts for kids and babies. For T-shirts and swimwear, check out the **Town & Country Surf Shop,** and for an excellent selection of sunglasses, knapsacks, and footwear to take you from the beach to the ridgetops, don't miss **Thongs 'N Things.** 1050 Ala Moana Blvd. ℰ 808/591-8411.

Victoria Ward Centers   This large, multi-block complex includes Ward Centre and Ward Warehouse mentioned above and is slated for enormous expansion throughout 2001 and 2002. A new entertainment center at the corner of Auahi and Kamakee streets is soon to open, and the 156,000-square foot center will include movie theaters, a 40,000-square-foot Dave & Buster's (with virtual golf, games, interactive entertainment, bars, and a restaurant), and about two more restaurants and six to eight retailers, as yet undetermined.

SURF & SPORTS

The surf-and-sports shops scattered throughout Honolulu are a highly competitive lot, with each trying to capture your interest (and dollars). But we can't live without them.

The Bike Shop   Excellent for cycling and backpacking equipment for all levels, with major camping lines such as North Face, MSR, and Kelty. 1149 S. King St., near Piikoi St. ℰ 808/596-0588.

Hawaiian Island Creations   HIC is a super-cool surf shop offering sunglasses, sun lotions, surfwear, surfboards, skateboards, and accessories galore. In the Ala Moana Center, 1450 Ala Moana Blvd. ℰ 808/973-6780, and other locations in Pearlridge (ℰ 808/483-6700), Waikiki (ℰ 808/971-6715), and Haleiwa (ℰ 808/637-0991).

Local Motion   Local Motion is the icon of surfers and skateboarders, both professionals and wannabes. The shop offers surfboards, T-shirts, aloha and casual wear, Boogie boards, and countless accessories for life in the sun. 1958 Kalakaua Ave. ℰ 808/979-7873, and other locations.

McCully Bicycle & Sporting Goods   Find everything from bicycles and fishing gear to athletic shoes and accessories and a stunning selection of sunglasses. 2124 S. King St. ℰ 808/955-6329.

Powder Edge Outdoor Gear   Some folks never take a trip without coming here first. Patagonia long underwear made of warm, light Capilene; the newest card-size Swiss Army knives; backpacks; waterproof bottles; water purifiers; sports shoes; clothing for all climes—this is an indispensable store for those who love travel and the outdoors. In Ward Village, 1142 Auahi St. ℰ 808/593-2267.

The Sports Authority   A discount megaoutlet offering clothing, cycles, and equipment, fishing gear, sports shoes, camping gear, beach chairs, and everything you can imagine for a life outside the office. 333 Ward Ave. ℰ 808/596-0166. Also at Waikele Center (ℰ 808/677-9933).

2 Windward Oahu

KAILUA

Long's Drugs and **Liberty House** department store, located side-by-side on Kailua Road in the heart of this windward Oahu community, form the shopping nexus of the neighborhood.

Agnes Portuguese Bake Shop *(Finds)*   This Kailua treasure is the long-time favorite of Hawaii's *malassada* mavens. *Malassadas*—sugary Portuguese dumplings that look and taste like doughnuts without holes—fly out of the bakery, infusing the entire neighborhood with an irresistible aroma. The Bake Shop also offers a variety of pastries, cookies, scones, Portuguese bean and other soups, and local- and European-style breads. 46 Hoolai St. © 808/262-5367.

Alii Antiques of Kailua II *(Finds)* Abandon all restraint, particularly if you have a weakness for vintage Hawaiiana. Koa lamps and rattan furniture from the 1930s and 1940s, hula nodders, rare 1940s koa tables, Roseville vases, Don Blanding dinnerware, and a breathtaking array of vintage etched-glass vases and trays are some of the items in this unforgettable shop. Across the street, the owner's wife runs **Alii Antiques of Kailua,** which is chockablock with all the things that won't fit here: jewelry, clothing, Bauer and Fiestaware, linens, Bakelite bracelets, and floor-to-ceiling collectibles. 9-A Maluniu Ave., Kailua. © 808/261-1705.

BookEnds BookEnds is the quintessential neighborhood bookstore, run by a pro who buys good books and knows how to find the ones she doesn't have. There are more than 60,000 titles here, new and used, from *Celtic Mandalas* to C. S. Lewis's *Chronicles of Narnia* and the full roster of current bestsellers. Volumes on child care, cooking, and self-improvement; a hefty periodicals section; and mainstream and offbeat titles are among the treasures to be found. 600 Kailua Rd., Kailua. © 808/261-1996.

Heritage Antiques & Gifts This Kailua landmark is known for its selection of Tiffany-style lamps ($200–$2,000), many of which are hand-carted back to the mainland. The mind-boggling inventory also includes European, Asian, American, local, and Pacific Island collectibles. The shop is fun, the people friendly, and the selection diverse enough to appeal to the casual as well as serious collector. Glassware; china; and estate, costume, and fine jewelry are among the items of note. Heritage has its own jeweler who does custom designs and repairs, plus a stable of woodworkers who turn out custom-made koa rockers and hutches to complement the antique furniture selection. 767 Kailua Rd. © 808/261-8700.

KANEOHE

Windward Oahu's largest shopping complex is the **Windward Mall,** 46–056 Kamehameha Hwy., in Kaneohe (© 808/235-1143), open Monday through Saturday from 10am to 9pm and Sunday from 10am to 5pm. The big news here is the 10-screen theater complex that opened in May 2001. The 100 stores and services at this standard suburban mall include **Macy's West** and **Sears,** health stores, airline counters, surf shops, and **LensCrafters.** A small food court serves pizza, Chinese fare, tacos, and other morsels, and the new theaters are a big draw for windwardites.

3 The North Shore: Haleiwa

Haleiwa means serious shopping for those who know that the unhurried pace of rural life can conceal vast material treasures. Ask the legions of townies who drive an hour each way just to stock up on wine and clothes at Haleiwa stores. Below are our Haleiwa highlights.

ART, GIFTS & CRAFTS

Haleiwa's shops and galleries display a combination of marine art, watercolors, sculptures, and a plethora of crafts trying to masquerade as fine art. This is the town for gifts, fashions, and surf stuff—mostly casual, despite some very high price tags. **Haleiwa Gallery** in the North Shore Marketplace displays a lot of local art of the non-marine variety, and some of it is appealing.

Global Creations Interiors   Global Creations offers casual clothing as well as international imports for the home, including Balinese bamboo furniture and colorful hammocks for the carefree life. There are gifts and crafts by 115 local potters, painters, and artists of other media. 66–079 Kamehameha Hwy. ℂ **808/637-1505.**

EDIBLES

Haleiwa is best known for its roadside shave-ice stands: the famous **Matsumoto Shave Ice** *⌖*, with the perennial queue snaking along Kamehameha Highway, and nearby **Aoki's.** Shave ice is the popular island version of a snow cone, topped with your choice of syrups, such as strawberry, rainbow, root beer, vanilla, or passion fruit. Aficionados order it with a scoop of ice cream and sweetened black adzuki beans nestled in the middle.

For food-and-wine shopping, our mightiest accolades go to **Fujioka Super Market,** 66–190 Kamehameha Hwy. (ℂ **808/637-4520**). Oenophiles and tony wine clubs from town shop here for the best prices on California reds, coveted Italian reds, and a growing selection of cabernets, merlots, and French vintages. Fresh produce and no-cholesterol, vegetarian health foods, in addition to the standards, fill the aisles of this third-generation store.

Tiny, funky **Celestial Natural Foods,** 66–443 Kamehameha Hwy. (ℂ **808/ 637-6729**), is the health foodies' Grand Central for everything from wooden spine-massagers to health supplements, produce, cosmetics, and bulk foods.

FASHION

Although Haleiwa used to be an incense-infused surfer outpost where zoris and tank tops were the regional uniform and the Beach Boys and Ravi Shankar the music of the day, today it's one of the top shopping destinations for those with unconventional tastes. Specialty shops abound.

In addition to Silver Moon (below), other highlights of the prominent North Shore Marketplace include **Patagonia** (ℂ **808/637-1245**) for high-quality surf, swim, hiking, kayaking, and all-around adventure wear; **North Shore Custom & Design Swimwear** (ℂ **808/637-6859**) for excellent mix-and-match bikinis and one-piece suits, custom ordered or off the rack; **Kama'ainas Haleiwa** (ℂ **808/637-1907**), the new gallery-gift store for quality island crafts, Hawaiian quilts, soaps, hats, accessories, clothing, and food specialties; and **Jungle Gems** (ℂ **808/637-6609**), the mother lode of gemstones, crystals, silver, and beadwork.

Nearby **Oceania,** 66–208 Kamehameha Hwy. (ℂ **808/637-4581**), also has some treasures among its racks of casual and leisure wear. Foldable straw hats, diaphanous dresses, dressy T-shirts, friendly service, and good prices are what we've found here. **Oogenesis Boutique,** 66–249 Kamehameha Hwy. (ℂ **808/ 637-4580**), in the southern part of Haleiwa, features a storefront lined with vintage-looking dresses that flutter prettily in the North Shore breeze.

H. Miura Store and Tailor Shop   Amid all these hip Haleiwa newcomers, the perennial favorite remains this old-fashioned, longtime neighborhood staple. You can custom-order swim trunks, an aloha shirt, or a muumuu from bolts of Polynesian-printed fabrics, from tapa designs to two-color pareu prints. The staff will sew, ship, and remember you years later when you return. It's the most versatile tailor shop we've ever seen, with coconut-shell bikini tops, fake hula skirts, and heaps of cheap and glorious tchotchkes lining the aisles. 66–057 Kamehameha Hwy. ℂ **808/637-4845.**

Silver Moon Emporium *(Finds)*   Top-drawer Silver Moon is an islandwide phenomenon, featuring the terrific finds of owner Lucie Talbot-Holu. Exquisite clothing and handbags, reasonably priced footwear, hats straight out of *Vogue,* jewelry, scarves, and a full gamut of other treasures pepper the attractive boutique. Tastes run from the conventional to the outrageous; you'll find shoes, handbags, suits, dresses, jewelry, bags, and accessories for all occasions, from weddings to the office, parties, and everything in between. Whether it's fragrances, crystal candleholders, or a special Sorrelli collectible, there's great style at Silver Moon. In the North Shore Marketplace, 66–250 Kamehameha Hwy. ✆ 808/637-7710.

SURF SHOPS
Haleiwa's ubiquitous surf shops are the best on earth, surfers say.

Barnfield's Raging Isle Sports   Barnfield's is the surf-and-cycle center of the area, with everything from wet suits and surfboards to surf gear and clothing for men, women, and children. The adjoining surfboard factory puts out custom-built boards of high renown. There's also a large inventory of mountain bikes for rent and sale. In the North Shore Marketplace, 66–250 Kamehameha Hwy. ✆ 808/637-7707.

B K Ocean Sports   Also owned by Barry Kanaiaupuni of Northshore Boardriders Club fame, this is a more casual version, appealing to surfers and watersports enthusiasts of all levels. In the old Haleiwa Post Office, 66–215 Kamehameha Hwy. ✆ 808/637-4966.

Hawaii Surf & Sail   Stop in for new and used surfboards and accessories for surfers, bodyboarders, and sailboarders. 66–214 Kamehameha Hwy. ✆ 808/637-5373.

Northshore Boardriders Club   Cream of the crop, this is the mecca of the board-riding elite, with sleek, fast, elegant, and top-of-the-line boards designed by North Shore legends such as longboard shaper Barry Kanaiaupuni, John Carper, Jeff Bushman, and Pat Rawson. This is a Quicksilver "concept store," which means that it's the testing ground for the newest and hottest trends in surfwear put out by the retail giant. In the North Shore Marketplace, 66–250 Kamehameha Hwy. ✆ 808/637-5026.

Strong Current Surf Design   This is the North Shore's nexus for memorabilia and surf nostalgia because of the passion of its owners, Bonnie and John Moore, who expanded the commercial surf-shop space to encompass the Haleiwa Surf Museum. From head level down, Strong Current displays shorts, ocean sportswear, hats, jewelry, towels, and popular new items of Hawaiiana; from head level up, the walls and ceilings are lined with vintage boards, posters, and pictures from the 1950s and 1960s. Although Strong Current is a longboard surf shop, the current popularity of longboarding among all age groups makes this a popular stop. World-famous North Shore shapers Dick Brewer and Mike Diffenderfer are among the big names who design the fiberglass and balsa wood boards. In the North Shore Marketplace, 66–250 Kamehameha Hwy. ✆ 808/637-3406.

Surf & Sea Surf Sail & Dive Shop   A longtime favorite among old-timers is this newly expanded, flamboyant roadside structure just over the bridge, with old wood floors and blowing fans. It sports a tangle of surf and swimwear, T-shirts, surfboards, Boogie boards, fins, watches, sunglasses, and countless other miscellany; you can also rent surf and snorkel equipment here. 62–595 Kamehameha Hwy. ✆ 808/637-9887.

Tropical Rush   Tropical Rush has a huge inventory of surf and swim gear: surfboards, longboards, bodyboards, Sector 9 skateboards, and all the accessories to go with an ocean-minded life, like slippers and swimwear for men and women. T-shirts, hats, sunglasses, and visors are among the scads of cool gear, and you can rent equipment and arrange surf lessons, too. An added feature is the shop's surf report line for the up-to-the-minute lowdown on wave action (© **808/638-7874**); it covers the day's surf and weather details for all of Oahu. 62–620-A Kamehameha Hwy. © **808/637-8886**.

9

Oahu After Dark

by Jocelyn Fujii

One of my favorite occasions in life is sunset at Ke Iki Beach on Oahu's North Shore. The entire day builds up to sunset—shopping for the mai tai ingredients, checking the angle of the sun, swimming with the knowledge that the big, salty thirst will soon be quenched with a tall, homemade mai tai on the beach I love most in the world. When the sun is low, we make our mix: fresh lime juice, fresh lemon juice, fresh orange juice, passion-orange-guava juice, and fresh grape-fruit juice, if possible. We pour this mix on ice in tall, frosty glasses, and then add Meyer's rum, in which Tahitian vanilla beans have been soaking for days. (Add cinnamon if desired, or soak a cinnamon stick with the rum and vanilla beans.) A dash of Angostura bitters, a few drops of Southern Comfort as a float, a sprig of mint, a garnish of fresh lime, and voilà! The homemade Ke Iki mai tai, a cross between planter's punch and the classic Trader Vic's mai tai. As the sun sets, we lift our glasses and savor the moment, the setting, and the first sip—not a bad way to end the day.

In Hawaii, the mai tai is more than a libation. It's a festive, happy ritual that signals holiday, vacation, or a time of play, not work. Computers and mai tais don't mix. Mai tais and hammocks do. Mai tais and sunsets go hand in hand.

IT BEGINS WITH SUNSET . . .

Nightlife in Hawaii begins at sunset, when all eyes turn westward to see how the day will end. Like seeing the same pod of whales or school of spinner dolphins, sunset viewers seem to bond in the mutual enjoyment of a natural spectacle. People in Hawaii are fortunate to have a benign environment that encourages this cultural ritual.

On Fridays and Saturdays at 6:30pm, as the sun casts its golden glow on the beach and surfers and beachboys paddle in for the day, **Kuhio Beach,** where Kalakaua Avenue intersects with Kaiulani, eases into evening with hula dancing and a torch-lighting ceremony. This is a thoroughly delightful, free weekend offering. Start off earlier with a picnic basket and your favorite libations and walk along the oceanside path fronting Queen's Surf, near the Waikiki Aquarium. (You can park along Kapiolani Park or near the Honolulu Zoo.) There are few more pleasing spots in Waikiki than the benches at the water's edge at the Diamond Head end of Kalakaua Avenue, where lovers and families of all ages stop to peruse the sinking sun. A short walk across the intersection of Kalakaua and Kapahulu avenues takes you to the Duke Kahanamoku statue on Kuhio Beach and the nearby Wizard Stones.

1 The Bar Scene

ON THE BEACH

Waikiki's beachfront bars offer many possibilities, from the Royal Hawaiian Hotel's **Mai Tai Bar** (© **808/923-7311**), a few feet from the sand, to the unfailingly enchanting **House Without a Key at the Halekulani** (✆ 808/ 923-2311), where the breathtaking Kanoelehua Miller dances hula to the riffs of Hawaiian steel-pedal guitar under a century-old kiawe tree. With the sunset and ocean glowing behind her and Diamond Head visible in the distance, the scene is straight out of Somerset Maugham—romantic, evocative, nostalgic. It doesn't hurt, either, that the Halekulani happens to make the best mai tais in the world. Halekulani has the after-dinner hours covered, too, with light jazz by local artists from 10:15pm to midnight nightly.

IN THE ALOHA TOWER MARKETPLACE

Unlike Waikiki, there are no swaying palm trees at Aloha Tower Marketplace, on the waterfront between piers 8 and 11, Honolulu Harbor (✆ **808/528-5700**), but the frequent appearances of the **Brothers Cazimero** at **Chai's Island Bistro** (✆ **808/585-0011**) have turned the waterfront into a thriving late-night spot reviving old-style Waikiki entertainment in a big way. Chai's offers live entertainment nightly from Hawaii's top musical artists: Hapa, Ho'okena, Olomana, and the indomitable Brothers Cazimero.

On the Aloha Tower Marketplace harborfront, **Don Ho's Island Grill** (✆ **808/528-0807**) is a local hotspot, with Willie K. and other musical icons taking the stage throughout the year. It's worth calling to see who's playing. At the **Gordon Biersch Brewery** (✆ **808/599-4877**), diners swing to jazz, blues, and island riffs with a changing slate of entertainers from sunset through the evening Wednesday through Saturday. And the food and beer are great, too. The roster of performers includes the cream of contemporary Island artists. Hours at the Marketplace are daily 8am to midnight.

Across the street from Aloha Tower Marketplace, the bar and lounge of **Palomino** (✆ **808/528-2400**) is a magnet for revelers, often two deep at the bar, partaking of the great appetizers, pizzas, service, and drinks.

See chapter 5 for reviews of all four of the restaurants mentioned above.

DOWNTOWN

The downtown scene is awakening from a long slumber, thanks to the **Hawaii Theatre** and some tenacious entrepreneurs who want everyone to love Nuuanu Avenue as much as they do. The occasional block parties along Nuuanu Avenue, called "Nuuanu Nights," are now a regular monthly event.

Hank's Cafe, between Hotel and King streets on Nuuanu (✆ 808/ 526-1410), is noteworthy and always jumping, a tiny, kitschy, friendly pub that spells FUN with its live music, open-mike nights, and special events that attract great talent and a supportive crowd. On some nights the music spills out into the street and it's so packed you have to press your nose against the window to see what's happening.

Down the street, **Havana Cabana** (✆ **808/524-4277**) is a clubby late-night cigar-smoker's paradise with live music ranging from jazz to rock and R&B.

At the makai (ocean) end of Nuuanu, **Murphy's Bar & Grill** (✆ 808/ 531-0422) and **O'Toole's Pub** (✆ **808/536-6360**) are the downtown alehouses and media haunts that have kept Irish eyes smiling for years.

2 The Club Scene

"Aloha shirt to Armani" is what we call the night scene in Honolulu—mostly casual, but with ample opportunity to dress up if you dare to part with your flip-flops.

HAWAIIAN MUSIC

Oahu has several key spots for Hawaiian music. A delightful (and powerful) element in the Waikiki music scene is Hawaii's queen of falsetto, **Genoa Keawe,** who fills the Hawaiian Regent Hotel's **Lobby Bar** (© 808/922-6611) with her larger-than-life voice from 5:30 to 8:30pm every Thursday. The rest of the week, except Monday, other contemporary Hawaiian musicians fill in.

The **Brothers Cazimero** remains one of Hawaii's most gifted duos (Robert on bass, Roland on 12-string guitar), appearing every Wednesday from 7 to 8:15pm at **Chai's Island Bistro,** in the Aloha Tower Marketplace (© 808/585-0011). On Monday from 7 to 7:45pm and Tuesday from 8 to 8:45pm, Robert Cazimero appears at Chai's, at the piano.

Impromptu hula and spirited music from the family and friends of the performers are an island tradition at places such as the Hilton Hawaiian Village's **Paradise Lounge** (© 808/949-4321), which (despite its pillars) serves as a large living room for the full-bodied music of **Olomana.** The group plays Friday and Saturday from 8pm to midnight, no cover charge.

At **Duke's Canoe Club** at the Outrigger Waikiki (© 808/923-0711), it's always three deep at the beachside bar when the sun is setting. Extra-special entertainment is a given here—usually from 4 to 6pm on Friday, Saturday, and Sunday, and nightly from 10pm until midnight. See chapter 5 for a dining review of Duke's.

Nearby, the Sheraton Moana Surfrider offers a regular program of Hawaiian music and piano in its **Banyan Veranda** (© 808/922-3111), which surrounds an islet-sized canopy of banyan tree and roots where Robert Louis Stevenson loved to linger. The Veranda serves afternoon tea, a sunset buffet, and cocktails.

Our best advice for lovers of Hawaiian music is to scan the local dailies or the *Honolulu Weekly* to see if and where the following Hawaiian entertainers are appearing: **Ho'okena,** a symphonic rich quintet featuring Manu Boyd, one of the most prolific songwriters and chanters in Hawaii; **Hapa,** an award-winning contemporary Hawaii duo; **Keali'i Reichel,** premier chanter, dancer, and award-winning recording artist; award-winning female vocalist **Robbie Kahakalau; Kapena,** contemporary Hawaiian music; **Na Leo Pilimehana,** a trio of angelic Hawaiian singers; the **Makaha Sons of Niihau,** pioneers in the Hawaiian cultural renaissance; **Fiji;** and slack-key guitar master **Raymond Kane.** Consider the gods beneficent if you happen to be here when the hula *halau* of **Frank Kawaikapuokalani Hewett** is holding its annual fund-raiser in Windward Oahu. It's a rousing, inspired, family effort for a good cause, and it always features the best in ancient and contemporary Hawaiian music. For the best in ancient and modern hula, it's a good idea to check the dailies for *halau* fund-raisers, which are always authentic, enriching, and local to the core.

LIVE BLUES, R&B, JAZZ, POP & WORLD MUSIC

The blues are alive and well in Hawaii, with quality acts both local and from the mainland drawing enthusiastic crowds in even the funkiest of surroundings. There isn't a regular blues club, however, so the best shows are usually at the Waikiki Shell, Hawaii Theatre, or Blaisdell Concert Hall.

For more late-night schmoozing, with a theater complex nearby, Restaurant Row's **Row Bar,** 500 Ala Moana Blvd. (© 808/528-2345), always seems to be full, smoky, and somewhat convivial. Also in Restaurant Row, **Sansei** (© 808/536-6286) keeps busy with its late-night karaoke, and **Baci at Restaurant Row** (© 808/550-8005) has live music regularly. See chapter 5 for dining reviews of both spots.

I also suggest that you call the **Aloha Tower Marketplace** hot line (© **808/ 566-2333**) to find out what's playing, because, with Gordon Biersch, Don Ho's Island Grill, and Chai's Island Bistro in the same complex, there's a lot of music filling the harbor air. (See "The Bar Scene," earlier in this chapter.)

Nick's Fishmarket, in the Waikiki Gateway Hotel, 2070 Kalakaua Ave. (© **808/955-6333**), is known for its seafood but also features live entertainment in its cozy lounge—with mild jazz or top-40 contemporary hits. See chapter 5 for a complete dining review.

Jazz lovers should watch for the **Great Hawaiian Jazz Blow-Out** every March at Mid-Pacific Institute's Bakken Hall.

At the south end of Honolulu, near Diamond Head, the sleek and flashy **Diamond Head Grill,** in the W Honolulu, 2885 Kalakaua Ave. (© **808/ 922-3734**), is Honolulu's hottest nightspot, with live music nightly. See chapter 5 for a dining review.

Tops in taste and ambience is the perennially alluring **Lewers Lounge** in the Halekulani, 2199 Kalia Rd. (© **808/923-2311**). **Bruce Hamada** and other local artists are a big draw, and when Diana Krall and other notables are in town for a concert, they often appear after the show and give impromptu performances in the intimate lounge.

In Moiliili, the grand dame of them all is **Anna Bannanas,** 2440 S. Beretania St. (© **808/946-5190**), the aging but beloved diva after 30 years in the business. Anna's offers an intimate setting for reggae, blues, and rock. Most shows start at 9:30pm, and the cover charge depends on the show.

The under-30 set throngs **The Wave Waikiki** (© **808/941-0424**), a small, dark, and edgy room that shakes with the rock and R&B groups that play there. Down the street, near the Hawaii Convention Center, decibels run amok at the **Hard Rock Cafe,** 1837 Kapiolani Blvd. (© **808/955-7383**). Most Friday and Saturday nights, you'll find live alternative, reggae, and classic rock.

Watch for **Sandy Tsukiyama,** a gifted singer (Brazilian, Latin, jazz) and one of Honolulu's great assets. Other groups in jazz, blues, and R&B include **Blue Budda, Bongo Tribe, Secondhand Smoke, Bluzilla, Piranha Brothers,** and the **Greg Pai Trio.**

DANCE CLUBS

In the bowels of industrial Kakaako, the party never stops at **Pipeline Café and Sports Bar,** 805 Pohukaina St. (© **808/589-1999**), the shrine of surfers and students and a magnet for revelers and the occasional visiting movie star. Pipeline's the place for cheap drinks, party grinds, and meeting people, whether it's to benefit surf movie premieres or Ladies Night with $2 drinks and pupus. (There's even a "Service Industry Night," where people in the business get discounts.) Open until 4am every night, Pipeline gets its gregarious crowd dancing to the loud DJ music in a nightlong party where fun is the mantra.

The current nightlife buzz is all about **Blue Tropix,** which opened in 2001 at 1700 Kapiolani Blvd. (© **808/944-0001**). It boasts a hip weekend crowd and a live monkey (shame on them) contained in soundproof glass behind the bar. (The grand opening was a benefit for the Honolulu Zoological Society—ha!) The nightclub features a restaurant, food service from lunch until 1am, and a 100-square-foot dance floor for the lively DJ jams of top 40s, hip-hop, and R&B dance music. There's a $5 cover charge. Dinner service begins at 5:30pm in the restaurant; the club is open from 10pm to 2am.

Aaron's Atop the Ala Moana, in the Ala Moana Hotel, 410 Atkinson Dr. (© **808/955-4466**), has the best view in town. From the 36th floor of the hotel (take the express elevator), watch the Honolulu city lights wrap around the room and cha-cha-cha to the vertigo! There's live music and dancing nightly, a great dinner menu, and an appetizer menu nightly from 5pm. See the restaurant review in chapter 5.

At Restaurant Row, the **Ocean Club,** 500 Ala Moana Blvd. (© **808/ 526-9888**), is the Row's hottest and hippest spot. Good seafood appetizers, attractive happy-hour prices, a fabulous quirky interior, and passionate DJs in alternative garb make up a dizzyingly successful formula. The minimum age is 23, and the dress code calls for "smart-casual"—no T-shirts, slippers, or beach wear. See chapter 5 for a complete restaurant review.

Downstairs in the lobby of the Ala Moana Hotel, **Rumours Nightclub** (© **808/955-4811**) is the disco of choice for those who remember that Paul McCartney was a Beatle before Wings. The theme changes by the month, but generally, it's the "Big Chill" 1960s, '70s, and '80s music on Friday; the "Little Chill" on Saturday; ballroom dancing from 5 to 9pm on Sunday; top 40 on Tuesday; karaoke on Wednesday; and an "after-work office party" to midnight on Thursday. A spacious dance floor, good sound system, and top-40 music draw a mix of generations.

3 The Performing Arts

Audiences have stomped to the big off-Broadway percussion hit, **Stomp,** and enjoyed the talent of the revered **Halau o Kekuhi, Tap Dogs, Momix,** the **American Repertory Dance Company,** barbershop quartets, and **John Ka'imikaua's halau** at the **Hawaii Theatre** (✰, 1130 Bethel St., downtown (© **808/528-0506**), still basking in its renaissance following a 4-year, $22-million renovation. The neoclassical beaux-arts landmark features a 1922 dome, 1,400 plush seats, a hydraulically elevated organ, a mezzanine lobby with two full bars, Corinthian columns, and gilt galore. Breathtaking murals, including a restored proscenium centerpiece lauded as Lionel Walden's "greatest creation," create an atmosphere that's making the theatre a leading multipurpose center for the performing arts.

The **Honolulu Symphony Orchestra** has booked some of its performances at the new theatre, but it still performs at the **Waikiki Shell** and the **Neal Blaisdell Concert Hall** (© **808/591-2211**). Also performing in the Blaisdell Concert Hall are the highly successful **Hawaii Opera Theatre,** now in its fourth decade (past hits have included *La Bohème, Carmen, Turandot, Romeo and Juliet, Rigoletto,* and *Aída*), and Hawaii's four ballet companies: **Hawaii Ballet Theatre, Ballet Hawaii, Hawaii State Ballet,** and **Honolulu Dance Theatre.**

Contemporary performances by **Dances We Dance** and the **Iona Pear Dance Company,** a strikingly creative Butoh group, are worth tracking down if you love the avant-garde.

SHOWROOM ACTS & REVUES

Showroom acts that have maintained a following are led by the tireless, disarming **Don Ho,** who still sings *Tiny Bubbles* and remains a fixture at the **Waikiki Beachcomber** hotel supper club, 2300 Kalakaua Ave., at Duke's Lane (© **800/ 923-3981**). He's corny as hell but attentive to fans as he accommodates their requests and sings nostalgic favorites. He's also very generous in sharing his stage with other Hawaiian performers, so guests are often in for surprise guest appearances by leading Hawaiian performers. Ho gives two shows an evening from Sunday through Thursday.

Across Kalakaua Avenue in the **Outrigger Waikiki on the Beach** (© 808/
923-0711), the **Society of Seven's** nightclub act (a blend of skits, Broadway
hits, popular music, and costumed musical acts) is into its third decade, no small
feat for performers.

Still sizzling in the Polynesian revue world is the Sheraton Princess Kaiulani's
"Creation—A Polynesian Odyssey" (© 808/931-4660) in the hotel's second-
floor Ainahau Showroom. Produced by **Tihati**, the state's largest entertainment
company, the show is a theatrical journey of fire dancing, special effects, illu-
sions, hula, and Polynesian dances from Hawaii and the South Pacific. Two dinner shows are held nightly at 5:15pm and 8pm. The first show costs $62, the
second show $55. Cocktail shows, priced at $32, are at 6 and 8:30pm.

LUAU!

Regrettably, there's no commercial luau on Oahu that comes close to Maui's Old
Lahaina Luau, or Hawaii Island's legendary Kona Village luau. The two major
choices on Oahu are **Germaine's** (© 808/941-3338) and **Paradise Cove Luau**
(© 808/842-5911), both located about a 40-minute drive away from Waikiki
on the leeward coast. Bus pickups and drop-offs in Waikiki are part of the deal.

Germaine's tries awfully hard and is a much more intimate affair, but
the experience is not as complete. Cost for Germaine's is $49 per adult, $39 for
14- to 20-year-olds, and $27 for 6- to 13-year-olds, including tax and trans-
portation. The shows are held nightly from 5:30 to 9:30pm.

Paradise Cove, too, is a mixed bag, with 600 to 800 guests a night. The small
thatched village makes it more of a Hawaiian theme park, with Hawaiian games,
hukilau net throwing and gathering, craft demonstrations, and a beautiful shoreline looking out over what is usually a storybook sunset. Tahitian dance, ancient
and modern hula, white-knuckle fire dancing, and robust entertainment make
this a fun-filled evening for those spirited enough to join in with the corny audi-
ence participation. The food is safe, though not breathtaking: Hawaiian kalua
pig, lomi salmon, poi, and coconut pudding and cake, as well as more traditional fare. Paradise Cove is extremely popular because of its idyllic setting and
good entertainment quality. Tickets, including transportation and taxes, are
$54.70 for adults, $33.85 for ages 6 to 12, $44.25 for ages 13 to 18, and free
for those 5 and under. Shows are held nightly from 5 to 8:30pm.

4 More Entertainment

FILM

A new 16-theater megaplex has opened in the **Victoria Ward** entertainment
center, at the corner of Auahi and Kamakee streets, and the **Windward Mall's**
10-screen megaplex is also bringing celluloid to the masses more conveniently.
This makes Honolulu's movie scene a galloping sprawl of more screens, more
seats and more multiplexes than ever before.

A quick check in both dailies and the *Honolulu Weekly* will tell you what's
playing where in the world of feature films. For film buffs and esoteric movie
lovers, **The Movie Museum,** 3566 Harding Ave. (© 808/735-8771), has special screenings of vintage films and rents a collection of hard-to-find, esoteric,
and classic films. The **Honolulu Academy of Arts Theatre,** 900 S. Beretania St.
(© 808/532-8768), is the film-as-art center of Honolulu, offering special
screenings, guest appearances, and cultural performances, as well as noteworthy
programs in the visual arts.

In the heart of Waikiki, on Kalakaua Avenue and on Seaside Avenue, three **Waikiki Theatres** are among the largest and most luxurious in multiplex-plagued Honolulu, showing major, mainstream feature films. In the university area of Moiliili, the **Varsity Twins,** at University Avenue near Beretania Street, specializes in the more avant-garde, artistically acclaimed releases. The Kahala Mall's **Kahala 8-Plex** and **Kapolei Megaplex** (a 16-theater complex), once the biggest movie theater complexes on the island, are eclipsed by the 18-screen **Dole Cannery** in Iwilei, the pineapple king of celluloid.

At the nine **Wallace Theatres** on Restaurant Row near downtown Honolulu, free parking in the evenings, discount matinees, and special discounted midnight shows take a big step toward making movies friendlier and more affordable.

DINNER CRUISES

The best news in the dinner cruise world is that the prominent cruises now offer more than a great sunset. Food quality has improved immensely, as in **Navatek's** (© **808/848-6360**) nightly dinner cruises off the coast of Waikiki. This means that the 140-foot-long, ultra-stable vessel not only promises spill-proof mai tais and a seasick-less ride, it is now in the gourmet dinner arena. The ride (and now the food, too) is worth a splurge.

Appendix:
Honolulu & Oahu in Depth

by Jeanette Foster

As the sun rises on the 21st century, other tropical islands are closing in on the 50th state's position as the world's premier beach destination. But Hawaii isn't just another pretty place in the sun. There's an undeniable quality ingrained in the local culture and lifestyle—the quick smiles to strangers, the feeling of family, the automatic extension of courtesy and tolerance. It's the aloha spirit.

1 History 101

Paddling outrigger canoes, the first ancestors of today's Hawaiians followed the stars and birds across a trackless sea to Hawaii, which they called "the land of raging fire." Those first settlers were part of the great Polynesian migration that settled the vast triangle of islands stretching from New Zealand in the southwest to Easter Island in the east to Hawaii in the north. No one is sure exactly when they came to Hawaii from Tahiti and the Marquesas Islands, some 2,500 miles to the south, but a dog-bone fishhook found at the southernmost tip of the Big Island has been carbon-dated to A.D. 700.

An entire Hawaiian culture arose from these settlers. Each island became a separate kingdom. The inhabitants built temples, fishponds, and aqueducts to irrigate taro plantations. Sailors became farmers and fishermen. The *alii* (high-ranking chiefs) created a caste system and established taboos. Ritual human sacrifices were common.

THE "FATAL CATASTROPHE" No ancient Hawaiian ever imagined a *haole* (a white person; literally, one with "no breath") would ever appear on one of these "floating islands." But then one day in 1779, just such a person sailed into Waimea Bay on Kauai, where he was welcomed as the god Lono.

The man was 50-year-old Capt. James Cook, already famous in Britain for "discovering" much of the South Pacific. Now on his third great voyage of exploration, Cook had set sail from Tahiti northward across uncharted waters to find the mythical Northwest Passage that was said to link the Pacific and Atlantic oceans. On his way, Cook stumbled upon the Hawaiian Islands quite by chance. He named them the Sandwich Islands, for the Earl of Sandwich, first lord of the admiralty, who had bankrolled the expedition.

Overnight, Stone-Age Hawaii entered the age of iron. Gifts were presented and objects traded: nails for fresh water, pigs, and the affections of Hawaiian women. The sailors brought syphilis, measles, and other diseases to which the Hawaiians had no natural immunity, thereby unwittingly wreaking havoc on the native population.

After his unsuccessful attempt to find the Northwest Passage, Cook returned to Kealakekua Bay on the Big Island, where a fight broke out over an alleged theft, and the great navigator was killed by a blow to the head. After this "fatal catastrophe," the British survivors sailed home. But Hawaii was now on the sea charts. French, Russian, American, and other traders on the fur route between

Canada's Hudson Bay Company and China anchored in Hawaii to get fresh water. More trade—and more disastrous liaisons—ensued.

Two more sea captains left indelible marks on the islands: The first was American John Kendrick, who in 1791 filled his ship with sandalwood and sailed to China. By 1825, Hawaii's sandalwood forests were gone, enabling invasive plants to take charge. The second captain was Englishman George Vancouver, who in 1793 left cows and sheep, which spread out to the high-tide lines. King Kamehameha I sent to Mexico and Spain for cowboys to round up the wild livestock, thus beginning the islands' *paniolo* tradition.

The tightly woven Hawaiian society, enforced by royalty and religious edicts, began to unravel after the death in 1819 of King Kamehameha I, who had used guns seized from a British ship to unite the islands under his rule. One of his successors, Queen Kaahumanu, abolished the old taboos, thus opening the door for religion of another form.

STAYING TO DO WELL   In April 1820, God-fearing missionaries arrived from New England, bent on converting the pagans. Intent on instilling their brand of rock-ribbed Christianity on the islands, the missionaries clothed the natives, banned them from dancing the hula, and nearly dismantled their ancient culture. They tried to keep the whalers and sailors out of the bawdy houses, where a flood of whiskey quenched fleet-sized thirsts and the virtue of native women was never safe. They taught reading and writing, created the 12-letter Hawaiian alphabet, started a printing press, and began recording the islands' history, until then only an oral account in remembered chants.

Children of the missionaries became the islands' business leaders and politicians. They married Hawaiians and stayed on in the islands, causing one wag to remark that the missionaries "came to do good and stayed to do well." In 1848, King Kamehameha III proclaimed the Great Mahele (division), which enabled commoners and eventually foreigners to own crown land. In two generations, more than 80% of all private land was in haole hands. Sugar planters imported waves of immigrants to work the fields as contract laborers. The first Chinese came in 1852, followed by Japanese in 1885 and Portuguese in 1878.

King David Kalakaua was elected to the throne in 1874. This popular "Merrie Monarch" built Iolani Palace in 1882, threw extravagant parties, and lifted the prohibitions on the hula and other native arts. For this, he was much loved. He also gave Pearl Harbor to the United States; it became the westernmost bastion of the U.S. Navy. In 1891, King Kalakaua visited chilly San Francisco, caught a cold, and died in the royal suite of the Sheraton Palace. His sister, Queen Liliuokalani, assumed the throne.

A SAD FAREWELL   On January 17, 1893, a group of American sugar planters and missionary descendants, with the support of gun-toting U.S. Marines, imprisoned Queen Liliuokalani in her own palace, where she penned the sorrowful lyric "Aloha Oe," Hawaii's song of farewell. The monarchy was dead.

A new republic was established, controlled by Sanford Dole, a powerful sugarcane planter. In 1898, through annexation, Hawaii became an American territory ruled by Dole. His fellow sugarcane planters, known as the Big Five, controlled banking, shipping, hardware, and every other facet of economic life on the islands.

Oahu's central Ewa Plain soon filled with row crops. The Dole family planted pineapple on its vast acreage. Planters imported more contract laborers from Puerto Rico (1900), Korea (1903), and the Philippines (1907–31). Most of the new immigrants stayed on to establish families and become a part of the islands. Meanwhile, the native Hawaiians became a landless minority.

For nearly a century on Hawaii, sugar was king, generously subsidized by the U.S. government. The sugarcane planters dominated the territory's economy, shaped its social fabric, and kept the islands in a colonial-plantation era with bosses and field hands. But the workers eventually struck for higher wages and improved working conditions, and the planters found themselves unable to compete with cheap third-world labor costs.

THE TOURISTS ARRIVE   Tourism proper began in the 1860s. Kilauea volcano was one of the world's prime attractions for adventure travelers, who rode on horseback 29 miles from Hilo to peer into the boiling hellfire. In 1865, a grass version of Volcano House was built on the Halemaumau Crater rim to shelter visitors; it was Hawaii's first tourist hotel. But tourism really got off the ground with the demise of the plantation era.

In 1901, W. C. Peacock built the elegant beaux-arts Moana Hotel on Waikiki Beach, and W. C. Weedon convinced Honolulu businessmen to bankroll his plan to advertise Hawaii in San Francisco. Armed with a stereopticon and tinted photos of Waikiki, Weedon sailed off in 1902 for 6 months of lecture tours to introduce "those remarkable people and the beautiful lands of Hawaii." He drew packed houses. A tourism-promotion bureau was formed in 1903, and about 2,000 visitors came to Hawaii that year.

Steamships were Hawaii's tourism lifeline. It took 4½ days to sail from San Francisco to Honolulu. Streamers, leis, and pomp welcomed each Matson liner at downtown's Aloha Tower. Well-heeled visitors brought trunks, servants, even their Rolls-Royces, and stayed for months. Hawaii amused the idle rich with personal tours, floral parades, and shows spotlighting that naughty dance, the hula.

Beginning in 1935 and running for the next 40 years, Webley Edwards's weekly live radio show, "Hawaii Calls," planted the sounds of Waikiki—surf, sliding steel guitar, sweet Hawaiian harmonies, drumbeats—in the hearts of millions of listeners in the United States, Australia, and Canada.

By 1936, visitors could fly to Honolulu from San Francisco on the *Hawaii Clipper,* a seven-passenger Pan American Martin M-130 flying boat, for $360 one way. The flight took 21 hours, 33 minutes. Modern tourism was born, with five flying boats providing daily service. The 1941 visitor count was a brisk 31,846 through December 6.

WORLD WAR II & ITS AFTERMATH   On December 7, 1941, Japanese Zeros came out of the rising sun to bomb American warships based at Pearl Harbor. This was the "day of infamy" that plunged the United States into World War II.

The aftermath of the attack brought immediate changes to the islands. Martial law was declared, stripping the Big Five cartel of its absolute power in a single day. Feared to be spies, Japanese Americans and German Americans were interned in Hawaii as well as in California. Hawaii was "blacked out" at night, Waikiki Beach was strung with barbed wire, and Aloha Tower was painted in camouflage. Only young men bound for the Pacific came to Hawaii during the war years. Many came back to graves in a cemetery called Punchbowl.

The postwar years saw the beginnings of Hawaii's faux culture. Harry Yee invented the Blue Hawaii cocktail and dropped in a tiny Japanese parasol. Vic Bergeron created the mai tai, a rum and fresh-lime-juice drink, and opened Trader Vic's, America's first theme restaurant that featured the art, decor, and food of Polynesia. Arthur Godfrey picked up a ukulele and began singing *hapa-haole* tunes on early TV shows. Burt Lancaster and Deborah Kerr made love in the surf at Hanauma Bay in 1954's *From Here to Eternity*. In 1955, Henry J. Kaiser built the Hilton Hawaiian Village, and the 11-story high-rise Princess Kaiulani Hotel opened on a site where the real princess once played. Hawaii greeted 109,000 visitors that year.

STATEHOOD In 1959, Hawaii became the 50th of the United States. That year also saw the arrival of the first jet airliners, which brought 250,000 tourists to the fledgling state. The personal touch that had defined aloha gave way to the sheer force of numbers. Waikiki's room count virtually doubled in 2 years, from 16,000 in 1969 to 31,000 units in 1971, and more followed before city fathers finally clamped a growth lid on the world's most famous resort. By 1980, annual arrivals had reached 4 million.

In the early 1980s, the Japanese began traveling overseas in record numbers, and they brought lots of yen to spend. Their effect on sales in Hawaii was phenomenal: European boutiques opened branches in Honolulu, and duty-free shopping became the main supporter of Honolulu International Airport. Japanese investors competed for the chance to own or build part of Hawaii. Hotels sold so fast and at such unbelievable prices that heads began to spin with dollar signs.

In 1986, Hawaii's visitor count passed 5 million. Two years later, it went over 6 million. Expensive fantasy megaresorts bloomed on the neighbor islands like giant artificial flowers, swelling the luxury market with ever-swankier accommodations.

The highest visitor count ever recorded was 6.9 million in 1990, but the bubble burst in early 1991 with the Gulf War and worldwide recessions. Airfare wars sent Americans to Mexico and the Caribbean. Overbuilt with luxury hotels, Hawaii slashed its room rates, giving middle-class consumers access to high-end digs at affordable prices—a trend that continues as Hawaii struggles to stay atop the tourism heap.

2 Hawaii Today

A CULTURAL RENAISSANCE A conch shell sounds, a young man in a bright feather cape chants, torchlight flickers at sunset on Waikiki Beach, and hula dancers begin telling their graceful centuries-old stories. It's a cultural scene out of the past come to life once again—for Hawaii is enjoying a renaissance of hula, chant, and other aspects of its ancient culture.

The biggest, longest, and most elaborate celebrations of Hawaiian culture are the Aloha Festivals, which encompass more than 500 cultural events from August to October. "Our goal is to teach and share our culture," says Gloriann Akau, who manages the Big Island's Aloha Festivals. "In 1946, after the war, Hawaiians needed an identity. We were lost and needed to regroup. When we started to celebrate our culture, we began to feel proud. We have a wonderful

---

Dancing the Hula

That naughty dance, the hula—once banned by missionaries and then almost forgotten in the rush to embrace America's consumer-based ideals—is today a movement of its own. In fact, it's rare to visit the islands these days and not see the real hula danced in traditional costumes.

culture that had been buried for a number of years. This brought it out again. Self-esteem is more important than making a lot of money."

In 1985, native Hawaiian educator, author, and *kupuna* George Kanahele started integrating Hawaiian values into hotels like the Big Island's Mauna Lani and Maui's Kaanapali Beach Hotel. (A *kupuna* is a respected elder with leadership qualities.) "You have the responsibility to preserve and enhance the Hawaiian culture, not because it's going to make money for you, but because it's the right thing to do," Kanahele told the Hawaii Hotel Association. "Ultimately, the only thing unique about Hawaii is its Hawaiianess. Hawaiianess is our competitive edge."

From general managers to maids, resort employees went through hours of Hawaiian cultural training. They held focus groups to discuss the meaning of *aloha*—the Hawaiian concept of unconditional love—and applied it to their work and their lives. Now many hotels have joined the movement and instituted Hawaiian programs. No longer content with teaching hula as a joke, resorts now employ a real *kumu hula* (hula teacher) to instruct visitors and have a *kupuna* take guests on treks to visit *heiau* (temples) and ancient petroglyph sites.

THE QUESTION OF SOVEREIGNTY   The Hawaiian cultural renaissance has also made its way into politics. Under the banner of sovereignty, many *kanaka maoli* (native people) are demanding restoration of rights taken away more than a century ago when the U.S. overthrew the Hawaiian monarchy and claimed the islands. Their demands were not lost on President Bill Clinton, who was picketed at a Democratic political fund-raiser at Waikiki Beach in July 1993. Four months later, Clinton signed a document stating that the U.S. Congress "apologizes to Native Hawaiians on behalf of the people of the United States for the overthrow of the Kingdom of Hawaii on January 17, 1893, with the participation of agents and citizens of the United States, and deprivation of the rights of Native Hawaiians to self-determination."

But even neonationalists aren't convinced that complete self-determination is possible. First, the Hawaiians themselves must decide if they want sovereignty, since each of the 30 identifiable sovereignty organizations (and more than 100 splinter groups) has a different stated goal, ranging from total independence to nation-within-a-nation status, similar to that of Native Indians. In 1993, the state legislature created a Hawaiian Sovereignty Advisory Commission to "determine the will of the native Hawaiian people." The commission plans to pose the sovereignty question in a referendum open to anyone over 18 with Hawaiian blood, no matter where they live.

3 Life & Language

Plantations brought so many different people to Hawaii that the state is now a rainbow of ethnic groups. Living here are Caucasians, African Americans, American Indians, Eskimos, Japanese, Chinese, Filipinos, Koreans, Tahitians, Vietnamese, Hawaiians, Samoans, Tongans, and other Asian and Pacific islanders. Add a few Canadians, Dutch, English, French, Germans, Irish, Italians, Portuguese, Scottish, Puerto Ricans, and Spaniards. Everyone's a minority here.

In combination, it's a remarkable potpourri. Nearly everyone, we've noticed, retains an element of the traditions of their homeland. Some Japanese Americans in Hawaii, even three and four generations removed from the homeland, are more traditional than the Japanese of Tokyo. And the same is true of many Chinese, Korean, Filipinos, and the rest of the 25 or so ethnic groups that make Hawaii a kind of living museum of various Asian and Pacific cultures.

THE HAWAIIAN LANGUAGE

Almost everyone here speaks English, so except for pronouncing the names of places, you should have no trouble communicating in Hawaii.

But many folks in Hawaii now speak Hawaiian as well, for the ancient language is making a comeback. All visitors will hear the words *aloha* and *mahalo* (thank you). If you've just arrived, you're a *malihini*. Someone who's been here a long time is a *kamaaina*. When you finish a job or your meal, you are *pau* (over). On Friday, it's *pau hana,* work over. You put *pupu* (Hawaii's version of hors d'oeuvres) in your mouth when you go *pau hana.*

The Hawaiian alphabet, created by the New England missionaries, has only 12 letters: the five regular vowels (a, e, i, o, and u) and seven consonants (h, k, l, m, n, p, and w). The vowels are pronounced in the Roman fashion, that is, *ah, ay, ee, oh,* and *oo* (as in "too")—not a*y, ee, eye, oh,* and *you,* as in English. For example, *huhu* is pronounced *who-who.* Most vowels are sounded separately, though some are pronounced together, as in Kalakaua: *Kah-lah-cow-ah.*

WHAT *HAOLE* MEANS   When Hawaiians first saw Western visitors, they called the pale-skinned, frail men *haole,* because they looked so out of breath. In Hawaiian, *ha* means *breath,* and *ole* means an absence of what precedes it. In other words, a lifeless-looking person. Today, the term *haole* is generally a synonym for Caucasian or foreigner and is used casually without any intended disrespect. However, if uttered by an angry stranger who adds certain adjectives (like "stupid"), the term can be construed as a mild racial slur.

SOME HAWAIIAN WORDS   Here are some basic Hawaiian words that you'll often hear in Hawaii and see throughout this book. For a more complete list of Hawaiian words, point your Web browser to **http://www.geocities. com/~olelo/hltableofcontents.html** or **http://www.hisurf.com/hawaiian/ dictionary.html**.

akamai   smart

alii   Hawaiian royalty

aloha   greeting or farewell

halau   school

hale   house or building

heiau   Hawaiian temple or place of worship

hui   club, assembly

kahuna   priest or expert

kamaaina   old-timer

kapa   tapa, bark cloth

kapu   taboo, forbidden

keiki   child

lanai   porch or veranda

lomilomi   massage

mahalo   thank you

makai   a direction, toward the sea

malihini   stranger, newcomer

mana   spirit power

mauka   a direction, toward the mountains

muumuu   loose-fitting gown or dress

nene   official state bird, a goose

ono   delicious

pali   cliff
paniolo   Hawaiian cowboy(s)
wiki   quick

PIDGIN: 'EH FO'REAL, BRAH

If you venture beyond the tourist areas, you might hear another local tongue: pidgin English. A conglomeration of slang and words from the Hawaiian language, pidgin developed as a method sugarcane planters used to communicate with their Chinese laborers in the 1800s.

"Broke da mouth" (tastes really good) is the favorite pidgin phrase and one you might hear; "'Eh fo'real, brah" means "It's true, brother." You could be invited to hear an elder "talk story" (relating myths and memories) or to enjoy local treats like "shave ice" (a tropical snow cone) and "crack seed" (highly seasoned preserved fruit). But since pidgin is really the province of the locals, your visit to Hawaii is likely to pass without your hearing much pidgin at all.

4 A Taste of Hawaii

by Jocelyn Fujii

TRIED & TRUE: HAWAII REGIONAL CUISINE

It was only a matter of time before the humble plate lunch became a culinary icon in Hawaii. These days, even the most chichi restaurant has a version of this modest Island symbol (not at plate lunch prices, of course), while the real-thing, carbo-driven lunch wagons have queues that never end.

Peter Merriman, a founding member of Hawaii Regional Cuisine, describes the current trend in Hawaii as a refinement, a tweaking upward, of everything from fine dining to down-home local cooking. "While fine dining is becoming finer, with more sophisticated wine lists and better service, the trend at the other end is that local food is becoming more refined as well," he explains. "Even the local, Hawaii-style cooks are using techniques they've learned from fancy hotels." Translated on the plate, this means sesame- or nori-crusted fresh catch on plate lunch menus, and huli huli chicken at five-diamond eateries, paired with Beaujolais and leeks and gourmet long rice.

At the same time, says Merriman, Hawaii Regional Cuisine, the style of cooking that put Hawaii on the international culinary map, has become watered down, a buzzword: "A lot of restaurants are paying lip service."

As it is with things au courant, it is easy to make the claim but another thing to live up to it. As Merriman points out, Hawaii Regional Cuisine was never solely about technique; it is equally about ingredients and the chef's creativity and integrity. "We continue to get local inspiration," says Merriman. "We've never restricted ourselves." If there is a fabulous French or Thai dish, chefs like Merriman will prepare it with local ingredients and add a creative edge that makes it distinctively theirs, distinctively Hawaii Regional.

Hawaii's tried-and-true baseline remains Hawaii Regional Cuisine (HRC), established in the mid-1980s in a culinary revolution that catapulted Hawaii into the global epicurean arena. The international training, creative vigor, fresh ingredients, and cross-cultural menus of the 12 original HRC chefs have made the islands a dining destination applauded and emulated nationwide. (In a tip of the toque to island tradition, *ahi*—a word ubiquitous in Hawaii—has replaced *tuna* on many chic New York menus.) And other options have proliferated at all levels of the local dining spectrum: Waves of new Asian residents have transplanted the traditions of their homelands to the fertile soil of Hawaii, resulting in unforgettable taste treats true to their Thai, Vietnamese, Japanese, Chinese, and Indo-Pacific roots. When combined with the bountiful, fresh harvests from sea and land for which Hawaii is known, these ethnic and culinary traditions take on renewed vigor and a cross-cultural, uniquely Hawaiian quality.

While in Hawaii, you'll encounter many labels that embrace the fundamentals of HRC and the sophistication, informality, and nostalgia it encompasses. Euro-Asian, Pacific Rim, Indo-Pacific, Pacific Edge, Euro-Pacific, Fusion cuisine, Hapa cuisine—by whatever name, Hawaii Regional Cuisine has evolved as Hawaii's singular cooking style, what some say is this country's current gastronomic, as well as geographic, frontier. It highlights the fresh seafood and produce of Hawaii's rich waters and volcanic soil, the cultural traditions of Hawaii's ethnic groups, and the skills of well-trained chefs—such as Merriman, Roy Yamaguchi, George Mavrothalassitis, Alan Wong, Beverly Gannon, Philippe Padovani, and Jean-Marie Josselin—who broke ranks with their European predecessors to forge new ground in the 50th state.

Fresh ingredients are foremost here. Farmers and fishermen work together to provide steady supplies of just-harvested seafood, seaweed, fern shoots, vine-ripened tomatoes, goat cheese, lamb, herbs, taro, gourmet lettuces, and countless harvests from land and sea. These ingredients wind up in myriad forms on ever-changing menus, prepared in Asian and Western culinary styles. Exotic fruits introduced by recent Southeast Asian emigrants—such as sapodilla, soursop, and rambutan—are beginning to appear regularly in Chinatown markets. Aquacultured seafood, from seaweed to salmon to lobster, is a staple on many menus. Additionally, fresh-fruit sauces (mango, litchi, papaya, pineapple, guava), ginger-sesame-wasabi flavorings, corn cakes with sake sauces, tamarind and fish sauces, coconut-chile accents, tropical-fruit vinaigrettes, and other local and newly arrived seasonings from Southeast Asia and the Pacific impart unique qualities to the preparations.

Here's a sampling of what you can expect to find on a Hawaii Regional menu: seared Hawaiian fish with lilikoi shrimp butter; taro-crab cakes; Pahoa corn cakes; Molokai sweet-potato or breadfruit vichyssoise; Ka'u orange sauce and Kahua Ranch lamb; fern shoots from Waipio Valley; Maui onion soup and Hawaiian bouillabaisse, with fresh snapper, Kona crab, and fresh aquacultured shrimp; blackened ahi summer rolls; herb-crusted onaga; and gourmet Waimanalo greens. You may also encounter locally made cheeses, squash and taro risottos, Polynesian imu-baked foods, and guava-smoked meats. If there's pasta or risotto or rack of lamb on the menu, it could be *nori* (red algae) linguine with *opihi* (limpet) sauce, or risotto with local seafood served in taro cups, or rack of lamb in cabernet and *hoisin* sauce (fermented soybean, garlic, and spices). Watch for ponzu sauce, too; it's lemony and zesty, much more flavorful than the soy sauce it resembles, and a welcome new staple on local menus.

PLATE LUNCHES & MORE: LOCAL FOOD

At the other end of the spectrum is the vast and endearing world of "local food." By that, we mean plate lunches and poke, shave ice and saimin, bento lunches and manapua—cultural hybrids all.

Reflecting a polyglot population of many styles and ethnicities, Hawaii's idiosyncratic dining scene is eminently inclusive. Consider Surfer Chic: Barefoot in the sand, in a swimsuit, you chow down on a **plate lunch** ordered from a lunch wagon, consisting of fried mahimahi, "two scoops rice," macaroni salad, and a few leaves of green, typically julienned cabbage. (Generally, teriyaki beef and shoyu chicken are options.) Heavy gravy is often the condiment of choice, accompanied by a soft drink in a paper cup. Like **saimin**—the local version of noodles in broth topped with scrambled eggs, green onions, and, sometimes, pork—the plate lunch is Hawaii's version of high camp.

Because this is Hawaii, at least a few licks of *poi*—cooked, pounded taro (the traditional Hawaiian staple crop)—and the other examples of indigenous cuisine are a must. Other **native foods** include those from before and after Western contact, such as *laulau* (pork, chicken, or fish steamed in ti leaves), *kalua* pork (pork cooked in a Polynesian underground oven known as an *imu*), *lomi* salmon (salted salmon with tomatoes and green onions), squid *luau* (cooked in coconut milk and taro tops), *poke* (cubed raw fish seasoned with onions and seaweed and the occasional sprinkling of roasted *kukui* nuts), *haupia* (creamy coconut pudding), and *kulolo* (steamed pudding of coconut, brown sugar, and taro).

Bento, another popular quick meal available throughout Hawaii, is a compact, boxed assortment of picnic fare usually consisting of neatly arranged sections of rice, pickled vegetables, and fried chicken, beef, or pork. Increasingly, however, the bento is becoming more health-conscious, as in macrobiotic bento lunches or vegetarian brown-rice bentos. A derivative of the modest lunch box for Japanese immigrants who once labored in the sugarcane and pineapple fields, bentos are dispensed everywhere, from department stores to corner delis and supermarkets.

Also from the plantations come **manapua,** a bready, doughy sphere filled with tasty fillings of sweetened pork or sweet beans. In the old days, the Chinese "manapua man" would make his rounds with bamboo containers balanced on a rod over his shoulders. Today, you'll find white or whole-wheat manapua containing chicken, vegetables, curry, and other savory fillings.

The daintier Chinese delicacy **dim sum** is made of translucent wrappers filled with fresh seafood, pork hash, and vegetables, served for breakfast and lunch in Chinatown restaurants. The Hong Kong–style dumplings are ordered fresh and hot from bamboo steamers from invariably brusque servers who move their carts from table to table. Much like hailing a taxi in Manhattan, you have to be quick and loud for dim sum.

For dessert or a snack, particularly on Oahu's north shore, the prevailing choice is **shave ice,** the island version of a snow cone. Particularly on hot, humid days, long lines of shave-ice lovers gather for the rainbow-colored cones heaped with finely shaved ice and topped with sweet tropical syrups. (The sweet-sour *li hing mui* flavor is a current rage.)

You may also encounter *malassadas,* the Portuguese version of doughnuts, and if you do, it's best to eat them immediately. A leftover malassada has all the appeal of a heavy, lumpy, cold doughnut. When fresh and hot, however, as at school carnivals (where they attract the longest lines), bakeries, and roadside stands (such as Agnes Portuguese Bake Shop in Kailua), this sugary, yeasty doughnut-without-a-hole is an enduring legacy of the Portuguese in Hawaii.

AHI, ONO & OPAKAPAKA: A HAWAIIAN SEAFOOD PRIMER

The seafood in Hawaii has been described as the best in the world. In Janice Wald Henderson's pivotal book *The New Cuisine of Hawaii,* acclaimed chef Nobuyuki Matsuhisa (chef/owner of Matsuhisa in Beverly Hills and Nobu in

Manhattan and London) writes, "As a chef who specializes in fresh seafood, I am in awe of the quality of Hawaii's fish; it is unparalleled anywhere else in the world." And why not? Without a doubt, the islands' surrounding waters, including the waters of the remote northwestern Hawaiian Islands, and a growing aquaculture industry contribute to the high quality of the seafood here.

The reputable restaurants in Hawaii buy fresh fish daily at predawn auctions or from local fishermen. Some chefs even catch their ingredients themselves. "Still wiggling" or "just off the hook" are the ultimate terms for freshness in Hawaii. The fish can then be grilled over *kiawe* (mesquite) or prepared in innumerable other ways.

Although most menus include the Western description for the fresh fish used, most often the local nomenclature is listed, turning dinner for the uninitiated into a confusing, quasi-foreign experience. To help familiarize you with the menu language of Hawaii, here's a basic glossary of island fish:

ahi   yellowfin or bigeye tuna, important for its use in sashimi and poke at sushi bars and in Hawaii Regional Cuisine

aku   skipjack tuna, heavily used by local families in home cooking and poke

ehu   red snapper, delicate and sumptuous, yet lesser known than opakapaka

hapuupuu   grouper, a sea bass whose use is expanding from ethnic to nonethnic restaurants

hebi   spearfish, mildly flavored, and frequently featured as the "catch of the day" in upscale restaurants

kajiki   Pacific blue marlin, also called *au*, with a firm flesh and high fat content that make it a plausible substitute for tuna in some raw fish dishes and as a grilled item on menus

kumu   goatfish, a luxury item on Chinese and upscale menus, served *en papillote* or steamed whole, Oriental style, with sesame oil, scallions, ginger, and garlic

mahimahi   dolphin fish (the game fish, not the mammal) or dorado, a classic sweet, white-fleshed fish requiring vigilance among purists, because it's often disguised as fresh when it's actually "fresh-frozen"—a big difference

monchong   bigscale or sickle pomfret, an exotic, tasty fish, scarce but gaining a higher profile on Hawaiian Island menus

nairagi   striped marlin, also called *au;* good as sashimi and in poke, and often substituted for ahi in raw-fish products

onaga   ruby snapper, a luxury fish, versatile, moist, and flaky

ono   wahoo, firmer and drier than the snappers, often served grilled and in sandwiches

opah   moonfish, rich and fatty, and versatile—cooked, raw, smoked, and broiled

opakapaka   pink snapper, light, flaky, and luxurious, suited for sashimi, poaching, sautéing, and baking; the best-known upscale fish

papio   jack trevally, light, firm, and flavorful and favored in island cookery

shutome   broadbill swordfish, of beeflike texture and rich flavor

tombo   albacore tuna, with a high fat content, suitable for grilling and sautéing

uhu   parrotfish, most often encountered steamed, Chinese style

uku   gray snapper of clear, pale-pink flesh, delicately flavored and moist

ulua   large jack trevally, firm-fleshed and versatile

5 The Natural World: An Environmental Guide to the Islands

The first Hawaiian islands were born of violent volcanic eruptions that took place deep beneath the ocean's surface, about 70 million years ago—more than 200 million years after the major continental landmasses had been formed. As soon as the islands emerged, Mother Nature's fury began to carve beauty from barren rock. Untiring volcanoes spewed forth rivers of fire that cooled into stone. Severe tropical storms, some with hurricane-force winds, battered and blasted the cooling lava rock into a series of shapes. Ferocious earthquakes flattened, shattered, and reshaped the islands into precipitous valleys, jagged cliffs, and recumbent flatlands. Monstrous surf and gigantic tidal waves rearranged and polished the lands above and below the reaches of the tide.

Oahu is the third-largest island in Hawaii (behind the Big Island and Maui), and the most urban. Oahu is defined by two mountain ranges: the Waianae Ridge in the west, and the jagged Koolaus in the east, which form a backdrop for Honolulu. These ranges divide the island into three different environments. The windward (eastern) side is lush with greenery, ferns, tropical plants, and waterfalls. On the leeward (western) side, the area between the Waianae Range and the ocean is drier, with sparse vegetation, little rainfall, and an arid landscape. Between the two mountain ranges lies the central Ewa Valley; it's moderate in temperature and vibrant with tropical plants, agricultural fields, and trees.

THE FLORA OF THE ISLANDS

Hawaii is filled with sweet-smelling flowers, lush vegetation, and exotic plant life.

AFRICAN TULIP TREES   Even from afar, you can see the flaming red flowers on these large trees, which can grow to be more than 50 feet tall. Children in Hawaii love them because the buds hold water—they use the flowers as water pistols.

ANGEL'S TRUMPETS   These small trees can grow up to 20 feet tall, with an abundance of large (up to 10 in. in diameter) pendants—white or pink flowers that resemble, well, trumpets. The Hawaiians call them *nana-honua,* which means "earth gazing." The flowers, which bloom continually from early spring to late fall, have a musky scent. *Beware:* All parts of the plant are poisonous and contain a strong narcotic.

ANTHURIUMS   One of Hawaii's most popular cut flowers, anthuriums originally came from the tropical Americas and the Caribbean islands. There are more than 550 species, but the most popular are the heart-shaped red, orange, pink, white, and even purple flowers with tail-like spathes. Look for the heart-shaped green leaves in shaded areas. These exotic plants have no scent but will last several weeks as cut flowers.

BANYAN TREES   Among the world's largest trees, banyans have branches that grow out and away from the trunk, forming descending roots that grow down to the ground to feed and form additional trunks, making the tree very stable during tropical storms.

BIRDS OF PARADISE   These natives of Africa have become something of a trademark of Hawaii. They're easily recognizable by the orange and blue flowers nestled in gray-green bracts, looking somewhat like birds in flight.

Marijuana

This not-so-rare-and-unusual plant—called *pakalolo,* or "crazy weed," in Hawaiian—is grown throughout the islands. You probably won't see it as you drive along the roads, but if you go hiking, you may glimpse the feathery green leaves with tight clusters of buds. Despite years of police efforts to eradicate the plant, its cultivation continues. If you're tempted to pick a few buds, don't give in. The captains of this nefarious industry don't take kindly to poaching.

BOUGAINVILLEA Originally from Brazil, these vines feature colorful, tissue-thin bracts, ranging in color from majestic purple to fiery orange, that hide tiny white flowers.

BREADFRUIT TREES A large tree—more than 60 feet tall—with broad, sculpted, dark-green leaves, the famous breadfruit produces a round, head-size green fruit that's a staple in the diets of all Polynesians. When roasted or baked, the whitish-yellow meat tastes somewhat like a sweet potato.

BROMELIADS There are more than 1,400 species of bromeliads, of which the pineapple plant is the best known. "Bromes," as they're affectionately called, are generally spiky plants ranging in size from a few inches to several feet in diameter. They're popular not only for their unusual foliage but also for their strange and wonderful flowers. Used widely in landscaping and interior decoration, especially in resort areas, bromeliads are found on every island.

COFFEE Hawaii is the only state that produces coffee commercially. Coffee is an evergreen shrub with shiny, waxy, dark-green, pointed leaves. The flower is a small, fragrant white blossom that develops into half-inch berries that turn bright red when ripe. Look for large coffee plantations on Oahu.

GINGER White and yellow ginger flowers are perhaps the most fragrant in Hawaii. Usually found in clumps growing 4 to 7 feet tall in areas blessed by rain, these sweet-smelling, 3-inch-wide flowers are composed of three dainty petal-like stamens and three long, thin petals. Ginger is so prevalent that many people assume it is native to Hawaii; actually, it was introduced in the 19th century from the Indonesia-Malaysia area. Look for white and yellow ginger from late spring to fall. If you see ginger on the side of the road, stop and pick a few blossoms—your car will be filled with a divine fragrance the rest of the day.

Other members of the ginger family frequently seen in Hawaii (there are some 700 species) include red, shell, and torch ginger. Red ginger consists of tall, green stalks with foot-long red "flower heads." The red "petals" are actually bracts, which protect the 1-inch-long white flowers; to see the flowers, look down into the red head. Red ginger, which does not share the heavenly smell of white ginger, lasts a week or longer when cut. Look for red ginger from spring through late fall. Shell ginger, which originated in India and Burma, thrives in cool, wet mountain forests. These plants, with their pearly-white, clam shell–like blossoms, bloom from spring to fall.

Perhaps the most exotic ginger is the red or pink torch ginger. Cultivated in Malaysia as seasoning (the young flower shoots are used in curries), torch ginger rises directly out of the ground. The flower stalks, which are about 5 to 8 inches in length, resemble the fire of a lighted torch. This is one of the few types of ginger that can bloom year-round.

HELICONIA   Some 80 species of the colorful heliconia family came to Hawaii from the Caribbean and Central and South America. The bright yellow, red, green, and orange bracts overlap and appear to unfold like origami birds. The most obvious heliconia to spot is the lobster claw, which resembles a string of boiled crustacean pincers. Another prolific heliconia is the parrot's beak; growing to about hip height, it's composed of bright-orange flower bracts with black tips. Look for parrot's beaks in spring and summer.

HIBISCUS   The 4- to 6-inch hibiscus flowers bloom year-round and come in a range of colors, from lily white to lipstick red. The flowers resemble crepe paper, with stamens and pistils protruding spire-like from the center. Hibiscus hedges can grow up to 15 feet tall. The yellow hibiscus is Hawaii's official state flower.

JACARANDA   Beginning around March and sometimes lasting until early May, these huge, lacy-leaved trees metamorphose into large clusters of spectacular lavender-blue sprays. The bell-shaped flowers drop quickly, leaving a majestic purple carpet beneath the tree.

MACADAMIA   A transplant from Australia, macadamia nuts have become a commercial crop in recent decades in Hawaii, especially on the Big Island and Maui. The large trees—up to 60 feet tall—bear a hard-shelled nut encased in a leathery husk, which splits open and dries when ripe.

MONKEYPOD TREES   The monkeypod is one of Hawaii's most majestic trees; it grows more than 80 feet tall and 100 feet across. Seen near older homes and in parks, the leaves of the monkeypod drop in February and March. Its wood is a favorite of woodworking artisans.

NIGHT-BLOOMING CEREUS   Look along rock walls for this spectacular night-blooming flower. Originally from Central America, this vinelike member of the cactus family has green scalloped edges and produces foot-long white flowers that open as darkness falls and wither as the sun rises. The plant also bears an edible red fruit.

ORCHIDS   To many minds, nothing says Hawaii more than orchids. The orchid family is the largest in the entire plant kingdom. The most widely grown variety—and the major source of flowers for leis and garnish for tropical libations—is the vanda orchid. The vandas used in Hawaii's commercial flower industry are generally lavender or white, but they grow in a rainbow of colors, shapes, and sizes. The orchids used for corsages are the large, delicate cattleya; the ones used in floral arrangements—you'll probably see them in your hotel lobby—are usually dendrobiums.

PANDANUS (HALA)   Called *hala* by Hawaiians, pandanus is native to Polynesia. Thanks to its thick trunk, stiltlike supporting roots, and crown of long, swordlike leaves, the hala tree is easy to recognize. In what is quickly becoming a dying art, Hawaiians weave the *lau* (leaves) of the hala into hats, baskets, mats, bags, and the like.

PLUMERIA   Also known as frangipani, this sweet-smelling, five-petal flower, found in clusters on trees, is the most popular choice of lei makers. The Singapore plumeria has five creamy-white petals, with a touch of yellow in the center.

Another popular variety, ruba—with flowers from soft pink to flaming red—is also used in leis. When picking plumeria, be careful of the sap from the flower, as it's poisonous and can stain clothes.

PROTEA Originally from South Africa, this unusual oversized shrub comes in more than 40 different varieties. The flowers of one species resemble pincushions; those of another look like a bouquet of feathers. Once dried, proteas will last for years.

SILVERSWORD This very uncommon and unusual plant is seen only on the Big Island and in the Haleakala Crater on Maui. This rare relative of the sunflower family blooms between July and September. The silversword in bloom is a fountain of red-petaled, daisylike flowers that turn silver soon after blooming.

TARO Around pools, near streams, and in neatly planted fields, you'll see these green heart-shaped leaves, whose dense roots are a Polynesian staple. The ancient Hawaiians pounded the roots into *poi*. Originally from Sri Lanka, taro is not only a food crop, but is also grown for ornamental reasons.

THE FAUNA OF THE ISLANDS

When the first Polynesians arrived in Hawaii between A.D. 500 and 800, scientists say they found some 67 varieties of endemic Hawaiian birds, a third of which are now believed to be extinct. What's even more astonishing is what they didn't find—there were no reptiles, amphibians, mosquitoes, lice, fleas, or even a cockroach.

There were only two endemic mammals: the hoary bat and the monk seal. The **hoary bat** must have accidentally blown to Hawaii at some point, from either North or South America. It can still be seen during its early evening forays, especially around the Kilauea Crater on the Big Island.

The **Hawaiian monk seal,** a relative of warm-water seals found in the Caribbean and the Mediterranean, was nearly slaughtered into extinction for its skin and oil during the 19th century. These seals have recently experienced a minor population explosion; sometimes they even turn up at various beaches throughout the state. They're protected under federal law by the Marine Mammals Protection Act. If you're fortunate enough to see a monk seal, just look; don't disturb one of Hawaii's living treasures.

The first Polynesians brought a few animals from home: dogs, pigs, and chickens (all were for eating), as well as rats (stowaways). All four species are still found in the Hawaiian wild today.

BIRDS

More species of native birds have become extinct in Hawaii in the last 200 years than anywhere else on the planet. Of 67 native species, 23 are extinct and 30 are endangered. Even the Hawaiian crow, the **alala,** is threatened.

The **aeo,** or Hawaiian stilt—a 16-inch-long bird with a black head, black coat, white underside, and long pink legs—can be found in protected wetlands. You can also see protected birds at the Goat Island bird refuge off Oahu, where wedge-tailed shearwaters nest.

There are 22 species of native **honeycreepers,** whose songs fill the forest. Frequently seen are the **apapane** (a red bird with black wings and a curved black bill), **iiwi** (another red bird with black wings but with orange legs and a salmon-colored bill), **amakihi** (a plain olive-green bird with a long, straight bill), and **anianiau** (a tiny yellow bird with a thin, curved bill). Also in the forest is the

elepaio, a small, gray flycatcher with an orange breast and an erect tail. A curious fellow, the elepaio comes out to investigate any unusual whistles. The **moa,** or red jungle fowl, was a chicken brought to Hawaii by the Polynesians.

Among the seabirds that frequent Hawaii are **red-** and **white-footed boobies, wedge-tailed shearwaters, frigate birds, red-tailed tropic birds,** and the **Laysan albatross.**

The **nene** is Hawaii's state bird. It's being brought back from the brink of extinction through strenuous protection laws and captive breeding. A relative of the Canada goose, the nene stands about 2 feet high and has a black head and yellow cheek, a buff neck with deep furrows, a grayish-brown body, and clawed feet. It gets its name from its nasal, two-syllable call, "nay-nay." The approximately 500 nenes in existence can be seen in only three places: at Haleakala National Park on Maui, at Mauna Kea State Park bird sanctuary, and on the slopes of Mauna Kea on the Big Island.

SEA LIFE

Approximately 680 species of fish are known to inhabit the waters around the Hawaiian Islands. Of those, approximately 450 species stay close to the reef and inshore areas.

CORAL   The reefs surrounding Hawaii are made up of various coral and algae. The living coral grows through sunlight that feeds a specialized type of algae, which in turn allows the development of the coral's calcareous skeleton. The reef, which takes thousands of years to develop, attracts and supports fish and crustaceans, which use it for food and habitat. Mother Nature can batter the reef with a strong storm or large waves, but humans—through seemingly innocuous acts such as touching the coral—have proven far more destructive.

The corals most frequently seen in Hawaii are hard, rocklike formations named for their familiar shapes: antler, cauliflower, finger, plate, and razor coral. Wire coral looks like a randomly bent wire growing straight out of the reef. Some coral appears soft, such as tube coral; it can be found in the ceilings of caves. Black coral, which resembles winter-bare trees or shrubs, is found at depths of more than 100 feet.

REEF FISH   Of the approximately 450 types of reef fish here, about 27% are native to Hawaii and are found nowhere else in the world. During the millions of years it took for the islands to sprout up from the sea, ocean currents—mainly from Southeast Asia—carried thousands of marine animals and plants to Hawaii's reef; of those, approximately 100 species not only adapted, but also thrived.

Some species are much bigger and more plentiful than their Pacific cousins, and many developed unique characteristics. Some, like the lemon or milletseed butterflyfish, developed specialized schooling and feeding behaviors. Hawaii's

---

Leapin' Lizards!

Geckos are harmless, soft-skinned, insect-eating lizards that come equipped with suction pads on their feet, enabling them to climb walls and windows to reach tasty insects such as mosquitoes and cockroaches. You'll see them on windows outside a lighted room at night or hear their cheerful chirp.

native fish are often surprisingly common: You can see the saddleback wrasse, for example, on virtually any snorkeling excursion or dive in Hawaiian waters. You're likely to spot one or more of the following fish while underwater:

Angelfish, often mistaken for butterflyfish, can be distinguished by the spine, located low on the gill plate. These fish are very shy; several species live in colonies close to coral for protection.

Blennies are small, elongated fish, ranging from 2 to 10 inches long, with the majority in the 3- to 4-inch range. Blennies are so small that they can live in tide pools; you might have a hard time spotting one.

Butterflyfish, among the most colorful of the reef fish, are usually seen in pairs (scientists believe they mate for life) and appear to spend most of their day feeding. There are 22 species of butterflyfish, of which three (bluestripe, lemon or milletseed, and multiband or pebbled butterflyfish) are endemic. Most butterflyfish have a dark band through the eye and a spot near the tail resembling an eye, meant to confuse their predators (moray eels love to lunch on them).

Moray and **conger eels** are the most common eels seen in Hawaii. Morays are usually docile except when provoked or when there's food or an injured fish around. Unfortunately, some morays have been fed by divers and—being intelligent creatures—associate divers with food; thus, they can become aggressive. But most morays like to keep to themselves, hidden in their hole or crevice. While morays may look menacing, conger eels look downright happy, with big lips and pectoral fins (situated so that they look like big ears) that give them the appearance of a perpetually smiling face. Conger eels have crushing teeth so they can feed on crustaceans; because they're sloppy eaters, they usually live with shrimp and crabs that feed off the crumbs they leave.

Parrotfish, one of the largest and most colorful of the reef fish, can grow up to 40 inches long. They're easy to spot—their front teeth are fused together, protruding like buck teeth and resembling a parrot's beak. These unique teeth allow them to feed by scraping algae from rocks and coral. The rocks and coral pass through the parrotfish's system, resulting in fine sand. In fact, most of the white sand found in Hawaii is parrotfish waste; one large parrotfish can produce a ton of sand a year. Native parrotfish species include yellowbar, regal, and spectacled.

Scorpionfish are what scientists call "ambush predators": They hide under camouflaged exteriors and ambush their prey. Several kinds sport a venomous dorsal spine. These fish don't have a gas bladder, so when they stop swimming, they sink—that's why you usually find them "resting" on ledges and on the ocean bottom. Although they're not aggressive, an inattentive snorkeler or diver could feel the effects of those venomous spines—so be very careful where you put your hands and feet in the water.

Surgeonfish, sometimes called *tang,* get their name from the scalpel-like spines located on each side of the body near the base of the tail. Some surgeonfish have a rigid spine, while others have the ability to fold the spines against the body until they're needed for defense purposes. Several surgeonfish, such as the brightly colored yellow tang, are boldly colored; others are adorned in more conservative shades of gray, brown, or black. The only endemic surgeonfish—and the most abundant in Hawaiian waters—is the convict tang, a pale white fish with vertical black stripes (like a convict's uniform).

Wrasses are a very diverse family of fish, ranging in length from 2 to 15 inches. Wrasses can change gender from female (when young) to male. Some have brilliant coloration that changes as they age. Several types of wrasse are endemic to Hawaii: Hawaiian cleaner, shortnose, belted, and gray (or old woman).

GAME FISH   Hawaii is known around the globe as *the* place for big-game fish—marlin, swordfish, and tuna—but its waters are also great for catching other offshore fish like mahimahi, rainbow runner, and wahoo; coastal fish like barracuda and scad; bottom fish like snappers, sea bass, and amberjack; and inshore fish like trevally and bonefish.

Six kinds of **billfish** are found in the offshore waters around the islands: Pacific blue marlin, black marlin, sailfish, broadbill swordfish, striped marlin, and shortbill spearfish. Hawaii billfish range in size from the 20-pound shortbill spearfish and striped marlin to the 1,805-pound Pacific blue marlin, the largest marlin ever caught with rod and reel in the world.

Tuna ranges in size from small (1 lb. or less) mackerel tuna used as bait (Hawaiians call them *oioi*) to 250-pound yellowfin ahi tuna. Other local species of tuna are bigeye, albacore, kawakawa, and skipjack.

Other types of fish, also excellent for eating, include **mahimahi** (also known as dolphin fish or dorado), in the 20- to 70-pound range; **rainbow runner,** from 15 to 30 pounds; and **wahoo** (*ono*), from 15 to 80 pounds. Shoreline fishermen are always on the lookout for **trevally** (the state record for a giant trevally is 191 lbs.), **bonefish, ladyfish, threadfin, leatherfish,** and **goatfish.** Bottom fishermen pursue a range of **snapper**—red, pink, gray, and others—as well as **sea bass** (the state record is a whopping 563 lbs.) and **amberjack** (which weigh up to 100 lbs.).

WHALES   Humpback whales are the popular visitors who come to Hawaii to mate and calve every year, beginning in November and staying until spring (Apr or so), when they return to their summer home in Alaska. On every island, you can take winter whale-watching cruises that will let you observe these magnificent leviathans close up. You can also spot their signature spouts from shore as they expel water in the distance. Humpbacks grow to up to 45 feet long, so when they breach (propel their entire body out of the water) or even wave a fluke, you can see it for miles.

Humpbacks are among the biggest whales found in Hawaiian waters, but other whales—such as pilot, sperm, false killer, melon-headed, pygmy killer, and beaked—can be seen year-round. These whales usually travel in pods of 20 to 40 animals and are very social, interacting with one another on the surface.

SHARKS   Yes, there *are* sharks in Hawaii, but you more than likely won't see one unless you're specifically looking. About 40 different species of sharks inhabit the waters surrounding Hawaii, ranging from the totally harmless whale shark (at 60 ft., the world's largest fish), which has no teeth and is so docile that it frequently lets divers ride on its back, to the not-so-docile, infamous, and extremely uncommon great white shark. The most common sharks seen in Hawaii are white-tip reef sharks, gray reef sharks (about 5 ft. long), and black-tip reef sharks (about 6 ft. long).

HAWAII'S ECOSYSTEM PROBLEMS

Officials at Hawaii Volcanoes National Park on the Big Island saw a potential problem a few decades ago with people taking a few rocks home with them as "souvenirs." To prevent this problem from escalating, the park rangers created a legend that the fiery volcano goddess, Pele, did not like people taking anything (rocks, chunks of lava) from her home, and bad luck would befall anyone disobeying her wishes. There used to be a display case in the park's visitor center filled with letters from people who had taken rocks from the volcano, relating stories of all the bad luck that followed. Most of the letters begged Pele's forgiveness and instructed the rangers to please return the rock to the exact location that was its original home.

Unfortunately, Hawaii's other ecosystem problems can't be handled as easily.

MARINE LIFE   Hawaii's beautiful and abundant marine life has attracted so many visitors that they threaten to overwhelm it. A great example of this over-enthusiasm is Oahu's beautiful **Hanauma Bay.** Crowds flock to this marine preserve, which features calm, protected swimming and snorkeling areas loaded with tropical reef fish. Its popularity forced government officials to limit admissions and charge an entrance fee. Commercial tour operators have also been restricted in an effort to balance the people-to-fish ratio.

All of Hawaii's reefs have faced increasing impact over the years. Runoff of soil and chemicals from construction, agriculture, erosion, and even heavy storms can blanket and choke a reef, which needs sunlight to survive. In addition, the intrusion of foreign elements—caused by such things as breaks in sewage lines—can cause problems; human contact with the reef can also upset the ecosystem. Coral, the basis of the reef system, is very fragile; snorkelers and divers grabbing onto it can break off pieces that took decades to form. Feeding the fish can also upset the balance of the ecosystem (not to mention upsetting the digestive systems of the fish). In areas where they're fed, the normally shy reef fish become more aggressive, surrounding divers and demanding food.

FLORA   The rain forests are among Hawaii's most fragile environments. Any intrusion—from hikers carrying seeds on their shoes to the rooting of wild boars—can upset the delicate balance of these complete ecosystems. In recent years, development has moved closer and closer to the rain forests.

FAUNA   The biggest impact on the fauna in Hawaii is the decimation of native birds by feral animals, which have destroyed the bird's habitats, and by mongooses that have eaten the birds' eggs and young. Government officials are vigilant about snakes because of the potential damage they can do to the remaining bird life.

Index

See also Accommodations and Restaurant indexes below.

FROMMER'S® COMPLETE TRAVEL GUIDES

Alaska
Amsterdam
Argentina & Chile
Arizona
Atlanta
Australia
Austria
Bahamas
Barcelona, Madrid & Seville
Beijing
Belgium, Holland & Luxembourg
Bermuda
Boston
British Columbia & the Canadian Rockies
Budapest & the Best of Hungary
California
Canada
Cancún, Cozumel & the Yucatán
Cape Cod, Nantucket & Martha's Vineyard
Caribbean
Caribbean Cruises & Ports of Call
Caribbean Ports of Call
Carolinas & Georgia
Chicago
China
Colorado
Costa Rica
Denmark
Denver, Boulder & Colorado Springs
England
Europe
European Cruises & Ports of Call
Florida
France

Germany
Great Britain
Greece
Greek Islands
Hawaii
Hong Kong
Honolulu, Waikiki & Oahu
Ireland
Israel
Italy
Jamaica
Japan
Las Vegas
London
Los Angeles
Maryland & Delaware
Maui
Mexico
Montana & Wyoming
Montréal & Québec City
Munich & the Bavarian Alps
Nashville & Memphis
Nepal
New England
New Mexico
New Orleans
New York City
New Zealand
Nova Scotia, New Brunswick & Prince Edward Island
Oregon
Paris
Philadelphia & the Amish Country
Portugal
Prague & the Best of the Czech Republic

Provence & the Riviera
Puerto Rico
Rome
San Antonio & Austin
San Diego
San Francisco
Santa Fe, Taos & Albuquerque
Scandinavia
Scotland
Seattle & Portland
Shanghai
Singapore & Malaysia
South Africa
South America
Southeast Asia
South Florida
South Pacific
Spain
Sweden
Switzerland
Texas
Thailand
Tokyo
Toronto
Tuscany & Umbria
USA
Utah
Vancouver & Victoria
Vermont, New Hampshire & Maine
Vienna & the Danube Valley
Virgin Islands
Virginia
Walt Disney World & Orlando
Washington, D.C.
Washington State

FROMMER'S® DOLLAR-A-DAY GUIDES

Australia from $50 a Day
California from $70 a Day
Caribbean from $70 a Day
England from $70 a Day
Europe from $70 a Day

Florida from $70 a Day
Hawaii from $80 a Day
Ireland from $60 a Day
Italy from $70 a Day
London from $85 a Day

New York from $90 a Day
Paris from $80 a Day
San Francisco from $70 a Day
Washington, D.C., from $70 a Day

FROMMER'S® PORTABLE GUIDES

Acapulco, Ixtapa & Zihuatanejo
Alaska Cruises & Ports of Call
Amsterdam
Aruba
Australia's Great Barrier Reef
Bahamas
Baja & Los Cabos
Berlin
Big Island of Hawaii
Boston
California Wine Country
Cancún
Charleston & Savannah
Chicago
Disneyland

Dublin
Florence
Frankfurt
Hong Kong
Houston
Las Vegas
London
Los Angeles
Maine Coast
Maui
Miami
New Orleans
New York City
Paris

Phoenix & Scottsdale
Portland
Puerto Rico
Puerto Vallarta, Manzanillo & Guadalajara
San Diego
San Francisco
Seattle
Sydney
Tampa & St. Petersburg
Vancouver
Venice
Virgin Islands
Washington, D.C.

FROMMER'S® NATIONAL PARK GUIDES

Family Vacations in the National Parks
Grand Canyon

National Parks of the American West
Rocky Mountain
Yellowstone & Grand Teton

Yosemite & Sequoia/ Kings Canyon
Zion & Bryce Canyon

FROMMER'S® MEMORABLE WALKS

Chicago
London

New York
Paris

San Francisco

FROMMER'S® GREAT OUTDOOR GUIDES

Arizona & New Mexico
New England

Northern California
Southern New England

Vermont & New Hampshire

SUZY GERSHMAN'S BORN TO SHOP GUIDES

Born to Shop: France
Born to Shop: Hong Kong,
  Shanghai & Beijing

Born to Shop: Italy
Born to Shop: London

Born to Shop: New York
Born to Shop: Paris

FROMMER'S® IRREVERENT GUIDES

Amsterdam
Boston
Chicago
Las Vegas
London

Los Angeles
Manhattan
New Orleans
Paris
Rome

San Francisco
Seattle & Portland
Vancouver
Walt Disney World
Washington, D.C.

FROMMER'S® BEST-LOVED DRIVING TOURS

Britain
California
Florida
France

Germany
Ireland
Italy

New England
Scotland
Spain

HANGING OUT™ GUIDES

Hanging Out in England
Hanging Out in Europe

Hanging Out in France
Hanging Out in Ireland

Hanging Out in Italy
Hanging Out in Spain

THE UNOFFICIAL GUIDES®

Bed & Breakfasts and Country
  Inns in:
    California
    New England
    Northwest
    Rockies
    Southeast
Beyond Disney
Branson, Missouri
California with Kids
Chicago
Cruises
Disneyland

Florida with Kids
Golf Vacations in the
  Eastern U.S.
The Great Smokey &
  Blue Ridge Mountains
Inside Disney
Hawaii
Las Vegas
London
Mid-Atlantic with Kids
Mini Las Vegas
Mini-Mickey
New England & New York
  with Kids

New Orleans
New York City
Paris
San Francisco
Skiing in the West
Southeast with Kids
Walt Disney World
Walt Disney World for
  Grown-ups
Walt Disney World for Kids
Washington, D.C.
World's Best Diving Vacations

SPECIAL-INTEREST TITLES

Frommer's Adventure Guide to Australia & New
  Zealand
Frommer's Adventure Guide to Central America
Frommer's Adventure Guide to India & Pakistan
Frommer's Adventure Guide to South America
Frommer's Adventure Guide to Southeast Asia
Frommer's Adventure Guide to Southern Africa
Frommer's Britain's Best Bed & Breakfasts and
  Country Inns
Frommer's France's Best Bed & Breakfasts and
  Country Inns
Frommer's Italy's Best Bed & Breakfasts and Country
  Inns
Frommer's Caribbean Hideaways

Frommer's Exploring America by RV
Frommer's Gay & Lesbian Europe
Frommer's The Moon
Frommer's New York City with Kids
Frommer's Road Atlas Britain
Frommer's Road Atlas Europe
Frommer's Washington, D.C., with Kids
Frommer's What the Airlines Never Tell You
Israel Past & Present
The New York Times' Guide to Unforgettable
  Weekends
Places Rated Almanac
Retirement Places Rated

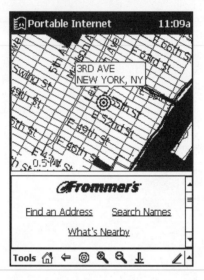

Frommer's®

Let Us Hear From You!

Dear Frommer's Reader,

You are our greatest resource in keeping our guides relevant, timely, and lively. We'd love to hear from you about your travel experiences—good or bad. Want to recommend a great restaurant or a hotel off the beaten path—or register a complaint? Any thoughts on how to improve the guide itself?

Please use this page to share your thoughts with me and mail it to the address below. Or if you like, send a FAX or e-mail me at frommersfeedback@hungryminds.com. And so that we can thank you—and keep you up on the latest developments in travel—we invite you to sign up for a free daily Frommer's e-mail travel update. Just write your e-mail address on the back of this page. Also, if you'd like to take a moment to answer a few questions about yourself to help us improve our guides, please complete the following quick survey. (We'll keep that information confidential.)

Thanks for your insights.

Yours sincerely,

Michael Spring

Michael Spring, *Publisher*

Name (Optional) ——————————————————————————

Address————————————————————————————————

——

City————————————————————————— **State**———— **ZIP**————

Name of Frommer's Travel Guide ——————————————————————

Comments————————————————————————————————

——

——

——

——

——

——

——

——

——

——

Please tell us a little about yourself so that we can serve you and the Frommer's community better. We will keep this information confidential.

Age: ( )18-24; ( )25-39; ( )40-49; ( )50-55; ( )Over 55

Income: ( )Under $25,000; ( )$25,000-$50,000; ( )$50,000-$100,000; ( )Over $100,000

I am: ( )Single, never married; ( )Married, with children; ( )Married, without children; ( )Divorced; ( )Widowed

Number of people in my household: ( )1; ( )2; ( )3; ( )4; ( )5 or more

Number of people in my household under 18: ( )1; ( )2; ( )3; ( )4; ( )5 or more

I am ( )a student; ( )employed full-time; ( )employed part-time; ( )not employed at this time; ( )retired; ( )other

I took ( )0; ( )1; ( )2; ( )3; ( )4 or more leisure trips in the past 12 months

My last vacation was ( )a weekend; ( )1 week; ( )2 weeks; ( )3 or more weeks

My last vacation was to ( )the U.S.; ( )Canada; ( )Mexico; ( )Europe; ( )Asia; ( )South America; ( )Central America; ( )The Caribbean; ( )Africa; ( )Middle East; ( )Australia/New Zealand

( )I would; ( )would not buy a Frommer's Travel Guide for business travel

I access the Internet ( )at home; ( )at work; ( )both; ( )I do not use the Internet

I used the Internet to do research for my last trip. ( )Yes; ( )No

I used the Internet to book accommodations or air travel on my last trip. ( )Yes; ( )No

My favorite travel site is ( )frommers.com; ( )travelocity.com; ( )expedia.com; other_____

I use Frommer's Travel Guides ( )always; ( )sometimes; ( )seldom

I usually buy ( )1; ( )2; ( )more than 2 guides when I travel
Other guides I use include _____

What's the most important thing we could do to improve Frommer's Travel Guides?

_____

_____

_____

_____

Yes, please send me a daily e-mail travel update. My e-mail address is

_____